FULL-TIME *at* THE DELL

First printed   November 2001
Reprinted   December 2001

First published in 2001 by
HAGIOLOGY PUBLISHING
170 Westbury Road
Bristol BS9 3AH

ISBN 0-9534474-2-1

Designed and typeset by Perry Associates, Bristol
Printed and bound in Great Britain by Bookcraft (Bath) Limited

FULL-TIME
at
THE DELL

From Watty to Matty 1898 – 2001

DAVE JUSON and DAVID BULL

in association with
SOUTHAMPTON FOOTBALL CLUB

&
Southern Daily Echo

The front cover illustration is a *Southern Daily Echo* photograph, taken from Overdell Court during the 1-0 win against Charlton Athletic on 30 April 1966. The back cover photos of Watty Keay and Matthew Le Tissier are from the collection and camera, respectively, of Duncan Holley.

The *Echo* was our main source of photos. The following list is of those *Echo* photos (and a few other illustrations), as used in this book at the pages indicated, all of which are available for purchase, at the terms set out in the **Echo advertisement on page 230:**

front cover; viii; 5; 58; 71; 82 (top photo); 95; 98; 100 (both); 102 (both); 105 (all); 106 (both); 107; 108; 111 (both); 115; 116; 117; 119; 122; 124; 125 (both); 130 (both); 133; 134 (both); 135; 136; 137 (both); 138; 143 (both top); 145; 147; 152 (left); 153 (both top); 154; 160 (top); 167 (top right); 170; 171; 173; 175; 176; 177; 178 (bottom); 179 (all); 181; 183 (both); 186; 187; 194 (both); 197; 199; 201; 202 (top); 203 (both); 204; 205 (all); 206; 207 (both); 208; and 210.

The above list of 81 illustrations is restricted to those of which the *Echo* is known to have copies. There are others that we have had to copy from the edition of the *Echo* in which they appeared. We have identified these as being in the "Hagiology collection", this being a catch-all name for a collection, mainly acquired and held by Duncan Holley, comprising not only the said copies from the pages of the *Echo* but also photos (obtained mostly from ex-players), where the copyright (if still in being) is unclear (we accordingly invite any copyright-holders to contact us, where their copyright material may have been used). Likewise, some of the photos in personal collections identified below are of unknown copyright or appear to be *Echo* photos not on the available-for-purchase list above.

Photos in the Hagiology collection are to be found at pages 23; 26; 27 (left); 29; 32; 36 (and back cover); 37; 40; 42; 43 (right); 47; 49; 53; 55; 70; 74; 75; 82 (bottom); 84; 86; 91 (both); 92 (top); 103; 109; 128; 148; 164 (both); 165 (both left); 166 (left); 178 (top); 198 (top left); and 209.

We have been pleased to borrow photos from personal collections: Helen Adlem (166, right); Crawford White (167, top left); Kevin Phillips (167, middle); Jack Broomfield (167, both bottom); Maurice Hockley (169); Mark Fickling (180); Robert Simons (190); Andrei Zhezlov (195, both); Pat Bryant (198, top right); Tom Kelly (198, bottom); and Dave Webster (202, bottom)

The other local collections drawn upon are those of Ray Mursell (8; 10; 11; and 52); Herbie Taylor (92, bottom); the Southampton City Archivist's office (27, right; and 132); and Southampton City Library Services (12 and 43, left).

We are pleased to acknowledge also the use of illustrations from the Ordnance Survey (50); *Sunderland Echo* (89); Mike Atkelsy (152, top right); the *Saints Matchday Programme* (153, bottom); and Oz cartoons (116; 142; and 208, with the permission of the late Don Osmond and Mrs Osmond).

Photos taken by members of the Hagiology collective or their friends (often especially for this book) have been used as follows: Dave Adlem (216 and 224); Gary Chalk (22 and 165, right); Shirley Gaulton-Wagg (160, bottom); Duncan Holley (196; 229; and back cover, right); and Dave Juson (16; 143, bottom; and 159).

Programmes used as illustrations are from the collections of Hagiology members or have been kindly loaned by Andrew Murray.

Contents

Appendices

DAVE JUSON
author of Part I

Attended his first game at The Dell on 3 November 1962. He watched Saints destroy Middlesbrough from the "comfort" of the boys' chocolate box. Since then he has watched football from just about every vantage point The Dell has had to offer over his 39 years of devotion – except the Directors' Box, the catwalks and the Press Box. Following a rich and varied working career, which has included freelance writing for a number of publications and the odd fee from BBC Radio 4, he attempted education, courtesy of Ruskin College in Oxford and the University of Leicester, from where he graduated, with a BA in History, in 1999. Since then he has had a rich and varied working career. Intends to invest any profits from this enterprise in breweries. Other than that, he will continue his rich and varied working career.

DAVID BULL
editor of Part II

His first visit to The Dell, in 1948, is recorded in Chapter 27. Soon after that, he left his native Salisbury to become in turn a Camberley teenager, an Exeter student and a university teacher in Exeter, Manchester and Bristol. Nowadays commutes from Bristol to the Itchen Stand. Has written for the Saints Programme – in three spells since 1981 – and for three Southampton fanzines. Edited two collections of fans' memories, *We'll Support You Evermore* (1992) and *Football and the Commons People* (with Alastair Campbell, 1994) as fund-raisers for the Child Poverty Action Group, in which he has long been an activist. His first two Hagiology Publishing ventures were *Dell Diamond*, a biography of Ted Bates (1998), and *Match of the Millennium* (edited with Bob Brunskell, in 2000). His biography of Terry Paine is due in 2003.

Conversion chart

There are so many references to pounds, shillings and pence (£.s.d.) that it would be cumbersome to keep showing, in brackets, the decimal equivalents. So, if you're too young ever to have handled "old money", all you need to remember is that there were 20 shillings to the pound, so that one shilling (1/-) became 5p in 1971.

Thus, when a huge crowd paid £112.12s.3d. to watch the Hants Senior Cup match described on pages 31-32, the bumper gate receipts were £122.61¼p. And when the mayor donated 200 shillings to help the Saints at the meeting recalled on page 90, this amounted to £10.

Foreword
by Nick Holmes

On 28 April 2001, I walked out onto the pitch at half-time in Southampton's game with Sunderland. I was not just part of a 25th anniversary parade by the Cup-winning squad of 1976; I was also saying farewell to The Dell, ending an association that had begun when I first stood on the terraces as a schoolboy, 39 years before to the very day.

I didn't last long on the terraces, I have to say. I was seven when my dad took me to see the last game of the 1961-62 season. It was a 5-1 win against Stoke, but we were standing under the West Stand and I didn't see a thing. Come August, I was a season ticket-holder, sitting with Dad just above where the players came out. It was a good time to be initiated as a Dell boy. Ted Bates was reshaping the side that had won the Division Three championship in 1960 into the team that would win promotion to Division One in 1966 – and was creating, along the way, the Cup-running XI of 1963.

That Cup run included, of course, the Sixth Round replay against Nottingham Forest that must rank as the most memorable of so many memorable Cup nights at The Dell. I was there. Two other members of the squad of '76 – Paul Bennett and Mick Channon – were also in the crowd. But, then, you'll have known that already if you've read about that evening in *Dell Diamond*, the biography of Ted Bates and the first book published by the small group of supporters who are producing a whole series of Saints memories, of which *Full-Time at The Dell* is the third.

I know I am not alone, as an ex-player, in having enjoyed my association with this series. When we got to the end of my interview for *Dell Diamond*, I couldn't believe that we'd been going for five-and-a-half hours non-stop, as I relived so many magic moments of my time at The Dell, fan and boy, man and player.

It was another way of renewing my life-membership of the Southampton FC "family". The label of "Family Club" may appear to be over-used, but you wouldn't think that if you'd experienced the togetherness at The Dell, where the office people were part of the Club: they weren't just there; they weren't being used.

Whenever I returned there, it still had that feel of a family club – even if all the smaller clubs like Southampton were being dragged a bit the other way by the changes in football finances.

I was adopted into the Dell family in 1970, when my parents took me, aged 15½ and dressed in my St Mary's school uniform, for an audience with Ted Bates, the man who had brought on so many local lads, including John Sydenham from our school. Pat Earles, a classmate at St Mary's, also joined and would play in that Cup-run of 1976 – yes, four home-grown players in a squad of 14.

As a schoolboy entering the first-team dressing room – where I would get to clean the boots of my hero, Ron Davies – I couldn't believe the industrial language. That was a real eye-opener, but all part of learning to belong in the *camaraderie*, an aspect of professional football which, along with the humour, some ex-players miss more than the game itself. Our dressing room wasn't exactly grand, but you should have seen the one reserved for our visitors. Lew Chatterley used to tell the tale of how he and his Aston Villa team-mates walked into it, in the baking closing-day sun of 1967, only to find the heating on and the windows fast shut. We beat them 6-2 and my hero bagged four to be the top-scorer in the entire Football League.

The impact of their dressing room on visitors to The Dell has understandably received less attention than the intimidating compactness of the ground – the "Fortress Dell" syndrome – and how many points this was allegedly worth to Saints. Knowing that your opponents didn't like coming to Southampton – that they had a fear of being so close to the crowd – inspired us and helped us to believe that we were, if not invincible, then very hard to beat at The Dell.

In that regard, there was nothing better than 1975-76, when we won 18 and drew two of our 21 home games, but were awful away from The Dell – except that we did what was necessary, of course, to win the Cup. Obviously, there were seasons when visitors were less in awe of The Dell, but I'm still concerned as to whether anything resembling that on-top-of-you atmosphere can be recreated at St Mary's – or "The New Dell", as I call it.

I made 266 of my 539 first class appearances at The Dell. Like many a contributor to Chapter 28 of this book, I find it difficult to pick out any one home game as my favourite, but I especially remember beating Everton 3-1 on 17 April 1984 – just three days after they'd beaten us in the semi-final. There was a lot of feeling that night.

Great games, great goals – in a great time at The Dell. I was pleased, then, to be invited to relive some of the highlights in the process of welcoming this book of memories of football (and many a related matter) at the ground that was for so long my "family" home. And my only one.

"Once a Saint, always a Saint," Terry Paine proclaimed at the launch of *Dell Diamond*. It may have been corny but it got a huge cheer. Loyalty always does. And, however much one acknowledges the need for change, this is perhaps the right moment for me to add

ONCE A DELL BOY, ALWAYS A DELL BOY.

Choosing my favourite goal is a lot easier. On 26 August 1980, I scored twice in our 4-0 League Cup win against Watford and one of them was from my own half. Chasing a through-ball, Micky Channon was just beaten to it by the 'keeper coming out of his area and kicking clear. He didn't catch it cleanly and it ran all along the ground to me, in the inside-right channel, just inside my own half. I struck it with my left foot and it didn't touch the ground until it had hit the net.

And I took part in what is generally reckoned to have been the greatest goal scored at The Dell in living memory – the 16-touch move against Liverpool in 1982. Chris Nicholl headed down, I exchanged passes with David Armstrong and hit the ball up the line from the left-back spot to half-way. Then I just watched in admiration as it all developed.

Whoever saw a better goal scored, team-wise, than you saw there?

On his final visit to The Dell in April 2001 – 39 years to the day since his first visit as a young fan – Nick Holmes holds aloft the FA Cup he helped to win 25 years ago.

Preface

GO, FOOTBALL FANS, AND TELL YOUR CLUB'S HISTORY, Nick Hornby urged us.

Within 18 months of the publication of *Fever Pitch,* the best-selling account of the agonies of watching Arsenal, its author was enjoining us to move on from the fad of recording our experiences as *fans* and to concentrate on being historians of our clubs.

Whether or not that advice was appropriate or necessary, both of us had already been dabbling in that recommended role and were in the fortunate position, as Southampton fans, of having available the works – S*aints: a complete record of Southampton Football Club 1885-1987* and *An Alphabet of Saints: a complete Who's Who of Southampton FC* – of Gary Chalk and Duncan Holley, who had been rightly recognized by the Club as its Official Historians and Statisticians.

Without their two priceless works of reference, everyone writing about the Saints, whether in books like this or in articles for the *Saints Matchday Programme* or the *Echo,* would struggle for accurate information.

In 1998, we were privileged to join with Duncan and Gary – along with local sports historian, Norman Gannaway – to form Hagiology Publishing. Norman has made 70 his voluntary retirement age from this collective and we would like to use this space to thank him for his unstinting contribution to our cause.

That cause is explained at page 229. Put simply, we are committed to producing a series of books on Saints' history, in association with Southampton FC and the *Southern Daily Echo.*

We have been, and will keep on, honouring that commitment in a variety of ways.

Our first book (*Dell Diamond,* 1998) entailed one of us writing a *biography* – of Ted Bates, who has been with the Club, from player to President, for 64 years.

The second (*Match of the Millennium,* 2000) involved 13 fans teaming up with Bob Brunskell of the *Echo* to write 100 reports of *matches,* from 1885 to 2000. Yet, if each book had a quite different focus, each needed to put that focus into context and generally to sketch in some kind of explanation of how Southampton FC got to where it is today.

And that – *literally and precisely* – is the topic of the first half of *Full-Time at The Dell,* in which Dave Juson charts the Club's journey from the Common to the Friends Provident St Mary's Stadium, focusing mainly, of course, on 103 seasons at The Dell. Part II of this book is also about The Dell, as seen through the eyes of almost 80 Saints fans.

Each of us will further explain, by way of an introduction to his particular part of the book – see pages 1 and 161 – how it came to be written and what ground it aims to cover.

We wish, in this shared preface, however, to acknowledge the many who have helped us to put this book together, whether for one of its parts or both.

Where better to start our "thankyous" than with the foreword? We wanted this to be written by a long-serving player whom we knew to have started young at The Dell as a fan. Nick Holmes fitted that bill exceptionally well, so he was our first choice. We were delighted, therefore, when he said "yes".

We have already acknowledged our debt to Gary Chalk and Duncan Holley for having written the two indispensable works of reference on which all historians of Southampton FC necessarily depend. And both of them have, as ever, supported our research, by checking all manner of facts and figures, while also helping, in various ways, with photographs and other illustrations, a task in which we also called upon Ray Mursell – who was so gracious about being omitted from the acknowledgments in *Match of the Millennium* – Andrew Murray and Dave Adlem. Gary was especially put upon in the injury-time of this book's production, tracking down information nobody thought was important when it was being written, some of which appears as Appendix I, which was utterly dependent upon his researches.

We have both enjoyed access, in recent years, to the minute books of Southampton FC, where our debt is to Brian Truscott, Barry Fox and the ever amenable Woggy Taylor. We acknowledge help, at page 225, from many other libraries and archives and from six people who consented to be interviewed. We are indebted, too, to Grant Coleman and Neil Stackley of Radio Solent for a tape of the game against Arsenal with which Part I of the book starts and ends.

As you can see on page 229, we enjoyed a photo-shoot with Matthew Le Tissier, whose efforts on behalf of Hagiology Publishing are so much appreciated. This included his posing for the back cover photograph, taken by Duncan Holley, who also supplied the shot of Watty Keay and several other older photos from his comprehensive collection, the copyright of which is invariably unknown (as explained at page (iv), we welcome overtures from any copyright-holders whose material we have used unattributed).

Most of the other photos have been supplied, at favourable rates, by the *Southern Daily Echo,* as part of their agreement, as aforesaid, to work with us and the Club in producing a series of books, our latest schedule for which is set out on page 229.

A big thankyou to all of those at Newspaper House who made this possible: from editor Ian Murray and the assistant editors who have condoned our access to all manner of material we had never seen before; to Paul Green and Jez Gale who tolerated Dave Juson's space-consuming activities in the *Echo* archive; to Paul Collins, who dealt with our last-minute needs; and for all the other favours and advice of staffers too numerous to single out.

The scanning of these photos depended especially upon Ainsley Adams, working tirelessly in his dark room, while David Ball cheerfully met our late needs.

Having done our best to assemble our two parts of this book in a way that was worthy of the various efforts on our behalf – including, of course, those contributions acknowledged in our separate introductions below – we depended, as ever, on Mark Perry, of *Perry Associates,* to craft the text and illustrations into a pleasing whole.

Pleasing *whole?* Well, we hope the two parts feel like a whole. From just looking at the illustrations, you may immediately perceive the two parts as very different from each other – the first full of photos of a ground, not always with people in it, while Part II is more reliant upon traditional action shots of those matches remembered by the fans.

And then, as you read the two parts, you will find that they are subjective in very different ways. In Part II,

neither of us ventures an opinion – save when it's our turn to record a memory of a first or favourite game, or in the last few paragraphs of the final chapter, as David Bull mops up.

By contrast, Part I necessarily includes Dave Juson's opinions, from time to time, not only of developments but of the people involved in making them happen or in ensuring that they didn't. Those are his personal views not necessarily shared by David Bull, who would sometimes have been less critical of personalities in the boardroom or dug-out; who has consistently argued, in the Saints programme, against aspects of Lord Taylor's reasoning and conclusions; and who never ever considered Stoneham a suitable site.

That said, we felt it might help you to appreciate the inter-relationship of the two parts if we were to cross-refer as appropriate. We could have done a lot more of that – "see the match details in Chapter so-and-so", etc – than we have and recognise that we'll have done too little for those who like cross-referencing as much as David Bull does, while doing too much for those who are irritated by it as much as Dave Juson is.

Likewise, we could have inserted invitations, chapter after chapter, to turn to *Match of the Millennium* for details of a match to which there is an allusion in Part I (where matches, especially away fixtures, are mostly of contextual significance only) or of which there is a restricted account in Part II (where brevity was the rule).

We have been content to include just a few such references to that book of reports on "The Saints' 100 Most Memorable Matches" – sufficient on the one hand, we hope, to advise those unfamiliar with that book that there is a source where match details can be explored; without, we trust, being so repetitive as to make it feel like a running advertisement for the book to which we both contributed a year ago.

And *pleasing?* Well, we're both pleased to have been able to collate and publish this memoir to "the atmospheric misshapen oddity of a ground that is called The Dell" – as one journalist put it on that last weekend (see page 4) – and hope that, whether or not you contributed memories to Part II of this book, you will find something in these pages to please you, too.

Dave Juson, Freemantle
David Bull, Bristol   October 2001.

The History: introduction

When it was first mooted that a book be compiled to mark Saints' passing to yet another ground, it seemed somewhat obvious that the subject matter should concentrate on their previous homes. As The Dell had been the Club's base for the previous 103 years, it was obvious, too, that it should be the main focus of the narrative.

No problem there, then: 30,000 words on the development of the "famous little ground"; 10,000 words, preferably less, on Saints' previous grounds; and Bob's your uncle. Nothing is that simple of course. Especially with Saints.

Most Football League grounds of Victorian and Edwardian vintage were built piecemeal. A single grandstand here, some banking there – which would evolve into terracing – and maybe a roof would emerge over one of the ends, after a time? Not so The Dell. It came complete with covered seating on both sides of the pitch and terracing all-round. True, the rear section of what became known as the Milton Road end was dubbed the "Brighton Beach" because it was just a shingle bank, but it was probably the most sophisticated stadium in the country in 1898.

Why? After all, Saints were not even a Football League club and, as any popular history of football will tell you, the Football League (up until the creation of the Premiership at least) was the be-all and end-all of professional football. Popular histories, especially popular histories about football, tend to skip inconvenient, and difficult to explain, anomalies. They tend to complicate things. Saints – wouldn't you just know it? – are an anomaly.

Gary Chalk, Duncan Holley and myself went some way to restoring Saints' Victorian/Edwardian reputation in Hagiology's previous publication, *Match of the Millennium,* but this book has provided the opportunity to elaborate on their early glories and expound on their development from church football team in 1885 to a side that was, in a little over a dozen years, destabilising the fabric of the game as the members of the Football League perceived it.

Of course, Saints have been doing that – notwithstanding the odd hiatus – for over a century now. The Friends Provident St Mary's Stadium will enable them to continue that fine tradition for the foreseeable future.

As for The Dell, it will be missed, but it's history. *This is it.*

Acknowledgments

My debts to those who have contributed to the research on Part I of this tome have been expressed in the Preface and/or in a list of libraries and archives under "Sources" at page 225. A special mention must be made of the help and friendliness of the Southampton City Archivist's Office and the Special Collections section of the Southampton Central Library. Thanks also to Brian Hunt, Ken Sweet, Nigel Bachmann and Alan Morton, the first two for consenting to interviews, the latter two for answering enquiries in respect of both Stoneham and Northam, and to my landlady, Jill White, for her patience regarding the rent. Also John Clements, for discussing the "good old days" with me.

In conclusion: I could write another book regarding all the support I have received during this project and on those who provided it. So, a big thank you to everyone I have ever discussed Saints with over the past 30-odd years and to all those many people who should have been included in my acknowledgments, whether here or in the Preface, but who have been excluded by the failure of a frazzled memory.

A note on this reprinting: Apologies if you had wanted this book for Christmas 2001. Having boldly printed 5,000 copies, we found ourselves unable, within two weeks of publication, to meet re-orders from the shops. Even allowing for the pull of Matthew Le Tissier – thanks again, Matt, for generously signing so many books – it seems that we under-estimated our fellow-fans' longings for The Dell.

We have corrected a few errors, including our embarrassing miscounts of Saints' seasons at The Dell (page ix) and their 1948 Cup rounds (page 172), but otherwise mostly of punctuation. An alternative identity has been suggested for the skater we thought might be Roper (on page 102) but we can't see it. And our attribution of the shot, on page 186, to Fisher has been challenged: the view that it is Gilchrist shooting accords with our own initial thoughts, but we accepted contrary evidence that this was indeed Fisher's famous goal.

Dave Juson and David Bull, December 2001

FULL-TIME *at* THE DELL

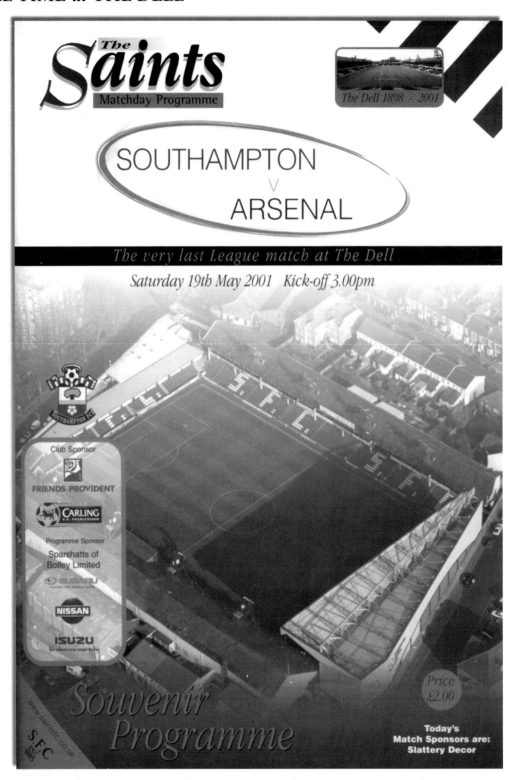

"The very last League match at The Dell" proclaims the programme.
It's the game with which Part I both begins and ends

Chapter 1
And in the End...

"You couldn't write it" was the greeting I received on ambling into the *Osborne* on the penultimate Sunday afternoon of May 2001. This salutation was proffered by Tom Dack, who began supporting Saints during World War II and knows more about suffering the slings and arrows of outrageous fortune than do most of The Dell's *cognoscenti,* not least myself. It was an apt salutation.

That morning I had religiously read every report of the Southampton v Arsenal Premier League fixture in the hope of finding a perfect... all right, a good opening for the first chapter for this book. Something like, but much better than:

> With a last minute pirouette, culminating in a perfect left foot volley into the top right hand of the Milton end goal, Matthew Le Tissier brought to an audacious climax over a century of truly fabulous football at The Dell.

But I hadn't.

For those of us there on Saturday 19 May 2001, nothing could sum up that incredible conclusion to The Dell's history better than *"You couldn't write it."*

For the legion of Saints' faithful unable to attend – the exiles or, worse, those excluded because of The Dell's paltry capacity – that evening's headline in the *Pink* came pretty close to capturing the moment:

LE TISSIER SECURES FAIRYTALE FINALE

As close as mere language is likely to be able to define a moment that combined a goal of artistic perfection, by a truly great player, with theatrical timing that would have made Shakespeare weep with admiration.

Words like fabulous, fantastic, stunning, incredible, unbelievable, outlandish, marvellous, spectacular, wonderful... etc. have been devalued by decades of misuse by football hacks groping to find synonyms for competent, good, not bad and my Granny could have slid it in. So it was only to be expected that, when trying to convey something as awesome and emotive as the last goal at The Dell – while trying to contend with a rapidly looming deadline, an insatiable thirst and a desire to make a dash for the very next train back to London – their shell-shocked vocabularies would not be up to the job. This isn't a criticism, because as the ball billowed the back of the net, my first reaction was to blub. Rising to acclaim the scorer, the quality of the goal, the happening itself, and the unique context it occurred within, came as an afterthought. My own clumsy attempt, above, to encapsulate the last strike at The Dell was the labour of an entire Sunday morning.

So, hats off to the Fourth Estate. Their stories may have been shoved into obscure corners of the sports pages by editors wishing to highlight more significant and auspicious footballing events – such as the acrimony between Alex Ferguson and the Manchester United board, David Ginola's feud with John Gregory at Aston Villa and the last broadcast of BBC's *Match of the Day* – and then butchered by subs, but they gave the neutrals, and the far-flung faithful, a flavour of the day; and, given that the press box at The Dell was at the very back of the Upper West Stand, how were they to know that many of us were crying as heartily as we were applauding after that winning goal?

> ROMANCE in football is not quite dead. For there could scarcely have been a more romantic ending to Southampton's 103 years at The Dell. Eighty-nine minutes had gone when Matt Le Tissier, so long the idol of the crowd, brought on as a substitute, spun on the ball to strike a glorious left-footed shot past Alex Manninger to win Southampton a game they seemed likely to lose.
>
> (Brian Glanville, *The Sunday Times,* 20 May)

> Southampton hero Matthew Le Tissier popped out of the shadows to bid a glorious farewell to his beloved Dell.
> Le Tiss has always had a wonderful sense of theatre, and there could not have been a more perfect script on an emotional day for Saints fans.
>
> (Kevin Moseley, *The People,* 20 May)

FULL-TIME *at* THE DELL

With one glorious sweep of his left boot, Matthew Le Tissier effectively paid for his new contract and then joked: "I wish I'd waited a week!"

The crowd favourite scored a dramatic last-gasp winner against runners-up Arsenal to provide The Dell with a perfect send-off in the last ever Premiership match at the old ground.

(Graham Hiley, *The Southern Daily Echo*, 21 May)

It had to be Matt Le Tissier. On The Dell's last day the player who had graced it so often came off the bench and in the 88th minute scored a great winning goal. …if anyone could provide a fairytale finish it had to be Le Tissier. Brought on with 15 minutes left, he brought the curtain down with a winning goal of such typical audacity that it rolled back the years to his youth. With two minutes left, the ball fell awkwardly to him in the penalty area. Somehow he got a foot high enough to control it, turned, and put the shot beyond Manninger to give a wonderfully fitting end to the story of The Dell.

(Norman Fox, *The Independent on Sunday*, 20 May)

He had started only two Premiership games all season and his late entry as a substitute yesterday initially seemed borne out of sentiment. But, as ever, Matt Le Tissier had saved a bit of magic for the finale as his first goal of the season was a spectacular 89th minute winning volley to bring the curtain down on 103 years of football at The Dell as only he can. Some parties will probably still be going on in Southampton today.

(Nick Callow, *The Observer*, 20 May)

Matt Le Tissier waved his magic wand and conjured up a Hollywood farewell to The Dell that was beyond the dreams of even Steven Spielberg. The Saints idol had a walk-on part but his 88th-minute winner will be the last goal at the famous old stadium – and probably the most famous in his golden collection.

(Nigel Whitefield, *News of the World*, 20 May)

…Le Tissier elated all present with his volley into the top corner.

(Adam Sills, *The Guardian*, 21 May)

Anyone who refuses to believe in fairytales need only have been at the atmospheric misshapen oddity of a ground that is called The Dell to realise that they do come true.

Matt Le Tissier, a peripheral figure for much of this season but still a cult figure in Southampton, ensured his club's 103-year reign here ended in rapturous fashion by coming off the bench to score a late winner.

(Richard Griffiths, *Sunday Mirror*, 20 May)

The Dell deserved something exceptional before the demolition squads break up 103 years of soccer history – and it was right that Matthew Le Tissier was the provider… no neutral, and certainly no Southampton fan, will be anything but delighted at such a thrilling end to the Dell's final competitive match before the club moves to their state-of-the-art home by the docks.

(Alex Montgomery, *Mail on Sunday*, 20 May)

Matt Le Tissier is almost as much a relic as the condemned Dell these days. But would you not just have guessed that the man whose magic has so often turned the ramshackle old stadium into Southampton's very own stadium of dreams should bring the curtain down with a wonderful winner in the 89th minute.

(Roy Collins, *Sunday Telegraph*, 20 May)

Matthew Le Tissier, a Southampton favourite for more than fifteen years, scored the spectacular goal that ensured his club's 103-year spell at The Dell ended in style.

(Steve Young, *Sunday Express*, 20 May)

Now, just in case you were so far from civilization as to have been out of reach of satellite television, or the BBC World Service, for the best part of the 2000-2001 football season; or you are, in the normal course of events, indifferent to the progress and/or regressions of Southampton Football Club; or are perusing this volume in a second-hand book store, some time in the distant future, it should be explained that a new stadium was nearing completion in Northam and that on Saturday 19 May 2001 AD, Saints played their last-ever fixture at The

Chapter 1

Dell against Arsenal, opponents who, no matter how many goals they won or lost by, would be Premier League runners-up, their place in the next season's European Champions League guaranteed. As for Saints, relegation had not been an issue for well over a month and the difference between a win and a hammering would be a place or two in the middle of the table.

So when the teams stepped out into the sunshine that afternoon, there was nothing much at stake other than pride. Pride, and the hopes of the Saints' faithful that it would all end in a bang rather than a whimper. Nobody wants to go out on an anti-climax.

The previous week, Premier League champions Manchester United had lost 2-1 at The Dell. Manager Alex Ferguson informed anyone who would listen (i.e. the media and fans from Barnstaple to Bangkok – maybe even some in Manchester) that he had been giving a run-out to a bunch of reserves, because United had a far more prestigious game later in the week (a friendly against Celtic in Glasgow) and he wanted his star players available for that.

Arsenal, on the other hand, are not given to banal excuses, but to pragmatic explanations. And, it has to be said, explanations, pragmatic or otherwise, have not been needed overmuch down the years: Arsenal had a good record against Saints, even at The Dell.

As the faithful made their way to the game, it was in the hope of a fitting end to The Dell's history as a football ground, with the expectation that Arsenal were not going to make any concessions to sentiment – the Gunners are perennially good, but they can rarely be accused of possessing a romantic streak.

Would we have wanted it any other way? Given the circumstances, and unaware of what was to unfold, yes. Probably.

The first-half was not promising. Arsenal looked eight places above Saints in the table. A neat move in the 25th minute saw Ashley Cole blast a shot, which Paul Jones failed to grasp, rebound back to the precocious defender, who lobbed the ball over the prostrate 'keeper's body.

Half-time: Southampton 0 Arsenal 1.

And all Saints had to show for it were outraged appeals for a penalty for an alleged Adams push on James Beattie.

The second-half started brightly for Saints. Hassan Kachloul chipped Alex Manninger to equalize before the visitors had worked out which way they were now kicking. He celebrated by executing an extraordinarily formal salute to his team-mates and the Milton crowd.

There followed a few dubious tackles, harsh words were exchanged, the referee wagged his finger a few times, then Thierry Henry hurtled along the front of the East Stand leaving Wayne Bridge, and several thousand spectators, spread-eagled in his wake, and squared the ball for Frederik Ljungberg, in front of the Archers goal, to tap home.

It was a classy goal. Only the most churlish of Saints' supporters could have resented it. They were perhaps still sorting their feelings out about it when Kachloul struck again, tidying up some confusion in the Arsenal penalty box caused by an audacious bit of ball-play by Gary Monk that had left Cole flat-footed. Again, that salute.

It was warming up to be a bit of a classic. Thoughts of it being the last game at The Dell were taking a back seat to the spectacle. And then Le Tissier was standing on the touch-line, the whistle blew and Kevin Davies ran off to a standing ovation for his substitute.

Matty was pushed up front, he reached balls first, knocked off some sublime passes, dropped deep, knocked off more sublime passes and, eventually, scored that goal.

"The Dell deserved something exceptional…"
Matthew Le Tissier provides it with the last league goal at The Dell

FULL-TIME *at* THE DELL

The reactions of supporters were solicited after the game. They were faithfully recorded in Monday's *Echo*:

Graham Bush of Bristol:
"Brilliant!"

Rob Heally from Hedge End:
"Great game, we definitely deserved to win. Just a great game really. I'm speechless."

Martin Hayes:
"It was awesome, absolutely awesome! It was worth the trip down from London. Matty just wrote the script didn't he!"

G. Ball of Bitterne:
"I thought you couldn't have written a better script to finish The Dell's history."

Steven Moore of Shirley:
"You couldn't have written it!"

Which is where we came in.

Postscript

Le Tissier's goal was not quite the end.

In a perfect world, that would have been it. Poetic perfection. Arsenal would have taken the kick-off. The referee would have blown-up, the crowd would have invaded the pitch (plenty of them did: there were fears for Matty's life – and his modesty – as he was mobbed and stripped), then picked up whatever part of The Dell they fancied as a memento: their seat, a "No Smoking" sign, the toilet block behind the East Stand, a director's car… then gone for a pint and an earnest discussion of the momentous events that had just taken place.

Reality, alas, is never quite that lyrical. Nobody could have predicted what actually transpired and plans were in motion to give The Dell a fond farewell to remember.

There was to be a well-deserved testimonial match for skipper Jason Dodd, a couple of six-a-side tournaments and, for the last kick of all, Brighton & Hove Albion were to drop by and play a sentimental recreation of the first-ever fixture at the ground.

The Dodd testimonial was something of a farce, with almost as many substitutions as spectators, but a fine time was had by all, even those who failed to get a kick and, especially, esteemed Club Chairman Rupert Lowe, who lurked sinisterly around the Woggy's Wanderers' penalty area and was eventually called upon to take a penalty – awarded for a less than masterly dive by Saints' acting manager, Stuart Gray. Young Mr Lowe's effort hit the post and the Jason Dodd XI (plus a cast of thousands) lost 2-1. The Chairman's attempts to live out a fantasy attracted some derision, mostly, I suspect, from personalities who would have mortgaged their families to have enjoyed the same privilege.

The six-a-side tournaments enabled a great number of sad individuals to do just that in the following two days. I can now galvanize acquaintances with my tale of playing in goal in front of a hushed Archers Road end. Hushed, because nobody was in it – this did not detract from the thrill one iota. Neither did being in a side that scored only one goal in eight matches. Nor did the eventuality that I spent more time leaping into the Lower East Stand to retrieve the ball than actually playing.

The Brighton & Hove Albion swansong took place on a bright, clear afternoon on Saturday 26 May. An occasion made all the more colourful by a larger proportion of the crowd than usual wearing replica Saints shirts of various vintages. And a respectable number of Seagulls' followers from along the coast to join the festivities and give their own side a last *hoorah* for their championship of Nationwide Division Three.

Ideally, the last game at The Dell would have been against the first visitors, but Brighton United were unable to fulfil the date, having been liquidated in 1899 – you just have to make do with what you can get – and, fair dos, Albion and their supporters did the occasion proud.

Uwe Rossler scored the last goal at The Dell, in a 1-0 win for Saints.

Then the better-equipped of the nostalgic supporters dismantled The Dell for memorabilia.

Chapter 2
The Dell Opens

FIRST MATCH OF THE SEASON AT SOUTHAMPTON

OPENING OF THE NEW GROUND

SOUTHAMPTON v BRIGHTON

MAYOR KICKS OFF

Nothing could have been more favourable than the general condition which attended the opening of the football season at Southampton on the fine new enclosure of the Southampton F.C. this afternoon. The weather was perfect, there was a lavish display of bunting on the grand stands, whilst the light and varied coloured costumes of the ladies who graced the opening match by their presence all helped to make the scene of exceptional brilliancy and charm. Everyone seemed to be in the best of spirits, and they had cause to be, as the Saints had commenced the season in a most auspicious manner by defeating both Bedminster and West Norwood, their goal average being seven to four. To-day , however, they had sterner stuff to contend with, the visitors being the newly formed Brighton United club, which had been admitted to the First Division of the Southern League at the first time of asking; just as Bristol City, then newly formed, was admitted into the charmed circle last year…

So opened the first published account of the first match at The Dell, in the first-ever edition of the *Football Echo & Sports Gazette* on 3 September 1898. It duly continued:

The gates were opened early, and the crown thronged in at the various entrances. The ground itself looked A1, but it was rather difficult to gauge the numbers of the crowd owing to the fact that they were spread all round the arena, thickly in some places and sparsely in others. There must, however, have been several thousands present long before the start.

It was the practice to give sports' journalists a byline, or rather a *nom de plume,* back in the latter half of the nineteenth century, but this particular report goes unattributed. However, the next couple of sentences identify the writer, fairly certainly, as "Echoist":

The interval was whiled away by the Southampton Town Band under the direction of Mr. Watts. The accommodation for the Press was somewhat of a primitive character; in fact not as good as provided at the County Ground last season, and even that was not

of the best. There was no desk, and the unfortunate football scribe had to get out his copy as best he could.

Echoist's commentaries were, routinely, the first chance the Southampton public had to read of Saints' fortunes – this by virtue of his working for the *Echo,* Southampton's only daily 'paper. Before the *Football Echo* was launched, the *Southern Daily Echo* issued a late "Football Special Edition" on Saturday evenings. For further insights on any particular game, or other goings-on at Southampton FC, the public had recourse to five other 'papers published on a weekly or bi-weekly basis; plus a singular publication by the name of *Southampton Amusements,* which added sport, and Saints' doings in particular, to its regular menu of musings on what and who was coming off where with regard to the local music halls, concert halls and theatres. Readers of that publication had to wait nine days to discover what "Burlington Bertie" made of the propitious event:

The weather on Saturday last was simply scorching, and made one fancy they were off to a cricket match, instead of to the opening of the magnificent new

FULL-TIME *at* THE DELL

football enclosure "The Dell" which Mr. George Thomas has so liberally provided for the Southampton Football Club. Mr. Thomas is to be congratulated on the success which has crowned his efforts, he… has spared no expense to make the enclosure one of the finest in the country. No wonder the "Daily Mail" representative was so pleased with the ground, it is something to be proud of.

On 20 August, he rhapsodised for "Arielites", as he called his readers, that: "It is perhaps safe to say that, not even excepting the Crystal Palace, there is no more scientifically constructed arena in the country."

And, a fortnight later, he insisted that, even those who had "seen several good grounds [had] become purple in the face in an endeavour to find superlatives to describe the beauties of the Southampton Ground."

The Mayor kicks-off "like an international"

Really? If the *Daily Mail* "representative" was "pleased", why weren't his readers advised of the new ground's glories? Was he just patronising the provincial hacks on the primitively-appointed press benches? After all, Saints had just spent two seasons playing out their fixtures on a cricket ground, albeit a county-class cricket ground, in front of a pavilion and a single grand stand; and a purpose-built football stadium, however rustic, was going to look pretty sophisticated to a public that had never seen a Football League venue.

Ariel, of the *Southampton Times,* was in no doubt that it was a home fit for heroes, having advised his readers, as early as June, to go and see "the new ground… down in the dingle at Fitzhugh":

No one without special knowledge on the subject would have thought it possible such a splendid ground could be made on the damp old dell with a stream running through the middle.

Then again, Ariel had a wicked sense of humour. Joseph Paxton's Crystal Palace was, of course, a magnificent structure and Ariel was deliberately courting confusion between the Great Exhibition Hall and the sports arena, a slightly more modest affair, that shared the same grounds in Sydenham. The latter was, however, functional and capacious enough to be the country's top athletics stadium and the FA Cup Final venue.

Given local interest, the *Southampton Observer* felt duty bound to give its readers – and posterity – a full description of "The New Football Ground situated between Archer's-road and Bedford-road," which had been transformed from what resembled "a railway cutting" into a "capacious arena, well adapted for the sport to which it will in future be dedicated. The lofty slopes on either side of the turfed parallelogram have been easily adapted for the accommodation of the spectators who assemble to watch the matches." There followed a most detailed guide to the facilities:

In the centre of the Eastern slope is A LARGE STAND covered with corrugated iron, with the lowest seats raised about six feet above the level of the turf. This stand is 200 feet long, 32 feet deep, and contains eight platforms for seats rising one behind the other. It will easily accommodate 2,000 spectators. Immediately opposite, on the West side of the ground, is what may be termed the grand stand, which will accommodate a similar number of shilling ticket-holders; several of the front rows are reserved for the purchasers of season tickets. This stand is 130 feet long, and 40 feet in depth. It is roofed with corrugated iron, and a large glass screen will protect the stand from wind and weather on one side, while the dressing-rooms, &c., afford sufficient protection on the other. The seats here are of a superior description, and the floor boards will be covered with linoleum. South of this a smaller stand is in the course of erection, and beyond that will be the refreshment rooms.

Over the refreshment rooms, is THE MAIN ENTRANCE to the ground opening on Bedford-road which connects Hill-lane with Milton-road. Here a number of turnstiles will be, and everyone admitted must either pay or give up a ticket previously obtained. A covered corridor gives access to the grand stand room from this entrance. One half of the south slope of the grounds will be covered with wooden platforms rising tier above tier, so that all can see the play, while the other half will consist of a series of gravelled terraces, each commanding a good view of the players.

THE OPEN PORTIONS of the slope on each side of the East stand and the whole of the north slope on the Archer's-road side are covered with narrow wooden platforms, rising one behind the other, and affording all who pass the gate an uninterrupted view of the play. The goals will be at the north and south ends of the ground and the latter has been so nicely levelled that there will be no advantage to either competing team except so far as light and wind is concerned. The position of the ground in a dell, surrounded by rising ground, will shelter the players to a great extent from windage.

It is difficult to estimate how many spectators can be accommodated, but we were told that there will, without crowding, be ROOM FOR OVER 25,000 SPECTATORS. There are other entrances besides those described… In order to facilitate exit on days when there is a large crowd a set of large double gates in the centre of the boundary fences on the south side can be thrown open to give spectators an opportunity of leaving the ground easily. There will be a private entrance through Glenside, confined to the directors, officials, and players, that property having been acquired for the purpose of offices, dressing-rooms, bath-rooms, &c [see page 46 below]. AN ASPHALT RUNNING TRACK has been laid down at the foot of the retaining wall of this property, which skirts the football ground on that side from north to south. This is reached by a flight of steps from the rear of the above mentioned property, and this also gives access to the playing ground.

On the space between Glenside and the grand stand are THE DRESSING ROOMS, LAVATORIES, AND BATH ROOMS of the playing teams. Those reserved for the Southampton team are most elaborately fitted, and are lighted from the roof. The bath room, which adjoins the dressing room, has a large plunge bath, two slipper baths and shower baths with wash hand basins, &c. Close by the entrance to the dressing room is a drying room fitted with rails for drying the clothing of the players on wet days, the heat being obtained from a number of hot water pipes. The floors are wood blocked, and the whole suite heated by pipes, while hot and cold water is laid on to each bath and basin. Adjoining is a suite of rooms for the visiting team, not quite so large, but equally comfortable… The teams will be able to reach and leave the ground without passing through the crowd, which alone is a great advantage.

In front of the dressing rooms is A TERRACE commanding a view of the whole of the playing ground…Altogether the grounds have been arranged to give the maximum comfort to the players and the spectators, and are the beau ideal of what a football ground should be. We do not think any ground in the United Kingdom equals that of Southampton, and we hope the results of the first season will show that the directors were justified in embarking upon this speculation.

FULL-TIME *at* THE DELL

These salubrious facilities were not provided by the Southampton Football Club, as the same publication acknowledged a week later, in an account of the Brighton United fixture: "Speaking of the Dell Football Ground reminds me that full justice has not been done to the part Mr. George Thomas has taken in providing such a capital home for Southampton Football Club. I understand that it is wholly and solely through that gentleman's exertions that this splendid ground has been constructed out of an unpromising looking piece of waste land." The account goes on to give statistics on the capacity of the individual ends and stands and a thorough breakdown on the plumbing and drainage facilities, which, for the time being, you, dear reader, will be spared.

corner of which was roofed over to protect the less hardy standing spectators from the worst excesses of the Mercian winter.

Everton's Goodison Park was another well-developed ground: its one covered stand had seating for 3,000 and, by 1895, one section of terracing also had a roof. Goodison had an estimated capacity of 55,000 and Villa Park had already played host to 35,000, making them far larger than The Dell; but, in terms of facilities, they were certainly not superior.

In fact, The Dell appears to have been the first football stadium in England with seating on both sides of the pitch; and, Villa Park aside, it had more buttock space than any other ground, too.

Brighton United attack the Milton end

Whatever, it would appear that "The Dell" – as *Southampton Amusements* had named it for lack of any lead from the Club on the matter – was an impressive undertaking for a Southern League club, at least. But how did it compare with the splendid stadiums of the North and Midlands, where the great clubs of the era entertained the industrial masses in their thousands? What would visiting spectators, players and directors from Manchester, Liverpool, Birmingham and Sheffield have made of it?

Simon Inglis, in his tome, *Football Grounds of Britain,* provides some answers to those questions. The mighty Villa Park had been opened the previous year and was probably the most impressive stadium in the country, with a single grand stand seating 5,500 and with the remaining three sides of the ground being banking, one

Most other arenas of this period appear to have been little more than a single grand stand and embankments: Burnden Park (another ground with an incongruous house sited in one corner), which hosted a Cup Final replay in 1899, had seating for a mere 1,600. In short, Southampton's new football ground was impressive by any standards; and it should be added that, very few games of football, other than Cup Finals, were watched by crowds in excess of 25,000.

First swing at the ball

The Mayor, Alderman J. Tilling JP, had the privilege of taking the first swing at a ball at The Dell. He kicked-off "like an international" towards the "Bedford-road end", which Saints' captain, Harry Wood, having won the toss, had chosen to defend.

The distinction of being the first goal-scorer went to Watty Keay, after less than five minutes. Tom Smith put in a cross, having sprinted the length of the field, "and Watty Keay, steadying himself, shot a lovely goal, amidst terrific cheers."

It was a rather one-sided affair. Perhaps the imposing surroundings unnerved the green-shirted Brighton side, despite having former Football League players in their ranks, but the fact that they were reduced to ten men after a high kick from Chadwick "accidentally" caught McArthur full on the chin, couldn't have helped their faint chances of a win.

turn-out at their former base at the County Ground, or any other Southern League fixture: why did the directors, George Thomas in particular, believe that Southampton required a state-of-the-art 25,000 capacity ground?

For the answer to that we must delve into Saints' past and the history of their former home grounds. The path to enlightenment is a devious one, but paved with good intentions and well-posted if you know where to look for the signs.

The journey, over the next five chapters, includes detours into the rise and fall of Rugby Union in Southampton; the rise, and further rise, of the Association

Saints attack the Archers end

The score was 4-1. But, all things considered, Saints were looking to win their third consecutive Southern League championship; they had four new signings, all with impeccable credentials; and, even had the game been played on United's home turf – on the East Sussex Cricket Ground – it would have turned a considerable number of heads, south of Luton at least, had Southampton failed to prevail. They were, in the small pond that was Southern professional football, big fish.

That said, the game was watched by a little over 6,000 individuals, less than a quarter of the actual potential crowd. This would have been considered a respectable

game in the town; and an introduction to a confederacy of earnest young men who decided to form a football club, which, ultimately, became the darlings of the local population. More, let it be placed on record, through chance than design. If it had been suggested in 1885 that Southampton would produce a famous football club, nobody, even in Southampton, would have considered the possibility of its being in the round-ball code or suggested it might emerge from St Mary's.

This is how things came to pass.

FULL-TIME *at* THE DELL

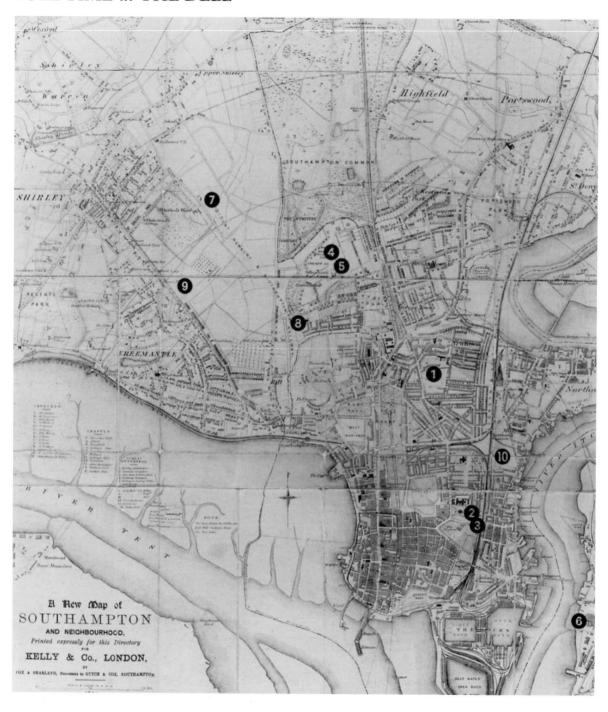

A local map of 1892, on which are marked, by numbers, 10 locations mentioned in this book, especially in the early chapters:

Already existing at that time: **❶** Antelope Ground, **❷** St Mary's Church **❸** The Deanery **❹** County Ground
❺ Banister Park School (later the site of the Stadium) **❻** Woolston Works

Projected: **❼** Route of the Didcot, Newbury & Southampton Railway

Sites of later developments: **❽** The Dell **❾** Freemantle's ground **❿** Friends Provident St Mary's Stadium

Chapter 3
Genesis

Southampton Football Club owes its origins, as everyone knows – or at least everyone who is anyone knows – to a meeting of the St Mary's Church of England Young Men's Association at the Grove Street Schoolrooms in November 1885, chaired by Rev A.B. Sole, one of the parish's curates.

The precise date, and anything that might have been discussed during the assembly, was not recorded for posterity. The bare facts are that an Association Football club was formed; that they played their first match on a "strip of ground in Northlands Road," later occupied by the Hampshire County Bowling Club, on 21 November; and that their opponents were Freemantle Association.

This enables us to deduce that Saints were formed sometime before 21 November 1885, but it does not tell us who the St Mary's Church of England Young Men's Association were. Neither has anyone ever bothered to explain where St Mary's was, or rather is. The following, given the current quality of information generated by the local media, is worth committing to memory.

Parishioners

At the beginning of the nineteenth century, the parish of St Mary's stretched eastwards of Above Bar to the banks of the River Itchen and out to Portswood, more or less; and, apart from the odd wharf and shipyard, it was predominantly rural.

At this time, Southampton was a genteel spa resort, albeit with busy Channel Island and Continental traffic from a much smaller Town Quay than today's. But, with ports such as London, Liverpool, Bristol and Cardiff being pushed to their limits to keep up with the awesome trade of the British Empire, it was only a matter of time before someone noticed the potential of Southampton Water as a major harbour. Astute men of business from Liverpool to London reached for their cheque books, Acts of Parliament were passed and, in 1835, work commenced on a railway line from Nine Elms to Southampton Docks. The foundation stone of the Docks themselves (the area now known as Ocean Village) was laid, "with full Masonic ceremony," on 12 October 1838.

Southampton was already experiencing a building boom and men of means were snatching up land in the Northam, Kingsland, Chapel and Crosshouse districts to meet the accommodation demands of the economic migrants pouring into the town. What had been an area of market gardens and meadows quickly became a densely developed network of terraced housing. The meanest and cheapest housing was concentrated in the low-lying areas of Chapel, Crosshouse and Northam.

To keep up with the population explosion, the Church of England began a rapid building programme of its own. Between 1847 and 1866, St Mary's was sub-divided into several parishes: Holy Trinity in Kingsland; St Luke's, Newtown; Christ Church, Northam (later to be replaced by St Augustine's); St James, Bernard Street (now the site of St Luke's Greek Orthodox Church); St Matthews in St Mary's Road (latterly the West Indian Club); and Christ Church, Highfield.

This left St Mary's, Southampton's "Mother Church", with Chapel, Crosshouse and part of Kingsland and in excess of 8,000 of the poorest parishioners in the town.

St Mary's was a problem parish. Something that Canon Albert Basil Orme Wilberforce, who became rector in 1871, was fully aware of. He was firmly of the opinion that the demon drink was, to a large extent, responsible for this state of affairs. This theory wasn't universally agreed with, as he conceded in the *S. Mary's Parish Magazine* of October 1887:

> Amidst the torrent of abuse poured upon me by angry liqueur dealers and their clients at Portsmouth and elsewhere, which abuse I cordially welcome as a proof that the shaft has told home, there have been some things said and written calculated to make the heart sad and anxious. One, residing in Southampton apparently, writes to a newspaper in these words:-

> Let me tell Canon Wilberforce that charity begins at home and that… he should recollect that the district in which he labours is sadly in want of his assistance,… the immediate neighbourhood of his church and residence

FULL-TIME *at* THE DELL

groaning under the curse of drunkenness and immorality: THAT A STREET IMMEDIATELY OPPOSITE HIS CHURCH TEEMS WITH BROTHELS: THAT THE PUBLIC FOOTPATH THROUGH HIS CHURCHYARD IS THE NIGHTLY RESORT OF PROSTITUTES, who solicit, aye, and ply their vile calling there; and that, lastly, under the very shadow of his church may often be seen scenes that were seldom equalled in the palmy days of old Portsmouth.

Let me commend the words printed in small capitals to the attention of the magistrates and Watch Committee of this town. Strip them of their obvious exaggeration, and there is enough truth in them to make every professed Christian in St Mary's throw aside indifference and guilty acquiescence and plunge into God's battle.

Despite its less than wholesome environs, St Mary's Church remained the leading centre of worship for the Town's most "respectable" personages. There are pointed references to the grandeur and status of the congregation members, their carriages outside the church, contrasted with the conspicuous poverty of the local residents. The humbler locals apparently preferred the less formal surroundings of the church's Dock Street Mission, or the dozens of chapels of other denominations in the district; those that were not part of the increasing Roman Catholic population at least.

From the pages of the parish journal, there appears to be no shortage of people fighting "God's good fight" – despite the odds piled against them.

"It is no slight privilege and responsibility," Wilberforce had written in 1886,

to preside over a devoted body of clergy and laity such as compose the staff of S. Mary's Parish. Your work in preaching the gospel, in visiting the sick, in teaching the young, in helping the doubtful, in stemming the tide of unbelief, in beautifying the Worship of God, requires special grace and power.

To this end, there are numerous organisations mentioned in the magazine, some given more prominence than others, testifying that largesse and self-help were alive and well in St Mary's. Among them the Working Men's Club; the Guild of St Mary; the Blanket Club; St Mary's Working Men's Cricket Club; the Band of Hope; the Guild of St Agnus; the Maternity Society; an Industrial Society; the Dock Street Mission; the Fo'c'sle, a "club for working lads"; the Crow's Nest Club, a night school "for a rough and neglected class of lads"; the Working Men's Rowing Club, run "on Total Abstinence principles"; and a Total Abstinence Society.

The statistics that have been preserved relating to some of these groups are impressive. The Sunday Schools claimed 1,159 scholars supervised by 118 teachers in 1886; while, between 1 December 1887 and 31 March 1888, 2,516 quarts of soup were dispensed from the Anderson's Road Soup Kitchen, one of three being operated by the church.

Which brings us the Young Men's Association. It gets more coverage in the *S. Mary's Parish Magazine* than most of the societies above, but there are frustrating gaps of information. We know that its members were obliged to carry out certain parochial duties, singing in the choir and teaching Sunday School being among them. The minimum requirement of members was to attend regular Bible Classes; but, although other options existed, they remain obscure. There is an intriguing claim in the parish magazine of July 1887, beneath an announcement of its "Annual Gymnastic Display and Assault at Arms",[*] that the Society was "doing large and valuable work among the young men of the town." The nature of this work is obscure, but there is an unqualified allusion to "mission work" in a *Southampton Times* report, of 15 January 1887, on a meeting of the YMA. The most obvious deduction is that some of its members were involved with the activities of the Crow's Nest and Fo'c'sle clubs. Certainly there were young men in the town in need of the guidance of a group of well brought-up young gentlemen with good educations. Reports of delinquency and crime in the local newspapers of the 1880s are depressingly similar to those carried in the *Echo* of today. And attitudes towards youths every bit as predictable.

The *Southampton Times* of 6 January 1883 carried a report of a meeting of magistrates discussing the "discreditable scenes which frequently occurred" in the "High-street". Sunday evenings, apparently, were

---

[*] Posh for "boxing".

14

especially problematical, "when gangs of youths from eighteen to twenty years of age banded themselves together on the pavements, forced respectable people into the road, and made use of very disgusting language." The article takes a Pythonesque turn towards the end, with the assertion that, on one Sunday evening, "there was a disgraceful scene occasioned by a lot of boys, who walked up the High-street and along Portland-street with false noses on, singing some abominable lines to one of the Salvation Army tunes."

Nobody questioned whether these lads had anything else to do, or anywhere else to go of an evening. If they had been from St Mary's, and had a mind to improve themselves, they would have had some options.

Being in the YMA was probably not one of them. As noted, it was very much a middle-class institution. The facilities at their disposal were a cut above what was on offer to the patrons of the Crow's Nest and Fo'c'sle clubs. By 1886, it had football, cricket, athletics and gymnasium sections; its own choral society; and an entertainments committee. And there were regular lectures on subjects as diverse as "A Voyage to China" and Cromwell. There is even a suggestion, in the parish magazine of February 1886, that it had its own gymnasium; but this is unlikely. Most probably, a room or hall at Grove Street School was made available to the lads and they had a place to stow their equipment.

The philosophy of the YMA is well set out in a remarkable article in the parish journal of March 1886:

> An invitation issuing from the Young Men's Association of the parish is being sent out, and will be gladly given to anyone applying to Mr. Harrison, the secretary, at the Grove Street School House, to come to a soiree, given by the society on Tuesday evening, the 9th, in their club rooms, Grove Street, at 7.30. There will be a gymnastic exhibition by the members, many of whom, by their constant practice have become proficient. All connected with the club are believers in muscular Christianity, and think that the advantage of strong developed limbs, a supple frame, and a quick eye, cannot be overestimated. Any may there be able to witness for themselves that in a "Christian Guild" there need be no lack of that true British manly spirit… May… our young men… use their physical strength and freedom as to make their

power the handmaiden to that moral strength and decision of character, that shall free them from the world's slavery and bondage…

Muscular Christianity emanated from the public school ethos so attractively presented by Thomas Hughes in *Tom Brown's Schooldays* and was promoted by the writings of such luminaries as Charles Kingsley (whose popular sermons were very much approved of by Canon Wilberforce and published in the parish magazine). It was a movement much respected in the late Victorian/Edwardian era and was a great influence on Baron de Courbertin, who founded the modern Olympic Games. Like the Olympic movement, many of its self-proclaimed adherents were capable of incredible cant – most especially when anyone not white and/or, at least, middle-class tried to involve themselves in top class sport. As for the lads of the YMA, fit, healthy, well-educated and, predominantly, from respectable homes they may have been, but this does not make it axiomatic that they all subscribed to the philosophical outlook attributed to them. Or even if they did, interpreted muscular Christianity in quite the same way as, say, the administration of the Amateur Athletic Association, or the Amateur Rowing Association and their ilk, who excluded anyone who earned a living from manual labour, including skilled craftsmen – as would the British Olympic movement when it got underway.

The only thing we can be sure of is, that like most middle-class teenagers and young men of the day, they were practising Christians. To that we can add that they were willing to give up spare time to parochial duties in the parish they prayed in. The fact that in exchange they were awarded sporting and social facilities was certainly an inducement, but this is not to say it was the only reason they sang at services or gave religious instruction to the children of the parish. However, it came to pass that the rector decided that the facilities were being abused. But before we discuss that, it may be as well to consider just why the Young Men's Association decided to form a football club.

A melancholy affair

The first captain of St Mary's Young Men's Association FC was A.A. Fry, a teacher and, latterly, the headmaster of Foundry Lane School. He recalled, in a *Southern Daily*

FULL-TIME *at* THE DELL

Echo article of February 1928, that he had originally played for another St Mary's team, Deanery Association, and that "the St Mary's Club was formed …by most of the same players and officials, and with the same president, the Rev. Canon Wilberforce."

Deanery players, who did battle in a splendid outfit of black stockings, white knickerbockers and white shirt bearing a black Maltese cross, topped with black and white caps "in halves", were influential in Saints' earliest days. Four or five of them appear to have ventured forth for St Mary's. But claims that there was an amalgamation are, at the very least, an exaggeration. The last report of a Deanery game appeared in the *Southampton Times* of 17 November 1883. The reason Deanery folded is unknown, but the fact that the Town Council had decided to convert their home patch, Porter's Mead, into a park (Queen's Park to be exact) may have been a contributory factor. The difficulty of getting a regular XI together may have been another. They had reported playing "men short" twice during the 1882-83 season. The problem of putting a full team out plagued even the most well-established outfits.

Formed in 1882, Deanery Association was an offshoot of The Deanery Cricket Club, which took its name from their home ground, within the expansive and pleasantly pastoral estate that surrounded the St Mary's rectory. A delightful location that was favourably compared to the best rural vicarages – and much handier for the shops, trains, docks and outlandish sinks of depravity.

The Deanery grounds were not a facility that the football club was able to avail itself of.

When Deanery Association formed, it was the only association football club in Southampton, while there

were at least seven Rugby sides. A football club that went by the name of Southampton Rangers had existed in the late 1870s, but they didn't make much of an impression. Dominated by Scottish sea-going engineers, they found it hard to maintain any consistency, in terms of team selection or form, and were best remembered as being easy pickings for Bournemouth-based sides.

The reason Deanery played "socker", as opposed to "rugger", is on record. A.A. Fry mentioned it while recalling Deanery's first game:

> So far as I know, the first organised association football match in Southampton was played between two teams of teachers, of which I was one, on the old Porter's Mead…
> Usually Rugby football was played there, and one day during a particularly fierce game one player was killed. This cast a shadow over the game for a time in the town, and it was then we began to play association football regularly.

To say that the death of Stanley Ernest Gibbs "cast a shadow over" rugby was something of an understatement: it brought Southampton national notoriety and then transformed it into a laughing stock.

Gibbs was a 19 year-old clerk in the employ of the Southampton-based newspaper, the *Hampshire Independent*. On 27 November 1880, he was playing for Trojans against Romsey Rangers and was injured when a scrimmage collapsed. He was quickly attended to by a doctor watching the game and was eventually stretchered home to his lodgings in the High Street, where his family looked after him.[*] His spine was damaged and even a specialist from the Royal Victoria Military in Hospital in Netley was unable to help him. The inquest, held in the Guildhall on 8 December, was informed that the victim had died the previous day "from congestion of the lungs, which always follows from such cases."

The jury returned a verdict of "accidental death" and that might have ended the matter; but both of the presiding magistrates – who were not inclined to

---

[*] His brother was a High Street butcher and his father, William Gibbs, a confectioner and baker. The location of the latter's shop is recalled by Gibbs Road, the alley linking Above Bar and Marlands Road.

The Deanery site as it is today

differentiate between the two popular codes – had words to say on the conduct of football.

What's more, Mr John Cooksey JP, who was also the mayor, promptly had the Town Clerk issue a handbill ostensibly banning football, of any code whatsoever, "in the Porter's Meadow-field, or upon any other part of public lands in Southampton."

Gibbs's "melancholy demise" and the inquest had attracted considerable interest in the press, all over the country. The ban was something of a sensation.

The Manchester-based national sporting bible, the *Athletic News,* reflected, on 15 December, that the accident had "been a positive godsend to the daily papers," offering, as it did,

> a grand opportunity for relieving the monotony of
> home and foreign politics . . . with a tasty entrée
> about the horrors and brutality of the game "only fit
> for a set of costermongers" . . . our "dailies" never
> miss an opportunity to bring what discredit they can
> on manly sports by the insertion of highly
> ornamented accounts of accidents incurred in the
> pursuit of popular pastimes. . .

Meanwhile, in London, the *Athletic World* poured scorn on the prohibition, accusing Mr Cooksey of being "maternally disposed" and bearing the "senile temerity of bumbledom" upon his face: it failed to see how he could "do anything to prevent the game being played in the public fields."

This thought had already occurred to several individuals in Southampton.

On 12 December a council meeting touched on the subject and Mr Le Feurvre (Conservative) demanded, of Mr Cooksey (Liberal),

> by what Act of Parliament or under what by-law the
> Mayor had power to stop football on the public lands?
> He did not want to open the question broadly, but he
> should like the Act or by-law pointed out to him.
> The Mayor said there was no endeavour or intention
> on his part to put down football. He had no desire to
> do so, but he had only done what he considered was
> his duty, and the bill he had issued itself fully explained
> its meaning. He had no desire to put down the game
> as long as it was played properly and decently.

Following on from its report of Gibbs's funeral, the *Southampton Times* noted the mayor's bill and the intention of the town's athletic community to hold an "indignation meeting". If it ever took place, there is no mention of it in the press, but the Trojans' committee were determined not be intimidated. Their minutes of

The Mayor's proclamation as it appeared in the *Times*

16 December include the entry: "With regard to the Mayor's handbill it was decided to play as usual unless we found out before that the Mayor had given any instruction to the police. In that case it was thought best to summon any offending 'arm of the law' for assault."

Southampton's other football clubs appear to have been of the same mind. There was no football in Southampton on the weekend of the funeral, out of respect for Gibbs, but the following weekend fixtures carried on as usual. The whole affair appears to have lost steam overnight.

The *Athletic News* could not drop the subject, though. Its edition of 29 December devoted several column inches to a new set of rules, 52 of them purportedly drawn-up by Mayor Cooksey. These included:

Rule 1 *Every player must wear carpet slippers, except in the case of a damp ground, when galoshes must be worn.*

Rule 12 *No talking aloud.*

Rule 36 *No married or engaged men, curates, or only sons may play; Irish landlords, mayors and orphans excepted.*

Rule 44 *No players may be collared by an opponent without the consent (in writing) of his parents, or, in the case of an orphan, that of the minister of his parish.*

FULL-TIME *at* THE DELL

Satire was absent from the local newspapers and it is impossible to know how many people in Southampton read the journals which, like the *Athletic News,* had a field day with the ban; but Fry, obviously, believed that rugby's popularity was affected by the affair, as do subsequent accounts of the matter.

The question is: was Fry correct? The number of rugby clubs in the town actually increased quite respectably in the following years. There were 14 mentioned in the local press during 1885 – although some of them appear to have been rather *ad hoc* set-ups – as opposed to six association teams. And four of those association sides were attached to institutions or clubs more usually associated with rugby: Trojans, for example, occasionally fielded an XI by the name of Somnambulists.

This state of affairs was to change radically in the next five or so years. By 1893, Southampton was teeming with soccer clubs and Trojans were the town's single representative of the Rugby Football Union.

The Common

The rise of Association Football, and the eventual eclipse of the Rugby Union game, in Southampton, and Hampshire for that matter, was not sudden. But it was certainly majestic. In Southampton, this rise can be charted from the fixture between St Mary's Young Men's Association FC and Freemantle, already noted, on 21 November 1885.

There are two accounts of the match and they are evidently the exact same report. The only difference being that the one published in the *Hampshire Independent* has had more edited out of it than the one that appeared in the *Southampton Times.* Curiously, both newspapers carry the same mistake in the heading, calling the Young Men "St. Mary's Y.M.C.A." This is an error that has been repeated interminably down the years by chroniclers thorough enough to check out the original match report, but too busy to read the first paragraph.

We do not know who wrote the report, but it was almost certainly somebody associated with the St Mary's team, who regarded their first game of sufficient social importance to place on record, especially as his side won 5-1. Vital information that failed to make it into print was the venue and the teams.

It is fairly certain that it took place on the "backfield" of the Hampshire County Cricket Club Ground, then frequently referred to as Banister's Park. And, thanks to a 1912 series on Saints' history in the *Southampton Pictorial,* we even have a team: R. Ruffell, goal; G.H. Muir and R. McDonald, backs; A.G. Fry, C. Deacon, and A. Gandy, half-backs; A.A. Fry, G. Gandy, E. Bromley, G. McIvor, and A. Varley, forwards. However, this line-up is dubious. Five of the Young Men's teams for the 1885-86 season featured in local newspaper reports and Ruffell and McDonald are mentioned in none of them; and, while former Deanery player, A.G. Fry, is named in two of the games, he is playing for Southampton Harriers in both of them. As "Recorder" of the *Pictorial* noted as he embarked on his pioneering hagiological work, "I have often found the recollections of men who took part in the games of the club's junior period at fault on many points." Bear this in mind as you read on.

The story of the development of the association game in Southampton, and of Southampton FC in particular, cannot be confined to relating what happened where to St Mary's. There were other clubs; and to understand why Saints emerged as the town's top club, and how soccer became something of an obsession with much of the local public, some attention must be paid to their rivals. Freemantle are a case in point; and their progress cannot be disentangled from Saints' until after professionalism is firmly rooted in the district.

L. Ghent, Williams, R. Williamson, Fowle, A. Coles (forwards).
St. Mary's Y.M.C.A. v. Freemantle Association Football Club.—The football club which has just been formed in connection with St. Mary's Young Men's Association, played their first match on Saturday last according to "Association Rules," when they showed that they have among their members the materials with which to form a fairly strong club by practice. During the first half St. Mary's scored four goals rather quickly, three of these being obtained from corner kicks. The game became much faster during the second half, and shortly after the change St. Mary's scored another point. Freemantle then obtained a goal through the ball from a corner kick passing off one of the St. Mary's team and so through the posts. Up to the call of time no further point was scored, so that St. Mary's were the victors by five goals to one. The goals were obtained by Bromley (three) and Fry (2). The Freemantle team showed some good play during the latter part of the game, while the good individual play of each of the St. Mary's team was well sustained throughout.

Avenue Rangers v. Arabs—played on the Southampton

According to Hampshire FA *Handbooks,* Freemantle were founded in 1884. As yet, though, no report of their games before their august confrontation with the Young Men has come to light. What we do know about them is that they were based at the *Waterloo Arms* and there appears to have been some connection with Christ

Church, in that one of the curates, Rev George D'Arcy, was a dashing figure in their ranks.

The two clubs would play a return game the following January, again on the County Ground – St Mary's won 1-0. It would appear, as Freemantle are often noted as playing there, that they were hiring the backfield on a fairly regular basis.

The YMA's home games were invariably played on the Common, which they shared with a number of rugby clubs and their second known opponents, Southampton Harriers. When they met on 9 January 1886, the *Southampton Times* carried the following report:

> **Southampton Harriers v. St. Mary's F.C.:-**
> A very exciting football match was played on Saturday, before a good concourse of people, on the Southampton Common, between these clubs, under Association Rules, both clubs putting very strong teams in the field, which was the result of some fast and good play on both sides.

The claim that this goalless draw was played in front of "a good concourse of people" is cryptic to say the least. A couple of dozen passers-by might have constituted a "good concourse" for an association match. An indication of just how healthy the "dribbling game" was at this time can be gleaned from a *Southampton Times* report of a charity game played at Westwood Park between Freemantle and the 93rd Highlanders on 17 April, which observed that "the weather was fine, but the attendance was not very large, this being no doubt owing to the fact that the match was played under Association Rules."

All football games in the Southampton at this time were "friendlies". The South Hants & Dorset Football Association had formed in April 1884 and was running Senior and Junior Cup competitions, but its members were concentrated around Bournemouth,[*] which was something of a soccer enclave in Hampshire. To the east, in Southampton and Portsmouth especially, rugby was king and the few association clubs that did exist probably lacked the facilities to host cup-ties.

The Young Men managed, during their first season, to arrange eight reported matches. There were undoubtedly

other games, but they didn't make the newspapers.[*] There were now five soccer clubs in the town: Harriers, St Mary's, Freemantle, Spring Hill and Banister Court School – who dabbled in both codes and were capable of fielding a formidable team, dominated by university-educated teachers, older boys and local residents – plus the Trojans' side, Somnambulists (who do not appear to have treated the game with any seriousness), and Geneva Cross, another club that dabbled in both codes and were based at the Royal Victoria Military Hospital at Netley.[†]

We can safely say, then, that Association Football was not well-developed in Southampton or Hampshire at the time the Young Men set forth on their career.

In sharp contrast, the game was undergoing a revolution further north. On 5 April 1885, a good seven months before the Young Men's Association had decided to form a football club, another nail had been hammered in the coffin of what had been regarded, barely two years previously, as very much a gentlemen's pursuit. The first FA Cup Final without either side dominated by former English public school boys had taken place: Blackburn Rovers had beaten Queen's Park of Glasgow 2-0. The previous year, the defeated finalists had been two-time winners Old Etonians, the victors being another Blackburn outfit, Olympic. A public school side was never to contest the FA Cup Final again.

During the summer of 1885, the Football Association had legalised professional footballers, albeit with severe misgivings and under very tight regulations. Clubs in the North and Midlands were poised to take the game over.

If there were any ideas of professional footballers booting the ball around on the open spaces of Southampton, Bournemouth, Portsmouth or the village greens of Hampshire, they were not articulated; but 1886 would see a revolution, of sorts, ignite on the central South Coast, not that St Mary's would have much of a part to play in it.

---

[*] For those readers too young to remember, Bournemouth was in Hampshire until 1974.

[*] For instance, they played Totton on 16 January. There is no report of the game in the local press and, while the game is noted as "lost" in the *S. Mary's Parish Magazine,* the score, venue and the team are not mentioned.

[†] Netley Hospital appeared to have had at least three football clubs at any one time: Army Medical Depot RUFC and Army Medical Students RUFC are also mentioned in the press during 1885.

FULL-TIME *at* THE DELL

The Works

The Young Men widened their horizon during the 1886-87 season, expanding their fixture list to include games at Cowes and Winchester, but they remained outside the South Hants & Dorset FA and continued to play home fixtures on the Common, wearing an improvised kit of white knickerbockers and white shirts with a red diagonal sash stitched across it. Other than a somewhat pretentious propensity to send reports of their games to the *Southampton Times,* there wasn't much to distinguish them from some *ad hoc* gathering hoofing the ball about on any open space in Southampton.

None of the hitherto mentioned Southampton clubs joined the Association either, but there was a new side, Woolston Works, on the scene; and such was their confidence, they immediately entered for the South Hants & Dorset Senior Cup. *

Meanwhile, in Portsmouth, association football – hitherto as prominent as it was in Southampton – was edging out from the shadow of the running game. The town's leading club Portsmouth Association FC decided to inaugurate their own – unofficial – tournament, the Portsmouth & District Cup. Woolston Works entered that too, as did Freemantle.

The major deterrent to Southampton teams entering the Hants & Dorset cups was probably the requirement that ties be played on an enclosed ground and that gate money be collected. The only such grounds in Southampton were the County Ground, The Antelope Cricket Ground, Westwood Park (where the field used for football was considered too restricted by the surrounding trees to play a good game) and Whithedwood Park, the base of Whithedwood Park RUFC. These venues required money to hire and were monopolised by the better-supported rugby clubs. This said, the St Mary's Young Men's Association Cricket Club had found the wherewithal to hire the Antelope for the summer of 1887.

St Mary's started their season on 2 October, with a practice match in the grounds of the Deanery, which – one 2nd XI game aside – pretty much accounts for their entire career of playing in the parish of St Mary's, while Woolston Works visited Portsmouth AFC and won 2-1.

The following Saturday, the Works played their opening Hants & Dorset cup-tie, thrashing Portsmouth Sunflowers 6-1 at Woolston Park.

This confrontation epitomised what had been going on in Association Football for the previous five years or so: the eclipse of "gentlemen" by "working-class" teams. The Sunflowers were a side run by Canon Norman Pares, who had been part of the Old Etonians team that had beaten Clapham Rovers in the 1879 FA Cup Final, and was predominantly made-up of relations (he had two footballing brothers and at least one cousin in the side at various times) and old chums from school and Cambridge University.

But Canon Pares was not the only man on the pitch with a Cup Winners' medal. Playing at right-back for the Works was a young soldier stationed at Netley Hospital by the name of Private J. Howarth, who had played for the ostensibly amateur Blackburn Rovers in their 1885 Cup Final defeat of Queen's Park.

Howarth was something of an outsider in the Works' side: most of the team were employees of the Oswald, Mordaunt & Co. shipyard, which occupied the site now (for the time being at least) known as Vosper Thorneycroft. It was a busy place in the mid-1880s and tradesmen were being brought to Southampton from all over the country. Mr Oswald, the Managing Director, appeared to have a predilection for hiring artisans whose skills were not confined to shipbuilding and repair.

In 1936, the Hon. Sec. of the South Hants & Dorset FA, William Pickford, recalled that

> The effect of this galaxy of Scotsmen on the game in Hampshire was electrifying. Up to then few local people knew anything about the fine points of the game, and the public troubled little about it as a spectacle. The opening of the Woolston Shipyard… turned Southampton into an Association hot-bed, and it woke up with a start.

Pickford remembered playing the Works at that time and it taking him several days to recover: "There was more than one free fight, and more 'tricks that are in vain' than we had been accustomed to."

The 1886-87 South Hants & Dorset Senior Cup Final was played on the Bar End Ground at Winchester. The protagonists were the previous year's beaten finalists

---

* Woolston was not in the County Borough of Southampton at this time, but – like Netley, Shirley, Freemantle, Millbrook, etc. – was generally referred to as being in Southampton.

Wimborne and, inevitably, Woolston Works. It was a keenly-contested game won by a single goal by McKechnie of the Works.

For the record, the two umpires were complemented by the distinguished presence of a referee from the Football Association by the name of M.P. Betts. Presumably the very same M.P. Betts who scored the first ever FA Cup Final goal, for Wanderers against the Royal Engineers, in 1872, playing under the pseudonym of A.H. Chequer.

The Works' victory over Wimborne was not the finale to the season. The final of the Portsmouth & District Association Cup was eagerly awaited and, according to the *Southampton Times* of 2 April, a remarkable 800 spectators duly turned up at the United Services Ground in Portsmouth to witness the Works take on Portsmouth AFC.

We know the crowd was remarkable because it was remarked upon; it appears to be the first attempt, in the Hampshire press, to enumerate the attendance at a game of football. But there was a clear sign that the Association game continued to paddle awkwardly in the wash of the stately sail-assisted steamer that was rugby: the match goals were rugby posts.

To general amazement, Portsmouth won 2-0. The indomitable performance of A.C. Smith – almost certainly the most famous footballer produced in Hampshire for several decades – between the rugby posts was regarded a contributory factor in the result. In the *Southampton Times*, Smith's name was given as Dr Doyle. Which was actually his real name. Why Arthur Conan Doyle played under a pseudonym is unknown.[*]

If the Young Men had yet to make a great impact on football, even within the confines of Southampton, they had earned the estimation of the *S. Mary's Parish Magazine*. Unable to resist a bit of spin, it judged the "Football Club" to be "winning golden opinions throughout the town and neighbourhood [for being] victorious 'all along the line'."

The Cup

On 13 April 1887, the South Hants & Dorset FA dissolved, at a meeting held at the Crown Hotel, Wimborne, and two separate county associations were formed in its place. The first "general meeting" of the Hampshire FA was held at the Spartan Club[*] in Southampton High Street on 20 April and sixteen clubs sent delegates: St Mary's were represented, according to the minutes, by "Varley & Bromeley". At a subsequent meeting, on 5 September, St Mary's entered the newly-created Hampshire FA Junior Cup competition. In the *Hampshire Football Association Handbook* for the 1887-88 season, they are entered as St Mary's Young Men's Association FC. Their home ground is given as Southampton Common and the nearest stations as Southampton West[†] and St Denys.

As the Common lacked the requisites for a cup-tie, it must have come as some relief to the St Mary's committee that, when the first round draw was made, the Young Men found themselves away to Totton. Given that the *Southampton Times* report was probably filed by one of the St Mary's party, one observation is especially significant: "the ground – in spite of the recent unfavourable weather – was in splendid condition, and the Totton Club have good reason to congratulate themselves on having the privilege of playing their matches on such an excellent ground."

The game, on 26 November, was decided by a single Saints' goal. The account concluded with the observation that "where each one worked so hard it seemed scarcely fair to particularise, though it was generally admitted that Carter's playing at the back was a distinct feature of the game."

George Carter, an engraver at the Ordnance Survey, had arrived in Southampton in or before October 1887, from Hereford, where he had an established reputation as a footballer, having played for the Hereford & Herefordshire FA. During a conversation with Saints' historian Gary Chalk, in 1999, Carter's daughter-in-law,

---

* See G. Stavart, *A Study in Southsea*. Doyle, in his autobiographical *Memories and Adventures* (1924), failed to mention that he played under a *nom de guerre* and was under the misapprehension that he had played for Portsmouth FC. Pompey were not formed until 1899, and the two clubs have but the loosest of connections.

* The Spartan Club was a short-lived venture that appeared to cater for sportsmen of all inclinations and backgrounds. Its pride and joy was several billiards tables.

† Southampton West was up-line, towards the tunnel, of the present Southampton Central Station. The town's main station was Southampton Docks, or Terminus, as it became known.

FULL-TIME *at* THE DELL

Nellie Carter, divulged that he was not at all happy about being posted to Southampton. Carter maintained that Dr Russell Bencraft, who, among his many other posts, was Medical Officer at the Ordnance Survey, arranged for his transfer specifically so he could play for St Mary's and, being employed by the army, he had no choice in the matter. It is unlikely Dr Bencraft had that sort of authority; but his being a Hampshire CCC colleague of Colonel Fellows, Director General of the OS, who certainly did possess the authority, the story has a distinct ring of truth to it.

What Mrs Carter did not reveal is what Carter thought of playing for what was, after all, a church youth club side that had never played a competitive game.

The Young Men drew Petersfield in the second round. The Antelope was secured, "by kind permission of the Pirates." Pirates being a rugby club, who were sharing the ground with Woolston Works at the time. It was not a good day for the visitors, who could muster only 10 men and claimed two of their best players were unable to travel. The result was 10-0.

Another home tie in the third round, on 21 January 1888, pitted St Mary's against Lymington. Pirates 2nd XV had a home fixture that Saturday and the Antelope was unavailable. St Mary's managed to secure a "fine field at Redbridge" owned by a Mr Steadfast.

Redbridge was about as far as you could get from Southampton without crossing a river, certainly beyond the range of the horse-drawn tram system, but there was a good rail link.

The field was behind the *Anchor* public house, but Mr Steadfast was not the licensee of that or any of the other pubs in the village. Whether the Club or Mr Steadfast had any ambitions regarding the field as a regular football venue remains unknown, but if they did they came to nothing.

The Anchor, Redbridge, today

Lymington were defeated 4-0, but it would appear that Mr Steadfast was not at all impressed. In his 1912 history, Recorder recalled:

Some of the hilarious St. Mary's supporters by some means greatly annoyed the owner of the field, whose indignation was expressed in a demand that the gate receipts should be sent to the Royal South Hants and Southampton Hospital. The Saints' officials went post-haste to tender an apology, which after some reluctance, was accepted, and there the matter ended.

Next up were Bournemouth Arabs, for the semi-final. The venue was the County Ground. The score was 2-1. The Young Men were in the final. Their opponents were one of the clubs who shared the Common with them, Southampton Harriers.

The Harriers were not, *per se,* a football club. They had started life as Temperance Amateur Athletic Association and had changed their name in 1885. The previous autumn they had been able to recruit some useful footballers. Freemantle had declined to enter for either of the Hampshire FA's cup competitions and half their team signed on for Harriers. This had led to a distinct rise in performance: Harriers had not only drawn with the Works on 11 February, but scored two goals against them.

On 10 March, the two sides met to contest the Final at the County Ground, just a few hundred yards from where both clubs played their home games. Neither team were strangers to the venue, but it may have been the first time they had played in front of the pavilion, or before a crowd that was estimated by the *Southampton Times* to number 600 people, "notwithstanding that the weather was rather threatening."

That same day, a *Southampton Times* report of a St Mary's victory of the previous week opened with the sentence: "The Saints journeyed to Cowes on Saturday to decide the return match with the town club." It was the first time "Saints" had been used to describe St Mary's in print. Another nomenclatural transformation was becoming evident as well: Y.M.A., which had never been consistently used in local newspapers, was now being routinely disregarded. When Saints took the field against Harriers they were most definitely St Mary's FC, not St Mary's Church of England Young Men's Association Football Club.

Saints, as we can freely call them now, struggled in the early part of the game but came from behind to draw 2-2. Plus, at some unspecified time during the game, Saints had scored a goal without noticing. An astounded

The first known photograph of the Saints,
with the Hampshire Junior Cup, their first-ever trophy.
Standing (left to right):
F.J. Montgomery, Carter, Warn, Sommerville, Fry, G. Candy.
Middle row:
Varley, C. Bromley, Muir, A. Gandy. Front: Deacon, Crossley, Ruffell

Bournemouth Guardian correspondent divulged that, "to the astonishment of both umpires and referee, the Harriers kicked off from the six yards' mark and no claim was made by the St. Mary's for the point, and the game proceeded. I can't imagine how the Saints, who must be kicking themselves with chagrin at their slip, lost sight of the goal. I don't think they will get the chance again."

It was this sort of incident that inspired J.A. Brodie of Liverpool to invent goal nets in 1890. It would be interesting to know where he was in March 1888.

Saints did get their chance again, a fortnight later at the same place, when the *Bournemouth Guardian* recorded an attendance of "over 500 people, exclusive of ladies who, bless 'em, are admitted free," to watch Saints win 2-1.

Going secular

The next Saturday, St Mary's FC gathered for a victory dinner at the popular sporting hostelry, Gidden's Restaurant. A notable absentee was their president, Canon Wilberforce, who would probably have baulked at entering licensed premises, especially if it was to enjoy the hospitality of one of his own church's guilds. Which is one of several reasons why Saints may have, by now, been known as plain St Mary's.

Another is that it seems that outsiders were being brought into the YMA on the basis of their footballing abilities rather than their adherence to Christianity, muscular or otherwise. George Carter was a case in point:

he may have been all that Canon Wilberforce wanted in a YMA member, but there was no doubt he was in Saints' ranks as a footballer, not a chorister or Sunday-schoolteacher.

The matter was settled at a meeting, in January, chaired by the rector and reported in the parish journal:

> After a full and interesting discussion it was finally resolved, *nem con* "That S. Mary's Church of England Young Men's Association should, in future, consist only of members who are either active workers in some branch of the parochial organization, or regular attendants at one of the Bible classes. For the purpose of effectively carrying this out, it was resolved to make a fresh enrolment of all those who desire to belong to the Association on this understanding."

How many football club members did, or did not, renew their membership is unknown. But it would appear to have been the point of no return for them.

They were not ostracised. Canon Wilberforce remained the president until he left the parish in 1894, although he is rarely mentioned in that capacity. Conversely, Doctor Bencraft, a highly active committee-man, was frequently referred to as such, although he did not "officially" become president until his predecessor's departure. Whatever, Saints' achievement was glowingly reported in April's parish magazine:

> S. MARY'S FOOTBALL CLUB. – We are glad to record a great triumph for the above club, which has now, by following up its many victories won the much coveted "Cup" for the year. We cordially congratulate them on their success.

The season was not quite over. It had been decided that the Junior Champions should tackle the Seniors. St Mary's v Woolston Works was staged at the Antelope Ground on 14 April. Could Saints do a "David" and claim to be Southampton's finest?

No. They were beaten 3-0. The *Bournemouth Guardian,* commenting on the result, offered the consolation: "Both teams have had a wonderfully good time of it on the whole and the people of Southampton ought to feel proud of their football population."

FULL-TIME *at* THE DELL

Elsewhere in the same edition, the *Guardian* observed that, "for a junior team St. Mary's appear to have the makings of a good club," while the vanquished Harriers were said to "have the makings of an excellent club with practice." But they faced a common obstacle: "they have no ground but the Common, which is a great drawback. An application to the Town Council for permission to play on the 'Hoglands' early in the season was unfortunately refused."

Quite right, too. The Hoglands was, and should remain, sacred to cricket – and informal kick-abouts. But the failure to find a suitable site, that could be enclosed, would continue, for some time, to ham-string the football clubs of the town especially the Saints. Given the demand for pitches at the County Ground and the Antelope, and the fact it cost between £2.10s and £3 (necessitating 240 spectators prepared to pay 3d each to break even) to hire them, the prospect of any of the town's teams getting a permanent pitch appeared remote.

Then one club did get their own ground: Freemantle took out a lease on a plot owned by the Atherley Estate, off Shirley Road, opposite the Stile Inn.*

By the start of the 1888-89 season, all the players who had defected to the Harriers had retraced their paths home, except "Banquo" Stride, who threw in his lot with St Mary's.

Meanwhile, from Birmingham to Liverpool, and east to Nottingham, the newspapers were discussing the radical proposal of Aston Villa director William McGregor to form what would become known as the Football League. The disparate gap between football in the North and the South was about to widen from a cherubic smile to the demonic yawn of a crocodile.

---

* The site was still in use as a football and cricket ground until recently, under the auspices of the Civil Service Sports Club.

Chapter 4
The Antelope Ground

Saints were still based on the Common as the 1888-89 season commenced. But they had a high enough profile to justify hiring the Antelope – and, at least once, the County Ground – for their more prestigious friendly games.

As with previous seasons, there is a problem working out whom they were playing where because reports did not always make it into the press; and when they did, information regarding location and teams was frequently hazy or squeezed out entirely.

The Luck of the Cup

The highlight of the season was another run into the Junior Cup Final. They had a little luck – they were gaining a reputation for their luck – but the lack of a ground and football politics almost did for them.

They defeated Havant at the Antelope Ground 5-0 in the first round, then drew the oldest football club in Hampshire, Fordingbridge Turks,[*] in the second. The date arranged coincided with a Hampshire FA Junior XI game for which four St Mary's players had been selected. A series of ½d postcards[†] was exchanged in an attempt to re-arrange the match; but, two days before the originally scheduled date, the Turks' secretary demanded the game be played as originally arranged. Come Saturday morning, St Mary's still did not have a venue and the committee must have been ruing the behaviour of their supporters in Redbridge the previous season – and the failure of Mr Steadfast to see the funny side of it. Woolston Works would appear to have taken over the management of the Antelope Ground at this time – either that or they had hired the ground for that particular day

and been unable to find opponents – for it was widely publicised that Mr A.L. Oswald "kindly allowed them to play at the Antelope." The result was given in the *Southampton Times* as "a win for the holders of the cup by three goals and one disputed goal to two." This put Saints in the semi-final for the second consecutive season. It is doubtful that many people got excited when it was announced that they had been drawn to play away to Cowes. Southampton was still perceived as a rugby town, if it was regarded as a football town at all. Interest in the dribbling game, unless Woolston Works were entertaining some "famous" London team at the Antelope, was, in the main, peripheral.

Saints' 1-1 draw at Cowes on 24 February heralded a complete change to this order of things. The four game saga – the two draws, Cowes's successful protest after Saints' 2-1 victory at the County Ground and the Southampton side's eventual passage to the Junior Cup Final – has been well-documented by Duncan Holley in *Match of the Millennium*. But there are certain points that warrant further consideration here – not least the fact that, when the two sides met for the replay at the County Ground, the attendance was so impressive (one estimate put it at 2,000) that Dr Griffin, the Hon. Treasurer of the Hampshire CCC, offered not only to stage the second replay at the County Ground, but to pay Cowes's travelling expenses. Despite this inducement, it was the toss of a coin that determined the third game would be played at Northlands Road.

As Dr Griffin anticipated, interest in the second replay was even greater than the first. He probably had to pinch himself when a third County Ground game became necessary. Even though Cowes went out 4-1, there were no losers: interest in the final game was phenomenal and the cash generated, for all the concerned parties, unprecedented. One, later estimate gives the attendance as 5,000, including "over 1,000 ladies"; this is doubtful, but there can be no gainsaying that both "footer" and Saints had made a very definite impression.

---

[*] The Turks has formed in 1868, as plain Fordingbridge, and adopted the *cognomen* Turks in 1879, in tribute to the Turkish defence of Plevna against the "dastardly" Russians. However, few readers will need to be informed that the verb Turk is a popular euphemism for copulation in the New Forest. Draw your own conclusions.

[†] A postcard with a ½d stamp on it could be relied upon to get to just about anywhere in the UK the following day in the 1880s. Within a town the size of Southampton, where there were five deliveries a day, you could expect a postcard posted in the morning to get to its destination by the same afternoon.

FULL-TIME *at* THE DELL

At the end of the season, Offside of the *Bournemouth Guardian* concluded that Saints' progress in the Cup had "aroused the wildest enthusiasm in the county and resulted in such large 'gates' that the County Association certainly owes a debt of gratitude to either them or Cowes or both for raising them from a hand-to-mouth state of existence to that of having a satisfactory balance in the Bank."

The final, at Bar End, Winchester, failed to live up to the encounters with Cowes. The challengers, Christchurch, were defeated 3-0, and most of the game was played so deep in the Christchurch half that Ruffle, in the St Mary's goal, "was enabled to get through a cigarette or two to pass away the tedious moments he had in goal."

No estimate of the gate was given, but it was reckoned that two-thirds of it came from Southampton with the team. The Saintly faithful appear to have made quite an impression in Winchester and "what happened on arrival at Southampton Docks can be better imagined than described, but jubilation is not precisely the word for it."

Not all the news was good for Southampton: the formerly near-invincible Woolston Works had been defeated in the Senior Cup Final by the Royal Engineers of Aldershot. Oswald, Mordaunt & Company were in financial trouble and many of their best footballers had departed for greener pastures, employment-wise and football-wise.

Their reign as Hampshire's best football outfit had been a short but glorious one: who, if anyone, could take their place?

Whatever, the demise of the Works left Saints clear to claim the Antelope as their home base. And on the occasions that their joint tenants, Trojans, had first call on its use, their close relationship with Dr Bencraft, the County Cricket Club's Honorary Secretary, would mean that they could always rely on The County Ground as back-up – on reasonable terms.

Home at the Antelope

The availability of the Antelope ground, just as St Mary's were becoming popular enough to justify booking it on a regular basis, was probably the largest single factor in their becoming Southampton's most prominent and well-supported football club.

It stood at the top of St Mary's Road, covering most of the area between what is now Brintons Terrace and

Dr (later Sir) Russell Bencraft, JP
An all-round sportsman and popular local councillor, of whom William Pickford said "a volume could be written," which was something of an understatement

Clovelly Road, as far as Exmoor Road, and took its name from the Antelope Hotel (which was situated on the site of the present Southern Gas Building), which faced it across St Mary's Road.

The ground had been established by the professional cricketer, Daniel Day, with the backing of Thomas Chamberlayne and other cricketing gentlemen, in 1842 or thereabouts. It became the headquarters of Hampshire County Cricket Club when it was formed at a meeting at the Antelope Hotel on 11 September 1863. The County Club developed their new headquarters – the County Ground – at Banister's Park in 1884 – thereafter, the Antelope was in demand by every cricket and football club, with means, in the district.

An unidentified building inside the Antelope Ground. The building beyond, the All England XI public house, was the home dressing room.
The magnificent and futuristic side elevation is of a 100 ft long (and four steps high) proposed stand, designed by Mr Bunday.
We have no idea whether it was ever built

Its great advantage for an ambitious football club – which Saints certainly were by this time – was that, since being enclosed as a cricket ground, the Antelope had become surrounded by relatively prosperous suburbs inhabited by just the sort of individuals who might have the inclination, the wherewithal and the time to enjoy watching a game of football on a Saturday afternoon.

Saints not only kicked off the 1889-90 in new, albeit familiar, surroundings, but in a new kit. The white shirt and red sash gave way to red-and-white quarters. F.J. Montgomery, who was at that time an active committee member, claimed many years later that a meeting of members baulked at the expense of new shirts; so he had coughed up for them out of his own pocket. It is an assertion that is unlikely, ever, to be challenged.

It was observed at the time that Saints playing another season in the Junior Cup was something of an absurdity, but they were intent on winning it outright. And that's what they did.

St Mary's contested their third Cup Final with Lymington at – where else? – the County Ground.

"Such a glorious afternoon," gushed the *Bournemouth Guardian,* "we have not had many of them this season, and the attendance at the County Ground cut the record. Altogether over 2,000 paid for admission, which with ladies, members of the County Club, Banister School, boys, and officials, would give an attendance of something like 2,800."

Moreover, the "gate" was reported to have been "the largest ever taken in the two counties [of Hants and Dorset], £51 3s 6d, and beats the big 'gate' at the Cowes match last year."

The score, 2-0, did not reflect Saints' superiority, although there is no reference to Ruffell having the odd discreet smoke. Nonetheless, the Saints' strike force came under severe criticism in the *Bournemouth Guardian:* "With forwards equal to the defence, St. Mary's might play a good game with better clubs than we often see in Hampshire; though I still have my doubts about Aston Villa."

At the end of the season, Saints had a balance in hand of £50, making it, in Offside's estimation, the wealthiest club in Hampshire: "We shall be having some Scotchmen [*sic*] in the town soon. Perhaps 'Captain' Carter will be taking a holiday among the Grampians this summer and coming back with a burly Highlander or two to help them to win the senior cup next year."

This was a jokey suggestion that they could afford to consider pulling in a "professor" or two [*] – there was one openly professional player in Hampshire at this time, Winkworth of Winchester Rovers. If Saints had any, they were very discreet about it; the most likely suspect might be Bod Kiddle, who spent his summers on the professional running circuit, sprinting for prize money.

---

[*] "Professor" was a euphemism for professional in the days before the FA legalised professionalism, usually referring to Scotsmen brought south and given generously remunerated, but bogus, jobs so they could claim amateur status. The term remained in use for some time after the FA's change of heart.

FULL-TIME *at* THE DELL

And even if he were getting paid, it would not have been a living wage. This is not to say there were not suspicions: Saints had an uncanny knack of poaching the best local talent. Then again, as William Pickford pointed out many years later, "It may or may not be that there were 'inducements', though without doubt the honour of playing with a brilliantly successful side was itself no inconsiderable one." He continued with an interesting insight into the difference in attitudes between Hampshire and those purportedly held in the rest of Southern England:

> Hampshire football sentiment never set itself against
> professionalism, and when the "Saints" picked up
> here and there a good back or forward to keep up to
> the mark it was applauded as a good move.

The chances of St Mary's emulating their Junior Cup success at Senior level were not highly-rated. But they had a relatively easy passage to the County Ground final, where their opponents were the club that had vanquished Woolston Works in 1889: Aldershot's Royal Engineers, who were widely expected to win the Senior Cup outright by taking the trophy for the third consecutive season.

The 1890-91 season had been a stimulating one for Saints and their growing regiment of devotees: they had widened their circle of friendly matches to include some big names. Given that there were no professional clubs in the South, the term "big name" is relative: south of the Thames, London Caledonians and the 93rd Highland Regiment were colossi, as were the Royal Engineers.

Which explains why Offside considered Saints' 3-1 triumph as

> almost the only event of any notion in the local
> football world… It was a victory highly creditable to
> the Southampton Club, for no other team in the
> County could have tackled the Engineers with the
> confidence that the Saints displayed.

Both teams retired to Gidden's Restaurant after the game. Saints were becoming almost as renowned for their post-match hospitality as their prowess in the field.

During the usual round of toasts, Dr Bencraft announced that "they might enter for the English Cup, just for the sake of competing, as he felt sure they could

hold their own against such teams as Swindon, and Reading, &c. and it would be a feather in their caps to get through a round or two."

A year later, on 19 March 1892 to be precise, Offside was telling his public how the cups were "all finding their resting places now one by one. On Saturday the Hampshire Senior Cup went back again to Dr Bencraft's sideboard as we all expected it would… This makes the fifth successive season in which St. Mary's have won the cup they entered for, first the Junior, and now the Senior, and never yet have they lost a cup tie. What is becoming monotonous with them would drive the footballers in other places mad with delight."

Saints had beaten the Army Medical Staff 5-0 in their second consecutive Senior Cup final.

The question was: where to now?

There was now, at least, a professional club south of Birmingham. In 1891, London Cup holders, Woolwich Arsenal, took the plunge – and probably regretted it. The London FA, to demonstrate their attitude towards clubs under their jurisdiction aspiring to compete with the likes of Aston Villa and Sunderland, expelled them from all their cup competitions, and from the association itself.

Quite how the St Mary's committee regarded this development is not, unfortunately, on record. But is fairly safe to assume that they took an interest.

Up for the Cup

In 1891 Saints ventured forth, into national competition. There was only one: the FA Cup. It proved an incredible experience, but they came through it with their record intact of never being defeated in a cup competition – unless you count "unofficial" tournaments, such as six-a-sides, the Portsmouth & District Cup and their ilk.[*]

St Mary's were not the first Hampshire club to take part in the "English Cup" – that honour fell to Bournemouth Rovers, who had made a short tilt at the trophy some years before – but they were certainly the first to stage an FA Cup match in the county, 19 years after the competition was launched.

They had a fairly comfortable start, travelling to and defeating Warmley, near Bristol, 4-1. F.J. Montgomery recalled that the referee was a Mr Lewis, "a highly

---

[*] Walt Disney was not born until 1901 and the term
"Mickey Mouse Cup" had yet to be coined.

placed official of the Association, who, I considered, took every opportunity to impress the players with the importance of his position." This is not the last time we will meet Mr Lewis.

Reading were drawn to play at Southampton in the Second Qualifying Round.

The elation was short-lived. It was Reading who went through to the next round. They progressed on a technicality. Fulminating against the injustice suffered by St Mary's, Offside claimed that "a thunderbolt has fallen in the middle of their camp. Innocent of wilful intent, they are punished severely, and added to this, is the

The entrance to the Antelope Ground

The St Mary's committee had pulled out all the stops to make sure the Antelope was up to the standards expected of a venue for the country's most prestigious football tournament, though it appears that they had not got the pitch marked out properly.

The *Bournemouth Guardian* correspondent, however, pronounced himself "knocked over" with the provision for the press:

> A long table in the shape of a shutter
> from the Old Pavilion front, open to the air, with
> chairs for the scribes, is a beginning certainly, but
> fancy if it had been wet. Really Mr. Hendin,[*] we
> must have a covered press box.

The estimated 4,000 crowd got a rare treat even by Saints' exemplary cup standards: a 7-0 win. "It was about the best game I ever saw the Saints play," gushed the *Bournemouth Guardian.*

feeling that Reading acted in anything but a sportsmanlike manner in this affair."

Which was fair comment. During the customary post-match hospitality at Dartnell's, the Reading secretary asked for, and was given, an advance of £3 on Reading's share of the gate money. A telegram, followed by a letter enclosing the mandatory two guinea fee, was sent to the Football Association claiming that Saints were fielding illegally registered players: Fleming and McMillan of the 93rd Highlanders. In fact, Saints had registered them both but, unwittingly (they claimed), had not complied with the letter of rule 28. The FA agreed that this rule was ambiguous, but expelled them from the Cup anyway.

The iniquity of this imperious decision was a further boost to Saints' local celebrity – and it was not as if they were going to win the thing. The only club in the South capable of taking on and defeating Football League sides were the elite amateur club, Corinthians, who disdained even to enter the Cup.

Corinthians paid a visit to the County Ground at the fag end of the season, taking on the Hampshire FA XI, in

---

[*] Mr Hendin being the St Mary's secretary

FULL-TIME *at* THE DELL

which St Mary's were well-represented. The visitors arrived a forward short and a Banister Court schoolboy by the name of Charles Miller was recruited to their left wing. It was an exciting week for the 17 year-old: two days earlier, on 18 April, he had made his debut for Saints in a 3-1 defeat of the army select side, Aldershot Division, and had opened the scoring. Corinthians won 1-0 and Miller, already a local favourite, was impressive. It was a good result for Hampshire, against a side with a fair sprinkling of England internationals. Miller was from São Paulo; Saints were almost certainly the first European club to field a Brazilian.

There are two ways of looking at the 1892-93 season. On the positive side: it was most certainly the first season of the rest of Saints' more than somewhat colourful history, in that they underwent a dramatic change of policy, determined – presumably – to establish themselves, beyond contention, as Southampton's football club.

On the negative side, however, the policy change blew up in their faces: it was, as far as the football was concerned, an unmitigated disaster – from start to finish.

St Mary's kicked-off the new term on 17 September, against the South Staffordshire Regiment, at the County Ground, and lost 4-0 in what was evidently a shambolic performance in every respect. They couldn't even provide matching shirts for the players. Ariel, of the *Southampton Times,* noted three different coloured shirts besides the "cherry squares", two of the Saints turning out in white.

The organisation of the Club was most certainly in a state of disarray. The cause of this would appear to have been the enforced absence of Hon. Sec. Mr Hendin, who had been convalescing in Brighton. In the last week of August, a fixture list had yet to be printed and a rumour that Saints were £50 in debt was circulating in the press. As if these were not problems enough, they were losing three of their best players. F.A. Delamotte's job as a surveyor was taking him to Derby, Ernie Nicholls was also leaving the district and Arthur Farwell's duties in the drapery department of Edwin Jones[*] would make him unavailable on Saturday afternoons.

---

[*] Please note, when directing visiting supporters to the Friends Provident St Mary's Stadium from the Above Bar area, that Edwin Jones is now called Debenhams, and has been for well in excess of 30 years. The refusal of Southamptonians to acknowledge this is gratifying, but confusing for strangers.

A professional solution?

Saints' need for new blood became manifest in August, when they made a bid to sign Freemantle's George Ridges on professional forms. There was nothing circumspect about this offer and Southampton's press took quite an interest in developments. Quite why the deal fell through is not made plain. Ariel complained of "a great deal of dilly dallying" on the matter, but does not reveal on whose part, and Ridges decided to remain at Freemantle as an amateur.

Saints did manage to lure away one Freemantle player. Jack Dollin was paid £1 a week and found a job, but his status as a professional was kept a secret for a number of years. This surreptitious style of professionalism was ubiquitous in the North, in the "bad old days" before the legalisation of wages for footballers. Given the attitude of many county FA's towards "players", such an arrangement was understandable. This said, the Hampshire FA harboured few, if any, prejudices on the issue and, given that Saints had already gone public on their intention to sign professionals, their skulduggery with regard to Dollin appears, in retrospect, to be decidedly odd.

The introduction of Dollin did not mark a significant improvement in form. There was a palpable sense of relief in the town when Saints defeated Newbury 4-1 in the First Qualifying Round of the FA Cup on 15 October, their first win of the season.

It all came to a head, horribly, on 29 October, when Maidenhead came to the Antelope to play in the Second Qualifying Round. Saints, having gone five years undefeated in cup competitions, capitulated by four goals to nil.

Despite this set back, they appear to have treated their victors with the usual hospitality at Dartnell's. In fact, the main agent of their destruction was so taken with the generosity of his hosts that he joined them.

What actually transpired in the debacle that surrounded F.W. Janes becoming a Saint has never been coherently explained, but Maidenhead officials maintained that, when he signed for Saints, "he was not in a condition to realise what he was doing." Which suggests that he signed-up while under the influence of intoxicants. Ariel warmly congratulated the Saints committee, on 19 November, on "taking the bull by the horns," when he announced that Janes was on his way. "He will play as a amateur," he told readers of the

Southampton Times, "if a berth can be obtained for him at his trade of engine fitter, otherwise he will be registered as a professional."

Actually he failed to materialise as either.

Maidenhead came to the Antelope to play a friendly on 3 December, with Janes still leading the attack. By this time, the whole affair had been dumped in the lap of the FA, who banned Janes for one week and Maidenhead for two. Which proved to Ariel that the attempt "to secure the services of Janes was all along fair and above board."

The St Mary's committee were now so anxious to sign new players, especially a forward, that they began advertising in the "athletic press" – not an uncommon method of recruitment back then.

But it was not until 7 January, when Saints tackled Freemantle at home, that the desperately sought-after new forward arrived, in the shape of former Royal Engineer (the regimental team based at Chatham not the Aldershot battalion side), Jack Dorkin. His status was, at the time, ambiguous. Ariel understood that he was coming to work in Southampton and would accordingly "be reckoned as an amateur player of the Southampton team." If there ever was a pretence that Dorkin was unpaid, it did not last long.

Saints managed a 3-3 draw with Freemantle, who were most certainly having a good year.

One other game worthy of note, before things get seriously depressing, is the arrival, on 10 December, of the South's only openly professional side – for a few weeks at least – Woolwich Arsenal.

Their fate demonstrated why Saints may have hesitated in signing Ridges and been keen to maintain Dollin's façade of amateurism. Arsenal were being treated as pariahs in London and the Home Counties and were finding it difficult to get fixtures. They had floated a proposal to form a Southern League the previous summer, but there were few clubs willing, or financially able, to make the necessary commitment and the Woolwich club found themselves in inglorious isolation. Saints' willingness to give them a fixture was a brave gesture in itself. They won 2-0, their first defeat of a professional club, at their first attempt.

Saints' form picked up for the Senior Cup, despite the fact that Dorkin's registration came too late for him to qualify for the tournament. The Royal Engineers and Portsmouth were disposed of, and it remained only for

Freemantle to be defeated in the final at the County Ground, for Saints to own the Senior Cup, like the Junior Cup, outright.

This was the hottest tie to be played in Southampton to date. Freemantle had been in Saints' shadow for eight years. Further, Southampton County Borough Council had announced its intention to apply to Parliament to expand the borough's boundaries to include Woolston, Bitterne Park, Shirley and Freemantle. This was not a proposal that was greeted with any great enthusiasm, particularly in Shirley and Freemantle, whose inhabitants were aghast at the thought of having to pay the increased rates that would follow the installation of a proper sewerage disposal system.

Given the vehemence of their objections, one might surmise that there was a great desire, even among those who had never seen a game of football, to see a blow struck against the evil empire – the one beyond Hill Lane.

Still, Saints had Delamotte back and Farwell had been given the day off, thanks to the generosity of Mr Edwin Jones himself. So what could go wrong?

The *Bournemouth Guardian* set the scene with some panache:

> The rivalry between St. Mary's and Freemantle over the final for the Hampshire Senior Cup stirred Southampton in particular and the county generally to fever heat. A glorious day gladdened the hearts of everyone interested and the way the people poured into the town from north, east and west by train, and from Cowes by boat, and rolled up the Avenue between 2 and 3 p.m. on Saturday was a grand sight. Preparation was made at the County Cricket Ground for a large crowd, but the attendance completely upset all ideas as to the accommodation that would be required, and the magnificent spectacle of between 6,000 and 7,000 excited individuals massed together round the field of play, crowding the stand [newly erected that season] and occupying every position of vantage within seeing radius, was one that Hampshire and indeed none of the counties south of the Thames and this side of London have ever witnessed at an Association football match. One need hardly say that the numbers were double those of any previous highest attendances on the ground, to evidence the enormous strides made by the dribbling

FULL-TIME *at* THE DELL

game in this part of the world. No less a sum than £122.12s 3d was taken in sixpenny and threepenny entrances at the gates, in addition to which a big majority of the County Club members were present, and a shoal of schoolboys from Banister Court, while the specially reserved entrance for ladies, admitted as usual free, was thronged with the fair sex, and judging from its prevalence green is the fashionable colour of the season… after two o'clock a steady stream of people began to pass the turnstiles. Many carried cards in their hats, black and white shields for the "Magpies"… and the well known scarlet and white squares of St. Mary's.

The game was tight, very tight. It was one-all with the last minutes ticking out. Then:

> Right in front of Ruffell, Horton was on the point of shooting, when Stride tripped him and the Freemantle forward stumbled. The whistle blew and at the same moment Horton recovered himself and drove the ball into the net. It was however brought back, the referee giving Freemantle a penalty kick.

At which point, William Pickford recalled many years later, "'Let me have it,' said the imperturbable Hawkins, and in the goal the ball flashed. That did it."

The Saints' reaction to this defeat was less than phlegmatic. The Southampton press handled the situation with kid gloves, but the *Bournemouth Guardian,* with its windows comparatively safe from the hot-tempered hurling of half-bricks, was frank and fearless:

> It was a battle worthy of an epic poem, excepting that it was spoiled to a great extent, by loss of temper on the part of the losing side. The "Saints," during the last year or so, have decidedly not improved in their temperament, and I am loath to put it down to a depreciation in the quality of true sportsmen… it does seem …that the crack Hampshire club cannot take a licking. The display of St. Mary's was far below form, and signs of temper were evident in the continued comments passed by some of the team at the referee and his decisions, their going for the man, and the numerous fouls given against them during the game.

It was reported that George Carter had approached the referee after the final whistle to tell him that the foul had been outside the penalty area and that he could take him to the spot. He was advised to have "a tombstone erected over it."

Saints protested the result.

In ignorance of this, or regardless of it, the Freemantle supporters went on a revel and legend has it the Cup was found in the early hours of the morning sitting unattended in the middle of the road outside a "well known hostelry", most likely the *Waterloo Arms.*

Freemantle, Saints' conquerors in the Senior Cup and contenders to be "Southampton FC".
"The imperturbable Hawkins" (with the apt first name of "Shirley") is in the middle of the back row.
George Ridges, who contemplated a move to St Mary's, cradles the ball

To Saints' credit, they withdrew their protest before the Hampshire FA could convene.

That was the nadir of the season, if not the Club's history, but there was more gloom to come. First Division Stoke were invited to the County Ground for an exhibition game and Charles Miller, who was now playing for the County's Senior team, was invited to take Bob Kiddle's place on the wing. He had little chance to shine: Saints were martyred, 8-0.

Nonetheless, the press congratulated them on their enterprise and felt the large crowd enjoyed themselves.

Having taken the first tentative steps towards open professionalism, St Mary's decided to sign a couple more "professors" in the 1893 close season. William Angus, formally of Third Lanark, chose the balmy South Coast breezes in preference to another season in the Second Division with Ardwick (now Manchester City), while Harry Offer decided to forsake the chance of experiencing Second Division football with Woolwich Arsenal – who had the great good luck to be the South's first Football League club as the result of a decision to expand its Division Two, from 12 to 15 teams, that summer.

There was another new face, too. E.J. Taylor, an amateur from Liverpool, came to work in the Southampton offices of the American Shipping Line. He proved well up to the standard of professional footballers – south of Birmingham, at least.

Facing the future

The committee's faith that they could attract respectable crowds at the Antelope for friendlies must have been balanced with the expectation, or at least the hope, that they would be able to sustain a decent FA Cup run in the regionalized qualifying rounds and, with any luck, get a home draw with a famous League side.

At this time, the Cup was far and away the most prestigious football competition, the Football League still being something of a parochial concern. National newspapers did report on professional football but, given the social pretensions of their readers, a match between the Old Wykehamists and Old Etonians would get more column inches than a top-of-the-table clash between Aston Villa and Sunderland.

That Saints were building for a future cannot be doubted – but what sort of future? With most of the South's county associations in cahoots with the London FA and hostile to professionalism, no league structure in Hampshire and their geographical remoteness from the Football League, their chances of maintaining a side capable of disputing honours with even a moderate Second Division outfit appeared limited indeed, especially as they were struggling to remain the town's premier club.

Saints were certainly on good form early in the 1893-94 season.

They lost just one game before Christmas, being comprehensively outclassed in every department by First Division Bolton Wanderers, by five goals to nil. Revenge was exacted on the Football League a little later, though, when Saints beat Woolwich Arsenal 4-2 at the Antelope

on 13 January. But, then, Woolwich were hardly setting the Second Division alight.

Saints' FA Cup run being perfunctory – they lost at Reading in the Second Qualifying Round – the pursuit of the Hants Senior Cup was again the business of the season. Hopes were high that Saints and the Magpies would once more contest the final, but it was in the semis that they came out of the hat together. Southampton went daft. A contributor to the local sporting weekly, the *Southern Referee*, was kissed by whichever muse is answerable for derby games:

> The topic of conversation
> Just now in this seaport town,
> Is of footer, footer, footer,
> From dawn till the sun goes down.
> Each person you meet will surely
> The subject at once begin,
> And start with the old, old question,
> "Will Saints or Magpies win?"
>
> It's vain to evade the question,
> 'Tis echoed both far and near,
> With your coffee in the morning,
> At night with your supper beer,
> On all sides it is repeated
> In one everlasting din,
> This all important question,
> "Will Saints or Magpies win?"
>
> To the speeches of Bicker-Carten *
> No more any interest clings,
> The bookies no longer offer
> To lay on the Sport of Kings;
> But all on this semi-final
> Are willing to plank their tin, †
> For who can answer the question,
> "Will Saints or Magpies win?"

The crowd at the County Ground on 3 February 1894 was larger than for the final the previous year. Interest

---

* Quite who Bicker-Carten was I am unable to ascertain. The name may be an obscure Victorian pun?

† Tin means money, and to plank it, in this context, to put it on the table.

FULL-TIME *at* THE DELL

generated perhaps by the chance of another upset, as Saints had been victims to a run of injuries. The indefatigable George Carter, who had been their most influential player for eight seasons, was certainly out, as was his preferred partner at the back, "Ginger" Price, who had been sidelined for most of the season.

The match was a draw and Saints won the replay 2-1, to restore a sense of normality to the ruffled sensibilities of the Southampton sporting public.

Meanwhile, on 12 January, at the initiative of Millwall Athletic, a meeting was convened at the Billiter Coffee Rooms, Fenchurch Street, London, to discuss, once more, the formation of a Southern League. The clubs represented, aside from Millwall, were Chatham, Clapton, Ilford, Luton Town, Reading and the 2nd Scots Guards. Of those clubs assembled, only Luton and Millwall had professionals on their books. A further meeting was called and a further seven clubs invited, only two – Swindon Town and the Royal Ordnance Factory – accepting the invitation.

At some point in the proceedings, the St Mary's committee wrote asking to be included, but were rebuffed.

Fortunately, the 2nd Scots Guards were obliged to drop out and St Mary's were invited to take their place in the nine-team league.

As it transpired, there were further applications, and a second division of seven teams was established; so Saints would have ended up in the Southern League, albeit in a humbler setting, even if the 2nd Scots Guards had not withdrawn.

But there was still that elusive third Senior Cup Final to be won. The Royal Engineers of Aldershot were the opponents, once again; the venue was the County Ground, once again.

Saints had certainly improved since they had beaten the Sappers in 1891, but their bad luck with injuries was continuing. George Carter was still absent, Angus too was out and, to make things worse, destiny decided to turn out for the underdogs.

Saints went down 1-0, having lost two players through injury: one after five minutes; the other, veteran goalkeeper Ruffle, in the second-half. It was a creditable result in the circumstances.

The season ended at the County Ground, where Saints played host to Stoke. There were complaints in the local newspapers that it was not Stoke's strongest team, but they were still good enough to beat the home team by the odd goal in five.

Charlie Miller was fielded and it would be fascinating to know if he was being considered as a Southern League prospect. As it happened, despite rumours towards the end of the summer that he would be playing for Freemantle, he packed his bags, early in the next season, and returned to São Paulo, where football was unknown. His arrival home, in November 1894, is celebrated in Brazil as the date football was introduced there.

Chapter 5
O Brave New World

It had been noted, from time to time, over the previous seven years, that among the many qualities Saints possessed was luck. Even their place in the original line-up of the Southern League's first division had a touch of Dame Fortune about it; although it could be argued that it was criminally foolish to have rejected their first application anyway. What would have been so dreadful about a ten-team competition?

However, luck is a finite resource and Saints' reserves of it had been stretched during the previous two seasons. The summer of 1894 would see it run out somewhat.

In the June 23 edition of the *Southampton Times,* a story buried on page 5 announced

THE LIVING OF ST. MARY'S AND ITS REVENUES
£5,000 WANTED FOR THE ANTELOPE.

Canon Wilberforce had left Southampton that year to take up a living in Westminster; and a committee, convened to look into the finances of St Mary's, decided that the parish funds needed a big cash injection rather than the steady dribble of rent that the Antelope provided.

This turn of events was a body blow to the town's sporting community, not least because the Royal Southampton Horticultural Society's lands at Westwood Park had been sold to property developers a short time before. Situated off The Avenue, over land now occupied by the housing in Winn Road and Westwood Road, it was a popular place of recreation, not just for high profile sporting events such as athletics, velocipede racing, tennis and somewhat constricted games of football, but military displays, exhibitions, fêtes and even balloon ascents. In 1887, to celebrate the Royal Jubilee, 10,000 children were treated to a tea there.

The vendors offered the Antelope to the council, as an open space, for £5,000, but this was regarded as too big a burden on the rates. There was also a campaign to get Saints to buy it, but it appears to have been somewhat half-hearted; and given that their turnover had been £892 11s 8d the previous season (and most of that had gone on wages and expenses), it is doubtful the committee entertained the proposal too seriously.

Commenting on their Annual Meeting in the *Southampton Times* of 30 June, Ariel pointed out that Saints would find it easy enough to move to the County Ground, where, he suggested, they would be better-off. Overlooking perhaps that the annual rent on the Antelope of £41 1s 6d was considerably less than they would need for a tenancy at Northlands Road.

A glance westwards over to Freemantle may have excited some envy. Not only did they have their own ground, albeit leased, but Tankerville Chamberlayne MP, their president, had been donating £30 a season to the club, which more than covered the annual rent.

St Mary's, or Southampton St Mary's as they were about to become, traditionally enjoyed far bigger crowds than Freemantle, but Freemantle's long-term future was far better provided for.

At last the League – but more Cup thrills

Saints undoubtedly took the Southern League seriously. They brought in Fred Hollands from Millwall and three Stoke players: "Lachie" Thomson, Charlie Baker and Alf Littlehales. Littlehales and Baker had featured in the notorious 8-0 thrashing at the County Ground in 1893. Thomson probably had.[*]

The confidence of the local press had more to do with "doing well" than actually winning anything. The public were not getting too carried away either. Ariel had his finger on the pulse:

> It is very wonderful to notice the pertinacity with which the prophets continue to prophesy. Southampton St. Mary's have not yet played in the competition, but their position at the end of the season has been positively fixed by some people, and I have not heard anybody place them lower than third on the list. Millwall Athletic and Luton only taking precedence.

---

[*] A player by the name of W. Thompson was listed as playing; it is likely a phantom "p" was introduced.

FULL-TIME *at* THE DELL

They were very good prophets as it turned out. Southampton St Mary's came third two seasons running.

In the Cup they were magnificent. In 1894-95, they struck 31 goals in the four qualifying rounds, 14 of them against Newbury at the Antelope.

The gap in quality between the Southern League and the Football League was brought home to Southampton when First Division Nottingham Forest triumphed 4-1, in the snow at the Antelope, in the First Round.

In 1895-96, the draw for the First Qualifying Round brought a one-and-a-third mile trek across town. Ariel, as usual, caught the mood to perfection:

> What ho my merry men! What ho! We are all bound for the village to-day to see what we should see, and to rejoice or regret, or do neither, as the case may be, after the game has been played and won and lost. A great day it is in the history of Freemantle, to be sure, to have an English Cup tie played on their own midden, and with the Southampton St. Mary's men too. What ho! Then, let us go up and form a serried line of human bodies ten deep round the ropes, watching the display of the locals.

Another chance for the Magpies to undermine Saints.

A record crowd was predicted. Sixty seats in the Freemantle Ground grandstand were reserved for two shillings (an extortionate 10 pence). And

> all along the west side of the field of play a platform has been raised some two feet from the ground, which will give another thousand or so spectators an uninterrupted view of the game. The ground has also been raised near the lower goal, and, taking one thing and another, I think the Magpies have made ample provision to deal with this great day in their history.

Monday's *Echo* claimed a crowd of 6,000, although Ariel put it at 5,000, all of whom "were all able to get a good view of the game."

Saints went through by five goals to one, and their most notable player, the commentators agreed, was Jack Farrell, a close season import from Stoke who had contributed two of the goals.

Farrell was not the only new player in the summer – or, rather, spring – of 1895. Chippy Naughton and Sam

Meston brought the St Mary's contingent of former Stoke men to six. Saints had also signed Watty Keay from Derby County, Joe Turner from Dresden United and A.E. Wood from Burslem Port Vale.

New signing Watty Keay, from Derby County, who has gone down in history as the first man to score at The Dell

The Club's predilection for players from the Potteries could simply be put down to Stoke's impressive performance of their team at the County Ground at the end of the 1892-93 season; but Alfred McMinn, the committeeman most responsible for recruiting Football League players, was a native of the Potteries and appears to have been at his most persuasive on his home turf.

McMinn's activities in the Midlands were notorious, but he had now definitely overstepped the mark. Stoke and Port Vale protested that their players had been "poached" before the season had finished and the FA concurred. McMinn was suspended for a year and Saints were censured and made to pay costs to the plaintiffs: £4 6s 3d and £1 13s, respectively. In addition, the registration of Wood was cancelled. He ended up at

Chapter 5

Stoke. Another new addition to the staff was Bill Dawson, who had been Stoke's trainer. He was not a football man at all, but had been a professional runner – in current parlance he would be termed a "fitness coach". He proved to be an astute acquisition.

If the episode did nothing else, it brought Southampton St Mary's to the notice of the Football League.

Saints again made it through the four qualifying rounds, earning themselves a plum home tie with Sheffield Wednesday. Ariel set the scene:

Ay! Lads, and it was a great day for Southampton. It was Sheffield Saturday on account of Sheffield Wednesday. The day had been looked forward to ever since the draw was announced, and the great fight that was to be was the sole topic of conversation in Saintly circles in season and out of season, and it has continued to be so all through the last week. Let it be said at once, and emphatically said, that the executive of the home team appear to have made the best possible arrangements for the accommodation of the people. And what a crowd it was to be sure! When I arrived on the ground about two o'clock the gates had been opened for over an hour, the South Hants band was playing merrily and the famous Antelope was fairly black with people. There were quite six thousand people present at this time, and they came pouring through every gate by hundreds until after the game had been well started.

All the world and his wife were there, including many of our "city fathers" and grave and reverend seigniors, whose curiosity had been aroused by the chatter that was going on in the town, and they had come to see what it was that caused the ordinary people to go close off their "nuts" over the kicking of a twenty-seven inch ball. It was a sight calculated to excite the feelings of the Saintly executive, and make them look as pleased and comfortable as if the very cockles of their hearts were being tickled. A sea of faces ten thousand strong bordered the field of play when Lieutenant Simpson, the referee, first tooted the whistle, and the people not only came from Southampton, but from all the county round for a radius of at least thirty miles…

Just before the Saints stepped out of their dressing-room an incident happened which might have had disastrous results. The Antelope is well suited to accommodate a large crowd at a football match, the embankment forming a natural grand stand.

But many wanted something better. They climbed on to fences and roofs of sheds to get a better view. Quite a crowd gathered on the roof of the old shed adjoining the dressing-rooms. With a loud crash this place came down with a run. The band stopped playing, the people held their breath, and things looked a bit awkward for a minute or two. No one could say how many people were under the debris, and Dr. Stancomb and Dr. Bencraft made their way to the place. It was with a sigh of relief that the people heard on their return to the grand stand that no one had been injured beyond a bit of a shake up which one or two might have sustained.

This Southern League line-up includes new signings from the Potteries and elsewhere in the Midlands

Standing (left to right) E.C. Jarvis, Meston, Marshall, Barrett, Littlehales, Cox, Wood, W. Dawson (trainer).

Sitting (left to right) Baker, Naughton, Rogers, Farrell, Thompson, Keay J. Turner.

FULL-TIME *at* THE DELL

As a matter of fact, one of the casualties had been badly hurt. On 19 January 1897, George Stephen Brett, a carriage maker earning £2 a week at Eastleigh Railway Works, who had been underneath the shed when it collapsed, brought a case for damages against the Club, claiming he had not been able to work for a year. The Club had sent him an unsolicited cheque for £4, as a gratuity, which had been returned. The Southampton St Mary's committee found themselves in the dock. The weight of evidence against them was considerable, in that there was no attempt by anyone to prevent people climbing on the roof or to clear those standing beneath it, but the Club won the case.

They had fared pretty well in the match itself, too, stiffly contesting the result to the end, before going down 2-1. Wednesday went on to win the Cup.

Full Time at the Antelope

Saints showed some good Southern League form, too, though not enough to challenge Millwall and Luton for either of the first two places. But they had an impressive run-in, scoring 13 goals without return in their last four games, which included a 2-0 victory over Millwall – the champions' first-ever Southern League defeat.

The committee, having decided that a side capable of defeating the "invincible" Millwall was still not good enough, went back into the transfer market. Bob Buchanan of Woolwich Arsenal, Harry Haynes of Small Heath (now Birmingham City) and goalkeeper George Clawley of – inevitably – Stoke arrived at the Antelope. Or rather: the County Ground.

Ariel had long since confirmed – on 18 January 1896 – that the Antelope was "to be built upon":

> The lawyers are now busy upon the necessary parchments, and before many months are over "eligible villa residences" will be raising their heads over the ground where so many "historic battles" have been fought and won and lost. It is not unlikely that Freemantle will benefit from this latest move, for by the removal of the Saints to the County Ground, the Trojans will probably have to make shift, and the "Mags" will receive them with open arms to share that excellent and spacious ground of theirs.

There had been much argument about the fate of the Antelope Ground, 18 months of it almost, but to no avail. And it would seem that the St Mary's committee had been resigned to the move up Rockstone Lane and across The Avenue well before the issue had been settled.

They would be welcomed with open arms, it is fairly safe to assume, by the Hampshire County Cricket Club's Hon. Secretary. Not just because he was their ever-supportive president, Dr Bencraft, but for the substantial extra revenue they would inevitably bring in.

The last game of football at the Antelope Ground was played on the evening of Wednesday 29 April 1896. A crowd estimated at 3,000 turned up to pay their last respects as Saints – sentimentally – defeated the Magpies 1-0. The very last goal scored was by one of the very few Southampton natives on the books, albeit a perennial reserve, Fred Hayter.

Chapter 6
The County Ground

What glorious times Saints' first season at the County Ground brought Southampton.

To start with, Saints' consistency in the Cup was acknowledged by the Football Association, who exempted them from the first of the four qualifying rounds.

Next, they justified the privilege by sweeping through to the First Round Proper, Reading biting the dust 4-1 in the Third Qualifying Round at Reading and the FA rejecting the, by now, traditional protest.

Saints then won, for the first time, their first tie in the competition proper, eliminating Derbyshire side, Heanor Town, in the First Round replay – away.

The reward was a home draw with Newton Heath (since re-branded as Manchester United). Given that the Heathens were a Division Two club, there were grounds for optimism, even if they were chasing promotion.

Disappointingly, Newton Heath managed a draw and won the replay at Bank Street, a venue noted for its "foul air", being located next to a chemical works.

Any distress endured was forgotten by 14 April, when the team returned by train from Wolverton.

> It had been decided to give them a public reception, and the news spread throughout the town. As a result there was a crowd of people, numbering many hundred [10 to 15,000 according to the *Echo*] at the Dock Station, awaiting the arrival of the seven o'clock train. The police band was also in attendance, and there were some wagonettes for the members of the team and their friends. The train was late, and the crowd increased. When the team stepped on the platform the "Southampton whisper" [a shout, with great vigour, of "Yi! Yi! Yi!"]gained such a volume that it almost raised the station roof. The vehicles were soon filled, and with the band playing and followed by a huge crowd the team had quite a triumphant march. The route was along Oxford-street, High-street to the top of town, and down St. Mary's-road to Kingsland. The procession was orderly, but they made themselves pretty well heard with the "whisper" and after the band played the National Anthem on the Square the people dispersed.

Not exactly Sunday afternoon, 2 May 1976, but pretty impressive nonetheless.

The reason for this display, so ably described in the *Southampton Times,* was a 1-0 win at Wolverton. A win at Wolverton, in itself, was not much to "whisper" about (they were bottom of the league and would finish the season with four points), but the two points so admirably taken placed Southampton St Mary's out of reach of Millwall Athletic, their nearest rivals, at the top of the Southern League. Saints were champions.

Granted, in Southampton, where the Junior and Senior championships of Hampshire had been celebrated with such gusto, it was understandable that this achievement should be fêted with some ballyhoo, but the Southern League championship was a comparatively meagre summit.

After all, read any popular history of football and the Southern League is something that, if the book is really comprehensive, might get mentioned in passing. In all truth, it was regarded as, at best, a third class competition. When Saints had beaten Bolton Wanderers 5-2 in an exhibition game back in 1894 the then assistant editor of the *Athletic News,* J.J. Bentley, reported that Saints were "up to the best Lancashire or Midland League standard." Which was meant, and received, as a compliment.

The Southern League's original champions in 1894-95, Millwall, were apparently invited to take a place in the Second Division, but turned the opportunity down. The expense of travelling considerable distances to play all but one of their away games and the poor share of gate returns they could expect at many venues were certainly a consideration. No more confirmation was needed than a trip across the Thames to Plumstead (Millwall were still resident on the Isle of Dogs), where Woolwich Arsenal were struggling financially and did well to exceed Millwall's crowds. In short, Division Two of the Football League was something of a morass. The Southern League may have been less glamorous than the Football League, but it was affordable, its gates compared favourably with the Second Division's and, with the

FULL-TIME *at* THE DELL

A close season view of the County Ground in the late 1890s
To the left of the pavilion can be seen the side of the football stand

increasing interest in professional football in London, and Woolwich being the capital's only Football League club, it had potential.

That potential was soon to be realised. The main agent in the competition's distinct rise of profile was the emergence to national prominence of Southampton Football Club.

This is what happened.

The long hot summer of '97

The Southern League shield as good as won and celebrated, the Southampton sporting public, for the most part, became somewhat blasé concerning football for the remainder of the season – not least because the weather was less than conducive to standing ten-deep around a roped-off field with no shelter.

This was a setback for the finances of Southampton St Mary's: there being only 20 league games a season at this time, they were still dependent on a heavy programme of friendly fixtures; and over Easter and up till the end of April, a busy and, hopefully, profitable list of prestigious opponents had been lined up, including

Darwen, Blackburn Rovers and Derby County, who were all beaten; and Woolwich Arsenal, to whom they lost 5-1.

In addition to these fund-raising games, the committee had the bright idea of running a prize draw. They went about it on a grand scale, taking over town-centre premises and placing "a large and attractive advertisement over the top," publicising a lottery, and …were promptly closed down by the police. Holding lotteries was an "illegal act". Chief Inspector Berry told the *Echo* that no animosity was involved: he himself was a vice-president of Southampton St Mary's and, as for rumours "of any kind of jealousy amongst rival football clubs in the town," he was not influenced by it.

Quite how much this enterprising misadventure cost Saints is unknown. As for rival football clubs in the town, there was only one candidate. The Magpies were, once again, breathing down Saints' neck – with a vengeance.

Having joined the Southern League Division Two the previous summer, Freemantle had got to third place, which entitled them to a test match with Northfleet, who had finished ninth in the eleven-team first division. The Magpies won 3-0 at Millwall's East Ferry Road on 1 May.

Chapter 6

After the game, Northfleet lodged a protest concerning the legality of one of the Freemantle team, Phillips, who played most of his football with the Portsmouth garrison side, Royal Artillery. Undaunted, the members gathered for the annual meeting of the Freemantle club at the Foresters Hall, on 4 May, "in a buoyant mood", according to the *Echo*. The main business of the evening was the necessity to strengthen the team for the First Division and there were plans to form a limited liability company with one thousand £1 shares. It then transpired that no balance sheets had been prepared and they were in some considerable debt.

Echoist noted, the next day, that Freemantle was "in a somewhat deplorable way financially," but the club would "not be allowed to go to the wall just as it is bursting into prominence and fame."

The meeting was adjourned until the Southern League had deliberated on the matter of Phillips and the accounts could be brought up to date.

The verdict on Freemantle was passed at The Mitre Tavern, London, on 8 May. The report by the "London Correspondent" of the *Echo* revealed that Phillips had signed Southern League forms both for Northfleet in September and for Freemantle in October. He had played for Freemantle in November, but had not turned out for Northfleet at all. More importantly, no transfer had been applied for. The committee ruled that Freemantle be deducted two points, which made them fourth, and that both sides involved in the test match stay in their original divisions.

The affair was a candidate for the most spectacular example of snatching defeat from the jaws of victory since the Trojans (those of ancient Asia Minor rather than the rugby club) had wheeled the wooden horse through their city gates in triumph. Still, there was always next year.

The good news: on the proposal of Mr Skeggs (Millwall), Dr Bencraft was elected the first President of the Southern League and the St Mary's representatives were presented with the championship shield.

Southampton United?

To say that the decision to nullify their promotion threw Freemantle into a state of crisis would be an understatement. But the St Mary's committee had problems too. The cost of hiring the County Ground was prohibitive and, during April, a sub-committee was formed to look into playing arrangements for the 1897-98 season.

Unfortunately, there are no extant St Mary's or Freemantle club minute books on which we can draw for this period. Fortunately, the St Mary's one did still exist in 1938, at which time it was employed for an article, on this very subject, in the *Hampshire Advertiser*.

It would appear that the sub-committee's main brief was to negotiate terms for another season at the County Ground, but it was also proposed "that enquiries be made as to the Freemantle Ground." There was one, emphatic, dissenter from this idea and there is no mention of whether Freemantle were approached or not.

Meanwhile, Freemantle re-convened their annual meeting on 21 May. Neither the Secretary nor Treasurer was present, each having sent letters of resignation instead. The collapse of their First Division aspirations being a *fait accompli*, the main talking point was the outstanding debt of £211 16s 2d.

The gathering appears to have been orderly enough, until Mr G. Kimber, chairing the meeting, produced a pamphlet proposing a merger with St Mary's. There were objections to the matter even being discussed – on the basis that it would be discourteous to the absent club president, Tankerville Chamberlayne. Yet, according to the *Echo*, "a letter from Mr. Chamberlayne [was produced], approving of the amalgamation."

Delegations from both clubs met. The advantages for Southampton St Mary's were obvious: the County Ground would be likely to cost them around £200 the following season, while Freemantle were paying £24 to the Atherley Estate – which was more than covered by Mr Chamberlayne's annual donation. The drawback was that the lease had only another five years to run; but, then again, that was a more secure arrangement than Saints had with the County Cricket Club.

The fine details of the negotiations go unstated in the *Hampshire Advertiser* story. Speculation, at the time, was rife, however. On 24 May, the *Echo* reported on "the general opinion... that a united club would be better than carrying on two professional clubs in opposition. In all probability the 'St. Mary's' will be dropped altogether next season, and Saints will be known as Saints no longer."

Five days later, Ariel of the *Southampton Times* weighed in to the contrary:

FULL-TIME *at* THE DELL

The proposal that Southampton St. Mary's should play their matches on the Freemantle ground, that they should change their name, absorb the Freemantle Club, take over their liabilities, and do goodness knows what else besides requires looking into pretty closely. I am given to understand that the rumour about the town that the County Ground authorities are asking from Saints twice as much as they paid last year for the use of the County Ground is mere bunkum. There has been no change in the attitude of the county people. The Saints know exactly where they are and what they can do at the County Ground, and so far as the Freemantle scheme is concerned they practically propose to make an experiment which may prove costly. The only possible gainers by the amalgamation, so far as I can see up to the present, will be the Freemantle Club and their creditors. Things have not been satisfactory up Freemantle way for a long time, and I fear that the proposed amalgamation, if it takes place, will not have an altogether happy result. I hope those who are personally interested in this matter will not allow themselves to be led astray, but will in due time make public all the facts necessary to enable us to size things up a bit.

They may have a splendid case in favour of their proposal, and it will have to be a very strong case indeed if it is to find favour in the eyes of a great many prominent supporters of the club. It is quite true that yard for yard the Freemantle ground is not much further from the tramway junction than is the County Ground, but everyone does not live at the tramway junction, and unless the attraction is particularly great the gate at Freemantle would probably be considerably less than at the County Ground, which is more easily accessible from all parts than is the Shirley-road enclosure… I hope that wisdom will prevail, and that unless it can be shown that a very substantial advantage will accrue to the game in Southampton, and to St. Mary's as the chief exponents of the game, by going over to Freemantle, things should be allowed to go on as they are for another year yet.

By which time, Freemantle would have gone into receivership and Saints could pick up their assets without

An engraving of the County Ground, as it regularly appeared in the Saturday evening football edition of the *Southern Daily Echo*

having to bail them out financially – perhaps? It is doubtful we will ever know how close Saints and the Magpies came to merging. It would be fascinating to know if the two sides got as far working out a name for the new club. It is apparent, according to the *Hampshire Advertiser,* that the identities of the Saints and Magpies were to be "suppressed". Whatever, by the time of the Saints' annual meeting, on 11 June, the subject was dead. In fact, there was only one major matter on the agenda: the proposal to turn Southampton St Mary's into a limited liability company – 5,000 shares at £1 each.

A home of their own?

The accounts were gone into and the necessity of raising money from shareholders noted: the Club were expected to have a bank overdraft of between £600 and £700 by the start of the next season. There was also the question of a new ground. How much time this occupied in the course of the evening cannot be ascertained. Just half of one sentence is devoted to the question in the *Echo* account, which revealed that "the Committee had a ground in view." The motion to form a company was "carried with acclamation." There is no clue at all as to which site the Committee had in mind. In fact, there is no press mention of a ground until October and then no indication of its location.

On the evening of 8 July, a "promoters meeting" was held at the Bedford Hotel, Bedford Place. Four brief paragraphs cover the proceedings of the meeting, the first entry in the first minute book of the Southampton Football & Athletic Company Limited. "Mr Newnham proposed and Mr R. B. Horne seconded that Dr Stancomb be voted to the chair." The provisional directors, G.A.E. Hussey, H. Ashton, G. Thomas and G. Payne, were then elected; and A. McMinn and E. Arnfield were appointed as Hon. Secretary and "financial secretary or treasurer". Finally, Dr Stancomb was "appointed trustee for the company to complete transfer arrangements with St. Mary's F.C." That was that. There is no indication of how many were present.

A further meeting, at the offices of Thomas & Mowat on 16 July, reviewed the prospectus and share forms and decided that the share issue be launched on 26 July and closed on 7 August. Other business included setting the price for season tickets, the signing of T. Nicol of Blackburn Rovers and the agreement that T. Chamberlayne Esq. become a shareholder and "accept a seat on the directorate."

It was an offer he graciously accepted, but he does not appear to have graced a meeting, either of the Board or of shareholders – not for the best part of a decade, at least.

One may ask: why invite a man, however much a gentleman, who was president of a rival club, to take an official position with a company he has no intention of getting involved with? A question that answers itself: Chamberlayne was very rich; very generous, especially to the many sporting organisations who had claims on his patronage; and not inclined to involve himself overmuch in sordid day-to-day details.

Indeed, as a Conservative MP for Southampton, he was not noted for his zealous attendance at the House of Commons. Chamberlayne was an Old Etonian, an Oxford BA, a fully paid-up member of the landed gentry – and fully paid-up members of the landed gentry were a greatly-prized asset in Victorian institutions.

They added tone and respectability; and they could often be relied upon to put their hands in their pockets when bank managers were getting nervous. Chamberlayne's financial guarantees had just prevented Freemantle from going out of business; although they had

Mr Tankerville Chamberlayne seeks election to Parliament, where his attendance record would be marginally better than that at Board meetings

Saints' financial secretary, Mr E. Arnfield (right), poses with Mr E.C. Jarvis, of the Hampshire FA, and a fine display of silver-ware

FULL-TIME *at* THE DELL

been obliged to go amateur and resign from the Southern League, they had survived.

As for the other directors, they are given on the Memorandum of Association as Ernest Stancomb, Medical Practitioner; G. A. E. Hussey, Brewer; George Thomas, Fish Merchant; R. B. Horne, Dairyman; H. M. Ashton, Engineer; W. Newnham, Law Clerk; Charles Robson, Mineral Water Merchant (he was also a Hampshire wicketkeeper); Edward Brown Jr., Butcher; and George Payne, Butcher. The company solicitor was Bernard Harfield.

They made an interesting coalition. Harfield was a Liberal councillor; George Hussey and George Payne were prominent Tories; and Dr Stancomb, whatever his political interests of the time, would be strongly associated with the Independent Labour Party (the official Labour party being hand-in-claw with the Liberals at the time). Given the supposed middle and upper-class sensibilities of the time, his presence on the Board does appear anomalous; but, like his medical colleague and outgoing president, Russell Bencraft, he was regarded as a person of great charm and exceptional persuasive powers. In addition, he relished a good argument.

Of the aims of the company, clause 3, subsection (1) states: "To purchase or otherwise acquire a football and athletic ground." The next five clauses deal with the maintenance of, and what diversions might be carried on at, any ground or grounds the company might choose to diversify into. There were not many enterprises the articles do not include: even hotel ownership is covered.

During subsequent meetings over the next month, it was decided that the financial secretary's salary "be fixed at one pound per week." And that the registered office of the company be switched from 26 London Road to 25 Derby Road. The London Road premises were those of Barton & Dorkin, "Athletic Outfitters". Victor Barton was a Hampshire cricketer; Jack Dorkin, as observed in chapter 4, was Saints' first openly professional player. The Derby Road address was the home of E. Arnfield, "Commissioning Agent", who was, as noted, Saints' financial secretary. He was expected to run Southampton Football & Athletic Co Ltd part-time and, presumably, keep the day job. Given that he had been doing much of the secretarial work for nothing (expenses may have been forthcoming?), the one pound a week was seemingly an improvement.

Strange to say, there is nothing in the following minutes concerning a football ground. The obvious reason for this is that George Thomas had already set the ball rolling on the project and it was none of their business. Not for the time being at least.

Chapter 7
The Saints are dead

No longer will football enthusiasts be able to call out "Buck up Saints!" No longer will reporters with a flowery style be able to write of the "Saintly ones." For the Football Association has acceded to the request of the powers, and the club will in future be known as Southampton Football Club.

The Saints are dead. Long live Southampton!

The team are a lively set of boys; and I will be surprised if the Southampton team will not play a better game than Saints of old. The shares in the Football Company have gone to allotment, but there are still a few, so I hear, which have not been taken up.

So Ariel informed his public on 22 August, as the 1897-98 season beckoned. He was quite emphatic about Saints being dead and steadfastly refused to use the word Saints for several months. The *Echo* and the supporters, however, continued to use it as if nothing had happened.

Ariel was correct about shares still being available, too. The issue was significantly under-subscribed. This actuality did not appear to discomfort the new Board.

There were other matters to ruffle their feathers, though, as the season went on. There was considerable disharmony in the Saints' dressing room. The conduct of Jack Farrell was especially problematical – he had been ordered out of a Board meeting and suspended early in the season, having used "abusive language" during a discussion of his grievances. Tom Nicol, who combined football with the tenancy of the *Kingsland Tavern,* was obliged to apologise to the Board; Chippy Naughton had his contract paid-off; Bob Petrie was reprimanded over his drinking; and, in November, Watty Keay asked to be relieved of the captaincy (a position that was, curiously, being rotated around the players on a monthly basis). He explained that he "was not comfortable in that position there being so much dissension amongst the players."

Whatever was going on off the pitch, it did not appear to affect results. Not until 22 January at least, when they lost 5-2 away to Bristol City. The London press – regarded in Southampton as heavily-jaundiced regarding Saints – took great delight in rubbing salt in the wound. It was, however, no more than a glitch

Saints' new ground

Meanwhile, in the FA Cup, they were through to the First Round Proper again. In deference to their impressive Cup record (for a Southern team at least), they had been

exempted till the Third Qualifying Round. Having successfully negotiated three Southern League rivals, they got a home tie with Leicester Fosse (now known as Leicester City), a side that had finished mid-table in the previous season's Second Division. The team was packed off to spend a week at Shawford, where most of them were lodged with Mrs Winn of "The Lindins", under the supervision of Bill Dawson. Such retreats were expensive undertakings, so here was a clear demonstration of the Board's lofty aspirations.

On 29 January, Saints beat Leicester 1-0. It was an historic victory. No Southern League club had eliminated a Football League side from the Cup before.[*] Its significance has been buried under a lot of other historic moments, many of which occurred during the same season. One of them, even less celebrated, was the first mention of the new ground in the company minutes.

In the account of a shareholders' meeting held on Thursday 11 November at the Royal Victoria Rooms, the chairman stated, in amongst many other items, "that all being well by next season the company would be in possession of its own ground which was at the present time in the hands of George Thomas Esq. who was devoting his time to its early completion." This is not the most elucidatory of passages. Was it under construction? And if so, where?

Most of the shareholders probably read the *Echo* on Saturdays, which devoted two full pages to football and a high percentage of that newsprint to Saints. Vectis, in his

---

[*] It was not the first time a "non-League" club had done so since the formation of the League. Sheffield Wednesday actually reached the Cup Final in 1890, only to be beaten 6-1 by Blackburn Rovers.

FULL-TIME *at* THE DELL

own fashion, gave the first update on the ground's progress on 30 October:

> Saints new ground
> Going on nicely
> Tremendous lot of stuff
> Being dumped there.
> Likely to make good ground.
> With every accommodation
> For players and spectators
> But more later on.

As to the location? Well, Southampton was a relatively small place and, evidently, word of mouth was a more effective form of communication back in the days before wireless and television.

The first coherent comment on the subject appeared in the *Bournemouth Guardian* of 11 December, which was reproduced in the *Echo* on the same day. It was penned by William Pickford:

> While in Southampton on Saturday, I had a look
> over the railings at the new ground in the dell
> that is not far from the County Ground, and nearer
> West Station and the town, and at the present time
> it is a narrow valley with a stone culvert running
> along the bottom.
> It will not be a large ground, but the natural banks
> on all sides will be a great help in arranging for the
> convenience of spectators… The Club directors,
> among whom Mr. Thomas takes the lead, are a very
> spirited lot, and mean no retrogretion [*sic*] in
> professional football.

Another unsung landmark in the ground's history was the first Board meeting there. It occurred on 4 February 1898. The minutes open with the statement: "A meeting was held at the house on the new ground Archers Road on Friday afternoon Dr E. Stancomb in the chair."*

When George Thomas acquired The Dell he also purchased a large villa by the name of "Glenside", standing in the northwest corner of the site, which remained in place as the ground was developed. A curious arrangement, as there were barely two yards between the

basement wall and the touch-line, but it had its uses: one of the rooms was converted into a boardroom.

The main business was a dispute with Mrs Winn, regarding the cost of accommodating the team at "The Lindins", and arrangements for the next Cup tie, also at home, against Newcastle United.

Shawford, unsurprisingly, was not considered, and it was decided that the directors take them out every night the week before the match.

The breadth of entertainment in Southampton at the time was staggering by today's standards; but the Southamptonians of 1898 did not have the choice of dozens of television channels regurgitating American and Australian soaps, sitcoms and blindingly banal sporting events and they had to walk into town, or catch a tram, to be amused. Some of it was, doubtless, just as inane as what appears on TV now but only the best was good enough for the Southampton players. On Wednesday evening, they were treated to an evening at the Philharmonic Hall; then on Thursday it was the Empire Music Hall; and on Friday they all trooped off to the Prince of Wales to see the Ben Greet Company in *Daughters of Babylon*.

The point of the exercise, one suspects, was to keep the lads, especially Petrie, out of the pub.

Did it work?

Echoist considered that, of the "many Red-letter days in the history of the Southampton F.C," their 1-0 defeat of Newcastle was

> the most remarkable of all, and in the language of the
> bard of Avon it deserves

> In Golden letter to be set
> Among the high feast in the calendar

> Last season the Saints set a record for the South by
> being the first professional club to survive Round
> One proper of the cup competition, but not content
> with that achievement, on Saturday they mounted
> still another rung of the ladder of fame and are
> now… one of the last eight to do battle for the
> national trophy.
> It is something to be proud of, isn't it? And if the
> present rate of progress is maintained we shall yet see
> our champions figuring in the final at the Palace.

---

* Mr Arnfield was not a great believer in the use of punctuation.

Buchanan scores the only goal of the win against Newcastle at the County Ground, on "the most remarkable of all" Saints' "red-letter days"

I am not sufficiently swelled headed to imagine that they will be seen there this season, though with a little luck the Southern League champions may reach the semi-final stage.

The little luck Echoist was hoping for was a home tie. Saints would need a lot more than a "little luck" to beat Bolton Wanderers anywhere. They drew Bolton Wanderers – away.

One, somewhat churlish, Geordie scribe was quoted in the *Echo* as informing his public:

> Southampton are making the trip to Bolton and by next Saturday night we will probably hear the last of the parrot cries concerning the great improvement in the game south of the Thames.
> The record score in the current contest stands to Forest's credit, and I will be hugely surprised if the Trotters don't go one better on Saturday.

In fact, Nottingham Forest had beaten two teams by 4-0 that season, Gainsborough Trinity and Grimsby Town. Given that bookmakers were offering 8 to 1 on Bolton to win the Cup, and 30 to 1 on Saints, a 5-0 defeat would not have been a disgrace.

The Board do not appear to have been betting men. They packed the team, Dawson and director, Harry Ashton, off to Matlock Bath for a week at the Chesterfield House Hydro – the La Manga of the era – for a week of special training. Each man was on an £8 bonus for a win and £5 for a draw.

At Burnden Park, they were greeted by at least 300 "whispering" Saints' supporters, who had arrived in a "special train" run by the Didcot & Newbury Railway. The journey would take eight hours from Southampton Docks to Bolton and another eight hours to get home. The round trip was 28 hours and cost 10/- (50 pence).

The *Daily Telegraph* described the goalless draw as "the biggest surprise of the day."

That was nothing to the surprise of the replay. Saints won 4-0. The gate was estimated, conservatively, at 12,000, netting gate receipts of £532. Not a bad turn-out for a Wednesday afternoon, when most of the population were at work – or at least supposed to be.

The *Daily Chronicle,* a publication of Southern bias, dared to think the unthinkable:

> It is an interesting question in football circles: "Will Southampton be the first Southern professional side to win the Association Cup?" At the outset of the season the suggestion would have been regarded as preposterous, but now Southampton is a team to be reckoned with…

Even the *Daily Mail* was impressed:

> Southampton's success against Bolton Wanderers marks the dawning of a new era for professional

football in the South, and it is now becoming more and more evident that absolutely first-class football is not to be for ever monopolised by the Northern organisations. While lamenting the methods by which this condition of things has been brought about – that is to say, the hiring of aliens – one cannot escape a feeling of gratification that the South is at last holding its own once more.

It is comforting to note that the *Daily Mail* has liberalised dramatically over the last century. While it remains patently obsessed by aliens, it no longer counts Scots and Northerners among them.

The *Echo* published a late "special edition". And it must be said Echoist was not happy with his contribution. It was not the pressing deadline and the primitive communication and printing technology of the day that was to blame:

> Owing to the wretchedly inadequate provision for the Press we are unable to give anything like as full a report as we should have liked. Long before the game commenced the crowd broke through the barriers and swept the reporters and Press tables before them. All this might have been obviated if the usual seats had been reserved for the "Fourth Estate," but as in previous cup ties, the Press representatives had to shift for themselves as best they could. Many were maimed in the scramble and few came out of the crush without… some personal injury or loss.

This was not the first time Echoist had switched from match commentator to war correspondent. The previous April he had pleaded, during his account of the home match with Millwall, at which a mere 5,000 were present, for the Saints' committee to

> show just a little consideration for the Press. The present apology for a table, within the rails might be of service at a pighunt, or in some outlandish village where such luxuries are unknown, but it is altogether inadequate for a club like St. Mary's.

Whatever, trooper that he was, he got the report out, and those who coveted their jobs more than being at the great event learned that Saints were in the semi-finals.

An audience at the Palace

It was just as well a new ground was being built, because it was already evident that the County Ground wasn't up to handling crowds of 5,000, never mind 12,000, or the sorts of crowds they were getting for cup games in the North. Burnley v Everton in the same round had attracted 20,000 and Nottingham Forest v West Bromwich Albion 17,000.

Nottingham Forest were Saints' semi-final opponents. It turned out to be one of the most controversial ties in the FA Cup's long and lively history.

It started off controversially and ended controversially. It was still causing controversy years later. If it hadn't been for two world wars, European Monetary Union and Ian Branfoot, there would probably still be evenings dominated by it.

When the Football Association decided that Derby County and Everton would play at Villa Park, while Saints and Forest would go to Sheffield United's Bramall Lane, the Board reasonably requested that the FA swap the venues.

The reply was minuted during the Board meeting of 11 March: "Letter from F.J. Wall saying Association could not see their way to change the grounds in the English Cup semi-finals." F.J. Wall, secretary of the Football Association, did not enter into arguments.

The directorate responded by buying a dozen sweaters from H. Ashdown, at 4s 11d each, marked "S.F.C.", for the players, and packed them off for another week at Matlock Bath.

Saints and Forest drew at Bramall Lane. Like the County Ground, it was a cricket arena, albeit with better facilities for football than those on offer in Northlands Road. The replay was fixed for the Cup Final venue, Crystal Palace, the following Thursday, 24 March.

The game itself has been well enough documented in *Match of the Millennium:* suffice it to say that it was goalless until the closing minutes, when, playing into the teeth of a gale-force blizzard, Saints conceded two goals.

The referee left the pitch to an uproar of protests. Not an unusual incident in the career of Mr John Lewis, who might be remembered from F.J. Montgomery's memoir of Saints' first-ever Cup match at Warmley, as reported in Chapter 4.

Lewis was a founding father, and director, of Blackburn Rovers and an important figure in both the

Football League and FA. Simon Inglis, in *League Football and the men who made it,* doubted "whether any other League referee ever became the subject of more physical attacks, hate mail or protests from angry clubs."

To that list of angry clubs add Southampton FC – they protested the result. Sympathy was almost universal. Even the London press, not renowned for their compassion for Southampton, were incensed with the injustice of it all, but the FA would not budge on the issue. Nottingham Forest went on to beat Derby County in the Final.

However, there is always someone determined to go against the grain. Ariel, after reviewing the whole sorry tale in his column of 2 April, continued:

> An anonymous correspondent signing himself "Southerner," has written a letter to a London sporting paper headed "Football By Proxy," in which he denies the recent success of Southampton in the Football Association Cup has benefited Southern Football. He concludes his letter in this way:- The demoralising effect of an imported team of mercenaries was evident in the behaviour of the Southampton partisans at Crystal Palace on Thursday. Anything more unsportsmanlike it would be difficult to conceive.

Dr. Russell Bencraft J.P., has written to the editor of the paper in the following terms:-

> Sir – If the gentleman who made the cowardly and uncalled for attack in your issue of to-day on the Southampton football team, which has proved itself to be one of the best in the country this season, will divulge his name instead of shielding his identity under the nom de plume of "Southerner," I shall be eager to join issue with him on the points mentioned in his letter. – Yours, &c., Russell Bencraft.

What happened thereafter was either nothing or kept between Southerner and Dr Bencraft.

As for Lewis, *Echo* readers were to gain a degree of consolation by reading regular updates on his further misadventures, which the paper religiously catalogued in following years – starting with the intelligence that he had been attacked by pitch invaders towards the end of the Ireland v Scotland international in Belfast on 26 March.

The season finished with a whimper: a 1-0 home reversal to Chatham. The first and last Southern League defeat at the County Ground – but by this time the championship was already Saints'.

Action, before the blizzard, from the controversial game at Crystal Palace, which earned Saints a more sympathetic London press than usual, yet had them denounced as "an imported team of mercenaries," having a "demoralising effect" on Southern football

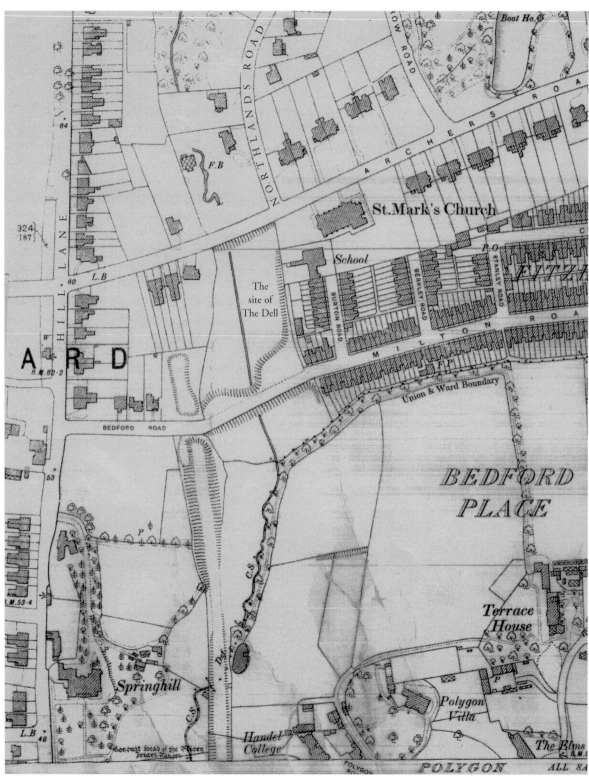

An Ordnance Survey Map of the Dell area about the time that George Thomas undertook to develop it as a first-rate enclosure for football.
For the convenience of the uninitiated, we have superimposed the site of The Dell and have inserted the names of Hill Lane and Northlands Road

Chapter 8
The Dell

One thing we are unlikely ever to learn is who spotted the suitability of The Dell as a site for a football ground.

Perhaps it was George Thomas himself? It would have been on his route home to Shirley from the County Ground. Then again, quite a few people involved with Southampton St Mary's lived in its vicinity: Charles Robson in Hill Lane; George Hussey in Northlands Road; Harry Ashton in Wilton Road; Dr Stancomb at the top of London Road; and E.C. Jarvis in Ordnance Road. Whatever their involvement, or lack of it, in the development of The Dell, they could never be accused of nimbyism.

…across a lovely dell

The Club possesses a sylvan painting of a small lake (or if you prefer, a large pond) purporting to be The Dell in its former incarnation, enclosed with towering trees and ducks coasting across its surface; but it is bogus. The picture might possibly be of the "fishing lake" situated immediately to the north. Which is not to say The Dell was not ideally idyllic. Philip Brannon, in recommending excursions, in his *Picture of Southampton: or Stranger's handbook* of 1850, felt obliged to draw attention to its environs. Having eulogised The Avenue, he continues:

> ARCHER'S LODGE stands to the left, shrouded in trees and shrubberies, amongst which are some comparatively rare exotics: above it appears the Friends' Burial-ground, a quiet resting place, planted with shrubs and flowers, and overhung with Scotch firs. Beyond this the path turns off through a wicket, winds round some fields to the end of the Crescent, and passes by another wicket into Fitzhugh's path, so named after a former proprietor of Bannisters, whose grounds it traverses; this is a most delightful walk, conducted with many a tortuous bend through a close irregular grove, then across a lovely dell with a gurgling stream and lofty aspens, through a field, and by rich meadows to the village of Shirley.

The "lovely dell" in question being The Dell, while Fitzhugh's Path approximately followed the present route of Wilton Road into Milton Road. And from The Dell to where St. James Road and Shirley Avenue now meet, it was farmland all the way; though, even then, Shirley was more sprawling suburb than village.

The "gurgling stream" was, and remains, Rollsbrook – which can still be traced for much of its length. It flows out of The Common, but first becomes recognisable as dividing it from the rear gardens of houses in Northlands Road. It then takes a swing to the south and runs under Overdell Court and The Dell; emerges beside the grounds of Springhill School, meandering parallel to Hill Lane through a thickly wooded valley; and then runs in, over and around various improvised dams of spent fire extinguishers, fork-lift truck pallets, easily detachable bicycle, motorbike and car parts and other essentials of modern living (some of them pretty revolting), before disappearing into a tunnel which channels it under a car park behind office blocks in Commercial Road. Thereafter, it flows under Central Station and goes on to merge with the complex drainage system under the Western Docks.

As late as the 1920s, before the land between West Quay and Millbrook was reclaimed, Rollsbrook emptied itself into West Bay after flowing under a bridge at the foot of Four Post Hill; and, back when Freemantle and Shirley were in Hampshire, became the county boundary south of Hill Lane, Southampton having been, since 1447, a county in its own right.

By the time The Dell had come to Thomas's attention, as a potential stadium at least, it had ceased to be in the least bucolic, or charming. It had been purchased in the 1880s by the Didcot, Newbury & Southampton Railway Company, who were intent on linking Southampton directly to the North and Midlands, as well as to London's Paddington Station, with a line that was to run east of Winchester, through Twyford, Otterbourne, Bassett and Shirley, under Winchester Road where the recreation ground stands at the top St James's Road, and where there was to be a station. After that, it would have cut through the farmland and then been taken beneath Hill Lane, a

FULL-TIME *at* THE DELL

little north of Archers Road, before running through The Dell. From there it was to run, on an embankment between Hill Lane and Rollsbrook, to a viaduct that would take it over Commercial Road and the London & South Western line near the present location of Central Station; and then run along reclaimed land outside of the Western Esplanade to a terminus at the foot of Arundel Tower. Very convenient indeed for the West Quay shopping mall – which, with this direct train link, wouldn't have required all those parking spaces.

The viaduct was at least partially built and the embankment leading to it can just about be discerned, but the scheme was scuppered by the Machiavellian stratagems of the L&SW, who were quite insistent that a rival railway in Southampton would be detrimental to the town. Ludicrous as this sounds, Parliament agreed with them and, short of time and money, the DN&S reached a deal with the L&SW to run their system into the London-Southampton line at Shawford, rendering the investment they had made in purchasing, digging up and developing the land in Southampton an utter waste. Among the now useless assets they owned was The Dell, which had been intended as a goods siding. As can be seen from the Ordnance Survey map of 1897 (on page 50), it had been stripped of vegetation, excavated and the stream through it channelled into a conduit.

The Dell had, indeed, already taken on some characteristics of an arena, albeit of a rough and ready sort and certainly not one that obviously identified itself as a football ground. Whoever did spot its potential had a well-developed imagination.

George Thomas, who probably purchased the site directly from the DN&S, may well have been a visionary. Wanderer of the *Southampton Observer* appeared to think so. On the Saturday after the historic opening game, he urged that "full justice" be

> done to the part Mr. George Thomas has taken in such a capital home for Southampton Football Club. I understand that it is wholly and solely through that gentleman's exertions that this splendid ground has been constructed out of an unpromising looking piece of waste land…

There followed an account of everything readers could possibly want to know about the new football ground:

It is hardly necessary to say that on Saturday last it quite realised the expectations which were then foreshadowed, and although 6,524 passed the turnstiles everyone not only had a clear view of the sport, but there was ample room for three or four times as many more. At the conclusion of the match all had cleared out in three minutes without any delay.

I may say… that although the whole thing has been taken in hand and carried out under the personal direction of Mr Thomas, the practical part was entrusted to Mr Bunday, of Clovelly-road, who superintended the whole of the work and the laying out of the ground, while Mr Stuchbury, of St. Mary's-road, did the whole of the plumbing work. The ground is most perfectly drained. Down the centre in line with the old ditch, runs a culvert 400 feet in length 4 feet 6 inches high and 2 feet wide. This acts as the main drain. In draining no less than 13,000 feet of agricultural drain pipes were used, all draining into the central culvert.

It is impossible at present to estimate the amount of timber used in the construction of the stands, and the number of bricks. But an estimate can be formed when we state that the rising staging on he north side of the ground will hold 5,500 spectators, who have of course to stand up; the covered east and west stands will seat 4,000 spectators comfortably, and the staging and sloping bank on the south side will hold 15,000 spectators. This totals up to 24,500. Considering that the playing space had to be levelled

Another view of the first-day action on the "splendid ground" that had been "constructed out of an unpromising looking piece of waste land"

up, in that the ground had actually to be made up and turfed, and considering the remarkable dryness of the past summer the ground on Saturday last was in wonderfully good condition. The squares of turf have taken a firm hold, and there is a good growth of root, and the surface has knitted together in a manner that can be hardly credited considering it has been down only a few months.

Other improvements, Mr Bunday told me, will be introduced as time goes on, among them being an improvement in the press box which occupies a portion of the front row of seats in the west stand. It was felt on Saturday by many who visited the ground for the first time that Mr Thomas's work in constructing this splendid ground for what is, perhaps, the most popular species of athletic sport of the century has not yet been properly appreciated. Nothing, I am sure, would give that gentleman greater pleasure than to see the accommodation he has provided fully tested at an early date, and I do not think he will have to wait long before that will be the case, at least I hope not.

People will soon commence to find out that at last they will be able to see first class football under comfortable conditions, and once having ascertained this fact by a visit to the new ground they will go there again. I was pleased to see so many ladies present on Saturday.

An innovation that passed Wanderer's notice was the imminent arrival of a 200-capacity cycle stand from the Birmingham and Coventry Cycle Company. When the facility was installed, in late September, it was not universally popular.

On 4 October, an indignant letter from W. Fulton of 56 Argyle Road was read to the directors, complaining about the two pence charge for using it. It was minuted that "No less charge could be accepted."

…by any other name…

It is curious that Wanderer refers to the new ground as the Dell Football Ground. The Board seems to have had no interest in naming it whatsoever. They kept the company address at Mr Arnfield's home at 25 Derby Road and, according to the local *Kelly's* street directories, did not change it to The Dell until 1907.

Even then the office address (Glenside) is given as "58 Archer's road" and a separate entry for the stadium reads: "Southampton Football Club Ground, Milton Road Fitzhugh & Archer's Road." Neither did the Board appear at all keen on the facilities available at the house, preferring, for most of the 1899-1900 season at least, to hold their meetings at the Bedford Hotel rather than in the boardroom.

It is some time before "The Dell" appears by name in the company minutes, and it is not referred to as such in *Kelly's* until 1946.

Glenside, otherwise known as 58 Archers Road, was part of The Dell in its early days

FULL-TIME *at* THE DELL

As for the press, they experimented with many variations. "The Southampton Football Ground" was popular, as was "Southampton's new ground", and sometimes "the new ground", and even the "fine new enclosure of Southampton F.C." *Southampton Amusements* were the first publication to call it "The Dell", in their 12 September edition (as seen in Chapter 2); but other local journals, while they did refer to "the dell", shrank from using "the Dell", needing to qualify the term. "The Fitzhugh Dell" was used occasionally. It is intriguing, but probably irrelevant, that the two articles that lay the heaviest emphasis on Thomas's responsibility for the new ground refer to it as The Dell. Could it be that that is what Thomas wanted to call it?

Some Saints' adherents were inclined to have an opinion on the issue, even if the directors were indifferent.

The *Echo*'s "Sport from Day To Day" column took the argument up on 31 October: "It is quite time the ground of Southampton F.C. was finally christened, if only to prevent confusion," it told readers, before publishing a lengthy letter on the subject from somebody addressing himself (or herself?) as "Memento" and who dismissed previous suggestions for "The Archer's Ground" and "Milton Park".

He or she went on to insist that Alfred McMinn was the man responsible for Southampton FC occupying the "proud position it does to day, viz., 'Champions of the Southern League.' In acknowledgement of this, I venture to suggest the ground be named 'Mac's Dell' to show appreciation of his work." A proposition that was probably not appreciated in the offices of Thomas & Mowatt, given the time, cost and energy Thomas had contributed to the cause himself. Nonetheless, by default as much as anything else, The Dell it was – thankfully without the "Mac".

Simon Inglis, in *Football Grounds of Britain*, supposes that "George Thomas must have been both wealthy and besotted with the Saints, because he charged only £250 a year for an eight year lease." This is, in all probability, true; but he was becoming less than enamoured of his fellow-directors. The Dell had cost him a tidy pile of money and there was a perceptible lack of appreciation regarding his commitment. As Southampton FC prepared to move into the new ground, an epic saga, worthy of dramatisation by Shakespeare, was unfolding. Unfortunately the *Bard of Avon* was not at hand, so before

we turn to some of the legendary confrontations that would unfold on The Dell's pitch, it would be as well to get the boring financial and political machinations out of the way.

The Battle for The Dell

There is no doubting that the 1897-98 season was phenomenally successful. Southampton had emerged, almost overnight, from relative obscurity to national celebrity and it is debatable whether getting to the Cup Final would have promoted their evident popularity to any greater extent (short of winning it) than had their contentious elimination, outlined in the previous chapter. Or, as it was expressed in the directors' report to the annual shareholders' meeting of 30 June 1898, "The team's performance in the English Cup and their retention of the Southern League championship entitled the club to rank among the best in the country."

In fact the whole Southern League would soon be basking in the reflected glory. The London-based national newspapers – those not antipathetic to professionalism, at least – now found they had clubs (Tottenham Hotspur and Millwall Athletic) in their own backyard worthy of promoting on a par with the better Football League teams. Hitherto, Second Division Woolwich Arsenal had been the capital's only professional side of distinction – being as distinctive, at least, as Burton Swifts, Darwen and Gainsborough.

The construction of a stadium as capacious and well-appointed as the one emerging around the dell in Fitzhugh, points to the actuality that the Board, and George Thomas in particular, were consciously building a club capable of competing on equal terms with the nation's elite. Which is not to say that the Board and Thomas were of one mind on all issues.

As already noted, the Board were not active in the development of what would eventually be known as The Dell: all arrangements, both technical and financial, were down to the fish merchant, so much so that there is no mention of a new ground in the reports of that year's annual shareholders' meeting. One would have thought its imminent opening might have warranted at least a passing reference.

It does not get many mentions in the company minute books either; and, when it does, a certain degree of tension is detectable.

There was "a long discussion" between Thomas and the Board on 14 June, at which he proposed that, if the Company could raise "£4,000 towards the purchase he would allow the balance to remain at 4½ per cent redeemable mortgage."

Failing that, he would accept a yearly rental of £200 per annum, "on same condition that they held the County Ground except that they should have possession for the entire football season." He further gave the probable cost of the "New Ground" at "about £7,000 or not more than £7,500 if purchased by the Company."

Quite where the Board were to get £4,000, never mind £7,000, is never mentioned, but the Club itself certainly did not have anything like the necessary reserves. On 18 July, it was moved by Dr Stancomb, and seconded by George Thomas *(pictured below),* that a call for five shillings be made on the first share issue.

The next item on the agenda was "the question of taking on the ground," which was deferred by Thomas, who had decided that it could wait until the end of September when it was completed and the license (presumably for the sale of alcohol) granted.

Nonetheless, the subject was revived on 3 August. On this occasion, the purchase price being discussed was £9,000, a jump in cost of £2,000 in a fortnight. It was then agreed that

> in the event of the purchase not being completed before the commencement of the football season then the Football Company offer to take the Ground and buildings therein for one year from the 1st of September 1899 at a rent to be calculated on the basis of 6% on the actual outlay on the ground such cost not to exceed 6% on £9,000 as before mentioned.

Other options were noted, but none of them was acted upon. Then, on 25 October, a final agreement was reached:

> After a long discussion between the board and George Thomas Esq. the following terms of tenancy of ground were agreed upon.

George Thomas Esq. agreed to let the Football Ground to the company for a period of three years [at an] annual rental of £250 for the football season only viz from the middle of August to the first day of May.

> At the end of the year the company undertake to pay 5% on any outlay that G. Thomas Esq. may be put [to] through making any extra accommodation on the ground by request of the Football Company. George Thomas Esq. further agrees to extend this agreement for a further period of seven years from the expiration of the above at the same terms (£250) per annum provided that he has not suffered any compulsory loss from injunctions against advertising spaces or loss of income for the license being withheld.
> The Company agree to pay gas and water charges for what they consume during the football season.

This was the agreement, apparently, that was ratified on 22 November 1898.

Quite what Thomas's expectations had been when he decided to develop The Dell is a matter of surmise; but leasing it on terms that would take him 36 years to break even on his investment was probably not one of them. On the other hand, he must have been as aware as the rest of the Board of the expense of running a successful club and of how poorly the share issue had fared.

The disillusionment of George Thomas

Whatever Thomas's aspirations – personally, or for the Club – they were certainly not met and his disaffection with his colleagues became manifest on Tuesday 18 April 1899. H. Thomas Esq. (almost certainly not a relation), the manager of the London & Midland Bank, was invited to a Board meeting, following a letter he had sent to the Club informing them that George Thomas had withdrawn his name as a guarantor on the overdraft.

It was decided to see a number of potential guarantors and meet again on the following Thursday. George Payne, Alfred McMinn, Harry Ashton, Charles Robson, E.C. Jarvis and E. Arnfield, in his capacity of company

FULL-TIME *at* THE DELL

secretary and minute-taker, met at the home of Dr Stancomb in College Place. If they talked over alternative financial backing, it is not disclosed: the main business, in fact the only business noted, was an agreement that Dr Stancomb would write a letter to George Thomas, which was drafted in the minute book:

> Dear Mr Thomas,
>
> The directors of the Southampton Football & Athletic Co. at their meeting requested me to write and inform you that they had received official notice of your action with regard to the Guarantee Fund. Taking into consideration the peculiarly embarrassing time that you chose for issuing a notice of withdrawal and in the absence of any formal notification that such a course was your fixed intention, the Board is obliged to regard your action as extremely hostile to your fellow Directors, to the Southampton Football Club, and to the many adherents and shareholders who have looked to you for direction and support. They will find it difficult to accept any justification for an action calculated to damage if not wreck the club at the period of its greatest need and when no income could be counted upon to meet even its temporary requirements. The Directors have made arrangements for the further financial conduct of the Company, but in the best interests of Southampton Football they sincerely trust you will see the advisability of reconsidering your present attitude to the Company.
>
> Yours Faithfully
>
> E.H. Stancomb
>
> Chairman of S'ton F & A Coy.

It was certainly a well-timed blow. When the letter withdrawing his support arrived, the Saints had three Southern League fixtures and one United League[*] fixture remaining, all of them away. The overdraft would stand at £1,095 9s at the beginning of May and the Club was anticipating a heavy summer wage bill without any further income (other than outstanding gate shares from a few away games) until September. Further, they were in the process of negotiating the transfer of former West Brom forward, Roddy McLeod, from Brighton United, at a knock-down fee of £5. It is most likely that Brighton wanted to off-load him because they couldn't afford to meet the cost of his close-season wages and he would not be a cheap addition to Saints' expenses. Regular first team players were getting between £2 10s and £5 10s a week, and McLeod would probably be expecting well over £3. Running at around £51.15s a week, it was the sort of wage bill that would spur many a Football League club director to shift his assets into the wife's name.

The transfer of McLeod was confirmed in the minutes on 27 April. Further down the agenda, it is noted that Thomas had resigned from the Board. Whatever was said about the situation goes un-noted, other than an instruction to the secretary to write acknowledging, and accepting, the resignation and to advise him that "we still hope to retain his support."

Evidently, other individuals had been persuaded to stand guarantee on the overdraft.

The most obvious conclusion, though not necessarily the correct one, is that Thomas expected his investment in the new ground to give him a controlling interest in the running of the Club; and that, when that was not forthcoming, he attempted to destabilize the Board, in the expectation that the resulting crisis would force the shareholders to call for him to take control.

If this is not the case, what might be the explanation?

There is precedent for the situation.

Back in the late 1880s, Everton FC had objected to increasing interference in their affairs by their President and landlord, John Houlding. Things came to a head in 1892 when Everton were left with a choice between letting Houlding take over and moving out of their Anfield Road ground. They opted for the latter, developing a new site at Goodison Road, across Stanley Park. Houlding, undaunted, recruited a team of professional footballers and set up Liverpool FC at Anfield in opposition.

If it ever crossed Thomas's mind to force Saints out of his ground, he probably wouldn't have considered the move for very long. They could simply have returned to the County Ground, where, beyond doubt, former president Dr Bencraft would have welcomed them back with open arms. Further, setting up another professional club in opposition was not a practical option:

---

[*] The United League was a competition, run between 1897 and 1899, in which most of the fixtures were played midweek. Saints were not inclined to take it too seriously.

Chapter 8

Southampton, unlike Liverpool, had neither the population nor the wealth to sustain two better-than-average football clubs.

Then again, if it was the case that Thomas wanted to take a controlling interest in the Saints, his scheming made very little impact.

There is little indication of crisis at that year's annual meeting, on 28 July.

Having reported on yet another Southern League championship season, gone through the accounts and divulged the staggering overdraft, Dr Stancomb captivated his audience with an oration on the increased financial burden brought about by their first season at what was being called The Dell.

The *Echo*'s account places great emphasis on the unexpected expense of the new ground:

> That deficit was caused through some considerable disappointment which they experienced in connection with the purchase and rent of the ground. Last year he told them they had every prospect of purchasing the ground at a very reasonable figure, and that, failing the purchase, they would have the option of renting the ground at a cost considerably less than had been the case at the County Ground. The directors were officially as well as privately of the opinion that they would have the ground practically rent free.

Stancomb placed no blame at anyone's door for this state of affairs and acknowledged that "the terms on which they held the ground were…, under the circumstances, perfectly fair."

No mention was made of George Thomas (by name anyway), of his resignation or of the problems he had caused by withdrawing as a guarantor.

Hereafter, Thomas, who continued to be an active supporter of Saints, appears to have made himself as amenable as possible to his former colleagues, even accompanying players going on international duty on their behalf; and if he made any further attempts to involve himself in the Club's internal politics – until 1904, at least – they have yet to be picked up on.

On 18 June 1904, the *Southern Daily Echo* reported on the previous evening's annual shareholders' meeting at the YMCA in Ogle Road. Rumour had had it that the Board

were in for a stormy time and the attendance was "a record one". But the anticipated "scene" did not materialise. Not that Dr Stancomb and his cohorts had an easy ride.

It transpired that a circular to attend a meeting, the night before the AGM, had been sent out by a pro-Thomas faction to a large number of shareholders, but not to the directors or their supposed supporters. Dr Stancomb, having taken no little time getting the preliminary business out of the way – the usual overdraft, the inevitable Southern League championship and the necessity of maintaining "a team capable of beating Aston Villa" – went straight for the jugular: if there was any dissatisfaction with the way the affairs of the Club were run then it should be brought up at the annual meeting. If the resulting answers

> were not satisfactory, if any information was withheld, and there was reason to suppose that the conduct of the club was not what it ought to be, then the shareholders had a just remedy, but he had never yet found such a policy in their club.

After a brief exchange with Thomas, whom he silenced, the Chairman addressed the circular's signatories one by one, asking them, more or less, if they were dissatisfied with the running of the company. Those who had complaints were not prepared to elaborate on them to any great extent and Thomas, whether out of choice or because the Chairman failed to acknowledge him (which is unlikely), or because he was edited out of the report, was not mentioned again.

As for the rest of the meeting, there was certainly some hard questioning about the running of the Club. But Stancomb appears to have handled the potentially volcanic affair with icy aplomb and, when it came to the election of directors, the four standing for re-election – Stancomb himself, Harry Ashton, George Payne and W. A. Hammock – breezed home fairly comfortably

If Thomas had been attempting a *putsch,* and it is hard to think what else he could have been up to, it was a marked failure.

Thereafter, relationships again appear to have normalised. And while, according to his obituaries, he continued to support Saints, Thomas became a director of the newly-created Chelsea Football Club in 1905.

The significance of that will be dealt with in good time.

FULL-TIME *at* THE DELL

This photograph shows how the Dell looked in 1889—ten years before it became the home of the Saints. I am indebted to Mr. C.J. Tofield, cycle agent, of Bitterne-road, for the opportunity of showing the Saints' followers what the Dell was like—when it really was a dell. Mr. Tofield owns the painting… and it hangs at his home, Warren Cottage, West Tytherley. It was given to him as a wedding present by his uncle, the late Mr. "Will" French, of the well-known Southampton boot firm, who was a collector of paintings. The picture painted by Mr. Masters, Mr. Tofield told me, from a house in Archer's-road overlooking the Dell.…
Football Echo, 13 September 1947

The above was printed in all good faith. Sadly, the painting, which hung in The Dell's boardroom in recent years, is bogus. It is probably what appears, on mid-nineteenth century maps of Southampton, as the Fishing Pond; which was a little to the north of the present Archers Road.

Chapter 9
The very Peru of football

If the opening of The Dell was not a great talking point in the national press, it certainly marked a point in time when Saints took another step-up in status. The most evident manifestation of this was the FA's decision to exempt them from the qualifying rounds of the FA Cup, this on the basis of their record in the competition, rather than an impressive new stadium.

The arrival of four internationals caused more comment. Scottish cap-holders, John Tait Robertson and Peter Meehan, who had both moved from Everton, were certainly accomplished and well-up to the standards the faithful had come to expect from signings over the previous couple of years; but the two Englishmen, goalkeeper Jack Robinson and inside-forward Harry Wood, were contemporary legends.

Wood's signing was especially remarkable. He was a real Wolverhampton Wanderers stalwart. As luck would have it, Saints' trainer, Bill Dawson, just happened to be in the area when Wood was in dispute with his directors and he persuaded the England international he would be happier at The Dell.

Robinson had answered an advertisement for players in the *Athletic News*. He had been playing for New Brighton Tower in the Cheshire League, but their election into the Football League Division Two meant he was unable to play for them, his Football League registration being held by Derby County.*

Their Dell debuts did not take place in the game against Brighton United. Nor was that game the opening of the ground – no more than the Premier League fixture against Arsenal was its closing, at least.

The Board wanted some pre-season events to enable the public to inspect the arena and, hopefully, buy season tickets. An actual game with some Football League or Scottish League club of renown was out of the question, as playing football in August, the height of the cricket season, was an absolute taboo.

But it was thought they might be able to hold a couple of practice matches.

The minutes of 18 July 1898 note a letter from the FA "saying… we should act improperly if we issued season tickets on our ground during the month of August with the view of the purchasers seeing the practice game." By this time, it had been mooted that some evening concerts be held at the ground and invitations to tender were sent out to the bands of the town.

There was further correspondence with the FA Secretary, who conceded that the Club could have races and ball dribbling "at our promenade concert if we wished to." And so it came to pass that the Town Band played and there were five athletic events held between the players: three sprint races, a ball-kicking competition and a ball-dribbling contest.

The *Southampton Observer* felt that,

> had the weather been more favourable the attendance no doubt would have reached into thousands. As it was only three or four hundred assembled. The rain fell in torrents during the sport, but it was pluckily resolved to go on with the events… Just as the sports concluded the weather brightened up. During the afternoon the Town Band played some excellent selections of music.

Not the most portentous of occasions but, then, the stadium was not built for brass bands and foot races: it was a temple to what J. B. Priestley would describe as "Conflict and Art." And there was to be plenty of that over the next ten decades.

Conflict and Art
The promenade concert done and dusted and that first – historic – game against Brighton United won, New Brompton came to Southampton and returned north

---

* The FA's policy on players' contracts was that they did not approve of them, but that they must not be broken during the season. The various leagues tended not to recognize each other's registrations; so, technically, players in dispute with their clubs could move between leagues without transfer fees being exchanged.

FULL-TIME *at* THE DELL

with both Southern League points. There was a great wailing and gnashing of teeth, but it was perhaps a relief to get the first defeat at The Dell out of the way before any unrealistic expectations were raised.

The 1898-99 season was not as sensational as the last season at the County Ground, but it was increasingly evident that both Saints and the Southern League were becoming regarded as a threat to the established order of things. Ariel observed in October 1898 that Millwall were getting bigger gates than Woolwich Arsenal. While the latter drew a crowd of 4,000 on 22 October, Millwall v Tottenham Hotspur had been watched by 15,000.

At the end of the season, Grasshopper, of the *Athletic News,* observed:

> As a representative Southern Club it cannot be said that the Arsenal have made so remarkable impression on the public as Southampton.
> The last named are undoubtedly in a better class and… I believe the club could have gone a good bit further in the Second-Division of the League had they been so engaged.
> As it is they have won the Southern League championship again with distinct honour and carried their banner into the thickest of Cup-tie strife.

One of the less significant games of the season was on 1 November, when the first international fixture took place at The Dell. A team from Havre came over to test the metal of Southampton's "soccer" aces. They were predominantly British ex-patriots, but the *Echo* insisted on referring to "a team of French footballers" and observed that, although they were a "decided novelty," they "failed to attract more than a hundred spectators to the Archer's Grounds." Their opponents were, uncannily, Trojans, who had forsaken the lozenge-shaped ball for one game and had recruited three Banister Court players and Councillor George Hussey to make up their XI.

Apparently not the most beguiling of spectacles, it provoked "endless hilarity" among the spectators, but Trojans upheld the honour of the Empire with a 3-2 win.

Saints' opponents were somewhat less exotic, but drew significantly larger crowds – who invariably got their money's worth. They ended their league fixtures at St John's Lane, Bristol, needing to take a point from Bristol City to regain the Southern League championship.

The interest in the game was, predictably, phenomenal, with large crowds waiting outside newspaper offices for telegrams carrying the latest intelligence to be posted in the windows.

There must have been some anxious faces around the Above Bar headquarters of the *Southern Daily Echo* that afternoon, as the news came through that Saints were 2-0 down and Robinson had been injured.

Saints, regardless, won 4-3. A dramatic come-back always brings that little extra zest to celebrations. The *Echo* chronicled the victorious return. The scenes at Docks Station were

> without parallel in the history of Southern football.
> Long before ten o'clock the streets at the lower end of the town were almost impassable, and joy triumphant reigned.
> At the stations en route pretty much the same sort of thing happened.
> The platform at Salisbury was crowded with Saintly enthusiasts, and at Romsey the team was hailed with the strains of "See the conquering hero comes."
> As a contrast, dead silence reigned at Eastleigh. Why? Ask me another.
> Verily, 'twas a great night. The procession through the streets reminded one of the conclusion of a great electoral campaign.

Ariel summed up the first season at The Dell, concluding:

> The great Cup-tie with Derby County of course formed the event of the Southampton season, and probably a record gate of £1,250 [allegedly 23,000 spectators, but see page 219] totalled on that classic occasion will take some time to eclipse. But undoubtedly the performance that conferred most distinction on the club was the splendid triumph over Notts County at Nottingham – the first actual victory… by the Saints on a First League ground.

That Saints had lost their first Cup game at The Dell was, fortunately, not any sort of omen but it was certainly galling. Derby County were not only lower in the First Division than Notts County, but had reported Southampton FC, and their former player, Jack Robinson, for making an illegal approach to their star

Chapter 9

forward, Steve Bloomer. A special committee of the FA heard the case, at the end of the season; and, like the reigning monarch, they were not amused. The *Echo* reported their finding that the charges were "as worthless as the paper they were written on… Thus ended one of the biggest farces of the past football season."

The season was given an ostentatious farewell at the Victoria Skating Rink. Speeches were made; music was rendered, not least a banjo duet from Messrs Ellaway and Williams; songs were sung, including a popular contribution from Dr Stancomb; medals were handed out; and Dr Russell Bencraft, as the league's president, presented the Southern League Shield to Jack Robinson, the "Prince of goalkeepers" and Saints' vice-captain (skipper Harry Wood being absent).

This sort of do was known as a "smoker". It was an evening that all present were supposed to contribute to: by singing, telling a story, reciting a poem or, at the very least, joining in the choruses of the songs. The grand event of the evening was the presentation of a silk flag, in the club colours and bearing the town crest, by R.H. Clark, representing the Southern League, to Southampton FC. A magnanimous gesture, albeit one for which the Club had to bear half the costs.

Pursuing the Villa standard

Meanwhile, Alfred McMinn was back in the North signing "tip-top" players.

The pick of the 1899 summer signings was not, however, an established League star, but Archie Turner of Camberley St Michaels. Reputedly recommended by a former *Echo* journalist working in Surrey, Turner was from Farnborough and the question must have been asked: could a Hampshire-born player make the grade in a side as accomplished as Saints?

Another question that must have been earnestly discussed in the four-ale bars of Southampton is whether Saints could continue their inexorable rise. They had emerged from local obscurity to national prominence in the space of a decade. And while the London and Northern press may have been comparing them favourably to Woolwich Arsenal, Dr Stancomb and Mr Arnfield were publicly stating that they were building a side to equal Aston Villa. Cloud cuckoo land?

The world was now Saints' oyster. Or at least the football world was. It was a rather small world to be sure, for while it held the attention of what careless sociologists and historians call the "masses" on the island of Great Britain, it had yet to galvanise the public in less-blessed countries.

The boy's paper, *Chums,* famous for its tales of daring-do on the Spanish Main, the Wild West and outlandish and perfidious parts of the British Empire, was inclined to agree with the masses. In a feature, headed

BUILDING A BIG FOOTBALL CLUB
THE STORY OF SOUTHAMPTON'S RAPID RISE,

it insisted that

> The Southampton club is the surprise packet of the football world. No team can boast of having fought their way to the front with such lightning-like rapidity as the champions of the South, and if the opinions of experienced judges are worth anything the Southampton men have absolutely no superiors. It is true they do not engage in first League duels, but the reason they do not do so is not that they consider they stand no chance of achieving premier honours, but that the departure would not pay them. There are no League clubs in the South,* the consequence being that if Southampton were to enter for the competition, about half their time would be spent in travelling to the North and back – a proceeding which would soon land them high and dry in Bankruptcy Court.

A lengthy interview with Mr Arnfield, "the popular secretary and manager of the club," ensued:

> "And what has been the cause of your astonishing success?"
> "In the main, our bold forward policy of engaging only tip-top players. No man is good enough for us who isn't good enough to take his place in any team in England. We shouldn't dream of engaging a player who wasn't worthy of inclusion in the Aston Villa eleven, for instance. This is our Standard."

---

* *Chums* had forgotten Woolwich Arsenal and Luton Town (who had defected from the Southern League in 1896), but most football enthusiasts did.

FULL-TIME *at* THE DELL

The growing realisation that the Southern League was shaping up as a challenger to the Football League was not confined to the London, and southern provincial, press. William McGregor, the man who initiated the League, felt moved to have an opinion, which was enthusiastically reprinted by the *Echo:*

> The South is now a great power in the land. What would certain clubs have given six seasons ago to have gained admission to the Second League? Now there are very few clubs of importance in the South who bother their heads about the League at all. It's scarcely to the credit of the once all-powerful League that the two members they boast in the South should be by no means the two representative clubs of the South.

William McGregor was not going to commit himself, however, to the growing assertion in the South that the Football League and Southern League should amalgamate.

Saints opened the 1899-1900 season with a swagger, hammering New Brompton 6-2. But there was trouble at the turnstiles, as the *Football Echo* pointed out:

> A great deal of interest was manifested in the dimensions of the gate, and it is only right to state that a vast majority of even those present consider the shilling charge to be mistaken.
> Outside the ground itself there was no doubt as to the popular opinion. A somewhat largely attended meeting of "anti-bobs" was held in Milton-road, and after grievances had been aired the participants therein wended their way to other haunts than the football field.
> Be that as it may, there is no getting away from the fact that the gate was disappointingly small, and at the time of the kick-off there were barely two thousand people present, whilst the stands were sparsely occupied.

Not the most portentous of launches to a season. But it is comforting to know that the Southampton Independent Supporters Association sprang from a traditional root. The same edition of the *Football Echo* (2 September) carried an interview with Mr Arnfield:

> "Now there is the delicate issue of the shilling gate. What do you think about it?"
> "Candidly I don't like it personally, but if we don't get enough 'tanners' we must have the 'bobs.' There is [an] alternative… to an occasional shilling gate, and that is to reduce the wages of players, which means inferior men. After all the brilliant players we have had, Southampton people won't put up with a mediocre team. Why, our people would throw bricks at us."

Arnfield went on to explain:

> The Board are particularly anxious to retain a good team, but you must remember we have a big deficit, and our summer wage bill is within £12 of our winter one, whilst for over four months we have not taken a penny.

And he couldn't resist a poke at the local media: "People get up in arms because you don't unveil to them every little detail of the club."

Saints – it is worth stressing again – were living beyond their means. They had a yearly bill for wages and bonuses in excess of £4,000; and when the FA introduced a maximum wage of £4 in 1901 (a piece of legislation the Southampton board supported), Saints had at least five players on their books whose earnings either matched or exceeded that sum. Their wage and bonus bill was modest compared with the £5,000 plus that Newcastle United were reported to have been shelling out for a First Division squad that was hardly in Saints' class; but it was probably more than all but five or six big clubs would have felt comfortable with.

The Southampton board were banking everything on regular Cup runs. As Dr Stancomb told the 1904 annual meeting, the Club's income "was about one-third of Aston Villa's, yet Southampton had to maintain a team capable of beating Aston Villa, and the club's income was only half of Portsmouth's."

He went on to point out that the Club's regular income would not support a wage bill of more than £35 a week.

The Board had come to the conclusion that the only thing to be done to make the Club a financial success was to maintain a team, the character of which, and the excellence of which, would enable them to pick the plums that were put in their way. It has to be said that, when it came to picking plums, Saints were serious contenders.

Twice the Bridesmaids

The 1899-1900 season was a case a point. By the end of February, they were sitting on top of the Southern League and were in the semi-final of the FA Cup. Everton, Newcastle United and West Bromwich Albion, each of them of the First Division, had all been eliminated at The Dell.

But it was Saints' semi-final opponents who had done most to shake the foundations of the Football League this time round. In the third of three epic confrontations, Millwall had beaten the League champions-elect, and by far the most consistent and outstanding club of the decade, Aston Villa, 2-1.

Semi-final day, 24 March 1900, was a red-letter date for the Southern League. In two years (since Saints had vanquished Bolton Wanderers), it had risen from an obscure regional competition to stand shoulder-to-shoulder with the Football League. Now one of its clubs must qualify for the Cup Final. The London dailies were full of it. The Saints' directors probably couldn't believe their luck: their boys were more than a match for Millwall. Just to be sure, they packed them off to Buxton for a week of special training, which, Mr Arnfield had informed *Chums,* consisted of taking a walk in the morning, "certainly the fat ones," ending with a bath:

> …in the afternoon sprinting and ball-kicking are the order. Baths are capital for removing stiffness from the joints. And, by the bye, everybody in training should go to bed early. Our fellows usually retire at ten, but the night before a big match they are all in bed by nine. They enjoy a long sleep, and don't appear for breakfast before nine.

He was then asked: "What about diet, smoking, etc.?"

> Our diet is an extremely plain one. We make our arrangements with the hotel proprietors some time before we embark on a tour. The customary fare consists of fish, chops and steaks. Vegetables and sweets are barred when a match is about to be played, and so are spirits. Half a pint of beer per meal, however, is allowed, and directly the match is over

the players can eat whatever they please. As regards smoking we only prohibit it on the morning preceding a big match. You might be surprised to hear that a week's training makes a big hole in £100.

Money well spent? Some 30,000 spectators watched a goalless draw at the Palace. The following Wednesday, 10,000 made there way to Elm Park, Reading and watched Saints win 3-0. It was something to take troubled minds off the dreadful events in South Africa, where the Boer War dragged on.

The final pitched Saints against Bury, on 21 April. Between the conquest of Millwall and the final, Saints played six Southern League fixtures. They won the first two, then fell to bits, suffering four defeats, two of them against Portsmouth.

Still, the Southern and Metropolitan press were fairly confident Saints were the better bet, but that it would be a very close game. Bury, who were mid-table in Division One, had a style of play similar to Millwall's and could hardly be said to be a whole lot better than the side that had eliminated Aston Villa. One of the few dissenting opinions regarding a close result was Frank Brettell, secretary of Portsmouth, who, the *Morning Leader* told its readers, was "unhesitating" in his opinion "that Bury would win the Cup by a comfortable margin. He thinks Southampton are stale."

He was right. The 1900 FA Cup Final was an unmitigated disaster for Saints.

Losing 4-0 was undoubtedly a humbling result. The least said about it the better, but masochists can find the grim details in *Match of the Millennium.*

It was later – 12 years later – revealed, in the *Southampton Pictorial* history of Saints, that the players had fallen out regarding the selection of Jack Farrell at centre forward; a choice approved by the English players, while the Caledonian contingent would have preferred the more direct Roddy McLeod. A somewhat simplistic explanation, but the only one that has been offered.

Saints pulled themselves together for the final two games at The Dell, but it was too late to revive their Southern League fortunes They finished the season in third place, behind Tottenham Hotspur and Portsmouth, who had quite enjoyed their first-ever season in the Southern League, having been elected straight into its First Division.

FULL-TIME *at* THE DELL

If the 1899-1900 season had ended in disappointment – one might even say bitter failure – it had at least firmly established Saints as what they had been for three years: a team that could take on and beat the best Football League sides. Not with ease, not every time (not even Aston Villa could do that), but as often as not. It had also boosted the esteem of the Southern League, which was almost certainly confounding the expectations of its founders.

The close season brought a drastic clear out. Petrie, McLeod and Farrell were among those not retained. The success of the season had been the young Archie Turner, who had not only had a great debut season on the right wing, but earned an England cap.

Whatever cash the Cup run had brought in, it was not enough: in July, the Board agreed to make another call on the shares. The response was disappointing. Letters were sent informing the recipients that they would have their shares rescinded if payment was not forthcoming. The response was equally disappointing. It would seem that supporting the Club by buying shares, with little hope of ever getting a dividend, was one thing. Throwing good money after bad was another.

Perhaps the most important development to take place during the summer of 1900 was the decision of Alfred McMinn to resign as a director. His ability to spot a "good 'un", and lure him South, had certainly been a crucial factor in the Club's progress.

The directors had an inspiration in 1900: why not recruit some top-class amateurs? There were still plenty about at the time, as Corinthians' results against professional sides could attest. Whether this was an actual formulated policy is debatable, but their audacious bids included approaches to three "gentleman" internationals.

The first was to L.H. Gay, an England goalkeeper (who was also an international cricketer, a Corinthian and Cambridge blue), who signed but never actually played for Saints. Yet having both of England's most regularly selected goalkeepers on the books certainly impressed the sports journalists. That Robinson would remain first

choice was never in doubt and, with him between the posts, Saints got off to a good start to the 1900-01 season, despite being somewhat light in the forward-line.

Another amateur double-international was signed in December and he *did* play. C.B. Fry, arguably the greatest all-round sportsman of his generation, made his debut at right-back against Tottenham Hotspur at The Dell on Boxing Day. Fry, who also played his football for Corinthians and had earned his single cap, to date, against Canada, was a national institution. He was most certainly the sort of player to bring extra punters through the gates – while the novelty lasted at least.

Unfortunately, he was signed too late to add his prowess to the Cup campaign: Saints were defeated 3-1, at The Dell by Everton, in the First Round.

An approach to another Corinthian, G.O. Smith, England's most accomplished centre-forward – whether unremunerated or otherwise – fell on stonier ground. His reaction to the offer is noted in the board minutes of 8 January 1901: "Post card from G.O. Smith saying he thought it impossible to assist our club in cup ties at same time wishing us every success."

Jack Robinson, C.B. Fry and Arthur Turner represented England in this, the only, international ever played at The Dell. The "home" side won 3-0, despite Turner leaving the field injured after 20 minutes

There were further improvements in The Dell's advanced facilities. Towards the end of September, the teams were chalked up on a blackboard carried around the pitch before games by Mr W. Walton. Back at a time when players did not have numbers (let alone their names) on their backs, this was a tremendous aid to serious critics of the game in identifying those players who needed tactical advice, or suggestions as to where their mothers might have been when they were conceived.

Despite the non-appearance of G.O. Smith, Saints again took the Southern League championship. The competition had administered another heavy blow to presumptions of Football League hegemony, when Tottenham Hotspur beat Sheffield United in the Cup Final. It was a splendid achievement for the Southern League – and, more especially, Spurs – but it must have dismayed a lot of people in Southampton, where it was taken somewhat for granted that upsetting the League applecart was a prerogative of Saints. This said, the dismay in the north was probably far greater.

Saints had the opportunity to put Spurs in their place the following January. They duly did so, but it was no easy task, the result, 2-1, being decided in a second replay. Thereafter, the passage to the Final was relatively trouble-free. Saints' stock was now so high that the 4-1 defeat of League Champions Liverpool at Anfield Road, in Round Two, was not regarded as an upset.

The Final, with Sheffield United, went to two games, both played at Crystal Palace. Again, Saints were fancied by the newspapers to win. Again they blew it. The result, 2-1, at least had the consolation of looking respectable on paper. And a generally sympathetic Southern press made polite noises that they were a little unlucky.

There was no consolation in the league either. Saints slipped to third, behind Tottenham Hotspur and Portsmouth, as they had been the last time they reached the Cup Final. With a twist, Pompey were champions.

Aftermath

Players came, players went; Saints continued to win more than they lost; George Thomas, we might presume, plotted; the overdraft waxed and waned; and Saints' fame continued to rise.

Under the leadership of Harry Wood, they won the Southern League championships of 1902-03 and 1903-04, though their Cup form dipped. Perhaps it was the 4-1 defeat at Bolton Wanderers that prompted Thomas's attempt to destabilise the Board at the 1904 Annual Shareholders Meeting? ·

Saints' reputation is wonderfully encapsulated in Arnold Bennett's 1908 story, *The Matador of the Five Towns.* The "Five Towns" were a metaphor for Bennett's native Potteries, so he might have had good reason to remember Alfred McMinn's activities there in the 1890s. Whatever, the narrator of the tale finds himself watching Knype (an allegorical Stoke?) – or, rather, the local crowd:

> I could hear specialists around me proving that though Knype had yet five League matches to play, its situation was safe. They pointed excitedly to a huge hoarding at one end of the ground on which appeared names of other clubs which Knype would

have to meet before the end of the season, and the figures indicated their fortunes on various grounds similar to this ground all over the country. If a goal was scored in Newcastle, or in *Southampton, the very Peru of first-class football,* it was registered on that board and its possible effect on the destinies of Knype was instantly assessed (italics added).

Peru? Well, in 1908, Southampton seemed, from the Midlands, no less far-flung or exotic and just as unlikely to possess a useful football team.

The Southern League, too, continued to hold out a threat. But this was not a threat Football League directors, other than William McGregor, were to take seriously in open conversation, no matter how loud the persistent demands, from the Southern and London press, for a "national league". An amalgamation would mean a minimum of three or four First Division clubs finding themselves in a reorganised Second Division, to make way for Saints and whoever might be adjudged their equal.

The *Football Echo*'s London correspondent had caught their mood as early as 14 April 1900:

> We can afford to wait. The Southern League is going well just now, but changes are sure to take place. S.L. Clubs affect to despise the League now, but they may have to change before long. We shall have them applying for admission some fine day, and they may find out their mistake. When they do come in the League will not suffer from the arrangement.

One Football League director pointed out that the clubs within the League

> were to be preferred before Southern League clubs, looking at them from all points of view, especially geographical position, old memories, and associations, and attractive power away from home, and the smaller amount of time and money absorbed in travelling… Arsenal would always rank before other Southern clubs for their past fidelity and sacrifices.

The reporter might have said, but he didn't, that the Football League was a cabal, devoted not to the propagation of football as a popular and lucrative

FULL-TIME *at* THE DELL

spectator sport, but to the narrow – and short term – self-interest of its members.

William McGregor re-entered the debate in 1906, courtesy of his contribution to the encyclopaedic *Association Football and The Men Who Made It*, within which he argued that his creation was too parochial and should include "influential clubs at present outside the organisation with the object sooner or later of making the league a truly national body. While it does not include Southampton, Portsmouth, and Tottenham Hotspur, it cannot be said to be truly representative."

But even with McGregor on the side of the angels, the turkeys of the Football League were not going to vote for a Southern League Christmas.

Decline and Fall

Even as McGregor wrote, the tide was turning in the Football League's favour. Bristol City had quit the Southern League in 1902, probably in sheer frustration; and, having been elected to the Football League's Division Two, were promoted to Division One in 1906. The third-placed side in the Second Division that year were Chelsea – an entirely new club, created to play games at the enormous Stamford Bridge Athletic Ground – who were promoted the following year.

How much influence George Thomas had on the Chelsea board is yet to be ascertained, but it is intriguing that their first manager – player-manager in fact – was former Saint, John Tait Robinson. He had left The Dell after one season, for Glasgow Rangers, after turning down the tenancy of the *Stewards Arms* public house. Quite what his objections to it were are not stated in the minute that recorded his evident disillusionment with the Club.

Clapton Orient had also deserted the Southern League for Division Two in 1905, but were less than successful. More offensive than all of this, though, was the promotion to the First Division of Woolwich Arsenal in 1904. That Arsenal were just as anonymous in the top flight as they had been in Division Two hardly mattered. Hitherto, Southampton were the star draws in the South: they were the side that all the other clubs were desperate to beat; they paraded a galaxy of famous players only a few sides in the League could boast the equal of; and they attracted big crowds.

By 1907, there were two clubs in London whose supporters could watch clubs with internationals playing nearly every other week; and at least a dozen of those sides were arguably as good as Saints.

The Southern League saw the writing on the wall and, in March 1907, formally approached the League's Management Committee with the aim of negotiating the formation of a National League. Simon Inglis, in *League Football and the men who made it,* records that the two sides met at the Tavistock Hotel, London on 11 March. The Management Committee circulated the League clubs on the matter, and had 38 replies, of which 26 were in favour, but "the Committee decided not to take the matter further, on the grounds that a three-quarters majority had not been reached."

It got worse: Tottenham defected to the Football League in 1908 and won immediate promotion, by which time Fulham had also been elected to Division Two.

Saints' last championship season had been in 1903-04 and, while they had an impressive Cup run in 1907-08, knocking Everton out 3-2 in a Dell third round replay (only to lose 2-0 to Second Division Wolverhampton Wanderers in the Stamford Bridge semi-final), their star, slowly but emphatically, waned.

They did not apply to join the League. It is unlikely they would have been accepted, being so far from its Northern axis, even had they been Southern League champions; plus, the financial implications were not much less than they would have been back in 1899 –when *Chums* concluded, as we saw, that such an undertaking "would land them high and dry in Bankruptcy Court."

There were complications other than the added expense of journeying to Birmingham, Manchester and beyond. While Saints would have to bear the cost of their own travelling expenses, they would also have to subsidise those of established League opponents. Fulham, Chelsea and Clapton were obliged to pay Northern sides £20 and Midlands clubs £15 on top of their share of the gate. Heaven knows what Saints would have been forced to cough-up.

This "tax" was not just for Southern clubs: Newcastle were compelled to make similar donations to their opponents when they joined the League in 1893.

Dr Stancomb left the Board in 1909 and was replaced as chairman by Tankerville Chamberlayne. It can be said, without any fear of contradiction, that it was the end of an era. Yes, another one.

Chapter 10
Promise unfulfilled

Saints marked their golden jubilee on Saturday 23 November 1935, by defeating Tottenham Hotspur, in a Football League Division Two fixture, at The Dell 2-0, and then moving on to the plush South Western Hotel for a slap-up dinner. It was, said the *Hampshire Advertiser,* "the happiest possible occasion, in that it gathered together leaders of the game and players of today with the old timers," even if the surfeit of speeches left "[in]sufficient time for the old 'uns to fight all their battles o'er again… However, they were good speeches. A great night in the estimation of everybody privileged to be present."

There were indeed many speeches. The *Advertiser* carried "points" from ten of them. Sadly, those points were somewhat perfunctory. Dr Stancomb's contribution reduced to: "Whilst I was on the board we were in the cup final twice and the semi-final four times – which goes to show you what one man can do." And his best wishes for the future.

We are not told how this statement was delivered or received. Did he expect a laugh, or was Dr Stancomb deadly serious, when he insinuated that he was responsible for Saints' best years? There must, however, have been many there who felt a serious twinge of nostalgia when Sir Russell Bencraft and he stood to address a gathering of many who had been involved in the 20 or so years that saw the Club rise from hoofing the ball about on the Common through to being acknowledged (grudgingly in some circles) as one of the country's leading sides playing at one of its finest grounds.

Judging from the report of this self-congratulatory event, the club officials were certainly on the defensive. Former chairman, Lord Portal, offered a challenge:

> When I joined the board of the Saints I imagined that a director's job was a highly paid one. I discovered, however, that the work the directors do is given for the love of the game. When people criticise I suggest that they ought not do so unless they can do better.

Then the Chairman of the day, Major Sloane Stanley, added his four-pennyworth: "There are great difficulties in maintaining a winning team, although I receive many letters, mostly anonymous, in which the writers seem to think that if I only followed their advice the path to glory would be very easy."

It would have been wonderful for posterity if the great event had turned into a heated discussion – or a brawl – on the plight of Southampton Football Club, but Stancomb appeared to be the only speaker prepared to drop a heavy hint that the Club were not the force they should have become.

Football had moved on somewhat from the era of Saints' Southern League heyday; and while the Club had moved with the times, in as far as they were now in the Football League, their reputation as a "first-class" side had not been maintained. They had enjoyed a purple patch from 1920 to 1927 (as we shall see in the next three chapters) in that they had three stirring Cup runs, but they had failed to realise their potential as a First Division force. When Saints had struggled in the Southern League before the 1914-18 War, there was a consensus that it was a brief hiatus. Now, it seemed, that mediocrity was the rule rather than the exception. The 1935-36 season was a case in point. Saints, having been in the Second Division for 13 years, were struggling for points and crowds.

In 1911, Bill Dawson had retired from coaching duties to become a full-time publican, Mr Arnfield's duties were confined to those of financial secretary and George Swift took over the management of the side. Swift had an impressive *curriculum vitae,* having been part of the 1893 Wolverhampton Wanderers Cup-winning team, and had seen service with Leicester Fosse and Notts County, before training, and being the secretary-manager of, Leeds City.

He was certainly not impressed with what he found at The Dell and, for the grand sum of £820, completely rebuilt the team on his arrival. It was ironic that it was young forwards from the Reserves, chucked in at the deep end, who saw Saints survive their first-ever Southern League relegation battle, after which Swift "resigned".

FULL-TIME *at* THE DELL

His replacement was James McIntyre, whose career had included stints with Walsall, Notts County, Reading and Coventry City, at the last of which he finished his career and took up coaching. With no money in the transfer kitty, he had an anxious first season, but again Saints survived and it was to be the last time they would struggle at the wrong end of the table during McIntyre's tenure.

If the results had been disappointing, there was cause for optimism: it had been proved, demonstrably, that the south could produce talented footballers.

The first, as already mentioned, was Farnborough-born Arthur Turner, who had gained two England caps during his two seasons at The Dell, before heading for Derby in 1902. By the time he had returned, in 1904, Fred Harrison, who had been spotted playing on the Common, was a regular fixture in the forward line, and had proved as prolific in front of goal as any of the stars signed over the previous decade. Frank Jefferis, another better-than-average forward, arrived from Fordingbridge Turks in 1905 and Bert Lee had come from Poole in 1900. Saints had, then, the potential to compete without recruiting established Football League players. Which was just as well because that was a diminishing option.

With the arrival of the maximum wage, big-name players had little to gain by moving South; and by 1912 the presumption that the formation of a National League would mean a new First Division, including Southern League clubs, was a dead letter. The Southern League could claim parity with Division Two, but even that contention was being undermined. Nor was there any hope of reclaiming its former glories.

In 1910-11, Woolwich Arsenal and Tottenham Hotspur were in Division One; Chelsea, having slipped back to Division Two, were mounting a serious challenge to get back up; and Clapton Orient and Fulham were more than holding their own in the Second Division. Even those London League clubs out of the top flight were playing the likes of Derby County, Wolves and West Brom, which looked a little more arresting than the posters on the walls around the capital's Southern League clubs advertising forthcoming attractions such as Southampton and, say, Watford.

The highlight of the 1913-14 season was the emergence of Southampton-born Arthur Dominy as a skilful inside-forward, who could distribute the ball and score with style. The future was looking bright.

Some of the more positive, and less politically aware, individuals in Southampton and, indeed, around the country, were looking forward to an interesting 1914-15 season. It proved to be a more interesting season than they might have cared to anticipate.

At two minutes past eight on the morning of August 1914, six battalions of German infantry and three divisions of cavalry, backed by artillery, crossed the Belgian frontier. As they marched on Liège, Europe went to war; one that had been on the cards for some time. Given the combined might of France and the British Empire, it was not expected to be a long one: the phrase "it will all be over by Christmas" became, and remains, a cliché. The Germans were every bit as Pollyannish. The Kaiser told his troops in that first week of the conflict: "You will be home before the leaves fall from the trees."

The 1914-15 season kicked off as if nothing untoward was occurring.

This was well-received by the supporters and by the War Office, who found football grounds fecund pastures for recruitment; but Rugby Union was abandoned for the duration and there was much sanctimonious comment regarding fit young men getting paid to play football while other fit young men (i.e. grammar school and public school-educated boys) were doing "their bit" for King and Country. That it was football played between the trenches by British and German troops on Christmas Day 1914 was little remarked upon, other than in hushed accusations of "letting the side down".

On top of that came a scandal. On Good Friday 1915, at Old Trafford, both teams were booed off the field after Manchester United had defeated Liverpool 2-0. Beyond any doubt, the result had been arranged. It transpired, after an interminable investigation, that the players, or most of them, had conspired to defraud bookmakers. That the result also saw to it that Manchester United avoided relegation from the First Division was not acted upon; although Chelsea, who were to be demoted in their stead, had plenty to say about it.

This was, though, academic, as, by the time the FA Commission had reached its verdict, professional football had been suspended.

Chapter 11
A Whole League Onwards

The 1915 FA Cup Final was played at Old Trafford on 24 April, between Chelsea and Sheffield United. It was a sombre affair, dominated by khaki-clad spectators, on a "murky, wet afternoon, and the drab silent crowd reflected the mood of the moment."

The war had not ended by Christmas. Geoffrey Green, in *The Official History of the F.A. Cup,* wrote that the temper of the nation was well expressed by Lord Derby when he presented the trophy and the medals at the finish:

> You have played with one another and against one another for the Cup; play with one another for England now.

Many Saints players went into the forces, but more found themselves employed in the shipyards and factories in and around Southampton. There was no league football for the rest of 1915, but there were a number of friendlies. Then, in the new-year, a seven-team competition, which recreated some of the spirit of the Southern League, was inaugurated. Pompey pipped Saints by a point to win it.

For the 1916-17 season, Saints and Pompey competed in the London Combination, a fourteen-club league called which proved a success; but the cost and trouble of getting to the Hampshire coast proved too much for Spurs, Arsenal and their ilk, so Saints and Pompey were cast out for the 1917-18 season, despite an offer from Saints to pay their opponents' travelling expenses.

Friendlies made up the bulk of the following two seasons, with Saints and Pompey resuming their rivalry in the South Hants War League.

A not very accomplished Saints side were eclipsed by Harland & Woolf and Thorneycrofts, each dominated by Southampton's own players, in 1917-18 and 1918-19.

The Great War ended, officially, on the 11 November 1918, too late in the year to recommence league or cup competitions. It all got going again in August 1919. The Southern League First Division was extended from 20 to 22 clubs, as was the Football League's First Division. This was expedient, as it enabled Chelsea – who, you will remember, were the victims of the rigged game between Manchester United and Liverpool – to stay in the top flight. It also allowed the Football League to elect the former Woolwich Arsenal (now styling themselves The Arsenal) into the First Division. This manoeuvre understandably upset Spurs, who had been the First Division wooden-spoonists in 1919. The year before the war, Arsenal had dropped Woolwich from their name and moved north of the Thames to Highbury, in the neighbourhood of Tottenham. Having Arsenal move in on their supporter base was bad enough; having them take your place in the top flight was adding insult to injury – especially when they hadn't even won the promotion.

This was not the only controversy the League was embroiled in. When West Ham United were voted into the Second Division, the Southern League were not at all happy about it, claiming that West Ham had applied for membership while still members of their organisation, in contravention of an agreement between the two leagues.

"I rather suspect," theorised Commentator in the first *Football Echo* published after the war,

> that members of the S.L. committee, like many other people, had grown tired of London clubs using the Southern League as a ladder on which to mount to fame and prosperity, and then throwing it away when it had served its purpose. The Committee must have felt annoyed, too, at the Football League facilitating this selfish action when the two Leagues were under a bond to protect each other's interests.

There was increased interest in football and Saints showed a good deal of promise. Dominy looked as good as ever and two youngsters, striker Bill Rawlings and left-back Fred Titmuss, were shaping up as stars in the making. But Pompey emerged as the top Southern League club, beating Saints 5-1 early in the season, and the interest in their visit to The Dell was manifest.

The match report in the *Football Echo* on 28 February 1920 has almost as much commentary on the crowd as on the goalless draw that resulted:

FULL-TIME *at* THE DELL

There was no doubt about the support which Portsmouth brought with them. Everywhere in the town before the match the blue and white colours of Pompey could be seen fluttering gaily. Long before the time of the match the gates at Archer's-road and Milton-road were packed with long queues of spectators eager to get into the ground. Half an hour before the kick-off the stands were absolutely crowded, and the terraces seemed to be so full that it was perfectly certain that all the men who wanted to get into the ground would be unable to do so. Every point of vantage was seized, and more than one adventurous sailor and civilian climbed to perilous places on hoardings and the wall surrounded the field. Considerable amusement was caused by many people trying to climb the tiled roof of the telegraph office at the Archer's-road end of the ground and slipping down the precipitous slope. Not only did the people crowd in all the available places on the terraces and stands, but they were packed along the touch-lines.

Arthur Dominy "looked as good as ever," when joined by "stars in the making," Bill Rawlings (left) and Fred Titmuss

The report estimated the crowd at not less than 20,000. A record Southern League crowd then? No. The official figure was only 17,879.

"What is required is better organisation, a system whereby islands of empty space are not allowed to form, and all available places on the terraces are filled," suggested Pointer in the following Saturday's *Football Echo*. He referred readers to the Southern League attendance record at The Dell of 19,291, for Pompey's visit in 1913, and to what he considered to be the Cup record (though see Appendix I at page 219), when Everton attracted 21,690 in 1908.

That the crowd for this derby game was 3,811 below that 1908 attendance must have upset the directors, given that they lost out on a substantial amount of money from the hundreds of people who were turned away; but there was the consolation that the Club made a record profit, of £3,360, that season. Those unable to get in must have been doubly vexed: before the war they could have popped into a pub for a consolatory pint, but licensing laws, introduced during the hostilities to stop workers loitering in bars when they should be aiding the war effort, now dictated that hostelries remained closed between 2.30 and 6pm.

Meanwhile, there were hints that the Southern League aspired to become a major competition once more. Exasperated by a number of slights to their self-esteem inflicted by the Football League, they decided to scrap the maximum wage, which the Football Association had abandoned but the professional leagues had retained. It meant, once again, that Southern League clubs could outbid Football League clubs for players.

This was an unlikely scenario. There were barely five clubs, if that, in the Southern League that had any immediate potential as first-class teams, and one of those, Cardiff City (who finished fourth in the Southern League), would be elected into the Second Division at the end of the season. So the abolition of the maximum wage was no more than one last, somewhat futile gesture of defiance. In May, the annual meeting of the Football League decided to inaugurate a Third Division, which would be made up of the 21 members of the Southern League First Division and the bottom club in the Football League Division Two.

Football League member

In the *Football Echo* of 28 August 1920, Commentator opened his first "Cherry Blossom" column of the 1920-21 season thus:

Chapter 11

THIRD DIVISION – BORN, 1920

The football season which commenced to-day will be regarded in later years as one of the mile-stones in the history of football progress in the South. For 25 seasons the Southern League filled the role of a complete combination for clubs in the South of England, but although it was productive of much good football and attracted some fine football clubs, yet it was lacking in one essential detail – there was no higher position for the clubs to strive to reach. It was, of course, an honour to win the championship, but there a club's advancement ended. So the stronger clubs in the League were always on the look-out to obtain admission to the Football league. The danger of losing its best clubs threatened the Southern League each season…

…There is an entirely new spirit in the new League; the spirit of keen competition to a definite goal, with definite reward – promotion. The championship of the Third Division means not merely the custody of a trophy for the season, but progress up the ladder of football fame.

Ron Moody depicts the Saint giving Echoist a free ride into the Football League

Quite what Saints' devotees of long standing made of this is unknown; but it must have been something of a let-down; after all, when the notion of a national league was first mooted, it was on the supposition that Saints would automatically be in the top flight. Then again, it had been well over a decade since Saints had successfully challenged presumptions of Football League hegemony; and now, as Commentator so pertinently indicated, a ladder was in place. There was now no impediment to Saints' First Division ambitions – other than the other 43 League clubs that desired to be in it, and the 22 determined to retain their place in it.

Saints' baptism in the Third Division was less than auspicious. They drew 1-1 with Gillingham, who had finished bottom of the previous season's Southern League First Division and who would finish in exactly the same position in the new competition.

Whatever, Saints had a fine season and there was genuine disappointment when they finished the season as runners-up to Crystal Palace; back then, only the champions were promoted.

The highlights of the season were the two matches with Portsmouth, especially as Saints did the double. The crowd management appears to have improved as 18,300 watched Saints win 2-0 at The Dell on 11 September and, the following Saturday, 20,585 spectators witnessed Saints win 1-0 at Fratton Park. On 28 March, with Saints running Crystal Palace neck-and-neck at the top of the table, The Dell entertained 20,000 spectators for their rivals' appearance, which ended in a one-all draw. Palace equalised in the closing seconds and a surge on the Milton end culminated in a number of injuries when barriers collapsed. The next day, Saints drew by the same score at Palace. The parity was not enough: Saints ended the season five points adrift of the Londoners.

The Third Division became the Third Division (South) for the 1921-22 season. There was no equivalent of the Southern League in the North, so the candidates for the Third Division (North) were culled from the Midland League, the Central League, the Birmingham League and several "goodness knows where" leagues.

This new northern division was not welcomed with open arms – there were enough Northern and Midland clubs in the League already. As to its success, it is significant that not one of its elected members has ever been in the top flight, as opposed to 10 of the Southern Division's members – albeit that some of those sojourns at the top have been fleeting.

Saints distinguished themselves by being the first champions of the Third (South); but it was, as Wellington observed of the Battle of Waterloo, "a damned nice thing – the nearest run thing you ever saw in your life."

FULL-TIME *at* THE DELL

Saints were two points behind Plymouth Argyle when they stepped out to play their last game of the season at The Dell on 6 May. Their opponents were a struggling Newport County. Plymouth, needing a single point to take them into the Second Division, were away to a useful Queen's Park Rangers side.

It was, the local press agreed, something of a forlorn hope that Saints could overhaul Plymouth at the death and the supporters evidently concurred: a below-average crowd of 9,000 turned up to what that day's edition of the *Southampton Times* headlined as "To-day's Feint Hope."

> It was queer that at the north end of the pitch the daisies were growing ever so thickly, while at the Milton Road end…
> Sudden and tremendous cheers. On the indicator near the West Stand somebody had put up plates showing that Queen's Park had a goal. The crowd jumped for joy. The 22 players looked and Rawlings made a break through. One wanted him to score in celebration of the moment, but he shot wide.

Saints won 5-0.

> At the close of the game nobody left the ground, and spectators swarmed across the pitch and assembled near the directors' stand to hear the full time announcement about events at Shepherd's Bush. The band played lively old tunes, until the final message came through, when the music was drowned by cheering.

The largest gate at The Dell that season had been, by some distance, the 19,291 that turned up to see Cardiff City on 28 January, in the Second Round of the Cup. But most games attracted over 10,000; and there must have been a lot of cursing that evening, as those who had apathetically shunned the Newport climax purchased their *Football Echo*.

The Cardiff game was a draw and Cardiff beat a depleted Saints side in the replay. But it gave a nameless scribe in the *Southampton Times* an opportunity to laud the delights of whiling away half-a-day outside The Dell:

> Queuing at the Dell for the Cup tie began at nine. "Light refreshments at twelve, Rolls Royces at five, if they win," said one of the early arrivals. By eleven the queues were long and lengthening, and a policeman remarked on the possibility of traffic being interfered with at the Junction.
> The queues were still young and stumpy when the favour-sellers and the queue-side musicians pounced on them. "Wearyer colour'n showyer favour. Cup'n colour sixpence. Colour'n Cup a tanner!" And the music! Men and women in football queues are the most helpless of mortals. They can't move or all is lost. They are there to be sang to, played to, sold colours, oranges and papers to; and one of these Cup days the street orators will go along, and have them at their mercy. But the music! How ever many loud "Whisperings" did the Milton queue hear? One singer finished the ballad thus:
> Whisper that I love but you.
> How much? Tuppence?
> this last whisper being to a man who had been along with the cap. He answered with a gloomy nod, and off they went to find a queue more responsive to affection.

Clearly all human life was there, street orators aside. Today, the "entertainers" would probably get an Arts Council grant and anyone queuing six hours before kick-off would be in with a fair chance of one.

·

·

Chapter 12
Second Division

Saints' debut season in the Second Division, 1922-23, may not have been spectacular but it was undoubtedly weird. They finished eleventh, exactly mid-table, with, perhaps, the uncanniest end-of-season statistics even they have put on record:

P 42 W 14 L 14 D 14 F 40 A 40 Pts. 42

Two more goals for and against would have made the figures just a little more eerie, but it proves beyond doubt that, even in an undistinguished season, Saints can exude panache unequalled elsewhere in the annuls of football.

They saved their best for the Cup. Newcastle and Chelsea, both of the First Division, were rolled at The Dell, as were Second Division Bury. All three matches were replays. This left them to contest a semi-final place with West Ham United. The tie went to a second replay at Villa Park, where the Hammers prevailed by the odd goal in one and went on to be the first losing Cup Finalists at Wembley. An event better remembered for the contribution of a white police horse than that of any of the players. Proving that destiny and posterity have well-developed senses of humour.

Happily, if somewhat frustratingly, Saints' League and Cup form improved over the next couple of seasons. They came fifth in 1923-24 – missing promotion by three points – and, in 1924-25, seventh. Some way off a promotion place, but they got to the Cup semi-finals, thanks to a Fourth Round defeat of Liverpool at The Dell.

Liverpool had drawn at The Dell (and won the replay) the previous season. Their visit had been keenly anticipated. And not just by Saintly devotees – an exile wrote home to the *Liverpool Echo* on the upcoming fixture. The ever-vigilant *Football Echo* picked the letter up and reprinted it, along with the editorial comment from Merseyside:

INNOCENTS ABROAD
Liverpudlian's Novel View of Saints:

Dear Bee, – There is a big crowd of Liverpool boys down here ("imported aliens" as the natives call us) spending a whole lot of money on lung tonic in readiness for the [cup-tie] at the Dell. We have been telling the only-one-team-point-of-view natives that they have as much prospect of seeing the Saints whop Liverpool as a snowball in – ; but kindly tell the Liverpool boys they just have to win, or our future lives here will not be on an equal with the proverbial dog.

We quite realise Liverpool will not have a walk-over on such a miserable ground, but there is nothing really great in the Saints' team to stop Liverpool… Any rate, we guess the Liverpool boys know their men [know] how to treat 'em, and all we can say in conclusion is: For God's sake whack 'em… We shall be at the Dell in force; in the meantime cheerio and good luck,

– yours etc. – A Whole Contingent Of Us.

As one who is looking to Liverpool to go a long way in the Cup (writes "Reds"), may I remind them of the peculiar ground at the "Dell," Southampton; it being very much on the small side (in fact the minimum), and many a First League club has come to grief in consequence. Very few games Southampton lose at home. If the Reds can adapt themselves to this ground, then I have no fear of the result; but there is a wide difference between the width at Anfield to that of the Dell, the players often being crowded out. Liverpool should take the tip for what it is worth. Let the Reds keep the game open.

Not the last unfavourable comment from Merseyside about our fabulous tabernacle to the golden spheroid, and it probably wasn't the first; in fact you could probably compile a hefty tome of caustic and uncomplimentary comments concerning The Dell from a trawl through the Liverpool and Manchester press over the last century or so, but it was becoming evident that The Dell was no longer among the best stadiums in the country. Even the

FULL-TIME *at* THE DELL

Football Echo was prepared to admit to its shortcomings or at least compare it unfavourably with Crystal Palace's new ground. Selhurst Park impressed Commentator in September 1924, despite the fact that the building work was still ongoing – there was no water for the players' baths or even their half-time cuppa. Yet this was, for Commentator,

> a site of immense possibilities. I was told that the "Glaziers" expect accommodation for 80,000 people, but in the programme 100,000 was mentioned as the figure when the site is fully developed. Selhurst Park has more spacious possibilities than any other well known club in London, and one could not help wishing that the site was near Southampton, for it is such a ground that the Saints need.

Saints had to make do with lemonade during the break, a contributory factor, according to the *Football Echo,* for their 3-1 defeat. This was presumably not a factor elsewhere, so their disappointing away form was hard to fathom. Jimmy McIntyre, who was still manager, was seemingly clueless as to why the results lacked consistency and resigned in December. The Board took over running the team, along with secretary George Goss, and Saints set off on another famous Cup run. Their failure to progress further than the semi-finals has been attributed to one of their most accomplished players, full-back Tom Parker, who not only scored an own-goal for Sheffield United in the first-half, but missed a penalty in the second.

The 1925-26 season saw the introduction of an altered off-side law. Now a mere two defenders between the goal and a forward would see him onside rather than, as formerly, three. Saints' lack of guidance on the new ruling appears to have rendered them bemused and they started off the League programme with four consecutive defeats, one of them a 3-1 home reversal to Pompey. In October, former Saint Arthur Chadwick, who had played in the first-ever game at The Dell, was recruited as manager. He had cut his managerial teeth at Exeter City and Reading and would prove, with hindsight, to be a good manager. But his first season was torrid. Fred Titmuss departed to Plymouth Argyle in February, in exchange for £1,750. On the whole, the supporters would have preferred the man; after all, he was an England international – not an easy accomplishment for a Third Division player, as he had been when he won his two caps. He was, however, being kept out of the first team by the precocious and meticulous, Milford-born, Mike Keeping. A few weeks later, Titmuss was followed out of The Dell by Tom Parker. He went to Arsenal for £3,250. It would be a long, long time before his maladroit performance against Sheffield United the previous term would be forgotten, but there was nobody that doubted his prowess or his usually reliable form.

The mood on match days turned ugly.

Dell-Buy date

Commentator, in the *Football Echo* of 13 March, attempted to deflect the indeflectable:

> A STORM OF PROTEST. – A storm of protest has been beating about the heads of the Southampton directors following the transfer of Parker to the Arsenal, but I am informed that they do not intend to expound their policy. In view of the action I tried to get the directors to talk, with the idea of receiving some information to pass on to the supporters of the club, but they do not wish to publish any explanations, and I was also told that the amount of the transfer fee will not be disclosed. It seems to me that there can only be two reasons for the transfer of Parker; to acquire money either for the purchase of a ground, or the acquisition of new players to strengthen the side… It is well known that the ground question has to be tackled in the very near future, and this will mean the expenditure of a big sum of money. The Dell, or some other ground, will have to be purchased…

Commentator was spot-on. On 1 May 1926, he kicked-off his "Cherry Blossom" column with the news:

> SAINTS BUY THE DELL. – A big move was made this week by the purchase of the Dell by the club. Now the ground is the property of the Saints the way

is open for an ambitious scheme of improvement. Not only the ground itself, but property and land adjoining have been secured, so that the plans for the extension of the Dell to accommodate 40,000 can be proceeded with so soon as the club consider the step, financially, justifiable. I am told that the gates this season average about 10,000 to 12,000 and that this figure is not big enough to enable the directors to move at once to provide a new stand and enlarge the ground. The club, for the first time in their history, have a ground of their own, and the outlook for the future is much brighter on that account alone.

Commentator went on to say that the Board considered "the deal… eminently satisfactory financially to the club." The cost was later reported as being £26,000, which went to Mrs Carvolth, George Thomas's widow. Yet the *Echo* reported, in January 1928, that the ground was "valued at £14,500 in April 1927"; and while it is not difficult to believe the directors may have paid over the odds, that they were gullible enough to be taken for £11,500 without considerable comment would appear unlikely. Whatever The Dell cost the Club it was certainly

This seriously boring photograph (which appears to have been cut from a seed catalogue *circa* 1922) does at least show the old West Stand at its best most of it at least. At the far corner of The Dell can be seen the roof and upper wall of "THE MAIN ENTRANCE" at the Milton (Bedford) Road end, described within the comprehensive depiction of The Dell from the *Southampton Observer* reproduced in Chapter 2. Contemporary photographs of The Dell (rather than the crowd) are something of a rarity from this period. In fact this is the only extant one we know of, including the pavilion-like structure, which accommodated the turnstiles into the West Stand.

This Spurs programme, from 1938, is something of an oddity, in that it features a drawing of the Main Entrance on the cover, around about 13 years after it had – apparently – been demolished, to make way for the new West Stand, in the summer of 1927

FULL-TIME *at* THE DELL

a positive move, although, by 1928, there was another venue in Southampton capable of staging competitive football matches.

Banister Court School had closed in 1927 and the site, immediately to the south of the County Ground, was purchased by a company formed by local entrepreneur, Charlie Knott. The old mansion and school buildings were demolished, the lake filled in and "The Stadium" erected. With a capacity of 28,000, it was primarily for greyhound and speedway racing, but a number of sports would feature there down the years. There was, too, plenty of land around it for expansion.

There is little doubt that Charlie Knott could, and would, have adapted it to host football on a regular basis, but it was something he was never called upon to do. Interestingly, Knott – very much a local boy made good – like Southampton's other stadium builder, George Thomas, made his fortune as a fishmonger.

Chapter 13
The West Stand

As the directors of Southampton Football & Athletic Company Limited deliberated on the advisability of what improvements were required where at The Dell, a slightly more ambitious undertaking was in the process of leaving the drawing board – one that would dramatically alter the geography of Southampton.

The *Echo*'s lead story on 3 January 1927 was

THE GREAT DOCKS SCHEME:
The great £13,000,000 docks extension scheme which is to be carried out on the Western Shore by the Southern Railway Co. and which will provide Southampton with 16,600ft of additional quayage, capable of accommodating 20 of the world's largest liners, was officially commenced to-day, when a unique ceremony was carried out in the River Test, opposite the Royal Pier.

It was reported that "Mayor of Southampton and Admiral of the Port", Alderman P.V. Bowyer, boarded "the mammoth dredger Foremost III" and gave the order, by ship's telegraph, to commence dredging operations that would set in motion the construction of what we now call the Western Docks.

These days, £13 million will buy a pretty useful footballer, but in the 1920s it was more than enough to buy every professional football club in the country, lock, stock, barrel, players and tea lady. The cost was not to be wondered at, its being the largest land-reclamation project ever undertaken in the United Kingdom. It was what American business moguls of the day might have quaintly termed "a big deal".

Less than three weeks after Alderman Bowyer removed a stone from the first bucket of mud dredged from the bed of Southampton Water and announced, "This is my souvenir of a very historic day in the history of the town and port," Commentator applied a proverbial boot up the collective behinds of the Saints' board:

SIGNS OF THE TIMES – AND THE DELL. –
The visit of Birmingham to the Dell next Saturday in the fourth round of the F.A. Cup has now completely gripped the attention of the supporters, and once again, I suppose, the ground will be full to overflowing. The signs of the times are so apparent that surely it cannot be long before the directors of the club tackle this question and proceed with the scheme which they have pigeon-holed to enlarge the enclosure and to build a new, up-to-date stand… DON'T "WAIT AND SEE." – I believe the Saints directors have been studying the question with increased seriousness recently, and I am not without hope that the improvement scheme will be commenced, perhaps sooner than most of us thought would be the case. I am one of those who believe increased support would follow quickly on ground improvements, and that it is the wrong policy to wait for increased support before tackling the question. It will be recalled that the directors at their annual meeting said they would build a new stand and enlarge the ground if and when the support justified this course. I agree that they are entitled to expect bigger "gates" than the present average, but I think the way to get those "gates" would be to go all out to show the supporters of the club that a forward policy has been adopted, and every effort is being made to cater for the needs of the spectators. Nobody disputes the fact that the Dell is hopelessly out of date, and as one tours the country and sees splendidly appointed grounds nearly everywhere, one regrets more and more that the Southampton club has fallen so far behind the times in the matter of a worthy ground.

Birmingham, of the First Division, drew a respectable 15,000 plus, most of whom went home happy with Saints' 4-1 win. By this time, First and Second Division clubs entered the Cup in the Third Round – which meant that, what with other adjustments, the semi-finals were no longer the fifth, but the seventh, round. Newcastle United were drawn at The Dell for the Fifth. It was the fourth occasion on which Newcastle had been pulled out of the hat with Saints since 1898. They had yet to win,

FULL-TIME *at* THE DELL

but they were a certainly a better side than the one that had been upset at the County Ground 29 years before; in fact, they were heading for the League championship. Saints would finish the season mid-table in the Second Division, so the result was easy enough to predict. Some 21,408 squeezed into The Dell and might have been disappointed by the margin of victory, only 2-1. The star turn was two-goal Dick Rowley.

If Saints were no longer the footballing power in the land that they had been 20 years before, they were, at the very least, perversely iconoclastic when it came to playing their "betters". Since promotion to the Second Division, four years previously, they had eliminated eight top-flight clubs from the Cup, all of them at The Dell. Unworthy of Saints their ground may have been, but it was becoming a graveyard of giants.

Ancient protagonist Millwall, of the Third Division (South) were beaten 2-0 in a Sixth Round replay at The Dell to earn Saints another semi-final tie, at Stamford Bridge against the Arsenal.

You might be thinking that there has been rather too much of Arsenal within these pages. This is not a matter of choice: it just so happens that the Victorian and Edwardian sporting press had frequently been given to discussing the relevant merits of Saints and Arsenal, being the two leading Southern teams in rival leagues. These comparisons had rarely flattered Arsenal. By 1927, however, "The Arsenal" were emerging as a power in the land. Not as yet legendary, but Herbert Chapman was now manager, the inimitable Charles Buchan was leading the forward-line and a legend was in the making – or, shall we say, in the process of being manufactured? Chapman was a master of public relations. This did not prevent the Arsenal, once more, being compared unfavourably to Saints. Alas, it was Arsenal who went to Wembley, winning 2-1, but the consensus among the nation's football scribes was that Saints were robbed and the referee was unanimously criticised for ignoring a blatant penalty when winger Bill Murphy was flattened by Cope in the Arsenal penalty box, denying Saints an opportunity to tie the score at 2-2.

Arsenal lost 1-0 to Cardiff City in the Final. Their keeper, 'Len Davies, let a soft shot squirm under his body and into the goal. The pristine and slippery fabric of Lewis's pullover got the blame for the mishap. Thereafter, it is claimed, new goalkeeper jerseys have always been washed before being donned by Arsenal custodians for the first time. So a great and immutable tradition was thereby born.

Another footballing tradition was established in 1927: the BBC made their first Cup Final broadcast. Those Saints' supporters wealthy enough to have wireless sets could at least enjoy Arsenal's defeat live from Wembley.

The semi-final result certainly excited resentment in Southampton, but optimism regarding the future was undimmed – not least because Saints were over £3,000 up on the season's workings and the team, on their day, looked capable of taking on anyone. And if Portsmouth could get promoted – which they did, as runners-up to Middlesbrough, that season – then, surely, there was no reason Saints couldn't make the jump. All that was required was those improvements to The Dell that Commentator was so anxious to see undertaken. As it happened, a good month before the historic confrontation with Arsenal, in the *Football Echo* of 19 February to be exact, he was able to enthuse on the ground's future:

> IMPROVING THE DELL. – I wrote in these notes a few weeks ago that probably the Southampton directors would start the ground improvements and alterations at the Dell sooner than perhaps some of us thought would be the case. This forecast was confirmed this week, when the directors announced their intention of starting the scheme next summer. It is a big scheme, and I am not surprised to learn that it will not be possible to complete it in the four months of the summer... Such a tremendous amount of work has to be done in clearing away the ground at the back of the present west stand before construction can commence, and then the new stand, I am told, will be no less than 500ft. long, for it will stretch across the breadth of the ground from Milton-road to Archer's-road... And also under the present east stand, terraces will be constructed.
> THE RIGHT STEP FORWARD. – The main fact, however, which emerges is that at last Southampton is on the way to having a ground worthy of the club... If in the course of a couple of seasons, the Dell is converted into an up-to-date enclosure, with accommodation for nearly 40,000 people... the difficulties which now arise whenever there is an

attractive match at Southampton should become something of the past.

Saints played their last game in front of the old "west stand" on 30 April, a Rowley goal giving them a 1-0 victory over Nottingham Forest in a Second Division fixture. Soon after, presumably, The Dell was invaded by an army of labourers and wheelbarrows.

Many of the architectural improvements in football grounds that Commentator was writing about were down to a Glaswegian engineer by the name of Archibald Leitch,* who had started out as a draftsman in the marine department of a Glasgow engineering company. After a thorough grounding in the trade, including service as a ship's engineer, he set up in business for himself in 1897. Quite how he came to get involved in the design of football stadiums, Simon Inglis (who outlined his career in the first edition of *The Football Grounds of England and Wales* in 1983) is unable to say, but his first commissions appear to have been at Ibrox, Celtic Park and Hampden Park. In England, he was responsible for the laying out of Stamford Bridge in 1904-05 and went on to design stands for Blackburn Rovers, Fulham, Spurs, Arsenal's new ground at Highbury in 1913 (though his single stand there was replaced in the 1930s), Huddersfield, Sunderland and so on. In 1925 he designed the South Stand at Fratton Park, a rather more modest affair than some he had built, but it was his favoured double-decker design with a white facing on the balcony crisscrossed with steel framing.

What was good enough for Fratton Park, Roker Park, Ewood Park and, indeed, Ibrox, was good enough for The Dell. Leitch was employed to build the new West Stand.

However, it wasn't Leitch's architecture that preoccupied Commentator in the first *Football Echo* of the 1927-28 season:

THE NEW DELL. – I suppose the reconstruction of the Dell has been the topic most discussed by the supporters of the Saints during the close season, and it is a pity – for all concerned – that the new stand was not ready for the opening of the season. "It won't be ready before Christmas," several people have said to me, but this is undoubtedly wide of the mark. My

latest information is that the stand will be in use about the end of September. The big trouble, I am told in official quarters, has been the difficulty of getting the steel work delivered quickly, and that has held up the construction in a way which was never anticipated…

SOLVING A PROBLEM. – Whilst I share the general feeling of regret that the work could not be completed in time for the first match, I must confess that I am more inclined to a feeling of relief that the remodelling of the ground was actually started this season. Even if it was delayed a few weeks, a step has been taken which the supporters of the club have so long desired, and I certainly think that, after the Dell has been put into "ship shape," it will be one of the most compact and convenient enclosures in the country. The accommodation has been increased, according to estimates, to 33,000. The record attendance now stands at 21,960. This roughly, will give accommodation for 16,000 additional people, and so, when the Cup-ties come round, there should be room for all. I understand that the biggest "gate" Portsmouth had last season was 28,000, and, therefore, it would certainly seem that the Saints' directors have at last solved their ground problem… I am told the terraces at Milton-road and Archer's-road end of the ground will be improved by "sinking" the front rows about two feet, which will have the effect of giving a better view of the pitch.

Even the pessimists had under-estimated the delay. The West Stand was not opened officially until 7 January. Presumably, the dressing rooms were operational, but there is scant information (other than a droll Ron Moody cartoon in the *Football Echo* showing the press watching the game from the subterranean boiler-room, their faces at pitch level) on how inconvenient it was to have the most capacious side of the ground closed – or at least mostly closed – for the first half of the season. Quite how many games were covered from the "Better 'ole"* (as

---

* Not to be confused with Cary Grant.

* This term derived from a popular Great War cartoon depicting two beleaguered Tommies sheltering in a small crater in a desolate no-man's-land with artillery shells whizzing past there ears. One is saying to the other, "If you know a better 'ole go to it." Or words to that effect.

FULL-TIME *at* THE DELL

Moody dubbed it) is a mystery: it can't be ruled out that the cartoonist was perpetrating an amusing fiction, but it illustrated the frustrations of just about everyone involved with Southampton FC at the time.

It certainly appears to have deterred spectators. The largest crowd in the first half of the season was the 14,000 that endured Chelsea's 4-2 win on 15 October; other than that, there was only one occasion on which more than 10,000 turned out.

The grand opening of the West Stand, and the visit of promotion-chasing Leeds United, was witnessed by 14,000. The *Echo's* "Final Edition" of 7 January carried a prominent back-page story on the new facilities and the ceremony with which they were opened:

NEW WEST STAND AT THE DELL
Official Opening This Afternoon
MAYOR TAKES PART IN CEREMONY
Ground Accommodation for 33,000 Spectators

An important occasion in the long and honourable career of the Southampton Football Club was marked today by the official opening of the new West Stand, which is regarded as one of the finest in the country, and the very last word in comfort and convenience for football enthusiasts.

This excellent and much-needed accommodation has been provided as part of a scheme whereby the Dell has been considerably altered and improved in several respects, so that now the ground is capable of catering for a crowd of 33,000, as compared with the original accommodation of 20,000 [*sic*].

SEATS FOR 4,500

The new stand extends the whole length of the ground – from the main entrance on either side – and covered seating has been provided in the upper portion for 4,500 including 1,200 reserved and numbered tip-up seats in the centre block, while beneath the huge structure there is terrace standing accommodation, also completely under cover, for 8,500. In the course of the development scheme, space for about 600 shilling patrons on the west side had to be absorbed, but to compensate for this the directors have provided accommodation for an extra 2,000 terrace places on the east side. The terraces on both sides slope up from below the level of the

ground, so that the whole of the spectators will have a clear view of the playing pitch and, what is even more important for enthusiastic fans, of every inch of the touch line.

200 TONS OF STEEL GIRDERS.

No expense has been spared in the construction of the West Stand, and the Saints' directors are to be congratulated upon their notable enterprise. The convenience of spectators, officials, and players alike has been studied in every respect, and the latest improvements in stand construction have been introduced. About 200 tons of steel girders have been utilised… while some idea of the area which is covered by the stand may be gauged from the fact that the roof is covered by about 7,000 Turner Trafford tiles, each measuring 4 feet by 3 feet 10 inches. The stand has a total length of 400 feet, and a depth of 43 feet, in addition to which there is a small lean-to sloping glass roof at the back which provides excellent lighting for the suite of rooms and offices for officials and players underneath. Plenty of light is also available in the upper part of the main stand by means of a wide strip of glazed glass running the whole length of the building.

Full use has been made of the available space underneath the stand, and facilities include a commodious Boardroom for the directors, adjoining which is the Secretary's office, a ladies' tearoom and cloakroom, referee's room, separate dressing rooms and excellent bathroom accommodation for home and visiting teams, and trainer's quarters, complete with lockers and the most modern arrangements for the drying of clothes.

"THE BETTER 'OLE"

The whole of the stand is centrally heated, boilers having been installed in the basement, which has been nicknamed "The Better 'Ole." One of the boilers heats the water for the players' communal baths, each of which measures 1ft. by 7ft., and has a depth of about 4ft. At the Milton-road end of the stand a tea-room for the use of the general public has been provided, while stalls for the sales of cigarettes and chocolates have also been fixed for the use of the stand ticket holders.

At the back of the stand, where there is a complete system of turnstiles to all parts, and plenty of

Chapter 13

entrances from either end, a private road has been constructed, through which cars will eventually be able to pass, and in the course of time it is the intention of the directors to provide parking facilities for motorists.

…the contracts for the ironworks and construction respectively were carried out by the Clyde Structural Company, of Glasgow, and Messrs. Humphrey's Limited, of Knightsbridge. Local labour was employed in the work of the new terracing.

To commemorate the completion of the work, Sir George F. Johnstone, Bart., one of the Directors, has presented a fine sideboard, of polished mahogany, for the new boardroom.

The report went on to describe "THE OPENING CEREMONY" in some great detail, speeches, community singing and all. Suffice it to say that everyone who was anyone was present. And that most of them had something to say, not least Southampton's first Lady Mayor, Mrs Lucia Foster Welch,[*] who

> expressed her pleasure at seeing so many sportsmen present, because she always realised those men and women who took a keen interest in sport were true sportsmen in every sense of the word. Not only were they sportsmen on the field, but they were sportsmen in the wonderful game of life.

The star of the proceedings was undoubtedly Miss Marion Knight, who "received a well-deserved ovation for her fine rendering of 'Land of Hope and Glory,' the resonant contralto voice of this popular vocalist reaching to all parts of the ground."

This was not a case of the game being unable to start until the fat lady sang,[†] for Miss Knight appears to have been of pleasant proportions.

She certainly gave better value than the Saints, who marked the occasion with a 4-1 defeat.

All the Club had to do now was pay for the thing, which was to prove problematic. Monday's *Echo* carried an announcement that £10,000 worth of Bearers Bonds were to be issued, the minimum subscription being £50 for ten shares. It was a good deal, as there was to be an annual draw in which 10 bonds would be redeemed, giving the lucky winners back their investment plus 10 years' interest and a £25 bonus.

This scheme was not an obvious success.

On 14 January, Commentator fulminated against the Board's short-sightedness and the team's precarious position in the league. The Club, he argued, needed "new blood":

> Granted that the last thing in the world they desire to do now is to spend more money – after expanding £30,000 on the ground since they bought the Dell – but the alternative may place them in an even more embarrassing financial position, for should the Saints descend to the Third Division, I do not see how the "gates" could possibly be expected to increase, or even maintain their present average…

That the Directors were more worried about money than the Club's shaky league position became manifest in March when leading scorer, Bill Rawlings, was sold to Manchester United. Jerry Mackie was immediately bought from Portsmouth to replace him, but although he scored six goals in seven games before being injured, he was hardly a replacement for Rawlings – a great local hero. Another departure in March was that of Colonel Wyndham Portal, who resigned as Saints' chairman to spend more time with his paper mills and the Great Western Railway (of which he was a director) and to be replaced by Major R.C.H. Sloane Stanley.

The press does not link the two departures, but…

---

[*] As John Edgar Mann observes in *Southampton People,* among many other "firsts", Lucia Foster Welch was the first woman admiral. The post of mayor of Southampton includes the office and title "Admiral of the Port".

[†] Isn't it galling how American clichés are infiltrating our sporting phraseology?

FULL-TIME *at* THE DELL

FIERY FINALE TO SAINTS' SE.

BIG BLAZE AT THE DELL.

Flames Fanned into Fury by Strong Wind.

EAST STAND "GOES WEST."

Firemen Prevent Fire Spreading.

:—: FINE PICTURE OF THE DELL FIRE. :—:

The above exclusive photograph of the fire at the Dell on Saturday evening was taken when the whole of the East Stand was in flames.

SENTENCES BY SOUTHAMPTON RECORDER.	BURGLARS TAKE K.C.'S GRAMOPHONE.	THE MURDER MYSTERY AT MANCHESTER.	ACROSS THE ATLANTIC IN 22ft. BOAT.
DECLARED TO BE	HIS WIRELESS SET	GREAT STRUGGLE	GERMAN'S OCEAN

(Above) The *Echo* of Monday 6 May 1929 insensitively boasted a "fine picture" of Saturday's fire.
(Below) They may joke about the quality of half-time Bovril, but their advertisements were built to last

Chapter 14
East Stand goes west

After vacillating as to whether the capacity of The Dell was to be 40,000 or less, the directors appeared to agree that an estimated 33,000 was probably enough to be going on with.

At the commencement of the 1928-29 season, the two ends were open terracing, the new West Stand stretched the entire length of the ground – the house in the corner, "Glenside", that had accommodated the Club's offices and the boardroom, having been demolished to make way for it. Facing the West Stand, the old East Stand (hardly commented upon) had been substantially modernised, having been extended to cover the entire length of the touch-line. In addition, the front of the seating tier had been cut back and a narrow row of standing terracing introduced. This "extension" had actually resulted in the loss of around 1,000 seats and in less standing room than had formally been available in the wings, but it greatly improved the view for those on that side of the ground.

Given the financial situation, and that the alterations to the arena were recent, it might be assumed that no further improvements were being envisaged – not unless the supposed capacity was to be tested on a fairly regular basis.

Optimism up in flames
In his first "Cherry Blossom" column of the season, Commentator was confident that attendances would improve. "Points picked up at the beginning of the season are worth more than they show in the League table," he reasoned, "confidence follows, and this means much to a team trying to find form. Optimism is everywhere – and why should it not be?"

Why not, indeed? There was a new, star signing. Willie "Farmer's Boy" Haines had moved up the coast to renew the partnership with Mackie that had taken Portsmouth into the First Division. A big man, but a very subtle player, he was an instant hit with the crowd.

Commentator observed that the gap between the First and Second Divisions was shrinking: "Tottenham Hotspur… one of the classic clubs of the country, are now in the Second Division, and no fewer than thirteen of the clubs in that competition this season have been First Division clubs." As for the attendance record, he made a bold prediction: "The Saints directors were longing all last season for an event to test the capacity of the 'new' Dell, but the early dismissal from the Cup-ties ruled this out. The occasion is provided early this campaign for the 'Spurs should attract a crowd to set up an attendance record, and give a good idea of how many spectators can now be accommodated."

A new Football League ground record for The Dell was indeed established for the Tottenham Hotspur game on 1 September: 22,574. Which, theoretically, left 10,000 vacant places. This record was short-lived: on 9 March, 23,829 watched Saints lose to Chelsea.

Saints finished the season in fourth place, seven points behind champions Middlesbrough.

Swansea Town came to The Dell on 4 May, to provide the season's swansong, as it were. A modest 6,510 turned out to show their appreciation of a not-too-bad season, and Saints won 3-0.

Echoist, in Monday's "Sports From Day to Day" column, observed that it was an enjoyable spectacle, but offered no comment on the most spectacular event at The Dell that Saturday. It had happened too late for inclusion in the *Football Echo* as well, but was the lead story in Monday's *Echo* – which had recently adopted the latest press innovation of news, rather than advertising, dominating the front page. The banner proclaimed FIERY FINALE TO SAINTS' SEASON and the very large heading over the main article announced a BIG BLAZE AT THE DELL, while the sub-headings inevitably included "East Stand Goes West."

A very full account of the incident suggested that a cigarette discarded by a spectator during the game was responsible for the inferno. No other theory has ever been published. It would be interesting to know whether the possibility of arson was ever discussed in the pubs of Southampton. Given the timing, it would be something of a surprise if some of the more suspiciously-minded citizenry had not leapt to that conclusion; especially after a couple of pints and a quick look around to make sure nobody connected with the Club was within earshot.

FULL-TIME *at* THE DELL

The likelihood of respectable gentlemen, such as the directors of Southampton Football & Athletic Co. Ltd., skulking under the stand with a box of *England's Glory* and some fire-lighters, would be pretty remote: for a start, it had only just been refurbished and extended and, more pertinently, the ground appears to have been under-insured, if it was insured for fire at all. The cost of replacing it would further hamstring the development of the team.

Nor was the timing convenient. There were two fixtures still to be played. Pompey were due at The Dell on Wednesday and, the following Saturday, Southampton Schoolboys were to play South Northumberland in the Final of the English Schoolboys' Trophy.

Saints and Pompey were contesting the Pickford Cup, an annual fixture to raise money for the Hampshire FA's players' benevolent fund. Another trophy, the Rowland Hospital Cup, was also contested between the same clubs most seasons between 1923 and 1935 – then again, occasionally the fixtures were merged.

Saints won both trophies this season. The game at The Dell, in front of less than 3,000, was played, for the most part, in a heavy rainstorm and became a farce. So bad were the conditions, the players were ordered straight off the pitch at the end of the game and into the baths, "to prevent them getting chills." The trophy was presented in the boardroom after they had all changed.

What is missing from the account of the game, and subsequent comment, is how the problem of the razed East Stand was mitigated. Naturally, that side of the ground would have been closed to the public, but there must still have been one hell of a clear-up operation to make it safe from debris falling onto the pitch, or to retrieve the ball from.

Reconstruction was being treated as a priority and Echoist reported that "the architect" had attended The Dell on 6 May. Presumably, this was Archibald Leitch.

Meanwhile, the schoolboys' game was switched to The Stadium in Banister Court. The officials there were taken completely by surprise by events. Quite how many they were expecting is anyone's guess, but there were only three turnstiles to cope with the crowd. The resulting chaos was a leading story in that evening's *Echo*: "the people assembled in a short road leading to them from Banister-road became so densely packed that one could move forward only by inches and to retreat was impossible."

The crush was so heavy an exit gate collapsed, which, fortuitously, relieved the dangerous crush. The number of people who paid to get in was recorded as 16,000, but the crowd was estimated at 20,000, while a host of others thought better of getting entangled in the scrum.

A scribe labouring under the *nom de plume* "Milton" opened the "Cherry Blossom" column in the first *Football Echo* of the 1929-30 season, with congratulations on "the expeditious way" in which "a modern stand" had been built. Which was not to say it was complete. The rapidity of the construction can be attributed to the fact that it had been built in prefabricated sections by Messrs Meston & Co. of Liverpool. How large the sections were and how they were transported is a bit of a mystery.

Another £10,000 was borrowed from the Norwich Union to build the stand which, in appearance, mirrored the West Stand: it was a double-decker, with the trademark Leitch steel work along the balcony wall. It was, however, narrower and far less sophisticated. There were no offices or dressing rooms to accommodate. There was seating for 2,600 spectators in the upper stand and, it was claimed, room for 6,000 to stand below. This, Milton reckoned, upped The Dell's capacity from 33,000 to 35,000, with 6,000 seated and 20,000 standing under cover. This might have added up if the rain was always driven in by an easterly wind; but anyone who ever sat in, or stood under, the East Stand, will tell you that the roof did not extend over the front dozen rows or more, and provided precious little cover from a "soft" westerly, even for those to the rear.

It is received knowledge that a section of the new East Stand was available for occupation quite early in the season, but there was no grand opening and quite when the entire structure was completed goes unrecorded in the press.

Work on the East Stand continued in 1929-30 and the team played on

The Dell's enlarged "capacity" was not tested for some years, but a new attendance record was set on Boxing Day when Spurs visited and 25,934 people shuffled through the turnstiles. This figure was not challenged until January 1935, when that fabulous estimate of 33,000 would be tested – and found wanting.

Depression and decline

The reason for the continually disappointing gates was, in all probability, Saints' declining form, but the economic situation did not help. In October 1929, the New York stock exchange had collapsed: "The Great Depression" was underway.

Manufacturing went into recession, unemployment rose and times became very tough indeed. Football, being a relatively inexpensive pursuit, did not suffer too badly and the economic ramifications in Southampton were not as dire as elsewhere. The Government, keen to show confidence in the economy, decided to issue the Southern Railway a Development Grant to continue the construction of the New Docks and, while trade had slumped, it still existed. And much of it was coming through Southampton. Nor had everyone gone bust. In 1935 alone, 75,000 cruise passengers came through the port and this – Adrian Rance observes, in *Southampton: An Illustrated History* – was "about one-seventh of the port's entire passenger traffic." Quite how many of the other six-sevenths were impoverished emigrants fleeing a hungry or hostile Europe is not mentioned, but it was a substantial proportion.

This is not to say Southampton was prospering – wages declined and unemployment queues lengthened just as they did all over the country. J.B Priestley, visiting Southampton in 1933 to research his book, *English Journey,* considered it a town "that had not let the universal depression master it and that was contriving to enjoy its unique situation, between forest and heath and deep blue water."

Priestley did not mention Saints who, by that time, were giving another new meaning to the word "average". They had slipped to seventh in Division Two in 1930 and continued to slip, by degrees, every season thereafter. And they had not had a Cup-run of any sort since their appearance in the semi-final of 1927. The one bright spot had been the introduction of a young Ted Drake to the side during 1931-32. Drake was not just a great centre-

forward in the making: he was about *the* most Southampton player to pull on the red-and-white striped shirt, having been born within the town walls. So when Arsenal made an offer that could not be refused (£6,000) in March 1934, the faithful were less than phlegmatic about it. Manchester United were the first side to visit The Dell after the transfer and the attendance reflected the disillusionment. A mere 4,900 came through the turnstiles. Another local boy, Norman Cole, took over Drake's No.9 shirt and, although he scored the only goal of the game, it was evident that he was not going to be an adequate replacement.

The poor gate also reflected the poor value of the two competing teams. United would finish the season one place and one point ahead of relegated Millwall and Saints, in their worst performance since 1928, would be six places and four points ahead of United. Drake, of course, would go on to become a legend at Highbury. Saints were once more the victims of short-term financial expediency. Or desperation?

The manager was now George Kay, Arthur Chadwick having resigned in April 1931. That Kay was a good manager cannot now be doubted – he took Liverpool to the League championship in 1947 – but at The Dell he was constantly deprived, like his predecessor, of his best players because of the ongoing financial problems.

Saints were trapped in a vicious circle. They sold players, results got worse, the supporters stayed away, another player was sold to make up the shortfall on the gate, form worsened, support declined further… and so on, *ad infinitum.* "The policy of selling players to pay the way had become such as an obsession," said one critic, "that it seemed natural to them to fall back upon that unsound policy… The public, whose confidence in the board was fast dwindling, quite rightly thought they were not getting a square deal."

The one source of reliable income was the Supporters' Club, which had been founded in 1926. Commentator had acclaimed them as early as 1929, when reporting on their annual dinner: while some supporters' clubs were "in the greatest disfavour with the directors of the football clubs they are supposed to support," he was pleased to say that this was "not the case in Southampton."

The chairman was Mr Charles F. Hoskins, who told those at the function that "the secret of our success is that we mind our own business, and do not interfere with the

FULL-TIME *at* THE DELL

directors of the football club." "No wonder, then," continued Commentator, "that a feeling of confidence in each other has grown up between the Saints' directors and the Supporters' Club." No wonder, indeed: the club's 2,203 members had raised £4,462 over the previous three years, through various fund-raising activities, which included a *Penny on the Ball* competition, regular social functions, a very popular monthly dance at the Royal Pier and other deeds and diversions that are part of the story in Chapter 26 below.

The Supporters' Club continued to warrant its motto – TO HELP NOT TO HINDER – by chucking cash at the Club, up to and beyond the Jubilee year and, while the committee may not have besieged the Board with demands of policy changes and threats of a financial boycott (which would not have been unreasonable in the circumstances), it cannot be doubted – as P.G. Woodhouse might have put it – that, while they were not openly disgruntled, they were far from gruntled.

As Southampton's officials and guests took their places for the Jubilee Dinner at the South Western Hotel on the evening of 23 November 1935, they were celebrating not just 50 years as a Football Club, but their fourteenth season in the Second Division. Perhaps "celebrate" is inappropriate. In 1923, when Saints had been promoted from the Third Division (South), there was a genuine belief that they were moving on to better things, that the glory days of the early twentieth century were there to be reclaimed. And while the newspaper accounts of the landmark event agree it was "a great night", there were, perhaps, too many reminders of "the good old days" for the comfort of the directors.

Arthur Wilson provides the foreground for this view of the 1930s scoreboard, the replacement of which features in the next chapter.

Chapter 15
A New Board

Saints' last FA Cup tie before World War II was at Chelmsford, on 7 January 1939. Chelmsford were a Southern League outfit; and it cannot be stressed too strongly that the Southern League was no longer the force it had been back in 1920 when its entire First Division decamped to the Football League (as you may recall from Chapter 11), never mind *circa* 1900, when (as you may further recall from Chapter 9) it was being regarded as a threat to the Football League. Saints lost 4-1[*]

It was the first time they had lost to "non-league" opposition in the Cup since Coventry City had beaten them back in 1912, when City were at least fellow-Southern Leaguers, albeit the first ever to beat Saints in a Cup match. There was no such consolation for the Chelmsford debacle.

Saints' first FA Cup game after World War II would beat home to Newport County on 5 January 1946. They won 4-3.

Between these two games quite a few things happened to Southampton, in general, and Southampton Football Club, in particular. So much so that events at The Dell depended more on decisions made in Germany than either in the boardroom or the chambers of the Football League and the FA. For those in Southampton not especially interested in the politics and foreign policies of Germany and Japan, life would become interesting at The Dell before it did in many of the other places that were to be swept up in the world-wide conflict.

Saints' Golden Jubilee game, as already observed, was a 2-0 victory over Tottenham Hotspur. A better indication of form was the return game at White Hart Lane on 7 March 1936, when Saints were defeated 8-0. They avoided relegation by five points.

It might be said that the Club had been in crisis ever since the East Stand had burned down. It might even be said that the erection of the West Stand was a grandiloquent gesture that led the Club to ruin, but the main criticism was that the Board lacked enterprise.

One might have expected the annual shareholders meeting of June 1936 to be dominated by recriminations and accusations of anything from the betrayal of the Club's glorious traditions to over-caution and even cowardice.

Nothing of the sort.

Boardroom clear-out

The report of the meeting not only dominated the *Echo*'s front page on 25 June, it got the banner headline: SOUTHAMPTON FC'S NEW BOARD OF DIRECTORS

Mr W. Penn Barrow, presiding, told the gathering that "decisions which will have far-reaching consequences have been taken" and that, "during the next few days we hope and believe we shall be able to inform you that negotiations have been successfully completed and that our financial position has been greatly improved."

Quite what these negotiations entailed was not divulged, but there had evidently been some tough deliberations in the boardroom some time prior to the meeting, resulting in the resignations of E. Arnfield, G.H. Muir and A.A. Wood.

The new Board was: W. Penn Barrow, H.H.G. Blagrave, C.F. Hoskins, A.E. Jukes, B.H. Ransom, J.R. Sarjantson and last, but far from least, Major R.C.H. Sloane Stanley.

B.H. Ransom had been co-opted onto the Board earlier in the year. The newly-elected Charles Hoskins was the most intriguing addition, being (as noted in the previous chapter) the Chairman of the Supporters' Club.

As the meeting continued, it was conceded by Mr Penn Barrow, that, although the Club had made a profit of £932 10s that season, this was due mainly to the transfer of goalkeeper, Bill Light (another local prodigy), the activities of the Supporters' Club and "the valuable services to the board of Major Sloane Stanley." Quite what these services were goes undisclosed.

Perhaps the testament was justified solely with regard to his duties as chairman of the Board, but Major Sloane Stanley was almost certainly one of the Club's key guarantors, had made a large financial investment in the

---

[*] Committed masochists can enjoy a full account in *Match of the Millennium*.

FULL-TIME *at* THE DELL

Club and, it later transpired, had loaned substantial sums of money to them. In fact, his importance to the Club was so great that the directors would take out an insurance policy on him in September 1937.

There followed a lot of talk along the lines of "facing a brighter future", but not a good deal of substance. "We intend to take the public into our confidence," said Mr Penn Barrow, "as soon as possible."

It would be August before the expectant (or otherwise) Southampton public got to discover what had actually been happening.

Before then, there was another blow – both, it would seem, to Southampton's future prospects and their esteem – when it was announced that First Division Liverpool had approached George Kay and offered him the position of their manager. The *Echo* confirmed his departure on 20 August.

It became the received wisdom that Saints had unfortunately lost their manager to a loftier club – until David Bull pointed out, some 62 years later in *Dell Diamond,* that the club minutes show how the new Board had asked Kay to resign: they needed to rationalise the wage bill.

Seven days after the manager's departure, the leading front-page story in the *Echo* was the annual meeting of the Supporters' Club, reported under the banner

SAINTS' FINANCIAL READJUSTMENT SAVES £840 A YEAR.

The Supporters' Club chairman, Charles Hoskins – now, of course, a director of Southampton Football & Athletic Co. Ltd. – explained how and why the board had been reorganised:

> He said that as far back as January last the old board had taken a very serious view of the financial position of the club. In spite of increased "gates" at the commencement of the season, attendances dropped when the team began to slip down the League table, and the financial position grew worse and worse, current expenses piling on the top of accumulated burdens.

He went on to criticise the old Board for the "unsound" policy outlined in the Chapter 14, before continuing:

the first move was a meeting in February, when a proposal was made to issue the remainder of the authorised share capital of the club, over £4,000, which he heartily supported.

Hoskins declared himself in favour of a new share issue of £20,000, adding that the "old directors were afraid that [any] new shareholders would lead to the loss of their places on the board." They had eventually stood down when the three principal guarantors agreed to take on all the minor liabilities and "a very generous offer had been received from the company holding the mortgage on the ground." What Mr Hoskins did not say was that the company in question was the Norwich Union. It was the new financial arrangement with them that would save the Club that vaunted £840 per annum.

The prominence accorded by the *Echo* to the Supporters' Club AGM and the nature of the "inside" information Hoskins was empowered to divulge is significant. It is obvious that the directors realised that they had the backing of a resourceful organisation and that it made sense to acknowledge openly its importance to the Club.

As for Charles Hoskins, he appears to have been recruited on his own merits – rather than a "fans' representative" – but his influence within the Supporters' Club (which reported assets of £1,703 and an annual turnover of £1,300 in 1937) would certainly have been considered useful to the Board.

One column to the right of the account of the Supporters' Club meeting was a picture of Mr C.J. Cosgrove, which has all the characteristics of a photograph discarded as too scary for a passport. The story under it announced not that he had been arrested on suspicion of murdering an inconvenient wife, but that he was "Saints' New Director".

The item noted that he was born in Norfolk, had "lived in Southampton for 32 years" and was "the local manager of an insurance company, and a very keen follower of football." It is probably not significant that the *Echo* – having twice had the opportunity, in two separate articles on the same page – failed to mention the Norwich Union. However, that Cosgrove was an executive of the Norwich Union was surely significant: had he been co-opted onto the Board in appreciation of the re-negotiated mortgage agreement – or as a condition of it?

Commentator was impressed with the changes, which he outlined in the first *Football Echo* of 1936-37:

> Seldom if ever, has so much happened to Southampton football, in a close season, as during the present summer. It has given me great personal satisfaction to see the club undergo re-organisation, a policy I have advocated for a long time, and I am certain too, the supporters of the club are now looking forward to a very interesting season.

Having reviewed the politics, he had a reservation or two regarding the management, however. George Goss, the secretary, had been placed in charge of the team, and captain John McIlwane's job description was expanded. "It seems to me," said Commentator, "to be asking a tremendous lot of one man to be player, captain and assistant manager. That looks to me to be an outsized man's job. He will need all the good wishes possible, and he has mine."

Commentator was actually underselling the task: McIlwane would also be responsible for coaching the first team and the reserves.

And good wishes were not enough. Saints struggled once again. They did have a red-letter day in the Cup, though. Sunderland descended to The Dell from the far reaches of the North East, and the farther reaches of the First Division, to contest a place in the Fourth Round. Saints lost 3-2, but they gave the eventual Cup-winners a hard fight and the directors got that long-cherished test of the ground capacity – 30,380 turned up – along with the record receipts that went with it.

A view of the record 30,380 crowd

Return of the native

Although the money raised on the Sunderland gate was undoubtedly welcome, a longer run in the Cup and larger League attendances would have been preferable and, as Saints again got embroiled in a relegation struggle, McIlwane, who had arrived at The Dell from Portsmouth in 1930 for a record fee of £2,650, resigned, not just as coach, assistant manager and captain, but as a player. Saints advertised for a manager and, in March 1937, out of an incredible 120 applicants (only three of whom were granted an interview), former Saint Tom Parker was given the job, while George Goss returned to concentrate on his secretarial duties – until the end of the season at least.

The new Board found money from somewhere. Parker was given £9,000 to spend on team improvements, the ground was lengthened by cutting back the Milton terracing and a half-time scoreboard became the latest technological wonder at The Dell. "It is the only one of its kind in the country," boasted the *Football Echo*'s "Olla Podrida"[*] column on 28 August 1937. It sat in the corner of the West Stand and Archers Road end ("Dockers' Corner") and bold white letters, from A to P, were painted on it. Each letter represented a game, the key to which appeared in the programme. In what way it differed from half-time scoreboards elsewhere was not explained.

Neither the scoreboard nor the new signings heralded greatly improved results, although Saints do appear to have become more entertaining to watch; gates increased. The great success of 1937-38 was Harry Osman, who was not one of the players that increased Saints' yawning overdraft, but a free transfer from Plymouth Argyle. He scored 22 goals that season, a more than respectable strike-rate for a winger.[†] Saints ended the season with five more points than the previous term, and in fifteenth place, but avoided the drop by a mere three points. It was tough at the bottom.

Still, the new Board were showing a degree of enterprise. They organised what can only be described as a rally towards the end of the season. The *Echo* of Friday 1 April 1938 proclaimed it the "Most Memorable Meeting in the Town's 'Soccer' History":

---

[*] It is Spanish for "odds and ends", according to *Brewer's Dictionary of Phrase & Fable*.

[†] A record total for a Saints winger equalled, in 1963-64, by Terry Paine.

FULL-TIME *at* THE DELL

Enthusiasm was the keynote of the mass meeting of the Saints' supporters, held at the Coliseum, Southampton, last night. Nearly 2,000 people packed out the hall, and all followed the speeches made with the closest interest.

The right note was struck at the very opening – indeed, before the opening of the meeting, when the Albion Silver Band played popular music – and the Mayor of Southampton (Councillor G.E.H. Prince) was cheered as loudly as though he had scored a goal in a cup final when he walked on to the platform at the head of a representative company of sportsmen, which included the Mayor of Salisbury (Councillor C. Thomas).

And there were special cheers for manager Tom Parker when he appeared. "Well played, Tom," shouted the crowd. Later in the evening, speaking with real emotion, he said: "I shall never forget this night," and there is no doubt it was an occasion unique in the history of football in the town – and probably in the whole of the country.

And so on.

It was a gushing write-up. The star of the evening was new chairman, J.R. Sarjantson, who held the floor for some considerable time. His "speech reached a high standard of clarity, His was a difficult task; to make figures interesting. He succeeded." He informed the meeting that gates were up, income was up and, after divulging all the relevant statistics, he concluded that these were

> cheerful figures, but the danger is to take too rosy a view of their significance.
>
> The great fact which stares us in the face at almost every board meeting is that, in spite of this great increase in our gates, the club is actually deeper in debt today than it was in 1935-36.
>
> A moment's thought will show that this must be so. To begin with, we have spent £10,500 on the transfer of new players to the club since the 1935-36 season commenced. We are spending more on managerial and administrative charges than we have ever done before. We have increased our staff, we have a larger number of players on our books, and we have spent considerable sums of money on improving our ground and premises…

The point being that the Club had a bank overdraft of £10,000, were paying £50 a week interest on the mortgage – which had been reduced from £30,000 to £20,000 – and they were about to spend four months without a game and with a large wage-bill to pay. Neither Mr Sarjantson nor his audience appears to have been dismayed by this prospect: it is not as though Saints had ever had a reputation as a cash cow for its shareholders.

He went on to make the delightful suggestion that, in recognition of the trade Saints brought to the town centre on Saturday afternoons, every business house should take up a season ticket: "some members of their staff would work all the better by enjoying an occasional match at the expense of the firm."

Having warmed up the congregation, Sarjantson stood aside for the Mayor, who hit them with the sting:

> "Are you going to let the club down?"
>
> "No." came the loud reply.
>
> "Well then," he added, "if we can get 300 new season ticket holders it would give the club the income they want, but I will do something now. I propose that a Shilling Fund be inaugurated, and that I will start it with 200 shillings." (Applause.)
>
> The Mayor added that if 49 other sportsmen would also each contribute 200 shillings he would give a further 200. "But," he added, "you can all do a little."

Then the suggestions for other fund-raising initiatives and pledges poured forth from the floor. That the Shilling Fund launch had been carefully planned became evident when Mr Sarjantson read out a letter from Sir Russell Bencraft, "our greatest sportsman and the most genuinely beloved citizen in this town," who had sent a donation of 500 shillings, together with 100 shillings from Mr Fred Hayter, also "an ex-Saint."[*]

---

[*] Fred Hayter, it might be recalled from Chapter 5, was the last Saint to score a goal at the Antelope Ground. His movements after leaving the Saints in 1898 have been lost in the mists of time, but it was said that Sir Russell Bencraft employed a chauffeur of the same name and that he and Hayter bore an uncanny resemblance. Dr Bencraft's letter implies that the player and the chauffeur are the same Fred Hayter.

A successful and positive evening. There was wit, big ideas, a bonding of club and supporters, even profundity – contributed by Canon R.B. Jolly, rector of St Mary's:

> I wish the dictators in Europe could see this meeting to-night. I am convinced that if Europe played with footballs more they would play with bombs less. (Applause.) In supporting football we are supporting peace. If Europe would learn to play the game and learn to pass the ball and not dribble it at their own feet, all the time, it would lead to peace.

Cutting back the Milton terracing

Southampton's inhabitants did not need to be seriously "informed" to understand the enormities being inflicted on the Continent. Since 1937, refugees from the Spanish Civil War had been pouring into the port – 4,000, mostly Basque children, in one shipment alone. The stories of German outrages in the re-occupied Rhineland, Austria, Czechoslovakia and, in particular, Germany itself could be authenticated by refugees passing through Southampton on their way to "popular" destinations such as the United States and South Africa.

There was not a lot the British people could do other than sit back and wait for their government to make some sort of decision as to what to do about the situation; football was as good a way as any of relaxing from the constant state of anxiety engendered by civil defence preparations and increasingly doom-laden headlines.

Despite the unbridled optimism of the "Shilling Fund" gathering of the previous April, the 1938-39 season got off to a horrible start, four consecutive defeats, and it didn't greatly improve after that; but gates, all things considered, were pretty buoyant. Over 11,000 turned up to watch Saints lose 2-0 at The Dell to Coventry City on 14 January, the week after the humiliation at Chelmsford.

Saints finished the campaign four points clear of relegation in eighteenth place, having managed to cull a mere two points from their last five games.

There was better news from the wrong side of Spithead. Portsmouth not only won the FA Cup by defeating overwhelming favourites, Wolverhampton Wanderers, but, according to the *Sunday Times,* "thoroughly outplayed" them.

It was not an especially popular victory as Wolves were the pin-up boys of the day, but it appears to have been greeted graciously in Southampton and it was a great morale booster for the Fleet.

That summer, the directors gave due consideration to the upkeep of The Dell. The West Stand had been painted the previous summer, but another coat was needed to save further, more time-consuming and expensive, work later on; and it was decided to paint the East Stand, which had not been painted since its construction in 1929.

The 1939 close-season was extremely tense, but the 1939-40 season kicked off as usual… well, almost as usual.

The Football League was celebrating its Jubilee and, as part of the celebrations, Pompey came to The Dell on 19 August, along with the FA Cup and all but one of the Cup winning side. Saints lost 3-0 in front of a respectable crowd, given the circumstances, of 8,747.

The League programme kicked off on 26 August and Saints went to Newport and lost 3-1. On the following Wednesday evening (kick-off 6.15 pm), they entertained Swansea at The Dell, generously. And lost 3-1 yet again.

The anonymous scribe penning the following day's "Sports Day By Day" column observed that new signing Bill Dodgin "was one of the few players to come out of

Pompey kindly brought the FA Cup for the Saints fans to fondle

FULL-TIME *at* THE DELL

the game with some credit," but appeared preoccupied with the latest innovation in player identification: numbers on the back of the shirts. Against Pompey, he had found the black numbers on Saints' striped shirts hard to distinguish, but they had now been placed on "white backgrounds" which was "a big improvement." He added, as an afterthought, that, "in view of the circumstances, the attendance – 7,155 – was quite good."

On the front page of the same edition, the main story was that the evacuation of schoolchildren would begin on the next day, 1 September.

A prominent proclamation, next to the article, announced the assembly times and points. First in line were Bitterne Park Boys, who were scheduled to get themselves to their school "Not Later Than 6.0 a.m." If all went to plan, the last children of school age would be heading for their designated railway station by 12 noon on Saturday 2 September.

On Friday 1 September, "Sports Day By Day" reported that Saints' players had been helping with the evacuation. That same day, Germany invaded Poland. On the Saturday, Bury came to The Dell and lost 3-0. The crowd was a little over 5,000 and the result provoked little jubilation. Nor was Monday's *Echo* in a congratulatory mood, being somewhat preoccupied with the "international situation": on Sunday morning, Prime Minister Neville Chamberlain had broadcast to the nation that they were at war with Germany. It was the end of football as the British public knew it.

Doug McGibbon (No.8) models the new shirt numbers in the pre-season practice match. Watched by Ted Bates, he challenges Dave Affleck

We have been unable to date this photograph, although there are indications to suggest that it is probably from the 1940s.
No matter when it was exactly, it serves as a reminder that The Dell did not always survive a season in such splendid condition as on its Final Day (see page 160)

Chapter 16
In the Firing Line

Nobody (nobody with the wit to inform themselves, at least) had any illusions as to what a war with Germany would entail. Those who had read Nevil Shute's novel, *What Happened to the Corbetts* – which was set in Southampton and predicted, with graphic accuracy, the devastation and social breakdown that air-raids would visit on the town – might have been relieved (relieved being very much a relative term in this context) that Shute's worst foreseen scenarios were greatly mitigated by the emergency services and, for the most part, an incredibly stoical and cooperative public.

As soon as war had been declared, all places of public entertainment were closed. The Football League Management Committee held their breath – as if in hope of Hitler backing down and withdrawing his troops from Poland – until 6 September, before shutting down the season for good. By which time, the Southampton board had already laid off their entire ground, and playing, staff and had arranged for Tom Parker to carry on the job of manager and secretary, in a part-time, caretaker capacity, from his Chandlers Ford home for £3 a week.

David Bull has charted, in *Dell Diamond,* the dispersal of many of the players into the local workforce, notably the police. For a few of them, including Ted Bates, this meant joining the War Reserve force, but most of these gave up being professional footballers to become full-time officers in the Borough Police Force – which soon had a formidable football team. By the end of the War, Bates and a few others were working in the aircraft industry and playing some of their football – unlike the Borough Police officers, they were still free to play for Saints sometimes – for the likes of Follands and Cunliffe Owen.

The German army was too busy in Poland to devote its attention to Western Europe and, while British troops prepared to embark for France and many less renowned areas of potential confrontation, there was a prolonged hiatus dubbed the "phoney war". Given the sky was not immediately black with *Luftwaffe* bombers, it was inevitable that the idea of a War League would be mooted before the first week of non-hostilities was out.

Barely had the Football League been aborted than there was talk of reviving the London Combination, that had run during the Great War. An *Echo* item on the subject was unable to hazard if Southampton would take part in it and disclosed that The Dell was "closed down". The restrictions on entertainment were soon lifted and

Tom Parker not only managed to arrange some away fixtures, but to assemble a team to play them. No mean feat given the circumstances under which he laboured.

This was not a situation that pacified Echoist. On 19 September, he demanded "Why Not Matches at Southampton?"

> I EXPECT Southampton people will ask: When will Saints play at home? I am afraid I cannot answer that at present, but there does seem to me to be an obligation on the part of the Saints' directors to do everything in their power to start football again at the Dell. Why should Southampton be the only – or nearly only place – without some football for those who follow the game?

That The Dell remained closed – when even Fratton Park, in the heart of one of the country's major Royal Navy ports, was open for business – must indeed have perplexed everyone. That Echoist continued to harp on about it must have irritated the Board beyond distraction. They certainly wanted to play matches at The Dell: they were desperate for the money.

At the Board meeting of 9 September, they considered a letter from the FA, "regarding the Army requisitioning the Dell." The minutes read: "it was decided to offer ground to government." An objection would hardly have got them anywhere. Another blow was delivered to them by the Supporters' Club, who had loaned their funds to the Government "interest free". The same meeting agreed "unanimously" to write to the Supporters' Club, "expressing surprise and regret." After all, wonderful and patriotic though the gesture was, it was merely a gesture; and the sum involved (whatever it was?) must have been a pittance in terms of the national interest, yet might have made a significant difference to Saints' short-term chances of survival.

The military did move into The Dell – and promptly. The minutes of a meeting, held at the Norwich Union Offices in the High Street on 16 September, record "a very full report of the activities at the Dell re the requisitioning by the military Authorities." Naturally, no details of these activities were set down. You never knew who might get hold of the minute books.

The Southampton board were able to hold meetings at The Dell again by early October and Saints were able to play in the "war league". It would appear that, whatever it was The Dell had been requisitioned for, it could be carried on circumspectly in the West Stand, within which certain rooms were apparently being used for storage.

The stand itself appears to have been out of bounds to spectators on match days. It was decided, during a Board meeting of 5 October, that the sum of £20 could be expended, "if required, to make the ground fit to re-open to the public."

They kicked-off in "League South B", a ten-team competition, on October 21, and in "South C", with a slightly different set of 10 teams, on 10 February 1940. Both leagues consisted of clubs from London and the South East.

War-time football has had a fair bit written on it in recent years. Jack Rollin's *Soccer At War: 1939-45* covers the national side of things quite comprehensively, while David Bull charts Saints' tribulations during this period in *Dell Diamond*. So suffice it to inform anyone not familiar with war-time restrictions that, whatever the inconveniences involved in keeping the game alive and whatever the football lacked in quality, it certainly made up for in novelty. Results were hardly considered important, though games could certainly be competitive. And, because professional footballers found themselves in the services or otherwise employed many miles from their own clubs, they were at liberty to turn out for whichever team they found convenient. Portsmouth were able to pick and choose from a multitude of great players passing through, or based, in the town; Aldershot, where many players were being trained as, or training under, PT Instructors for the army, emerged as one of the country's most attractive and consistent sides; and Saints... partly because many of their pre-war side were playing, for reasons already noted, at least some of their football for

local works' sides and particularly because of a reluctance to pay out excessive expenses, depended on promising local youngsters.

This is not to say they didn't have their sprinkling of star "guests". Charlie Mitten, Eddie Hapgood, Walley Barnes, Jack Stamps and, an as yet relatively obscure, Tom Finney were among the "greats" that found themselves in the "cherry stripes" during these years.

London clubs repeated their action of 1917-18 and collaborated, for the 1940-41-42 seasons, in the London Combination, a competition that excluded Saints. A Southern Regional League of 32 clubs was set up, which included London sides, but did not guarantee fixtures against them, its being what can only be described as a merit table. Saints went as far east as Brighton, as far west as Cardiff and as far north as Watford, but never to London. Following a 3-2 defeat at The Dell by Reading, on 23 November 1940, they played only away fixtures for the rest of the 1940-41 season.

The Blitz

On 10 May 1940, the German army poured into the Low Countries; by 20 May, they were entering France; and by 26 May, the British Army had been driven back to Dunkerque. The evacuation of Dunkirk (as we British usually refer to it), which rescued 338,226 troops from the beaches by use of just about everything that could float, was hailed as one of the highpoints of the war. That Western Europe was now "occupied" was almost forgotten in the euphoria.

This left the way open for the *Luftwaffe* to move their bomber squadrons to western France, giving them easy access to the sky above England. The South Coast, and London, were within easy reach. Plymouth, Portsmouth and Southampton, being large ports with plenty of industry in and around them, were prime targets – and they got pasted.

The raids on Southampton commenced on the evening of 19 June 1940 and continued for four years, ceasing on 15 July with a "doodlebug" that crashed, as they were designed to do, into an "Army camp" in woodland off the Bursledon Road, damaging 150 houses. Neither raid appears to have caused casualties. In between, according to Tony Brode's *The Southampton Blitz*, 2,361 bombs and 31,000 incendiaries were dropped on the town, leaving 630 dead and 1,877 injured, 898 seriously. The homes that were destroyed or damaged beyond repair numbered 3,589, with another 40,000 or so damaged to one extent or another. Given the collateral damage, the number of dead and wounded appears miraculously small.

What did the people do? They got on with their lives. A lot of their lives, granted, were spent in air-raid shelters or camping in the countryside – if they had access to transport – but they worked, went to the cinema and, given half a chance, many went to The Dell, despite the fact that these diversions were frequently interrupted by the wail of the air-raid sirens.

The reason the young Saints' side spent the 1940-41 season, from December onwards, roaming grounds from Cardiff to Southend was not because Southampton was too risky, but because The Dell, like most of the rest of the town, had become a victim of the blitz.

On the evening of 30 November, a bomb was dropped on the Milton end penalty area, which, according to the board minutes of 30 December, "caused the storm water culvert to be badly damaged, consequent flooding followed." Other sources note that an 18 foot-wide crater was created, which presumably dammed the tunnel carrying Rollsbrook under The Dell. The resulting flood was said to be three feet deep: a little damp underfoot for even English footer to continue.

The fire-damaged West Stand in 1941

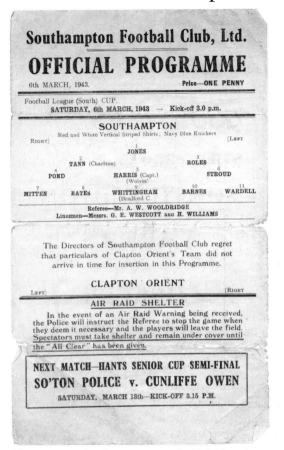

This programme describes arrangements for Air Raid warnings.
It also announces a forthcoming cup-tie between two
of the works' teams fielding acquisitions from Saints

FULL-TIME *at* THE DELL

The man-hours and materials required to repair such damage were not readily to hand. There was more pressing repair-work to be done in the town, so much of it imperative.

The Dell was a victim of the war once again in March 1941. This time, it was the West Stand that suffered. The received wisdom is that it was hit by an incendiary; but Ken Sweet who, at dusk on the day in question, was inspecting recent bomb damage in the Shirley area with his brother, is adamant that this was not the case. A teenager at the time, he claims there was no raid going on (he would hardly have been roaming the streets if there were) and that, as he reached the Hill Lane end of Howards Road, "Bang! Bang! Bang!… The Dell went up like that." (He raised both hands, as he described this to me in August 2001). "My God, the flames were right up in the air." His brother insisted they get away as fast as possible, "before the Germans see it."

Ken recalls the widely-held belief that "the military had stuff put in there."

He was absolutely correct in that regard and there was no raid that evening, which was 8 March. The board minutes of the meeting of 17 May 1941 note that the fire damage in the West Stand amounted to "£4,000 approximately." And that the "Royal Air Force admitted neglect." It would be 18 October 1941 before The Dell turnstiles revolved again.

Saints competed in the League South in 1941-42. This comprised sides as far flung as West Brom, Nottingham Forest and Swansea, but it was another merit table, which meant Saints went no further than Cardiff and Luton. Again, London clubs played in their own League and Saints were excluded.

They kicked off their home games that season against Cardiff on 4 October, not at The Dell but at Pirelli's Dew Lane ground in Eastleigh, which proved an unhappy venue, as they lost 3-1.

The following season, Saints had the chance to test their metal against London sides again. The capital's clubs had been persuaded to venture as far as Southampton and Luton. As the country adjusted to the travails of war, communications became easier and Tom Parker was no longer spending a lot of time borrowing cars and begging petrol to get to and from away fixtures: he could rely on an increasingly dependable train service. Football was regaining a semblance of normality.

Commentator noted this when pronouncing on the Christmas derby games with Portsmouth in 1942:

> SOUTHAMPTON and Portsmouth had two holiday matches, which – true to form – were spiced by keen rivalry and drew big crowds. There were 10,000 people at Fratton Park on Christmas Day, and 17,000 at the Dell on Boxing Day. This "gate," by the way, was easily a war-time record for the Dell, and about 6,000 larger than when Arsenal visited.

Statistics aside, Commentator was especially interested in the crowd's mood at The Dell:

> It was reminiscent of the old-time clashes between the two clubs to see the spectators thronging to the ground, and I saw several men – in festive mood – with coloured paper hats on their heads, and banging triangles.
> There was also a mouth organ group, and another party of spectators who lustily sang the "Pompey Chimes" as Guthrie led his side on to the field just before a policeman had "directed" a soldier and a sailor, who were kicking something about on the pitch – probably a cap – back to their places in the crowd.

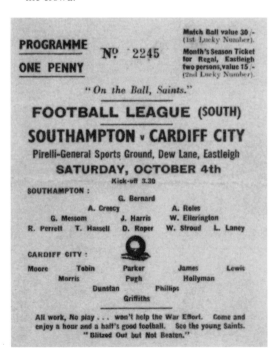

Yes. The stage was set for a real "local Derby." Sadly, Saints lost 2-0, but they had stunned Fratton Park, and most of Southampton, the day before by winning 3-2; they remained what they had been almost from the abandonment of the Football League programme in 1939, a side dominated by local youngsters, led by Wolves' stalwart, John Harris, while the Pompey team were as formidable, if not more so, as the side that had won the FA Cup – which they were to retain, uncontested, for the six years of hostilities. An enviable, if somewhat quirky, record.

Parker knell

During the 1943 close season, Tom Parker left The Dell, asking to be relieved of duties until "happier times returned." He had been offered a job and, given that he was on a part-time wage, was hardly in a position to turn it down – unless, that is, the Board offered him better terms. These were not forthcoming. The chairman, John Sarjantson, resigned from the board of directors to take up the position of secretary-manager, while former player, Arthur Dominy, took over the duties of "Team Manager". By all accounts – and they are mostly his – it would appear that Mr Sarjantson was the one doing most of the running around; and he appears to have enjoyed himself doing it.

Tom Parker's departure caused a good deal of comment in, and correspondence to, the *Echo* and, while the Board decided not to perpetuate matters by entering into the public debate, they were left with some explaining to do when the Annual General Meeting took place on 4 August. Parker's role in the vastly-improved form of the previous season (they came fifth in the eighteen-team League South) was somewhat churlishly played down, as the *Echo*'s account of the gathering shows. Mr Jukes, the Club's new Chairman, claimed that

the wonderful season the Saints had last season was, in the main, due to four things over which Mr. Parker had no control.
One was the fact that for the first time in war football the club had competed in a proper wartime league. Another was a stroke of luck that many star players were in this district, and remained throughout the season without being drafted away. A third was that in spite of restriction on travel, no club

failed to keep an engagement. The fourth was the weather.
Success on the field was due to a wonderful team spirit, which was due just as much to the club's own players as to guest players.
"Our Manager resigned," added Mr. Jukes.
"We regret it, but we bear no ill-will."

It was further noted that the Club's net income in the previous season was £8,975 3s. 5d, including a profit on catering, programmes and advertisements of £244 5s. But after expenses, by far the largest consideration being Entertainment Tax, the year's profit was £730 11s 9d. Which didn't make a large dent in the Club's liabilities, that now stood at – brace yourself – £40,390 14s.

The following two seasons were much like the previous one, with bizarre score-lines a feature – a 7-0 defeat at Queen's Park Rangers and a 10-1 reversal at Aldershot being the outstanding results in the League South in 1943-44; while The Dell played host to a 9-0 defeat of Watford, a 7-2 triumph over Aldershot and 12-3 romp against Luton during 1944-45.

By the beginning of the 1944-45 season, the War was, as far as air-raids were concerned, as good as over. In the weeks leading up to June 1944, Southampton became overwhelmed by American troops and, on 5 June, they – along with an enormous Allied armada, launched from every harbour of consequence between Shoreham and Plymouth – set off from the docks for Normandy.

No sooner had they departed than even more American and Commonwealth troops replaced them.

Germany's surrender on 8 May 1945 provoked celebrations that some of the participants were reminiscing about on the evening of 1 May 1976. Superficially, there appears to be no reason why the Football League could not have been up and running for the 1945-46 season, but the country was still on a war footing; the Japanese were refusing to back down; rationing – especially of fuel – was still in place; and reliable bus and train travel was still problematical.

The Japanese surrendered on 14 August 1945. The news came to Southampton, according to the *Echo*'s "Topics of the Hour" column, when most of the population was asleep. A few minutes after midnight on the morning of 15 August, ships in the harbour sounded V (for victory) in Morse code on their sirens:

FULL-TIME *at* THE DELL

It was a signal for the mass awakening,
and crowds trekked to the centre of the town.
In a few minutes rejoicing had begun.
Fireworks were cracking, bonfires were lit (some in
the streets). Service men and civilians surged through
the streets with linked arms…

The 1945-46 season kicked-off, as scheduled, less than
a fortnight later, with no proper League programme as
yet; but the FA Cup was to be re-instated.

For football, the War was over.

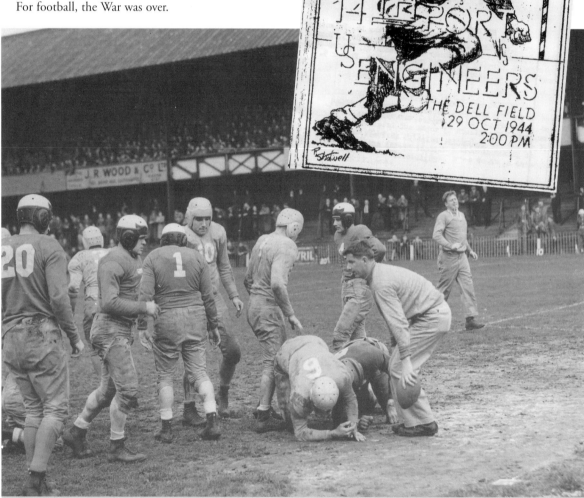

American Football at The Dell?
An American army side – basing themselves at "The Dell Field" – represented Southampton towards the end of World War II.
They played several games under the name of 14th Port.
"It was all very unlike the football of these islands…" wrote a bemused A.E.R. in the *Echo* of 23 October 1944.
"The programme told us that 'from Caesar to Eisenhower the game of football has constantly improved from the original game of brute force…'
I suspect that none of the regular Dell 'fans' who were present would look upon the American game as an improvement on that
ordinarily seen on that pitch, and rugby players probably thought the same. But perhaps we are prejudiced."

Chapter 17
Post-War transition

The date: Saturday 25 August 1945. The place: The Dell. The event: the first competitive – or, rather, semi-competitive – match in the first post-war season. Monday's *Echo* headlined the 5-5 draw with Plymouth Argyle a SPARKLING GAME AT THE DELL. It must have been a jolly occasion for the 13,000 witnesses, being, at long last, *sans* gas-masks and tin helmets.

And especially exciting for the youngsters, who had come of football-going age while being evacuated and were now able to experience the joys – and aggravations – of Saintly devotions.

Rob Holley, who movingly evoked this "return-of-the-native" moment in *Match of the Millennium,* recalled meandering home from the game with friends, "kicking a tennis ball around in streets almost devoid of traffic."

A further indication that the bomb-ravaged town was slipping back to some sort of normality was flagged-up a fortnight before the Japanese capitulated, when a "Sports Day to Day" heading drew attention to "Improvements At Dell." Improvements in this case being the intention to have "the west stand re-roofed …accommodation will be more comfortable before the really winter weather arrives for spectators in the stand." It was also recorded that The Dell's pitch had been extensively re-turfed.

The bad news?

Season tickets had been "advanced" to £4. 4s: "it would be a mistake," Commentator pronounced, "to imagine that the club will reap a harvest. In point of fact, all the club will get out of the £4. 4s. is £2. 5s 3d. (for 21 first team matches). The other £1.18s. 9d goes on entertainment-tax."

The prolonged delay concerning repairs to the West Stand may puzzle younger readers; but, while the war was over, as far as British civilians were concerned, there remained shortages of just about everything. Rationing of food, fuel and even clothing was, at this time, actually being tightened. The availability of building materials was problematical, especially in towns like Southampton, which were having to be extensively re-built.

It was not just bricks, mortar etc. that were in short supply, as an *Echo* report on a council meeting highlighted on 2 August. Alderman Fred Woolley informed the assembly that there was a shortage of architects and surveyors and that the town needed "something like another 1,500 building trade operatives."

More good news: A headline in the same edition of the *Echo* vouchsafed: ORANGES ON WAY TO SO'TON.

The League South had been extended to 22 clubs from as far north as Birmingham and Nottingham, giving Saints fixtures against First Division clubs such as Aston Villa, Arsenal, Wolverhampton Wanderers and… well, even Portsmouth.

Again, it was another season in which entertainment was widely considered more important than results and which would beguile many beyond just those who regarded themselves as football-lovers. The Plymouth result was by no means untypical: Saints belted home 97 goals, one more than champions Birmingham City. However, their defence, unlike Birmingham's, was not quite up to speed with the forward line and conceded 105.

The cavalier attitude to defensive frailties was pretty universal; attendances boomed countrywide; and while Saints finished an unassuming sixteenth, the support was more than respectable. Gates averaged 15,547.

This all made for a cheery AGM at The Dell on 16 August. Making his financial report, Mr Cosgrove announced that, after all allowances had been made, there had been a profit of £1,445 2s 6d and that the total liabilities of the company had been cut by £4,737 2s 6d, leaving £30,917 8s 9d outstanding. Mr Cosgrove added that Major Sloane Stanley's loan had been "practically covered by an insurance policy."

The *Echo* account continued with the observation that the restoration of the fire-damaged "west stand" had cost £1,107 11s 6d and that The Dell appeared as an asset of £24,785 13s 8d.

Mr Jukes had earlier promised that more improvement "had already been decided on" and that the Club was waiting on permits (official permission being required for substantial building works) to "make the Dell one of the cosiest grounds in the country."

FULL-TIME *at* THE DELL

The great thing about the 1945-46 season was the return of the FA Cup. It was decided to play all ties, up to the semi-finals, on a two-leg basis. A blow against tradition that did not meet with unanimous approval, as Geoffrey Green intimated in *The Official History of the F.A. Cup* in 1949:

> Gone for the moment was the true character of the Cup Competition; gone the sudden thrill of the knock-out blow. We were to become adding machines, working out aggregates on our finger tips. David had now to face Goliath twice and his chance of glory was diminished. But praise be! It was only to be for the one season of 1945-46.

Saints had relatively easy pickings with their first post-war Cup opponents: Newport County. The Welsh club were to finish the season one place ahead of wooden-spoonists Plymouth Argyle in the League South. Then again, Saints had been two divisions above Chelmsford, who had been their last Cup opponents.

Newport came to The Dell on 5 January – a week after Saints had mutilated a star-studded Chelsea 7-0 – and were two goals up after 10 minutes. Saints roared back to win 4-3. They also won the second-leg, 2-1, to go

Restoration of the West Stand in progress

through to only their second Fourth Round tie since 1927. According to Commentator, their opponents, Queen's Park Rangers, a Third Division (South) club in peacetime competition, "out generalled" them at The Dell in the first leg and won 1-0. They also won at Loftus Road, 5-3. Saints went out on a 6-3 aggregate, as convincing a margin as Chelmsford had managed, over one game, in 1939.

Return of the FA Cup: Newport County come to The Dell

Chapter 18
The Ecstasy and the Agony

If one is forced to seek out a game that marked the absolute nadir of Saints' fortunes (since the 1900 Cup Final or the Hants FA Senior Cup Final of 1893, anyway), one can at least take a crumb of comfort in that few of the leading candidates took place at The Dell.

Among the blackest days in the Saints' miscellany of pathos, bathos, disaster, farrago, farce and fiasco was almost certainly 30 April 1949, when Saints dragged themselves off Chesterfield's Recreation Ground, having lost the final Second Division fixture of the 1948-49 season 1-0. Pedants might argue that the preceding three games at The Dell, having raised a miserly two points from a possible six, were every bit as pathetic; but as Saints stepped out that afternoon, their fate was in their own hands. A single point would have seen them, after 26 years in the Second Division, promoted to Division One.

Post-war football had all started so promisingly. Optimism had been rampant. Not just in Southampton, but everywhere. And why not? So many players had come to the end of their careers during the war (some tragically) and any number of lads had emerged, their talents yet to be tested in regular competition, that there was no way of assessing which clubs would emerge as post-war giants. Why shouldn't supporters of Second Division Newcastle United aspire to achieving the lofty position occupied by Stoke City in 1939; or West Ham rise to be the equals of the mighty Preston North End; or Tottenham Hotspur emulate Grimsby Town?

Saints appeared to have a promising side rather than one that might bounce straight into the First Division. Ted Bates, a young inside-forward whom Tom Parker had recruited from Norwich City, the club he managed before coming to Southampton, was a case in point. Now 27 years of age, he had matured well during the war and had looked a better-than-average player the previous year. Others fortunate enough to continue where they had left off were Eric Webber, George Smith, Doug McGibbon. Len Stansbridge and Billy Bevis. Retained, from the young men who were blooded during the conflict, were Bill Ellerington, Eric Day, Alf Ramsey, Don Roper and Bill Stroud. The big-name signing was the experienced left-back, Bill Rochford, who had played for Portsmouth when they lifted the Cup in 1939.

Another pre-war player staying at The Dell was Bill Dodgin. A veteran of 30 when he arrived, he had made the grand total of two appearances in the three games of the aborted 1939-40 season and had featured in 84 war games. Under Sarjantson's management, he had taken on coaching duties, as well as playing, in the 1945-46 season.

It had been decided not to re-appoint Tom Parker as manager and, in February 1946, his contract was paid off. The following month, Dodgin was appointed "Acting Team Manager", leaving John Sarjantson as General Manager and Secretary. At the same meeting, Mary Bates, wife of Ted Bates, who had been working at the club since the previous summer, was given the title of Assistant-Secretary. Dodgin's appointment was, and continues to be regarded as, important. That of Mary Bates was singular on a number of points, the significance of which has been explored by David Bull in *Dell Diamond*. Women at football clubs had made tea, done the laundry and cleaned; they did not take on important administrative work. As David Bull observes, when the national newspapers – specifically the *Daily Mirror* – heard of what was a landmark appointment, they trivialised it – the suggestion being that her main responsibilities were making tea and keeping the office tidy: "no mention here of how she was having to learn the game's laws and regulations and take over many such matters from Mr Sarjantson, as the authorities prepared for the return of 'proper' football."

No matter that, over the previous 30 years and during two world wars, women had successfully accomplished "men's work", from clerical duties to building battleships and even driving buses, the idea that they could carry on running businesses or riveting steel in time of peace was generally regarded as laughable.

That first "proper" football season, of 1946-47, also saw the return of the *Football Echo,* or the *Football Echo & Sports Gazette* to give it its full title. It looked a little different: an "Editorial Note" regretted the inability to

FULL-TIME *at* THE DELL

In "the most ghastly winter on record," the players and trainer take advantage of another postponement to skate on the pitch.
The hatless skaters are easily identified as (left to right) Stroud, Bradley, Grant, Stansbridge, Lewis and Warhurst.
The leading pair are more of a challenge but we suggest Webber (left) and Roper

provide the "familiar yellow coloured paper… It may be possible later, to flood the High-street on Saturday night with 'golden rain' of other days – but that time is not yet." The reason for the lack of yellow paper, and the failure to publish at all the previous season, was the rationing of newsprint. Still, shortages aside, life was returning to normal; Saints went to Newport County for their first Football League game and the leading headline in that first edition was SAINTS' MATCH RAINED OFF.

Inclement weather turned out to be the main feature of the season. It was the most ghastly winter on record. There were floods, followed by blizzards, sleet and more rain – and more floods. The disruption, to industry and transport, was as bad as anything that had been caused by the blitz and there were record numbers of respiratory diseases. Just what was needed after six years of war.

On top of this was the housing shortage. In the *Football Echo* of 7 September, Commentator (whose column no longer bore the title "Cherry Blossom") observed that even professional footballers, especially in Southampton, were having problems finding property to rent. Bill Dodgin, who was now manager, had "been all over the town and the district trying to get accommodation for his players." And that wasn't the worst of it: "'I've now got to get out of my house,' he told me, 'but where I shall go I just don't know'." Squatting was a widespread solution to the problem and, according to Commentator, even Saints' players had contemplated such a recourse.

The Dell saw a couple of innovations during the season and an ambitious scheme to enlarge the ground

was hatched by J.R. Sarjantson (*below*). One advance was a commendable system to improve crowd control; the second would revolutionise facilities for a hitherto neglected section of the supporters. Commentator announced the first on 7 September, in the light of increasing gates:

TALKING of ground capacity leads me to the new police control system at the Dell. The police have installed a telephonic system, with a central control in the West stand, whereby they can be kept in touch with the situation, both inside and outside the ground, all the time spectators are coming in and during the game.
With the system working, spectators can be directed to the turnstiles where there is the least congestion, and away from the points where the crowd is piling up.
Everything is being done to get spectators in and out of the ground with the least possible inconvenience.

That inconvenience was becoming a major factor in going to The Dell was becoming more and more manifest over the next three seasons as crowds, all over the country, continued to rise. When the FA Cup Sixth Round draw brought Spurs to The Dell on 28 February 1948, the newly-introduced ticket allocation system broke down, to

Assistant-Secretary, Mary Bates, trapped in a "snowstorm" of applications for Saints' first Sixth Round tie for 21 years

massed howls of complaint. The major problem was caused by the bright idea of allowing firms to make block purchases of tickets for their employees. There was a "snowstorm" of applications, which were impossible for the Club to fulfil. Commentator claimed "that there were 66,000 application for the 6,000 Milton-road terrace tickets." And that another 7,000 tickets went to White Hart Lane.

"The first all-ticket cup-tie to be played in the town was," Commentator observed in his *Football Echo* report, "a red letter day in soccer history."

An all-ticket tie meant that the ground capacity was cut down somewhat, and the official attendance figures this afternoon were 28,425, and the gate receipts £3,296 16s. 6d.

The actual gate turned out to be 30,240. This, being approximately 2,000 under the "official" capacity. It demonstrated, beyond doubt, that there was a considerable disparity between the number the directors thought could get into The Dell; the number that could be physically shoe-horned into The Dell; and the number of those who, once sardined in, could actually see anything of the game.

Another front-page story in that edition of the *Football Echo* was headlined:

CROWDED DELL Those Unable to See Walk Out.

> A number of would be spectators at the Saints-Spurs clash walked out of the Dell this afternoon before the kick-off because they claimed it was impossible for them to see the field...
> Ticket-holders wanting to gain entry to the West Stand enclosure were also delayed in getting into the ground because gangways at the back of the West stand, which are normally kept clear, were blocked by spectators inside. Ticket-holders gathered outside the booking-office and shouted: "What about it."

Eventually all the ticket-holders got into the ground – most of them 15 minutes late – and their protests were taken up by people who had walked out of the Milton-road entrances. Some demanded their money back.

COULD ONLY SEE BRICK WALL

One who walked out, Mr. E.W. Bryant of Testwood-lane, Totton, told me he arrived about an hour before the game was due to start. He paid his money, and was admitted to the 1s. 3d. Milton-road enclosure, but on getting inside he was unable to reach the terraces. He said: "All I could see was a brick wall." He added that about 150 other people walked out of the enclosure with him.

Other complaints followed. One interviewee compared the conditions inside to "being in prison." What made it worse is that those locked-out, or that had begged to get out, had nothing else to do other than get themselves a cup of tea or do some shopping – World War One licensing laws still prevailed. Understandably, continued the report,

> thousands of people waited outside the ground, even after the kick-off, to hear reports on the game inside. A long line of police officers stood on the scaffolding at the Milton-road end of the ground to prevent anyone scaling the walls of the ground.

The reference to the scaffolding on the Milton end indicated some sort of attempt to improve facilities. The improvements at that end included the second innovation at The Dell that season – a ladies' toilet. Two turnstile booths were converted to accommodate it – this having the dual effect of creating both longer queues in Milton Road and a queue that had not previously existed inside the ground.

In that historic first post-war *Football Echo,* of 31 August 1946, Commentator had picked up on a letter in the *Southern Daily Echo* dealing with a subject "very near my heart", that of a Central Sports Stadium. "I have long advocated this idea. And so far as a football club is concerned I think it is really a question of financial life and death." The letter in question was from Councillor S.M.G. Mitchell, Chairman of the council's Borough Estates Commission, who made the point that if "Saints

FULL-TIME *at* THE DELL

reach the First Division – or even if they do not – the Dell capacity is not enough to meet the accommodation demanded of a boom." Commentator claimed that "there was a proposal, at one time, to make the Banister Stadium such a centre – I think it is still a good idea, though I do not know how the people concerned now regard the idea."

There was certainly plenty of room for expansion around Banister Stadium – although the ice rink may have had to go – but access would have been something of a problem, with the County Ground on one side; housing on the other three; and only one access road.[*]

A better option would almost certainly have been a completely new ground on West Bay. The Borough Council and the Club most certainly discussed, as early as 1948, the possibility of a stadium being built there. A site opposite Central Station had been ear-marked and the scheme "in principle" had Council approval. Among the board minutes of the time is a draft statement that notes how the scheme would

> incorporate running and cycle tracks of international standard and a dirt track. These could be available for training for instructional purposes for the Education Authority. There would also be stands capable of housing 60/70,000 spectators. They hope to plan the stands at one end of the Ground in such a manner as to provide an Open Air Theatre.
>
> It is felt that receipts from Football Matches alone after all expenses have been deducted would not leave sufficient to pay heavy overhead charges which would be involved if the stands and accommodation is to be on the scale which is desirable.

The Directors also envisaged "Lecture Rooms, extra Dressing Rooms (Male and Female), Gymnasium, a cinema for technical films, and so on which they feel would be of service to the Education Committee, for the probable increase in sports and physical training Instructors for Schools." They also wished to emphasise that they regarded the Southampton Football Club as a "Public Utility Sports Company not run for the distribution of profits."

---

[*] Recall the scenes before the Southampton Schoolboys' game in Chapter 14.

The drift of this document was that what Saints were hoping for was, if not a municipal stadium, then one in which the municipality would take-on a substantial portion of the financial input. This was not a forlorn hope at the time: there were municipal stadiums all over Europe and the United States, so why not England?

There is little doubt that, before the war, when Alderman Sidney Guy Kimber – who was the driving force behind the concepts and realisations of both the Civic Centre and the Sports Centre in the 1930s – was the head honcho of local Conservative politics, such a project would have been given serious consideration. However, in 1948, the military were still occupying the site in question; building materials and labour were, as already noted, in short supply; and the nation's economic situation was precarious.

The Western Esplanade remained a "new Jerusalem" for Southampton FC until the 1990s; but in the meantime, the constraints of the era demanded that the directors concentrate on exploiting the full potential of The Dell.

Mr Sarjantson told Commentator in November 1947 that his ambition was "to see the whole of the spectators at the Dell able to come to matches and stand under cover from the weather before I hand over the secretarial reins to somebody else."

Commentator continued: "the Saints' directors plan to put both Milton-road terraces and Archers-road terraces under cover as soon as possible, and – this is a very long term policy – build a 'double-decker' at Milton-road." But there was a problem: the shortages of materials and manpower already referred to above. So the directors were "not even hoping they can carry out their full plans for some time."

Somebody somewhere pulled the proverbial finger out. The first stage of the improvements was underway in a little over a year.

In November 1948, in the 29 November edition of the *Football Echo* to be exact, Commentator announced that there would be increased "accommodation for spectators at the Milton-road end of the ground," work on which would be "started next close season. When the scheme is completed there will be standing room for more than 2,000 additional spectators." There follows a lengthy description of the intended re-building work, which would entail the building of a new wall along the Milton Road end, and inside that an inner retaining wall: so that there will be a passage between the two walls of about six or seven feet. This inner retaining wall will form a buttress to which the terraces can be built up, and consequently extended. There will be concrete steps up to the new terracing at the West Stand end of the ground, and eventually, probably, also about three "feeds" along the length of the terraces leading from the seven foot passageway.

The Chocolate Boxes

Preparing the ground

Construction continues while the Clerk of the Works watches the players practise

With one box yet to be completed, fans pack around the scaffolding for the Christmas 1949 fixture with Luton. And not a Health and Safety inspector in sight

It was also proposed, at some time, to throw a roof over the end.

This was to be the first stage of what would become known, affectionately, as the "Chocolate Boxes" or – less affectionately – as the "Ashtrays". An intriguing ergonomic solution to The Dell's limitations: three concrete balconies mounted on pillars at the back of the Milton end and, according to Simon Inglis, the only example of uncovered double-decker terracing on a British football ground.

The much-desired roof never materialised and the Chocolate Boxes themselves provided scant cover for those few who could shelter under them and still observe what was happening on the pitch. Then again, if you could get up the front, they provided a wonderful view of the play – so long as you didn't mind missing the climax of John Sydenham's exhilarating runs in front of the East Stand; or his corners.

While all this was being planned and executed, Saints thrilled and confounded the faithful. The 1946-47 season saw Bill Dodgin's side finish in mid-table; and eliminated from the Cup away to another Second Division club, Newcastle United. Their executioner was Charlie Wayman, who scored a hat-trick.

There was no evident disharmony among the supporters with regard to the less-than-sensational form. Like a lot of people around the country, with nothing much better to do on Saturday afternoons, they appeared happy enough to watch a good game, which is generally what they got. The directors, noting the potential offered by the booming gates, were not disheartened either. The Chairman, A.E. Jukes, addressing a Supporters' Club dinner in April 1947, told them that, "with one or two additions to their side, the Saints would have a championship team next season."

They did not exactly get off to a racing start and the failure to sign "one or two additions to their side," or at least significant ones, must have been a contributory factor. There was plenty of news regarding Bill Dodgin trying to sign a big-name, but nothing to show for it. After a 5-0 thrashing at Newcastle, on 25 October, he finally nailed his man: Charlie Wayman. While no footballer, however good, however many goals he may score, could possibly have been worth the outrageous £10,000 that Wayman cost, the faithful would never begrudge a single penny of it.

FULL-TIME *at* THE DELL

Results improved, not dramatically to start with, but Saints began a gradual climb up the League ladder.

There were further moves to improve The Dell, too – for the players at least. On 15 November, the *Football Echo* reported on new equipment for the "treatment room", which had been completely modernised, courtesy of a donation from the Supporters' Club the previous

year. The training staff, Sam Warhurst and Sid Cann (*left to right, above*), now presided over a treatment room with a wide range of electrical equipment, which was second to none in the country, Bill Dodgin told Commentator: "We now have a more modern treatment room than they have at Highbury."

The latest hi-tech wonder was "sun-ray equipment."

In the following edition of the *Football Echo*, another change was announced: the pitch was to be widened. "The 'old' marking gave the Dell a width of 70¾ yards," explained Commentator. "Now with the touch line taken back 18 inches on each side of the ground, the pitch will measure 71¾ yards."

Bill Dodgin professed that "you can play better football on a wider pitch… The extra yard in width should make some difference; the wingers will have a little more room in which to work. An extra yard may not be very much, but it is something." The pitch now, apparently, measured 108 yards by 71¾ yards.

Naturally, this alteration also brought officials and players 18 inches closer to the spectators, meaning advice was even closer than had hitherto been the case; a convenience that has not always been appreciated. It also added an extra smidgeon of excitement to two of the most visceral pleasures enjoyed under the stands at The Dell down the years: the vision of the stark terror on the face of players, careering after a ball running into touch, as they realised they were not going to be able to pull up in time to stop falling into the crowd; and, subsequently, the sensation of being hit by the full bulk of a hot, sweaty athlete on an irresistible trajectory.

Saints' run-in to the end of the 1947-48 season was promotion form: they took nine points from their last five games; but they had left it too late, finishing four points below runners-up, Newcastle United.

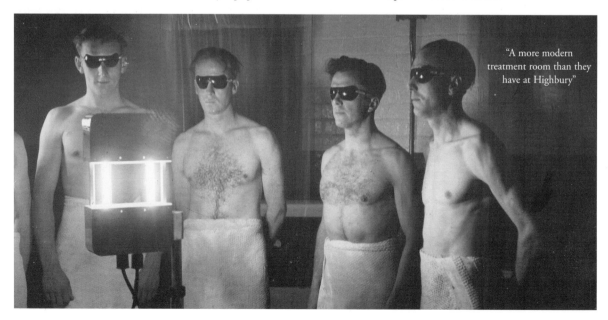

"A more modern treatment room than they have at Highbury"

As soon as the season ended, with a goalless draw at Filbert Street, Saints were transported back to Southampton to spend a night in a hotel, before embarking upon the good ship *Andes* for Rio de Janeiro. They were to be the first team to tour Brazil since the war. The voyage alone was a culture shock for the players: there was no rationing aboard ships; and there weren't many of the party that had seen a steak for seven years. In fact, it's doubtful some of the younger ones had seen one in their lives.

Brazil was an education. Saints played in immense stadiums, under floodlights, with white balls, against players who were more skilful and faster than they were. "It was," as one player, Ted Ballard, told David Bull, "an entirely different game."

Something of Brazil rubbed off on the Saints. The following season, they were magical. With the stands echoing to the plea of "Up the middle to Charlie", they were never out of the top three; and, come April, they were six points clear at the top of the table, with eight games remaining. What could go wrong?

Well, Wayman could tear a thigh muscle. And that is what happened at White Hart Lane on 2 April. Saints won that game, with Wayman scoring the only goal – after he was injured – to go eight points clear.

Wayman was an exceptional player; yet even without him, they should have been able to secure the six points that would have been needed to guarantee promotion, but five was all they got. The only hope they had as they stepped off the field at Chesterfield was that Fulham would lose by double figures at home to West Ham on the following Saturday. They won 2-0.

To add insult to injury, Bill Dodgin left The Dell, during the summer, to become Fulham's manager.

The physiotherapist, Sid Cann, took over the management of the team. He would, later in the season, also take over the job of secretary, when J.R. Sarjantson stood down and returned to the boardroom. Mary Bates retained her post as assistant-secretary: it was

one thing to have a woman responsible for running the Club; it was another to give her any actual authority.

Saints responded to Dodgin's departure, or Cann's elevation (or both), appallingly. Three consecutive defeats were followed by a home draw with Barnsley, who were less than scintillating that term. After which their form improved, in so far as they became erratic. They had 10 points from 10 games by 1 October and were in thirteenth position.

The good news was that the finances continued to be healthy. The Club's income had been £82,607 for the 1948-49 season, the highest in history.

The bad news was that their entertainment tax contribution had doubled. Nevertheless, the mortgage on The Dell had been reduced by £1, 246 over the previous year and now stood at £9,172.

This unprecedented wealth (or, rather, relative lack of debt) provided the incentive to increase the capacity of The Dell. Commentator revealed all – or all that was divulged – on 21 January 1950:

SOUTHAMPTON Town Planning Committee have accepted certain plans which have been laid before them for the extension of the west stand at the Dell, and terracing at the Archers-road end of the ground.
…One point, I understand, on which agreement has not yet been reached is whether to add seats to the stand by taking it back, out over the car park, or to lengthen the wings, carrying them round the corners at each end of the ground.

A special edition of the *Football Echo* in September 1948 celebrated the 50th anniversary both of that exemplary journal and of The Dell

He cautioned that it was, however, "unlikely the scheme will reach the practical stage for some years" and it would, in the meantime, "be nice to have a crowd at the Dell to test the present accommodation capacity. The new work at the Milton-road end was designed to increase the ground capacity to 34,500."

It would be some time before that capacity would be tested to the limit. The post-war boom in soccer crowds was beginning a gradual

FULL-TIME *at* THE DELL

downward curve; and there must have been plenty of supporters who had decided not to risk life and limb in the sort of conditions endured when Spurs had come to The Dell the previous October.

Meanwhile, Saints' form improved and they were making an ominous climb up the table. In their last nine games, they dropped only two points and, in front of large Dell crowds, they beat their two closest promotion rivals, Sheffield Wednesday and Sheffield United. Both games were won 1-0 and Wayman scored both goals.

Saints' last two games of 1949-50 were both at The Dell. Good wins were required, because the promotion race was so close that the runners-up spot might well be decided on goal average.*

Saints won those games, against Leicester City and West Ham, 5-3 and 3-2, respectively.

This gave them a goal average of 1.333. Which was not quite good enough.

They lost out to Sheffield Wednesday, who had 1.396. Saints were edged out by 0.063: another three goals would have been enough. Spare a thought, though, for Sheffield United, who came third, pipped by their neighbours, by 0.008.

---

* In those days it was goal average, not difference, that decided placings when points were tied. That is the goals for were divided by the goals against. A nightmare in an age before the pocket calculator.

Rugby goals at The Dell?

On 8 November 1947, 8,000 spectators turned out to see the Australian Rugby Union touring side play a Hampshire & Sussex XV.

The *Echo* reported: "To be beaten by no more than 14 points to 5 by a national side which has lost only one of its 17 games on these islands was an achievement of which the counties' players could be proud, and the Wallabies themselves paid tribute to the hard game they had."

Chapter 19

Going Down

The idea that 34,500 could now be packed into The Dell may not have been all that fanciful. With expert stewarding, and the full co-operation of the spectators, it almost certainly could have been achieved. The question is: how many of those 34,500 would have had sight of enough of the pitch to have any clear idea how the game was progressing? Anyone under six feet tall who experienced, from the Archers or Milton end, any of the near-capacity gates of the 1950s and '60s, will attest that, while the atmosphere was terrific, the crush on the terraces was, at the least, worrying and that the view was hopeless.

It would be some time before Saints would get as close to promotion as they did in 1949-50. Wayman departed for Preston North End during the summer, pleading his wife's inability to settle in the South, and in a cloud of inaccurate rumours regarding both his finances and the perfidy of the directors.

If Saints were doing little to impress on the field, they were bounding into science fiction around it. Whatever Sid Cann's limitations as a team manager, there can be little doubt he was forward-thinking with regards to technology. He was mainly responsible, after all, for equipping the treatment room, which was now "more modern… than they have at Highbury." On 15 October 1949, *Football Echo* readers were informed that a telephone system had been installed between his seat in the West Stand and the "trainer's box near the touch-line, where Sam Warhurst sits." He could now order positional changes without leaving his place. Another, more dramatic, installation was also germinating: floodlights.

Sam Warhurst sits in his "trainer's box" with Charlie Wayman (left)

A Mr Corry was invited to the Board meeting of 19 October 1949 "and gave some advice on the question of floodlighting." He afforded the directors a long lecture on how the technology worked and on the best way of approaching the scheme:

> there was only one such installation to be seen in this Country and this was prepared for night Rugby League games at the White City Stadium, the total number of floodlights installed is 120; 1,000 Watt units, mounted 120 feet above the playing field level. The lighting results proved most satisfactory and such an installation is the ideal necessary for night football… if floodlighting was to be established to meet the wishes of Mr. Cann… it was certainly a much more expensive scheme than seemed to be anticipated by the directors (original punctuation).

After Mr Corry had gone, the Board agreed that the expense involved in installing floodlights seemed to be "financially impracticable." In fact, the initial estimate was £5,000. It was then decided to approach the Supporters' Club to see if they were prepared to help out.

At this time, it does appear that Mr Cann, and the directors, were more interested in providing a facility for evening training than for actual games; and, anyway, playing under lights was proscribed by the Football Association and the Football League. So after a lot of umming and erring, the floodlights were installed, by Mr Corry, at a cost of "less than £700."

It would appear that, although training was the main priority, the thought of playing actual games under lights was certainly on the agenda. During a Board meeting on 9 September 1950, following consultation with the police, it was agreed to pay Mr Corry £60 to install lights

FULL-TIME *at* THE DELL

in the East Stand – so that spectators there didn't have to find their way out in the dark. Now there was no technical reason why evening matches could not be played at The Dell.

At the same meeting, it was decided to adopt *The Bells of St Mary's* as the club's signature tune. Customised lyrics, commissioned from local musician, Monty Warlock, duly appeared in the programme of 7 October (*as seen below*), in the hope that this would provide "a War Cry to compete with the 'Pompey Chimes'."

The song would prove, however, to be less enduring than the floodlighting introduced three weeks later. Commentator set the scene in the *Football Echo* of 28 October 1950:

Match Under lights

Saints' supporters will have the opportunity to see football under floodlights at the Dell next Tuesday, October 31, when Bournemouth will send their first team to play the Saints.

This will be an exhibition match and will show the possibilities of play under lights – in this case 16 1,500-watt lamps, arranged eight-a-side along the two stands.

The installation, the item went on, was provided by the Supporters' Club. The match would "kick-off at 6.30p.m., and the standing accommodation under the two stands will be open free to the public. The teams will play half-an-hour each way."

This was not the first game of football to played under lights in Southampton. In November 1878, Trojans had played a game at the Antelope under a system rigged up by a Mr Tasker, who had been touring the country with it, staging sporting events from Sheffield to Bournemouth. Opinions were mixed as to his success, but he was dogged by bad weather. The Trojans game was played on a tempestuous evening and the crowd was a small one.

The conditions for the Saints-Bournemouth "experiment" were hardly the best, although it was not wind and rain that were the problem, as the *Echo* account, of 1 November, makes clear:

The fog was so dense for the greater part of the match that sitting in the West Stand, I could not see the opposite side of the field, but when the fog began to clear, towards the end, it was possible to see – though even then some of the players were shadowy figures – nearly the whole of the pitch.

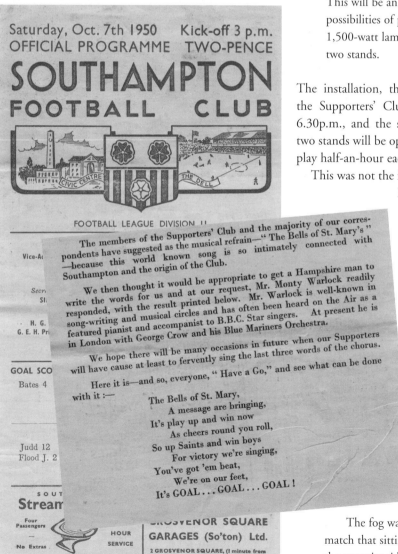

Saturday, Oct. 7th 1950   Kick-off 3 p.m.
OFFICIAL PROGRAMME   TWO-PENCE

SOUTHAMPTON FOOTBALL CLUB

FOOTBALL LEAGUE DIVISION II

The members of the Supporters' Club and the majority of our correspondents have suggested as the musical refrain—" The Bells of St. Mary's "—because this world known song is so intimately connected with Southampton and the origin of the Club.

We then thought it would be appropriate to get a Hampshire man to write the words for us and at our request, Mr. Monty Warlock readily responded, with the result printed below. Mr. Warlock is well-known in song-writing and musical circles and has often been heard on the Air as a featured pianist and accompanist to B.B.C. Star singers. At present he is in London with George Crow and his Blue Mariners Orchestra.

We hope there will be many occasions in future when our Supporters will have cause at least to fervently sing the last three words of the chorus.

Here it is—and so, everyone, " Have a Go," and see what can be done with it :—

The Bells of St. Mary,
A message are bringing,
It's play up and win now
As cheers round you roll,
So up Saints and win boys
For victory we're singing,
You've got 'em beat,
We're on our feet,
It's GOAL ... GOAL ... GOAL !

Floodlight pioneers:
Wally Judd prepares for the historic kick-off against Bournemouth, flanked by George Curtis (left) and Ernie Stevenson
As Kirkman stands by, goalkeeper Stansbridge looks for the ball against Spurs Reserves, in "the first 'official' match under lights in England"

Discussion on the floodlights, understandably, dominates the story; careful scrutiny is required to discern that the score was a goalless draw.

Understandably, too, Commentator's column in the following *Football Echo* is dominated by the event:

> The several thousands of Saints' supporters – a guess of something up towards 10,000 might not be so very far off the mark – who saw the club's experimental floodlit match at the Dell on Tuesday evening may well have been in on a first-night which they will talk about to their grandchildren one of these days.
> In fact I would not hesitate to suggest that floodlighting of football pitches has been taken out of the experimental stage by the game played between the Saints and Bournemouth. It was proved even on a foggy night you can play football under lights.
> And the fog was so dense that the referee, Mr H.G. New of Portsmouth, "lost" the coin used for the toss-up, and one of the photographers who went out on to the field to take a picture of the captains tossing, found himself at the Archers-road goal when he walked off expecting to finish up near the players' entrance.

Simon Inglis (an author not prone to error) notes, in *The Football Grounds of England and Wales,* that a friendly match between South Liverpool and a Nigerian XI was the first post-war game to be played under lights; and Headington United (now Oxford United) played a number of floodlit games, under a somewhat jury-rigged system, from December 1950.

He further claims that Swindon Town's County Ground became "the first League club to install lights, eight behind each goal, first used on 2 April 1951 for an exhibition match v. Bristol City." However, Arsenal (who had followed Saints to Brazil in 1949) do appear to have had lights installed (at a cost of £6,000, a far more sophisticated system than the Dell's) around the same time as Southampton; and the Bournemouth match certainly preceded the experimental games at Oxford and Swindon. Indeed, it was attended by Swindon manager, Louis Page, who was "thinking", the *Echo* reported, "about the installation of a floodlight system at his ground."

Other notables were there, too, and it would appear that the FA received a favourable report on the experiment: they duly lifted their ban on floodlit games in December 1950. The following month, January 1951, Inglis tells us, "the FA had added a qualifying clause to its original lifting of the ban. This stated that no competitive

FULL-TIME *at* THE DELL

matches were to be played under floodlights without permission from the FA or the County FA and the organisers of the competition concerned."

The first time permission was obtained was for a Football Combination fixture – on 1 October 1951, 11 months after the Bournemouth experiment, between Tottenham Hotspur Reserves and Saints Reserves, at The Dell – which has gone down in history as the first "official" match to be played under lights in England.

Not everybody was besotted with the idea of floodlit football, however; there were still only 36 Football League clubs with lights by 1955; and when Saints proposed to Walsall that any Dell replay of their second round FA Cup tie of December 1955 be played under lights, they were turned down flat. As it happened, Saints lost 2-1 at Fellows Park.

To be fair, Walsall's conservatism on the matter may have had more to do with the quality of illumination rather than the principle of electric illumination itself. While The Dell's floodlights had certainly been improved since installation, they were hardly top of the range. Their being slung under the eaves of the roofs over the East and West stands, the elevation was not as high as it needed to be for maximum effectiveness and there were twilight zones.

The 1951-52 season started badly and got worse. Sid Cann was "released from his duties" in December and, in March, after running the side themselves, in concord with a committee of playing and coaching staff, the Board recruited Exeter City manager, George Roughton. The results improved even before Roughton's arrival and they clawed their way into mid-table. It was merely a postponement of the inevitable.

Roughton had little luck at all in 1952-53. There was a plague of injuries and illnesses and performances varied between the sublime and the dire. The best came in the Cup when Saints drew 1-1 against Blackpool – Stanley Matthews and all – at Bloomfield Road in the Fifth Round of the Cup.

The replay, on 18 February 1953 at The Dell, is still regarded as a classic.[*]

The game had to be on a Wednesday afternoon; and in business premises and factories all over town, notices went up announcing that the management would take a dim view of those absenting themselves, no matter how many grandmothers' funerals they had to attend.

Ford's in Swaythling, legend has it, threatened absentees with dismissal. The entire work-force walked out in high dudgeon – which left them free to attend *en masse*. A crowd of 29,223 turned up – which would have been a remarkable attendance on a Saturday. It was the largest Dell gate since the League game with Tottenham in October 1949. Saints came close, tantalisingly close, to winning; but scoring chances were spurned and Blackpool prevailed by two goals to one, going on to the famous "Matthews Final." And Southampton… went on to Division Three (South).

The consensus was that Saints, what with the team having to be constantly shuffled, were unlucky rather than poor, but the chances of winning the last home game of the season, against Blackburn, seemed pretty remote. Contrary unto the death, Saints won 6-1. Alas, it was too late. They went to Nottingham Forest on the last day of the season, their fate sealed, and won 3-2.

Saints had been in Division Two 32 years. Plenty of other clubs had been in it: many had gone up, many had dropped down and quite a few of them had returned, but Saints, idiosyncratic (as well as contrary) in all things, were the only ones who had just stayed there.

After 59 years of league football, they had been relegated – for the very first time. The faithful might have derived some comfort if some well-meaning time-traveller had dropped by and told them it would be another 21 years before they got relegated again – and from a more exalted position at that – but there are no claims of such a happening.

---

[*] See Rob Holley's account in *Match of the Millennium.*

Chapter 20

Onwards...

Will The Saints get back to the Second Division at the first attempt? I have found quite a lot of optimism among supporters of the club – optimism which I do not feel I can share completely... I must say that I do not think the side is strong enough all-round to command the Third Division title.

So ran Commentator's prognosis in the first *Football Echo* of the 1953-54 season. He was right. Saints would take seven years to return to Division Two.

The club's potential can be gauged by the fact that the attendances for the first home games of each of those seasons was more than respectable, the lowest being 17,242 for the visit of Walsall on 28 August 1957. The reality of the performances was reflected, however, in the lower average gates, which failed to exceed 15,000 until 1959-60 and dipped to less than 13,000 in 1955-56. Whereas their average Division Two gates, from 1947-48, had exceeded 20,000 until their relegation year. An indication, of sorts, that, while hope sprang eternal, it died early.

Not that Saints didn't flirt with promotion a couple of times. But – and we have been over this ground before – lower gates meant lower income, meant cutting the wage bill, and ... so on. It was a return to the bad old days before the 1937 board re-shuffle – which must have hurt Mr Sarjantson deeply. He resigned from the Board in October 1955, after some 40 years' involvement with the Saints. He died in September 1958.

Needless to say, there was not much talk in these days of grand new stadia on the Western Esplanade or of any radical expansion plans for The Dell.

About the only improvements at the ground during this period – bar a lick of paint here and there – was the installation of further secondary lighting, to facilitate the regular programme of floodlit friendly matches. There was also talk in the boardroom of improving the floodlighting, but more procrastination than action. This was understandable given the reservations harboured by the Football League and the Football Association concerning the novelty. It seems absurd now but, at this point in time, if there was poor light towards the end of a game, a referee could call for a white ball to make it easier for players, officials and spectators to follow the game; yet it was not until the 1956-57 season that the League

sanctioned the use of floodlights on gloomy afternoons. This enabled clubs to set their kick-off times, all season round, to 3 pm – as opposed to 2.15 pm during British winter-time.

Thus it was that another milestone in The Dell's rich and glorious history took place on Wednesday afternoon, 5 September 1956, when, 20 minutes from the end of a match with Colchester, the field of play was bathed with artificial light. The first time Saints' supporters – or detractors – had experienced floodlighting during a Football League game.

Commentator, having noted this momentous event in the 8 September edition of the *Football Echo,* went on to announce the logical extension of it:

> For the next home midweek game – against Norwich City on October 3 – it will be floodlights all the time, for the kick-off will be at 7.30.
> A number of suggestions from supporters have been received at the Dell that seven o'clock would be a more convenient time than 7.30 for matches played wholly under floodlights.
> But this is impracticable. Current for the floodlighting system is obtained at "off-peak" rates and this cannot be switched on until seven o'clock. As a certain amount of floodlighting is necessary before the game starts for the comfort and convenience of the crowd an earlier start is impossible.

The new technology was not without it problems, especially at The Dell. Commentator complained, in the *Football Echo* of 8 October, that the Norwich game was spoiled because "it was difficult to tell one side from the other on the far side of the ground." He returned to the theme the following week. A number of supporters had written to him on the matter, one suggesting that Saints should change to white shorts. "For a long time I have thought that the Saints should play in white shorts (perhaps with a red stripe). This would be smarter strip altogether than the present one and would be a great help in recognition on dull days or in floodlit games." It was an interesting notion, but a little radical in a world where playing strips evolved rather than changed. And too soon after Saints' kit revolution of 1950, when the *Football Echo* of 18 February had explained their move from navy blue shorts to black: "Owing to the poorness of blue dye these days the blue shorts take upon themselves a very washed-out appearance after only a few washes. Black holds very much better."

Manager Bates

With regards to team matters: George Roughton turned out not to be the messiah (which, given the situation, was all that would have saved them). On 8 September 1955, a little over two seasons after Southampton FC had been delivered into the "un-promised land," the Board resolved to ask for his resignation and to offer his job to Ted Bates, who by now was doing great things as Reserve team coach. Roughton packed the game in altogether, while Bates's appointment was arguably the most astute bit of business any Saints' board has ever conducted. It was probably more luck than judgment, because all they wanted to do at the time was slash the wage bill in an effort to placate the bank manager. They were already in the process of trying to get the majority of the playing staff to accept part-time contracts.

Present vice-chairman Brian Hunt, who joined the Board in 1988 but who has had a long association with the Club (beginning as a promising player on the books back in the late 1940s), is adamant that the only reasons the Club did not end up going semi-professional at that time were the shrewdness of Ted Bates and the financial generosity of director John Corbett who, not infrequently, paid wages out of his own pocket.

David Bull's biography of Ted Bates demonstrates pretty emphatically that the new manager had inherited a set-up that was out of luck and ideas – other than having a director or two willing to take his cheque book to Board meetings. This said, Ted had organised a very useful reserve team, having won the Football Combination Cup with them in 1954. He also had the great good fortune to have an outstanding, but so far unsung, striker on the books, Derek Reeves. He then had the sort of luck few

Third Division managers ever get, the signature of a young lad who not only had the potential to be a world-class player, but actually realised it. The luck was that Arsenal were after him as well; but, as David Bull records, somebody at Highbury "had neglected to send the right forms at the right time."

On 16 March 1957, the 17 year-old Terry Paine made his first-team debut against Brentford at The Dell. It was a 3-3 draw, which, given that Saints were promotion candidates, should have been something of a disappointment. But that is not what anybody recalls about the game.

Ted Bates's sides, like those of his predecessors, were prone to false promise. They scored goals with gay abandon and lost games inexplicably.

The 1957-58 season was a watershed, both for Saints and the Football League. It had been decided to re-jig the two regional Third Divisions into Third and Fourth Divisions. The method was simple enough: the top 12 teams in each league would make up Division Three; and the bottom 12 in each the stiffs. It was a season in which Saints gave a new meaning to the word enigmatic as they yo-yoed up and down the top half of a very close competition, in which nobody was sure if they were flirting with the Second Division or the Fourth.

In the *Football Echo* of 7 December, a week after defeating Brentford 4-2 at The Dell – a result that saw them sitting in a precarious twelfth position in the table – the headline over Commentator's half-page of Saintly goings-on was

MORE OF THIS "FIGHT-BACK" SPIRIT AND IT'S PROMOTION TALK AGAIN

Except that it was not Commentator who was now commentating – his baton had passed to Observer.

Saints smacked home 112 goals that season and finished on 54 points – six points behind Brighton & Hove Albion, who went up as champions, and nine ahead of Northampton, who were the unlucky thirteenth.

The all, new "improved" Division Three of 1958-59 brought a fresh *frisson* to lower league football. Before there was promotion for the champions and, for absolute failure, the humiliation of applying for re-election; but now there were two promotion places and the prospect of relegation. Saints never looked like being involved in a struggle to do either. But they kept up the goalscoring – Derek Reeves again being the most adept practitioner in front of goal, with 16 strikes. Something of a let-down after the 31 he had netted in 1957-58.

A rare bright spot was a Third Round cup visit by Blackpool, which had them queuing behind the West Stand for tickets (*as seen right*) to be part of a crowd of 29,265 that saw Saints lose 2-1.

When Ted Bates reviewed a disappointing campaign, he put 14 players on the transfer list and begged, borrowed and half-inched nine new ones. Of those on the way out, the most significant was a successful young pretender to Derek Reeves's position as goal-scorer in chief, by the name of Charlie Livesey. He went to First Division Chelsea in a deal that saw a half-back, Cliff Huxford, come in the other direction. Another new face was inside-forward George O'Brien, who had been kicking his heels at First Division Leeds.

Unlike the departure of Livesey – which provoked director Rex Stranger to resign – these new arrivals generated little obvious excitement. Even so, the 1959-60 season began with the long forgotten emotion of optimism again suffusing The Dell. It was, however, a slow start and the biggest change looked, for a while, as if it was going to be in the floodlighting. On 17 October, Observer tentatively mentioned plans to "double the standard of the present lighting." By 26 March, he was able to reveal all:

Floodlight Improvements

The Saints, who were the pioneers of floodlight football in England (remember that foggy October night ten years ago when one wit described them as the "Wraith Rover", playing a goalless draw with Boscombe) are to install an entirely new system at the end of the season at the Dell.

The work has been delayed until then because it will involve building a catwalk on the roof of both the East and West Stands ten feet up, on which lamps in clusters of three will be fitted.

In all there will be 80, plus four behind the goals, providing altogether over 100 kilowatts, or double the present power.

The whole thing will cost about £6,500 and will be a tremendous improvement.

The Saints of course would have preferred to have

pylons, such as there are at Fratton Park, Maine-road and Chelsea, but this is out of the question at the Dell.

I hope that under the new installation the Saints will sparkle with ever increasing brightness in the years ahead.

By then, Saints' season was indeed "sparkling" in ways that could not have been predicted at the end of August. Three games into the season, they had two points and were in the bottom half of the table. By 3 October, they had 16 points from 13 games and were sixth; and local teenager Bob Charles was now guarding the net. As Christmas beckoned, they were top of the division with 32 points from 23 games and, thereafter, never dropped out of a promotion place. In fact they were top of the pile from 20 February till the end of the season.

As if that wasn't heartening enough, they got through to the Third Round of the Cup, drew First Division Manchester City at Maine Road and beat them 5-1. Southampton was ecstatic. Crowds of 20,000 plus once more became the norm – even after being defeated by Watford (of Division Four) in a Fourth Round Cup replay at Vicarage Road.

Ted Bates (understandably, given his experience of 1949) was far from complacent about elevation. In early March, he signed Spurs' goalkeeper Ron Reynolds. He was brought straight into the side and retained his place till the end of the campaign.

Saints clinched the championship on the last day of the season with a 2-0 home win over Bradford City. Champagne awaited the triumphant team in the dressing room. Reeves and O'Brien, the scorers, had, perhaps, the

FULL-TIME *at* THE DELL

most to celebrate. They had brought their respective total of goals to 39 and 23, a useful contribution to an overall aggregate of 106. But every bit as important was the wing partnership of Terry Paine and another Saints' prodigy, John Sydenham. Paine was quick, elegant, skilful and full of guile. Sydenham was a streak of lightning with a cannonball cross on the end of it.

Saints were on the march.

After 40 years of being in the Football League, it was about bloody time, too!

The new catwalks are discussed on the opposite page.
Here we see (left) a preview by Oz of life in
Division Two and beyond, under these new
floodlighting arrangements.
We can just see below the original floodlights
on the East and West Stands,
before the catwalks were introduced

Chapter 21

…and upwards

"The past," any soccer enthusiast (and L.P. Hartley) will tell you, "is a foreign country: they do things differently there." How true. Ask anyone about their experiences at The Dell between 1960 and 1966 and they will go into raptures about the rock-hard effectiveness of Cliff Huxford, "Docker" Walker and Tommy Traynor; the artistry of Ken Wimshurst and David Burnside; the elegance of Stuart Williams; the cobra-like instincts of George O'Brien; and the power and the glory of Martin Chivers in front of goal. Without exception, they will dwell lovingly on the audacious Terry Paine and the meteoric John Sydenham.

If you cannot change the subject quickly enough, they will then proceed to sermonise on how this was in the years before Alf Ramsey's "wingless wonders" and all that faffing about with 4-3-3 and 4-4-2. These were the days of five forwards and… "All right, we conceded a good few goals, but we scored a whole lot more. Great days."

It is fascinating, 35 and more years later, to thumb through old copies of the *Football Echo* and read the letters from exasperated supporters complaining about the use of a deep-lying centre-forward, Paine playing as an inside-forward, Sydenham playing "too deep", Ted Bates's selection policies … and much else besides.

On the whole, though, the nostalgists have got it right. In those six seasons in the Second Division, there was only one in which Saints didn't show, at least fleetingly, as potential promotion candidates, and that turned out to be one of the most memorable in the Club's history.

The summer of 1960 saw a lot of work on The Dell. Most of it was up-grading and general sprucing-up the already-existing facilities, but the new floodlighting system, forecast in the previous chapter, was installed and made an indelible impact on the look of the ground. The gantries, or catwalks, along the roofs of the East and West Stands appeared, the lights being affixed to the goalpost-like brackets along the front of them.

There were also the "four behind the goals", which had been heralded in Observer's forecast: a most curious arrangement of elongated lamp posts that were positioned against the barriers behind each touch-line, approximately 10 yards either side of the goals, with a single, shaded, bulb on each of them. They were a singular solution to the problem of lighting a penalty box, and would have been incongruous in any setting other than The Dell. They were certainly a cause of amusement among

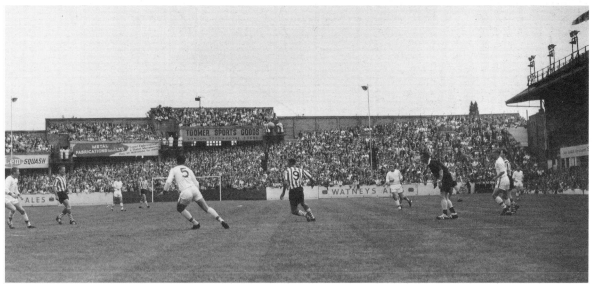

This action shot from the early 1960s shows the catwalk on the West Stand and the "elongated lamp posts" behind the Milton end goal

FULL-TIME *at* THE DELL

patronising supporters from grander surroundings and would sway when hit by particularly firm, wayward shots.

A gift of £2,000 from the Supporters' Club reduced the bill for the new lights. These were further up-graded in 1963. The *Football Echo* of 9 February reported the installation of "a good many extra lights… and the power of the lamps have been increased, so that it is estimated there is a 28 per cent improvement in the lighting."

The new system was certainly better than the old one, even before the 28 per cent improvement. The investment was justified by the fact that the Football League had abandoned all caution on floodlit football.

In fact, the 1960-61 season saw the introduction of a new knock-out competition, the Football League Cup, with the very idea of providing mid-week fixtures to be played in the evenings.

The new tournament was not greeted with universal acclaim. But Saints entered it and it soon provided one of the most memorable, and time-consuming, matches at The Dell: on 5 December 1960, 13,488 spectators spent from 7.30 to 10.30 pm in the ground to see, through to the end, a Fourth Round tie between Saints and Leeds United. Owing to failures of the local electricity supply, the lights failed twice (the delays added up to 70 minutes). The game became all the more remarkable because Cliff Huxford was forced to take over from the hospitalised Ron Reynolds early on; and George O'Brien spent most of the game as a passenger after a leg injury. Substitutes being unknown at this time, Saints were effectively down to nine men. Which was all quite astonishing in itself, but the result, a 5-4 home win, with Reeves netting all five goals, was more so. It was a rare highpoint in Reeves's post-Division Three Saints career: he was never the destructive force he had been before promotion.

The Third Round of the FA Cup provided another match of the millennium, a 7-1 hammering of Alf Ramsey's all-conquering Ipswich Town at The Dell. Ipswich would go on to take the Second Division Championship and the First Division Championship in successive seasons – so it was a pretty good result.

While all this was going on, the Professional Football Association, under the astute leadership of Jimmy Hill and Cliff Lloyd, was fighting a protracted campaign for the abolition of the maximum wage. From November 1960 through to the end of January 1961, there was a distinct threat of a strike. It was averted and the country's

top players were no longer restricted to an earnings limit of £20 a week during the season and £17 during the summer (exclusive of discreet, untaxed, illegal back-handers). Johnny Haynes of Fulham, famously, had his wages raised to £100 a week. In the not-too-distant future, some Saints would be getting as much as £35 a week, plus "appearance money". The age of "soccer slavery", which had commenced in 1901, was over – apparently?

Limits of The Dell

Naturally, a higher standard of football meant higher attendances. The Dell's capacity was tested at the second home game of 1960-61 – and was found wanting.

"After 33 Years – Snappy Saints Outclass Pompey" proclaimed the *Football Echo* of 27 August. Observer's match report of the 5-1 win noted that the gate of 28,845 "was not quite as great as anticipated, although the gates were shut before play started."

He subsequently blamed those who had got in for the fact that others were locked out and that the attendance record was not broken: they "did not pack together quite so closely as they might have done. Perhaps they had comfort in mind!" "Comfort", in this situation, being able to breathe.

The Dell did not come under siege again until 3 April 1963, when the "Town Final" edition of the *Echo* carried the headline, FANS IN CUP TICKET ROW:

> There were angry scenes at The Dell, today, after the remaining tickets for the Saints FA Cup quarter-final replay with Nottingham Forest had been quickly sold.
> Hundreds of fans who had queued for hours – some from midnight – refused to disperse. They could not believe the tickets sold so rapidly.… Twenty minutes after the ticket box opened it closed. The fans were shouting angrily nearly an hour later.
> "Don't bother with my name," said an old age pensioner, "I'm 75 and I come to all the matches. I was here three hours on Monday and three hours this morning – and I haven't got a ticket."

For those who failed to be part of the congregation of 29,479 that evening – and there were plenty of them – something of a disappointment was in store. Saints, trailing 3-0 with 16 minutes left on the clock, took the game into extra time, in, arguably, the most dramatic match ever played on the verdant emerald sward that was the Dell's stage. Though it had been one of the hardest winters on record and, by this time, grass was at something of a premium.

The second replay was at White Hart Lane on 8 April.

"Out of the 42,000 crowd some 20,000 belonged to the south coast," the *Times* informed its readers the next day, "where the factories were closed in mid-afternoon. It might have been Wembley again…" Their "Association Football Correspondent" might have added that schools and offices were near-deserted and that a few thousand more adherents were still stuck in traffic jams outside London when the match kicked-off.

Saints won 5-0. Nottingham Forest were well-placed in the First Division at the time, so the result was a bit of an eye-opener. Sad to relate, Saints lost the semi-final 1-0, to a less than scintillating Manchester United.

The Forest game aside, 1962-63 was a disappointing season for gates – an average of 15,252. There were two contributory factors. The first was a very poor start to the season, which saw Saints holding up the entire division until 29 September. Between 18 and 27 September, Ted Bates spent an astounding £48,000 on three players: Welsh international full-back, Stuart Williams, and Dave Burnside, both from West Brom; and the robust but "gentlemanly" George Kirby, from Plymouth Argyle. From which point, form definitely picked-up – when there was a game to play.

Which brings us to the second factor. It was a bitterly cold winter and not only was an evening in the stands or on the terraces a far from alluring prospect, but there was a high probability that public transport would be disrupted. The sight of passengers pushing skidding buses up hills was not an uncommon one. Nation-wide, football was an exception rather than the rule over Christmas and well into February. Between 22 December 1962 and 9 February 1963, Saints had seven matches postponed and one, at Charlton, abandoned in a blizzard. By the time the weather improved, the League and Cup programmes were in utter disarray and the season had to be extended by a very congested fortnight – it was the year they introduced the Pools Panel.

The disappointing League attendances may have owed something to a third factor, articulated in a letter to the *Football Echo* of 3 March:

One of the big problems is the ground. The only way spectators can see is to go up in the stands. Take the game against Sheffield [United – when 20,049 attended]. The stands were full but there was room for at least another five thousand spectators. They will not come and pay good money to stand at the back and see nothing of the game.

The writer went on to claim that many supporters felt the same way and suggested steepening the terraces.

In fact, improvements were already in-hand at The Dell. But these did not include provision for more spectators. At the Board meeting of 13 September 1963, it was decided to build a new gymnasium (*below*) and

convert the one they had into a new boardroom, chairman's room, kitchen and toilets. The work, begun and finished in the summer of 1964, included the provision of extra admin offices and the re-seating of the centre of the West Stand. According to the *Football Echo* of 22 August 1964, the cost was a cool £30,000. The turnstiles were also replaced with brand new ones. Whether the cost of these was included in the £30,000 is a matter of speculation, as Observer failed to list this particular enhancement.

He was not, it transpired, the only one in the dark. A letter from Fred Clark of Bitterne Park featured in Observer's column on 28 November 1964:

Would you be so kind on behalf of myself and several thousand other Saints' regular supporters to give us space to protest at the appalling conditions of entry at the Archers-road entrance to the Dell. As the

FULL-TIME *at* THE DELL

Saints get nearer the top of the league it is getting worse. These early Roman-type turnstiles would be much more appreciated at a scrap yard than at their present location.

It's a sore point with me (and I am sure I speak for a lot of regulars) to have to queue for anything up to half-an-hour, often miss the kick-off, and in a lot of cases, the best move of the match, to be unable to get in.

These old turnstiles have never been altered since the game began at the Dell. It's surprising to me that the local residents have not asked for a reduction in their rates, through having to look out on this old unpainted, untidy relic and antiquated front to a football ground.

Observer had fun at Mr Clark's expense the following week (the club having pointed out to him the turnstiles were brand new), but – notwithstanding his tardiness in getting out of the Hulse Road Club, the British Legion or whatever den of iniquity he frequented before games – Mr Clark had a valid point: The Dell was antiquated; and inadequate even for Division Two football.

Saints had their chance, in the Third Round of the next season's FA Cup, of revenge for their semi-final defeat by Manchester United. On 4 January 1964, 29,164 turned up expectantly at The Dell to see Saints vanquish the Cup-holders. An item at the bottom of that day's *Football Echo* avowed:

> All Was Quiet At The Dell this afternoon… and there were even tickets to spare.
> "People took advice and got here early; some started going in about one o'clock," said a policeman.
> Although police were watching the gates in Archers and Milton-roads in anticipation of trouble, fans quietly queued for their places and everyone was in the ground apart from one or two latecomers before the whistle blew for the kick-off.

The lack of "trouble" was some relief. Rowdyism, vandalism, random acts of violence and football were becoming inextricably linked about this time. Though nobody (nobody of much consequence at least) had yet described football hooliganism as worse than mod and rocker confrontations at seaside resorts or, indeed, what

the Teddy Boys had inflicted on "polite society" in the 1950s. Observer tackled the subject the next Saturday, under the heading "Peculiar People":

> I am sure nearly everyone must regret the behaviour of those young hooligans who indulge in the present craze of throwing toilet rolls… even when the match is in progress.
> There is a lunatic fringe in every community, and in football crowds it seems to express itself in this peculiar way… It is the same sort of person who has been in evidence this season in smashing up railway carriages on the way back to matches.

He went on to say that carriages had indeed been wrecked on the way back to Manchester and that "the disorders that have occurred at a good number of grounds this season have fortunately, not been repeated at the Dell." Unfortunately, this "craze" would hit Southampton soon enough.

As for the game, we can leave fans writing in Chapters 27-29 to account for the blowing of a 2-0 lead: the United supporters who vandalised their train on the way home were "celebrating" a 3-2 victory.

Manchester United aside, the 1963-64 season was a funny affair. Saints popped into the promotion reckoning two or three times, but would, once again, enrich the meaning of the word enigmatic.

The young Martin Chivers established himself in the first team alongside George Kirby, being preferred to George O'Brien, and scored 21 goals in 28 appearances – which made him joint-top scorer with Terry Paine. Then, to a fair measure of dismay, Kirby was transferred to Coventry City. O'Brien returned as Chivers's strike partner, after an 18-game absence, and brought his goal tally to 16 goals in 24 matches. The new combination looked ready to set the world alight towards the end of the season: in the last four games, Saints hit the net 20 times.

Only 12,539 turned up for the season's last bow, a Monday evening game at The Dell. Southampton turned on the style and tore the baffled visitors to pieces, urged on by the modest crowd vociferously chanting *We want a hundred!* The 6-1 victory gave them the goal aggregate of 100 for to 73 against. They finished fifth.

The 1964-65 season was a funny one, as well. They began with a 3-0 home defeat to Middlesbrough. Won, lost, lost, then went on a seven-game winning spree that took them from twenty-first to sixth in the table. Thereafter they got booted out of both cups by Crystal Palace and tormented the supporters into a state of neurosis by winning just enough games to look as if they might creep into promotion contention – if only they could put a little run together – and not quite doing it. It is little wonder that the gates tumbled towards the end of the season. Saints improved their position by one point and one place on the previous term, and the faithful, all but the masochists, welcomed the cricket season with profound relief.

Going up

And so to the 1965-66 season, at the end of which England would be playing host to the World Cup. To nobody's surprise, The Dell was not selected as a venue. There was hope of Southampton involvement, as Terry Paine was by now an established international; and while Martin Chivers was a mite callow as yet, he was playing for the England Under-23 side and was being tipped as a certainty for future international honours.

There was also a daring new innovation this season: substitutes. If a player was injured, and *only* if he was injured, a designated "twelfth man" could take his place. There was much debate about this: football was, after all, a man's game. What if a player just pretended to be injured, so that a tactical change could be made? Why, it would wreck the game as we knew it. After the one season, the proviso was dropped and a substitution could be made on the mere whim of the manager. Surprisingly, the world did not collapse around our ears.

Saints got off to roaring start. Their first seven games brought six wins and one defeat and they went to Coventry, on 14 September, at the top of the division and looking irresistible. They left Coventry having been well-beaten by five goals to one. Four days later they entertained Wolverhampton Wanderers and won 9-3 (of which much more in Chapter 27). Thereafter, the season came apart at the seams. Hindsight informs us that an injury to Charlie Wayman cost Saints elevation to the First Division in 1949. No amount of hindsight or even a book dedicated to it – however detailed – will ever adequately explain what happened in 1965-66.

Injury followed injury; players were played out of position; youngsters were chucked in at the deep end;

past-it players were dragged out of the reserves and "A" team… the catalogue of mishap, calamity, mischance and adversity was piled on misfortune, affliction and disaster.

It all began with the home game against Coventry on 8 September, when 'keeper John Hollowbread sustained a leg injury. Cliff Huxford took the green jersey, to make yet another heroic stand between the posts, and Ken Wimshurst climbed out of the dug-out to become the first Saints substitute in a League game. Saints won 1-0.

The following week, left-back Denis Hollywood sustained a knee injury. In November, George O'Brien contracted hepatitis. O'Brien had scored 32 goals the previous season and 11 in 16 games until his illness. On 30 October, he had overtaken Bill Rawlings's Saints' goal-scoring record, of 187 goals, which had stood since 1928.

The most conspicuous success of the youngsters chucked in on a "sink-or-swim basis" was centre-forward Norman Dean, who played 18 games and scored 11 goals: a respectable goals-to-game ratio by any standards.

In all, 24 players made League appearances that season. Only two of them were brought in during the season: goalkeeper Campbell Forsyth; and defender Dave Webb.

Webb came in a part-exchange deal from Leyton Orient that saw George O'Brien go the other way. George's 188th goal for Saints was his last. His departure caused an outrage. An Eton schoolboy, David Mabey, spoke for many in the 12 March edition of the *Football Echo*: "I am disgusted that Saints have sold O'Brien: I have been a Saints supporter since I was six (10 years ago), and have always regarded O'Brien as their best player."

There were probably those that thought Ted Bates got all he deserved when Chivers, Saints' leading scorer, retired from the game at Bristol City on 8 April and missed the two following matches with a back injury. A 17 year-old reserve called Micky Channon took Chivers's place, beside Norman Dean, for the return fixture against City on 11 April, fell over a lot, scored a goal, was brought down in the penalty area and awarded an indirect free-kick… and Saints got a 2-2 draw. Not nearly enough.

By 16 April, they were in fifth place, three points behind second-placed Wolverhampton Wanderers but… they did have three games in hand.

If the *Football Echo* of 26 March is anything to go by, some supporters had by then given up: "Surely the Dell executive can no longer seriously consider the present team as likely promotion candidates," bewailed Doug

FULL-TIME *at* THE DELL

Forder of Shirley, in a very long, and poetic, letter. "Their embryonic potential has blossomed, bloomed, matured and now begins to fade, leaving our fervent hopes once again to be frustratingly unfulfilled." While D.D. Stockwell of Hedge End, wrote:

> Southampton, now a city, is growing in size and stature day by day but Southampton Football Club surely is dropping in status before their home supporters every time they play. The management year after year promise their supporters First Division football but when are we going to get it, this year, next year, sometime or never…

While all this was going on, Southern Newspapers publishers of the *Echo* and *Football Echo* presented the Club with an "honours board" (*as seen right*). A handsomely-finished section of wooden panelling with one panel devoted to the chairmen of the Southampton Football and Athletic Co. Ltd., listed in gold, and a further four sections devoted to the individual international honours. There were 24 players and 70 games listed on it when it was presented. It was continually updated, in the finest gold calligraphy, until full. A further two boards have since had to be crafted and they hung proudly in The Dell's boardroom until the Club moved out.

Saints battled through the last twelve games of the season without losing. They scraped six draws and in only one of them, a 3-1 home win over Middlesbrough on 2 April, did they defeat a side by more than a single goal. It was a tenacious struggle, by a very determined team.

The penultimate result of the season, a 1-1 draw at relegated Leyton Orient (a score that would have filled Observer's postbag with letters signed "Disaffected Fan", or some variation thereof, a week or so before) was greeted with hysteria.

Saints needed only to avoid a 6-0 defeat in their final game. It was just their luck that it was away to the team most likely to achieve such a scoreline – Second Division champions, Manchester City.

The date: 19 May. The time: 9.10 pm.

The result: Manchester City 0 Southampton 0.

It was party time.

Chapter 22
The road to Wembley

Lawrie McMenemy recalled, in his *Echo* column of 18 August 2001, accompanying one of the directors, Mr Chaplin, to the Civic Centre Council Chamber in 1976. They took the FA Cup with them and were greeted by a full assembly of councillors who, regardless of political affiliation, wore large Saints rosettes:

Mr Chaplin made a very correct and courteous speech then I got up and said, without much diplomacy, "you all look very comfortable, ladies and gentlemen in those nice, leather bound seats. I'm delighted you all support Saints but isn't it time you tried to get some better quality seats for the supporters on a Saturday? In other words, how about a new stadium?"

I got suitably admonished a couple of days later by our legendary chairman George Reader who basically said "right speech, wrong time" but he did have a twinkle in his eye.

Saints' need for a new stadium had been obvious since it had been decided to build the West Stand and on the cards since 1948 when, as we saw in Chapter 18, the Club and the Corporation had discussed developing the Western Esplanade. The problem then was lack of building materials, manpower and money. The project had been raising its head ever since, but money was always going to be the problem, both for the municipality and the Saints – especially for the latter when they slid from being a potential Division One club to a mid-table Division Three (South) one.

However, Saints' eventual, and well overdue, elevation to the top flight in 1966 coincided – portentously – with England winning the World Cup, and the nation had gone football crazy. Gates – which had been steadily declining from Perth to Plymouth since the post-war boom – were expected to take a steep upward curve. Everything was falling nicely into place. Southampton was a prosperous city, one of the world's busiest ports, and it had a football team with a growing reputation; all it needed now was a stadium worthy of its growing status and of the footballing aspirations of its citizens.

That the Council were pleased with Saints' achievement could not be doubted. They held a Civic Reception for the Club and offered the Supporters' Club the use of the Guildhall for a celebration Dinner Dance. Sensing the mood and the moment, the directors agreed, on 23 June, to apply to the "local Authority for consideration to be given to the building of the Sports Stadium on the Common so it could be used by this club. The board felt that there would be no harm in sending such a letter…"

The idea had one merit: it would have taken the club back to its roots. It also demonstrated a worrying degree of dislocation from the sensibilities of most Southamptonians – even the Saints' daft. While there had been incursions on the Common down the centuries, it is not a matter of chance that it has remained as an open space: it has been jealously guarded since the twelfth century. The Board were fortunate that the proposal was not picked up by the local media.

While this suggestion does not appear to have been entertained, a dialogue regarding the need for a new ground had at least been established. Evidently, the dialogue was not as intense as the club would have liked and they also contacted the County Council with a view to at least considering a move outside Southampton.

By June 1967, sites at Hut Hill, Chandlers Ford; Wide Lane in Eastleigh; West End; and North Stoneham were being investigated. These were still being considered in September 1997 when a connection from the past was rekindled: the McDonald Chamberlayne Estate offered a site on the Bursledon Road, which would now face the *Tesco* hypermarket across Hamble Lane.

There were discussions, consultations, deliberations and, maybe, discreet exchanges in dark, smoke-filled rooms, but very little in the way of progress towards a new ground.

Meanwhile, for the big bow in the First Division, The Dell received another dramatic transformation. The roofs of the East and West stands were reinforced and embellished with imposing steel fabrications supporting

FULL-TIME *at* THE DELL

banks of floodlights – four of them on each roof. They were as distinct an improvement as the lights mounted on the catwalks, back in 1960, had been on the original lights attached under the roofs. This was not the only change on The Dell's skyline: a ten-storey block of flats, Overdell Court, was being built in Archers Road, the top floors of which provided an excellent view of the pitch – and a vantage point from which to take photographs like the one on the front cover of this book.

The new high lights

As to the playing staff, the only significant addition was an unsung Welsh centre-forward from Norwich City, who cost an astounding £55,000. He had made the Welsh international team, but had no First Division experience. There were distinct reservations as to whether he would be up to the job; but if he had a reputation for being good in the air and if he could knock down balls for Martin Chivers in the box... all well and good. His name was Ron Davies.

With Paine and Sydenham running down the wings, and Davies and Chivers in the centre, Saints' attack was awesome. The defence – less so.

They smacked home 74 goals in 1966-67, a total bettered in the division only by League champions, Manchester United. Ron Davies outstripped the entire League strike-force with 37 of them. The defence conceded 92 goals. Only Doncaster, relegated from Division Three, managed to concede more – a fabulous 117.

Saints avoided an instant return to Division Two by five points, having given the nerve-frayed supporters a delightful climax to the season with a 6-2 demolition of a doomed Aston Villa.

Gates for the 1966-67 season were definitely better than they had been for the Second Division, the average rising from 18,920 to 25,526. Thereafter, more or less following a nation-wide trend, they gradually declined.

A number of explanations were mooted for this, the most ubiquitous being the perceived increase in violence – on the field and on the terraces. And while letters to what was now called the *Southern Evening Sports Echo* reflected this national consensus, The Dell's limitations as an arena for those standing on the terraces was almost certainly an added factor locally. Not that there was a shortage of those prepared to suffer extreme discomfort for special occasions.

Manchester United had come to The Dell on 19 November and, for the third time in three months, the turnstiles were closed before the game got underway. The *Sports Echo* published a number of complaints in the 26 November edition, one, from someone in Hythe (wisely writing anonymously), suggesting the Common as a site for a new, larger stadium.

The United game, and the Liverpool match at The Dell earlier in the season, saw the not unusual situation of supporters attempting to watch games from the trees in Archers Road and one unfortunate fan fell down the unfinished lift shaft in Overdell Court.

Ted Bates concentrated on strengthening his defence throughout the first couple of terms in the top flight. Midfielder Hughie Fisher – and goalkeeper Eric Martin, to replace the injured Campbell Forsyth – had been the significant signings of the 1966-67 season. Scottish international Jimmy Gabriel came from Everton in the summer of 1967. Full-back Joe Kirkup and centre-half John McGrath arrived during the 1967-68 season. The most significant departure was in January 1968, when local hero Martin Chivers packed his bags for White Hart Lane for £80,000 plus Frank Saul. The deal, estimated at £125,000, was a record for a British player.

Joining the European community

Saints finally got to grips with the First Division in the 1968-69, qualifying for the 1969-70 European Fairs Cup. This competition, for those too young to remember, was the predecessor of the UEFA Cup, with a vital difference: only one club per city (or town) could qualify for it. Saints had actually come seventh that year, but Leeds United were champions, placing them in the European

Chapter 22

Cup, followed by Liverpool, Everton, Arsenal, Chelsea, Tottenham Hotspur. Fairs Cup rules dictated, therefore, that Everton, Chelsea and Spurs had not qualified. Still, as Brian Hayward pointed out in the *Sports Echo* of 15 November 1969, "just ten years ago [Saints] were playing such teams as Accrington Stanley, Chesterfield, Brentford, Port Vale, Newport County and Grimsby Town." They had, under Ted Bates, made tremendous progress.

Rosenborg of Trondheim in Norway thus became the first European side to play a competitive match at The Dell. The occasion was enhanced by the fact that George Curtis – who had graced Saints teams between 1947 and 1952 – was Rosenborg's manager. The tie brought 22,329 spectators into The Dell on 1 October 1969. Saints went into the Second Round courtesy of a 2-1 aggregate, having won 2-0 at The Dell.

Vitoria Guimaraes of Spain were next up. They were dismissed 8-4, after a 5-1 victory at The Dell. Saints were in the last 16. From the cream of Europe, they were drawn against the defending Fairs Cup champions, Newcastle United – which was a bit of an anti-climax.

After a goalless draw at St James' Park, they drew 1-1 at The Dell and departed from their first crack at European competition on away goals (a disappointment relived in Chapter 29).

Saints qualified for the Fairs Cup again in 1971, having finished the 1970-71 season in seventh place, and played one tie, losing to Athletic Bilbao 2-3 on aggregate. Given that they struggled in the League that season, going out by one goal to a team as experienced in Europe as Athletic Bilbao was not a bad result.

Throughout this period, Terry Paine, who was now more often seen in midfield – in a 4-4-2 or 4-3-3 formation – than on the wing, was the Saints' most influential player.

Having been responsible for the pinpoint crosses that had maximised the effectiveness of strikers such as Derek Reeves, George O'Brien, George Kirby, Martin Chivers

(Left) The first European fans (competition-wise) come to The Dell
(Below) Fred Kemp follows in as Ron Davies, hidden behind the foremost Rosenborg defender, scores Saints' first competitive goal in Europe

and, briefly, Norman Dean, he was now gliding balls, with deadly intent, through opposing defences, for the quicksilver Mike Channon to run on to. Paine's distribution could make a limited forward dangerous, but Channon had developed into one of the country's few world-class forwards: by 1973 he had become a fixture in the England teams that failed, under Alf Ramsey and Don Revie, to qualify for the 1974 and 1978 World Cup finals. Unfortunately for England, it seemed that there was no mid-fielder of Paine's class capable of exploiting Channon's talents as effectively as they were at Southampton. Quite why Paine was never selected by England after the 1966 World Cup remains one of the more curious of English football's many conundrums.

Meanwhile, gates continued to fall. On 31 March 1973, Manchester United were due in Southampton. In appreciation of the fact that every previous First Division fixture with them had seen thousands of disgruntled supporters locked out of the ground, it was decided to make the game all-ticket. Even given that the average gates that season were approximately 3,000 down on the previous term, the response was disappointing: 23,161 turned up. Yet the attendance was less of a disappointment than the result. Saints, who were fairly comfortably situated in mid-table, lost 2-0 to a United side fighting a relegation campaign.

On the evening of the game, the *Sports Echo* published the results of a survey, under the heading "Gate slump: Fans want more flair."

The number of those questioned was not revealed, but there were some worrying statistics. When asked if football in general was "less entertaining than ten years ago," 79 per cent replied yes, while 91 per cent thought Saints less entertaining than they had been 10 years before.

The most intriguing results were from the question "What do you consider the main reason for falling attendances?" Some 64 per cent plumped for lack of entertainment, 8 per cent for hooliganism and 11 per cent for "lack of facilities". Those aged between 20 and 40 appeared most concerned about the facilities; while, of the over 40s, only 9 per cent ticked that box. Most remarkably: only 6 per cent of females (all ages) expressed any concern regarding facilities. The most comforting statistic was that 82 per cent thought Saints had done well to stay in Division One, while the most depressing was that only 53 per cent felt they deserved better support.

Letters, accompanying the questionnaires, covered many aspects of football's decline, including the standards of football journalism and The Dell's suitability as a first class venue. One published extract averred:

> The Dell is the worst ground in the First Division, both for the players and spectators. I am sure it is responsible for much of the lack of entertainment for you cannot expect good football on a cramped ground. I have vowed never to see Saints again until they have a new ground.

Letters to the local newspapers down the years decrying The Dell were, as already observed, nothing new. They continued to be sent and they continued to be published. The *Sports Echo* of 9 October 1971 featured a complaint from Douglas Forder. Last seen in the previous chapter, berating the directors for the inadequacies of the players, he was now accusing them of naivety on the issue of falling gates:

> Surely, it must be obvious to Mr. Reader and the Board that the real reason is people are utterly fed up with the grossly inadequate and cramped Dell. Those who man the terraces strongly resent the apparent disregard for their welfare.
> I invite Mr. Reader, at the next home match to stand with me behind the Archers Road goal for 80 minutes before kick-off, as I did at the Arsenal match.
> He would soon get the message that in this day and age fans are entitled to value for their 35p, irrespective of what transpires on the pitch.
> No, Mr. Reader, your missing fans literally will not stand for it. They have opted out, preferring peace of mind and a less exciting Saturday afternoon.

Mr Forder recommended a 50,000-capacity stadium as being the solution to Saints' problems, as it would guarantee "average gates of 30,000 plus." He did not, however, recommend where such a stadium might be built or where the money to build it might come from.

It was also becoming evident that it was not just discomfort and a failure to get into big games that was concerning spectators. During a game against Crystal Palace, on the evening of 28 December 1971, police had to wade into visiting supporters on the Archers Road end "to prevent spectators near the bottom of the terrace being crushed or toppled."

The reason for the crush was, according to *Echo* staff reporter, Mary Ackroyd, jostling among the supporters at the top of the terracing. What was probably happening was the latest craze among idiots, of jumping into the back of the crowd. If three or four spectators towards the rear could be unbalanced, they fell forward, each unbalancing two or three people in front, and the effect rippled outward and downward. Properly done on a terrace with inadequate crush barriers and one could break a limb or two or three and crush a few ribs. Great fun.

Saints' secretary Keith Honey told the *Echo* of 28 December that "additional crush barriers" would probably be put in at the Archers Road end. They were installed before the next home game, at the cost of £250.

Mr Reader opened his heart, on the subject of a new ground, to a meeting of the Dell Supporters' Club on the evening of Monday 23 October: "I have been trying for five years, both with the city and with the county, and I am still in the hands of the planning authorities. I cannot give you any hope at the moment." He later added: "Until somebody can tell me where we can get three million pounds, we can get nowhere."

It was not that the Club lacked ambition as far as a stadium was concerned: a number of possibilities had been considered, but there were always drawbacks. The site on the Bursledon Road proved far too expensive and interest was lost in the Hut Hill land when it proved that there were three different vendors to deal with. Nursling also emerged as a contender, but the Western Esplanade continued to be the most likely location; and the City Council appeared keen for Southampton FC to take it. Presumably price was the sticking point?

According to the minutes of 20 August 1970, "The Board discussed the proposal of the City Planning Officer for the siting of a new stadium near Central Station, and he had sent maps together with plans of the Flamengo Stadium Rome, which had a capacity of 55,000 people."

There appears to have been a transcription error here: Flamengo is a Brazilian side based in Rio De Janeiro: the ground being referred to was almost certainly the Flaminio Stadium, the home of Lazio in Rome. It was, and still is, a handsome arena, but presumably the City

planning officer had something with more cover in mind, as the Flaminio had only 8,000 seats under cover.

It was encouraging that the City had grand plans for Saints' future; but according to an *Echo* article of the 18 June, it looked as if Saints would remain at The Dell for "another five years at least... but it is possible to say that the way ahead seems more clearly focused than for some time past." Any development would have to wait for the publication of "a new South Hampshire plan," which would be based on a thorough survey of "jobs, people, quality of farmland and present urban area problems. The needs of The Dell are included in the report on recreation."

Presumably, the South Hampshire plan recommended out-of-town hypermarkets and ribbon housing developments? Certainly, no coherent strategy emerged for sport, professional or amateur.

Saints' gates, against the national trend, actually began rising during the 1973-74 season. To start with, there was nothing to indicate this would be the case. For the First two home games, against Wolverhampton Wanderers and Norwich City, the gates were 17,457 and 17,658 respectively, but it became evident early on that, after some years of following the prevailing trend of somewhat cynical footballing tactics, Saints had turned over a new leaf. They were playing bright attacking football and interest started picking up again.

The credit for this was largely attributed to "Team Manager Designate", Lawrie McMenemy, who had arrived from Grimsby Town during the summer.

In November, Ted Bates took a step up to be Saints' "Chief Executive" and Lawrie McMenemy was made manager. Brian Hayward, on his "With The Saints" *Sports Echo* page of 17 November 1973, commenced:

> AT A TIME when managerial changes are so often accompanied by intrigue and ill-feeling, how pleasant it is to record that the re-organisation at The Dell this week was accompanied with goodwill and the most friendly atmosphere.

In detail, the managerial reign of Ted Bates came to an end after 18 years in which he guided Saints from Third to First Division, while Lawrie McMenemy, the ambitious 37-year-old Geordie, succeeded to the position for which his grooming began back in the summer.

FULL-TIME *at* THE DELL

The hand-over from Ted Bates (right) to Lawrie McMenemy

McMenemy was promoted when Saints were eighth in the table. A couple of weeks later, Mr Hayward was talking in terms of "aiming for a place in Europe next season." They surely were. On 15 December, they beat Ipswich Town 2-0 at The Dell and rose to fifth in the division.

It might be said – it certainly was at the time – that, like all Ted Bates's sides, they were two or three players short of being a really top class team, but they were a good footballing side and …then the wheels fell off. What transpired is even more bewildering than the failure of the

1949 promotion campaign. They lost, they drew, but more often than not they lost. The accomplished David Peach was brought in to mitigate the defensive frailties in January and the imperious Peter Osgood was rescued from Chelsea, at a record club fee of £270,000, in March. But while they played some smooth football, the confidence visibly drained out of them.

After that mid-December defeat of Ipswich, they won only two more matches. On 5 February, they beat Newcastle United 3-0; and, on the last day of the season, they went to Goodison Park, hoping for a win, and praying that bottom club Norwich City would win at Birmingham City.

"Despite a magnificent 3-0 victory at Everton, Saints, tragically, are relegated," opened Brian Hayward's *Sports Echo* account of Saints' final game of the season. "A 2-1 win over Norwich City hauled the midlands' club out of Saints reach and to First Division safety. Manchester United join Saints and Norwich in the plunge to the Second Division."

Saints finished twentieth. It was somewhat typical of their luck that they should be third from bottom in the first season of the three-up, three-down system.

It was received knowledge at this time (as it was in 1894 and will be in 2004) that the difference between the first and second divisions (whatever names they may masquerade under) was more marked than it had ever been. It was logical, then, to assume that all three clubs that had gone down would be strong contenders to bounce straight back.

So nobody was surprised when Manchester United stormed away with the Second Division title and Norwich slid into the third promotion place fairly comfortably, while Saints… Saints spent a lot of the season looking uneasily over their shoulders.

Quite what the problem was continues to perplex, though everyone has an opinion, but McMenemy became the most obvious target for blame.

That Terry Paine had departed for Hereford United on a free transfer during the summer did not help his case – there were many who fancied Painie as a future Saints' manager. McMenemy's marches along the touch-line to and from the dug-out on Saturdays afternoons, and weekday evenings, became something of a trial.

Brian Hayward, in his end of 1974-75 term report, observed that,

Despite the wretched return of only 19 points
half-way through the season (21 games),
Saints reached a situation in February where
a really good string of results could have brought
a challenge for promotion.

It was not to be, however, but at least Saints improved in the second part of the season with manager McMenemy introducing a number of youngsters in his search for a successful formation. That first season back in the Second Division gave Saints and the faithful – and its contingent of "peculiar people" – the opportunity to reacquaint themselves with a forgotten corner or two. Fratton Park, among other forgotten theatres of dreams, beckoned.

Portsmouth came to The Dell on 14 September 1974. The police segregated the rival supporters by keeping "a 25-yard open space between rival sets of fans" on the Milton end; where the bar was not opened at half-time.

As an indicator that there was a widespread perception that the game was not the auspicious event it used to be, the crowd was only 19,361. Saints won 2-1.

Not a lot happened at The Dell during the summer of 1975. Only one player of significance was signed: veteran Welsh international defender, Peter Rodrigues, arrived on a free transfer from Sheffield Wednesday. Given that Wednesday had been relegated from Division Two that year, this was not a development that caused much of a buzz in the pubs and clubs of the city when discussion shifted to the prospects of promotion in 1975-76.

Saints were actually top of the league by 30 August – for a week. They were not to reach that exalted position again; and when April dawned, their chances of returning to the top flight were being considered as remote. Unless, as Brian Hayward pointed out in his 3 April *Sports Echo* article, one of the leading contenders did what Saints had done in 1949.

If there was any despondency regarding the prospect of a further year in Division Two, it went unregarded, as Saints were in the FA Cup Final.

To say Southampton were underdogs would be something of an under-statement. To say Southampton, regardless of age, sex or sexual persuasion, took an interest would also be an under-statement.

I have a friend who, being completely uninterested in sport and blind to the significance of the Cup Final, went into town on the Saturday afternoon. It was so quiet that he thought, to begin with, that it was Sunday. Having found the shops open, he then found it difficult to get served, as most of the staff were riveted to televisions.

We need not go into the niceties of the game here.* Suffice it to say that just as everyone at Wembley Stadium – and half the population of Manchester and the entire population of Southampton – who were following the game on television, were bracing themselves for extra-time, Bobby Stokes moved on to a Jim McCalliog through-ball and, calmly and elegantly, stroked the ball wide of Stepney and was running back up field with his right arm raised in salute before the ball crossed the Manchester United goal-line.

There have been some spectacularly-enacted goal celebrations at The Dell down the decades, but this was something special. Thirty-thousand Saints' supporters raised the roof at Wembley and, by every account, every space in front of a television set in Southampton was the scene of unseemly cavorting. People who had never taken the slightest interest in football became, at an instant, Saints barmy.

If you had asked anyone of them at that time if Southampton FC could demolish their houses to build a new football ground, they would have handed over the deeds and happily moved into a tent. So when Lawrie McMenemy rose to his feet in the Council Chamber a few weeks later and re-ignited discussions on a new stadium, it was plain that not one person there, or anyone else for miles around, was going to contradict him.

---

* This historic event is given ample, illustrated coverage in *Match of the Millennium.*

FULL-TIME *at* THE DELL

The scenes of jubilation, on Sunday and Monday 2-3 May, that gave such an impetus to Lawrie McMenemy's bid for a new ground

(Left) Saints supporters hail a bus, as Bobby Stokes shows off the Cup

(Below) The Milton end shows its appreciation of Mick Channon's "immaculate timing"

Chapter 23
The road to West Bay

The summer of 1976 will be remembered for a number of things – record levels of sunshine and water shortages for a start – but, in Southampton at least, the abiding memory will be of the Southampton team circumnavigating the main thoroughfares of the city's suburbs aboard a cream, open-topped, double-decker bus (advertising a well known brand of chewing-gum), on Sunday 2 May.

Quite what was so attractive about the proposition of standing around for hours on a pavement waiting for a bunch of footballers taking turns to hold the FA Cup aloft is mystifying. But every man, woman, child and dog was there – an estimated 200,000 – and a further 50,000 were outside the Civic Centre for, in all likelihood, the most colourful, cheerful and chaotic spontaneous assemblies that have been witnessed anywhere.[*]

The crowds were so thick around the triumphant procession that the bus got to the Civic Centre three hours late for the civic reception, but the councillors appear not to have taken this as an affront to their collective dignity. In fact they looked every bit as chuffed as the hordes witnessing their big hello to the players on the Civic Centre steps. It would have surprised nobody if the entire crowd had been invited in for a drink.

Quite when things returned to normality nobody appears to have any clear idea. There are some that vaguely recall Heart of Midlothian coming to The Dell a week later, and a heavy contingent of their supporters failing to cope with the beer on offer in the hostelries of Bedford Place. Everyone appears to have a story concerning solicitously frogmarching befuddled young Scotsmen to the Archers Road end and leaning them against the wall; a degree of concern probably excited by the dim memory of hangovers on the previous Sunday and Tuesday mornings. The story is told that there were so many people, incapable of getting home and sleeping the drink off in the Parks on the night of the Cup Final, that the Police went round wrapping them in blankets.

As for Monday…

Mike Channon, whose timing was never less than immaculate, had scheduled that evening for his testimonial. The world and her husband turned up. The

Echo reported that 5,000 had to be turned away and gave the official gate as 29,508. Not quite a record crowd, but anyone there will tell you that this was an under-estimate. The crowding was so great, and the spirit of the occasion so high, that thousands were allowed to sit on the touch-lines behind the goals – a situation that would never have been countenanced, either by the Club or the police, at a League or Cup fixture.

The game, if it could be called that, because several of the Saints' side gave the impression of having been celebrating from the final whistle at Wembley to the kick-off, ended in total farce as more and more spectators climbed over the Milton end and Archer end walls and, in due course swamped the pitch, as the referee was blowing for full-time. The final score was given as 2-2.

The team appeared in the directors' box, with the Cup. The crowd sang *We'll support you evermore* until they were hoarse. And everybody went home, or to the pub, exhausted, and exultant.

Councillors in support

There can be no doubt whatsoever that the City's councillors, on the whole, were every bit as besotted with Saints as the rest of the population. On 10 November, they gave the Club the Freedom of the City, during a ceremony at the Council Chambers in which the Lady Mayor Mary Key gave Chairman George Reader a scroll enclosed in a "12-sided casket… made at the Southampton College of Art. A silver replica of the city seal was fixed to the cap."

The *Echo* report continued: "Council leader Councillor [Norman] Best, who revealed he had been a Saints supporter for 21 years, sang the praises of the football team which had brought 'pride, fame glory and unity' to Southampton."

The same edition of the *Echo* (12 November 1976) reported the Council's giving

---

[*] It made Mardi Gras in New Orleans look like a village fete. No, really.

FULL-TIME *at* THE DELL

the go ahead for the first steps towards a £15-million scheme produced by Lord Lucas of Chilworth to build a giant complex on reclaimed land between Western Esplanade and West Quay Road...
Lord Lucas is keen to get ahead with feasibility studies immediately and he hopes to have the whole project completed by 1980...

Councillor Norman Best then launched into a panegyric on "a project, which would provide Southampton 'with so many superb recreational facilities.' It was a now or never opportunity for Saints to get a new ground, something which had been talked about for 30 years."

Labour leader Pat Allan was less enthusiastic, seeking "assurances that the city will not be spending any of its money on this scheme." He had a point: as yet there was nothing on the table other than a location and a few fine words from Lord Lucas.

Lord Lucas's grand plan, as far as it went, had been public knowledge for at least a month. The proposed £20-million pound hotel, sport and leisure complex – which the planners (*right*) had named "The Dell" – had hit the *Echo* headlines on 6 October, when it was stated that "A MYSTERIOUS consortium" headed by the "50-year-old peer" was already in discussions with the City Council. This claim was substantiated by Norman Best. The following day, the *Echo* announced that "OIL-RICH ARABS may provide the financial backing for the ambitious plan to provide Southampton Football Club with a new home in the heart of the city." But it went on to say that Lord Lucas preferred not to be drawn on the subject and that some councillors were sceptical "about the scheme, since few developers would be prepared to risk such a large amount of money in the current economic climate."

It might be added that not only was the economic climate poor at this time, but football, as a spectator sport, continued its decline in popularity and was gaining a reputation, in widening circles, as a pariah pursuit. It

was possible to stop a "polite" social gathering dead by a mention, however passing, of the recent fortunes of the team you followed. Football fan = hooligan, QED.

In the meantime, Saints had promotion, domestic cup and European Cup Winners' Cup campaigns underway.
In Europe they did well.

A memorable evening was conjured up at The Dell on 15 September when Saints took Olympique Marseille 4-0. On 29 September, they went to Marseilles and, on a night notorious for violence both on and off the pitch, escaped, just, with a 2-1 defeat. Survivors returned with hair-raising stories confirming that hooliganism was not confined, by any means, to the British.

In October, Carrick Rangers were defeated 9-3 on aggregate and this meant that all Saints had to do was

defeat Anderlecht to move on to the semi-finals. Anderlecht were a side of Belgian and Dutch internationals, but Saints were considered hard done-by to lose 2-0 in the away leg. In the return leg, at The Dell on 16 March, Saints had them on the rack, especially in the second-half. Leading 2-0, Saints were pressing to get a third. Then Jim Steele, whose performance had been no less magnificent than in the Cup Final, over-elaborated in front of Van der Elst, the ball got held up on the sticky surface and the Dutch star gratefully ran off with it and smacked it into the Archers Road goal. Collapse of stoutly confident party.

The result, after such a sterling performance, was a disappointment, but Saints had proved beyond doubt that, despite being a Second Division team, they possessed class and that, on their day, could go the distance with anyone.

Or one would have thought so. Peter East, who was now the Saints' correspondent of the *Sports Echo*, claimed in the 2 October edition, that their start had been the worst for 14 seasons. This was the same week they had removed Marseille from the Cup Winners Cup. There was better news on the front page: "SAINTS rediscovered all their old magic with a superb sensational victory over star-studded Fulham in this afternoon's Second Division game at the Dell." Score: 4-1. Gate: 28,489.

Recent signing, Ted MacDougall, scored a brace, as did centre-back Mel Blyth. MacDougall's ability to materialise in front of goal and convert a half-chance certainly improved the team, but form remained erratic. Then, in December, McMenemy made one of his "historic signings", rescuing England international, Alan Ball, from Arsenal. Ball was 30 years-old and was still regarded as a world-class player everywhere but Highbury. And his decision to join an unfashionable club, in a footballing backwater, struggling at the wrong end of Division Two, was regarded as questionable by Fleet Street's lord high priests of footy.

Thereafter, Saints rose steadily up the table and got as far as the Fifth Round of the FA Cup, where they were defeated, narrowly, by Manchester United, in a replay at Old Trafford, after Jim Steele had been sent off.

Saints' rise up the table was too late and too inconsistent to see them in the promotion frame, but they made up for it the following season. Catching up after the usual slow start, they were soon among the contenders and promotion, beyond all but the most improbable mathematical convolutions, was secured, at the same ground, Brisbane Road, by the same score as in 1966 – a 1-1 draw with Orient (who had, at this time, dropped Leyton from their name).

The final League game of the 1977-78 season was on 29 April 1978 at The Dell. The opposition were Tottenham Hotspur, who required a draw to see them promoted in third place – just supposing Brighton & Hove Albion could not beat Blackpool by nine clear goals at the Goldstone Ground.

There had been a pronounced increase of disturbances in and around The Dell that season. The opening game, on 20 August, had witnessed Brighton supporters fighting among themselves on the Archers terraces, which were now designated the "away end". Spurs had their own contingent of "peculiar people". In anticipation of trouble, wire-mesh fencing was erected at the front of the Archers Road end. Peter East set the scene in that Saturday's *Sports Echo:*

> There was trouble before the kick-off, but it was contained to the Archers Road end which had been allocated to the Tottenham fans.
> They jostled with policemen, threw missiles including at least one policeman's helmet and a smoke bomb on to the pitch. Great holes were also kicked in the fencing.

Whether this behaviour acted as a disincentive to score is impossible to say, but it was evident that Spurs had come for a goalless draw and Saints' interest in taking the championship, which a win would have brought them, appeared to cool appreciably in direct relation to the growing number of police taking up positions behind the Archers Road goal.

Thus it was that Bolton Wanderers won the Second Division championship and Saints were, once again, runners-up.

A crowd of 28,846 turned up to the Spurs game. It would be 23 years before a larger crowd attended a football match played in Southampton.

While discussions on the Western Esplanade continued and before the First Division became a reality, alterations at The Dell, to comply with the 1975 Safety at Sports Grounds Act, as well as just improve the place generally, had to be carried out.

In 1976, numbers 64 and 66 Archers Road (*as seen below*), the stately Victorian semi-detached villas, that stood in glorious isolation beside the West Stand – and

had accommodated administration offices, the Saints' Social Club and a room for the programme sellers to pick up their wares and to cash-up afterwards; had housed the Hampshire FA; and had provided a flat for a number of Saints' players, including Ted Bates – had been demolished to make way for a purpose-built social club.

There had also been a small innovation. In May 1977, it was announced that the eastern end of the Milton terrace was to be sectioned off as "family area". The number of applications was so great that, in July, the Club announced that they were doubling its size, from a capacity of 900 people to 1,800. This would, because it was a reserved enclosure for adults and children, further reduce the ground's capacity.

In 1978, even before the most myopically optimistic Saints adherents had started counting First Division chickens, there was some doubt as to whether The Dell would be able to comply with new government regulations, within such provisions of the 1975 Safety at Sports Grounds Act as pertained to the First Division. "Saints know that work has to be done... but it is understood they have not yet been given a list of jobs to do," averred Peter East in the *Echo* of 15 April. "There are items which would require decisions on the planning side. No decisions have been taken... and even if they were taken next week, it could be as long as a year before they were actually put into practice."

Despite East's pessimism, the required work, plus other alterations, was underway before the players' kits had been laundered and stored for the close season. Some radical transformations were in the offing.

The first brought future director Brian Hunt's expertise as a builder to the forefront. The terraces under the East Stand were restructured and aluminium bench seating was introduced.

A novel solution was concocted to please both those who preferred to stand and those who liked to rest their feet. A barrier was constructed diagonally from just north of the half-way line southward to the rear of the paddock. The seating was fixed in front of the barrier, enabling those behind it to see over the seated spectators' heads. The angle was such that those seated could see more of the pitch than was ever visible when they were standing. The reason for this change was, primarily, to reduce the capacity. The exit gates were not sufficient to evacuate a crowd, speedily enough, should there be an emergency.

Another development was far less charming. Peter East described it in the *Echo* of 17 August:

FOUR PENS
The Archers Road terraces have been split into four pens and the number of pens allocated to the visiting fans will depend on the anticipated travelling support. For instance Bolton and Middlesbrough, next week, may have one or perhaps two pens as they are not normally followed by massive groups, whereas the likes of Manchester United or Liverpool or any of the big London clubs could possibly occupy most, if not all, of that end.

Installing seats under the East Stand

The four pens at the Archers end

What a way to treat your guests! There cannot have been many less pleasant places any person could spend 90 minutes – not without being arrested; or visiting another football ground. Luton's Kenilworth Road being especially oppressive.

Just to make sure that those in the Archers end got the full benefits appropriate for those interned in a Stalag, the police control point was moved from the centre of the upper West Stand into the corner under the half-time scoreboard. Another change was that a section of terracing to the south of the West Stand paddock was sectioned off and reserved for season ticket-holders. These alterations reduced The Dell's capacity to 26,000.

There were further changes. A commentary box (*as seen above*) for television cameras was erected on the roof of the West Stand, a new press room was fitted-out inside it and the "players' tunnel" – which remained a set of steps leading down to the pitch, through a door, at the Milton Road end of the West Stand – was "improved".

Talks pertaining to the eagerly anticipated re-location to the Western Esplanade apparently continued. There was also a proposal to demolish the garage at the end of Wilton Avenue, re-routing Milton Road through it and extending the Milton end back across Milton Road's former path, but the council would not entertain it.

Saints' return to the First Division was accomplished despite the temporary absence of Mike Channon, who had left for Manchester City in the summer of 1977. In his place came Ted MacDougall's former strike partner at Norwich City, Phil Boyer. Who proved a sound investment. Another notable addition to the team was centre-back Chris Nicholl from Aston Villa. Meanwhile, a young midfielder from the youth team, Steve Williams,

had stepped up to partner Alan Ball and the redoubtable Nick Holmes, and was looking to have international potential. Late in the season Peter Osgood had departed to play football in the United States.

During the summer of 1978, there were two new players, Yugoslav international full-back Ivan Golac and a winger from Derby County, Terry Curran.

Summing-up the 1978-79 season, Peter East concluded that it had been about one question: could Saints stay up?

The answer to that question being an emphatic "Yes." In fact it has been consolidation with a bonus for, as well as settling nicely into a mid-table position at the rate of about a point per game, Saints reached the League Cup Final for the first time.

And there was definitely no fluke about that, with four First Division sides beaten on the way to Wembley…

Saints had also got as far as the Sixth Round of the FA Cup before losing a replay to Arsenal at Highbury. A game notable for a rare sighting of another "historic" McMenemy signing: Charlie George – whose early career at The Dell was restricted by a series of bizarre injuries.

In passing, it is worth mentioning that Saints' 3-2 defeat by Nottingham Forest, in the League Cup Final, was a glorious game to watch and was judged to be "one of the best finals for years," as Bob Brunskell reminds us in *Match of the Millennium*.

The summer of 1979 saw more alterations at The Dell. The terracing under the West Stand was ripped up, to be replaced by a system of standing areas spliced with bench seating, as had been introduced the previous summer under the East Stand. Wooden seating, rather than aluminium, was installed, which brought another reduction in the ground's capacity, but relief to those prone to haemorrhoids.

Talks regarding the Western Esplanade continued and another potential stadium site was mooted. Eastleigh Borough Council hatched a scheme to build a stadium complex, including a 200-bed hotel, conference centre and shops, on an 80-acre side at Wide Lane, north of the M27.

Saints appear to have had little, if any, input into this whatsoever (not publicly at least) and, intriguingly, not only did Hampshire County Council turn the proposal down, but Conservative councillors in Southampton voiced objections to it.

FULL-TIME *at* THE DELL

The prospect of a new stadium on the Western Esplanade site is pronounced dead by Chairman Alan Woodford.
Seated (left to right): Malcolm Price, Commercial Manager; Lawrie McMenemy; John Corbett, Director; Brian Truscott, Secretary

The debate rumbled on and a 2,000-signature petition from outraged local residents was handed in at Eastleigh Town Hall. About the only person to say anything in its favour seems to have been Southampton councillor, Ernest Lewis, who was quoted in the *Echo* of 2 August 1979 as saying "that the Dell was in his ward and normally he would welcome any proposals to get rid of it. 'It makes the life of my constituents one of misery with all the vandalism and so on'."

George Reader had died during the summer of 1979 and the burden of overseeing a club trying to compete with the likes of Manchester United and City, Liverpool, Everton, Chelsea, Spurs, Aston Villa – to say nothing of Stoke City, Wolverhampton Wanderers and any other side with a ground that held over 24,000 people – fell to solicitor Alan Woodford.

On 24 March 1980, he issued a statement:

> THREE WASTED YEARS has [*sic*] seen the end of our hopes of moving to a new Stadium on the Western Esplanade site. We have felt obliged to respect the Council's request for confidentiality concerning the discussions we have been having with the Council's working party since early 1977. Today that request has been lifted and I am, for the first time, able to set out the Club's position.

And that is what he did. In great detail. Anybody who cares to read the statement can look up the *Echo* of that day or get hold of a copy of the 29 March programme for the Norwich City League game. Suffice it is to say that the scheme put forward by the Council would have financially crippled the Club. It was also mentioned that, since 1966, a number of other sites had been proposed but the local authorities had found them unacceptable. Given that one of these was the Common, the local authorities may have had a case, in some instances.

Mr Woodford went on to say that plans had already been submitted to the council "for improving facilities at The Dell," although he believed that the Western Esplanade site could have been financed "if there had been sufficient political will and muscle. As this is not to be, it is my hope that the necessary planning permission, WHICH IS ALL WE ASK, may be forthcoming, to enable the Club to progress even if not at the Western Esplanade." (original capitals).

Plans to modernise the ground must have been well-advanced because during the summer of 1980 the Archers Road end was completely demolished and rebuilt. The terracing was improved, a lower perimeter wall erected, new toilets and turnstiles installed and a tea bar built. A new network of anti-hooligan fencing was also put in place.

One Chocolate Box down. Two to go

During the following summer, The Dell experienced a far more dramatic metamorphosis. It was heralded in the *Official Matchday Programme* of Saturday 4 April 1981 (a 2-0 win over Nottingham Forest) with a fine drawing, courtesy of architects W.H. Saunders & Son, and a blurb headed: "Close Season Redevelopment of Milton Road". What the script did not mention (though it was obvious it would have to be done) was that the "Chocolate Boxes" would be demolished.

An insensitive omission, because there were those that cherished these vantage points: the central one – known as the "boys" – had been a baptismal font for generations of lads, and the odd girl, by providing an adult-free zone in which youngsters could get a good view of the pitch without the need to keep standing on tiptoe and craning their necks over fully-grown shoulders. This was the theory. More often than not a bunch of gigantic teenagers would bully their way to the front 10 minutes after the kick-off and burn objectors with cigarettes.

Fond memories.

The new end would consist of two tiers of terracing, both of which followed the old contours of the Milton Road end but would, cunningly, accommodate a further 1,000 spectators, the lower level having a capacity of 4,500 and the upper tier, which was fearsomely precipitous, 3,000. This upper terracing was designated as the "Family Centre."

On 4 April 1981, Bob Brunskell told his *Echo* readers that these changes to the Milton Road end would "push Saints' capacity up to 25,000" and would include improved "toilet and refreshment facilities, turnstiles and crush barriers." And that part of the cost would, hopefully, be defrayed by a grant from the Football Grounds Improvement Trust, which received its funding from the Spot the Ball competition on Football Pools coupons. The contribution from the FGIT amounted to £76,670.

The last game at The Dell that season was a 1-1 draw with Tottenham Hotspur on 20 April. As the spectators exited the ground into Milton Road, they passed the demolition gang and their machinery waiting to move in.

The "eccentric angles" of the Milton end, as seen from the road

FULL-TIME *at* THE DELL

They had to make a quick start if the project was to be completed for the 1981-82 season, which was due to commence in 18 weeks' time. Bar the odd lick of paint it was. The "new" Milton was impressive and ingenious, but lacked the romance of its predecessor.

This was not the only change at The Dell during the summer of '81. A section of terracing at the Milton end of the lower West Stand was remodelled and sectioned off for the used of wheelchair users. Responsibility for allocating spaces in the new facility was handed over to the Federation of the Clubs for the Disabled.

The following summer, it was proposed to redevelop the Archers Road end with a similar, but slightly less eccentrically-angled, construction than the new Milton end. But this hit difficulties at the planning stage. An *Echo* article of 30 March 1982 told readers that the Southampton Council's chief engineer had "branded" it "a potential traffic hazard." The projected upper terracing would overhang the pavement by 1.4 metres and the city engineer reasoned that this would give "the impression of narrowing to drivers, at a point close to the junction of Northlands Road and Silverdale Road where disruption of smooth traffic flow already occurs."

The Club responded to the objection by pointing out that cutting back the overhang would reduce the ground's capacity by 200, which would result in the loss of £10,000 a year. Needless to say, planning permission was not forthcoming.

In 1983, Collins Willow published a revolutionary book by Simon Inglis: *Football Grounds of England and Wales* (which has proved, as previous references testify, essential for this tome). Not only did it explain the evolution of stadia, with particular emphasis on football grounds, but it contained details on the histories of all Football Leagues venues. The fact that Inglis placed trust in some dubious secondary sources, not least in his section on Southampton, does not diminish the quality, or the innovativeness, of the work whatsoever.

Inglis's observations on The Dell end with a paragraph that makes for intriguing reading in the 21st century:

> It is unquestionably a Southern ground, in atmosphere and hue, yet however small and basic it may seem compared with fellow stadiums in Division One, The Dell has one major asset – an administration that cares for its surroundings … Southampton is a club with advanced ideas living in a small, old ground. In view of football's receding audiences, it is probably happy to stay that way.

This just might have been true at the time, but then came three incidents – none of which involved Southampton Football Club – that had a profound effect on English football. They would come close to ruining Southampton FC and, ultimately, lead to The Dell, already an anachronism, becoming a liability.

A Piano Lid appeared at the Milton end, in place of the Chocolate Boxes

Chapter 24
No Road to Stoneham

The first "incident" happened on 11 May 1985, at Bradford City's last game of the season at Valley Parade. During the closing stages, the Main Stand burst into flames. The fire killed 55 and hospitalised another 200. A little over a fortnight later, on the evening of 29 May, a TV audience of millions sat down to watch Liverpool and Juventus contest the final of the European Cup at the Stade du Heysel in Brussels, and witnessed the catastrophe when a grouping of Liverpool "supporters" charged spectators and sections of fencing and terracing collapsed. Thirty-nine people died and 450 were injured.

As a result English clubs were banned from European competition "indefinitely". This was harsh, but not unreasonable. The travelling supporters of Southampton and Norwich (two of the clubs expelled) were hardly synonymous with overt aggression, but English fans had been a byword for ignorance, stupidity, cowardice and violence on the Continent for a couple of decades. It was not UEFA's role to judge which clubs' followers were fit to be allowed across the Channel. Fingers could be, and were, wagged at other miscreants but UEFA stood firm: European football would have to get by without the English.

The next disaster was at Hillsborough, the home of Sheffield Wednesday, on Saturday 15 April 1989. The event was an FA Cup semi-final between Liverpool and Nottingham Forest. A "crush" in one of the cages on the Leppings Lane terraces resulted in 95 deaths on the day and over 400 casualties. Those at the front of the terracing were unable to seek safety by getting onto the pitch because of the anti-hooligan fencing that stretched across the entire end. Furthermore, the police, seeing supporters attempting to climb the fencing, mistook the chaos as "crowd disorder" and kept the emergency exit locked.

Much has been written on the above incidents, much of it tabloid tosh, and does not need to be rehashed here.

Lord Justice Taylor was commissioned to head the Inquiry into the Hillsborough disaster and to produce a report taking into consideration what had, or should have, been learned from Bradford and Heysel. There is a comment from the second of his two reports that is well worth quoting:

> Amazingly, complacency was still to be found even after Hillsborough. It was chilling to hear the same refrain from directors at several clubs I visited:

> "Hillsborough was horrible – but of course it couldn't happen here."

Couldn't it? The Hillsborough ground was regarded by many as one of the best in the country. It was selected by the FA for the Cup semi-final and thought by them to be entirely suitable.

There were several important, and positive, recommendations emanating from the Taylor Reports. Two of which would have a profound effect on the experience of attending professional matches and radically change the look of every football ground in the country, while another would result in the ditching of the government's plans to introduce ID cards for all spectators at football matches. This ludicrous scheme, the major clause of the Football Spectators Bill 1989, would have prevented casual supporters (not least those visiting from abroad) from attending games. Taylor further proposed the abolition of the oppressive and, frankly, insulting anti-hooligan fencing and the provision for seating for all spectators. This latter recommendation was met by howls of anguish from traditional fans who insisted that they have the right to stand in the pouring rain being jostled while gingerly handling boiling hot Bovril in an un-insulated plastic cup, but there were plenty of others who thought the concept of paying to get into a game and not having to suffer pushing and shoving and actually being able to see the whole pitch would be a distinct plus.

There was also the view that terracing could be made safe, which is undoubtedly true, but then you have to decide the individual merits of every standing section of every ground in the country – an exercise that would have been fraught with logistical difficulties: as Lord Taylor

FULL-TIME *at* THE DELL

pointed out, pre-Hillsborough, Leppings Lane had been considered exemplary.

Years of glory

This was all in the future. Saints had five glorious years ahead of them, with a cohort of young players who were maturing quickly and blending well with experienced campaigners like Alan Ball, Mike Channon, Charlie George and Chris Nicholl. Some of the football at The Dell was breathtaking. But you cannot please all the Saints' faithful all of the time, as Matthew Engel observed in his *Guardian* report of the Saints v Brighton game of 10 February 1980:

> The moment Southampton scored their fifth goal, the man in the bobble hat in the next seat rose slowly to his feet and headed for the exit. "That's it," he groaned. "I've had enough." He was not alone, for outside Southampton supporters trudged away, in small groups, dolefully discussing what went wrong.
> "That were a shocking miss."
> "That other were Hebberd's fault."
> "Bloody Channon should have had that."
> Perhaps they are hatching a new South Coast answer to the Hampden Roar – the Archers Road Whine.

Having reviewed Saints' 5-1 win, Engel returned, whimsically, to his opening theme.

> West Bromwich are the next visitors, but the Southampton forwards had better watch it; with these fans, if they score more than five, McMenemy could be lynched.

The Dell had never been short of "the hard to please" or, for that matter, "the impossible to please". There is a largish contingent of curmudgeons who can derive satisfaction only from carping on about how bad Saints are. A good run provokes sour facial expressions and Cassandra-like predictions of doom. Quite what satisfaction they derive from this attitude is hard to fathom. Most of them would swim through shark-infested waters to get to a game, and write abusive letters to the *Echo* if they turned up to find it called off. How many of these characters were among the 18,000 season ticket-holders The Dell had in 1979-80 is anyone's guess.

In February, McMenemy called a press conference at the Potter's Heron Hotel near Ampfield. A large press contingent turned up in the expectation that Saints were, at last, to unveil concrete plans for a new stadium. What he actually did was to introduce them to England international and European Footballer of the Year, Kevin Keegan of SV Hamburg, and announce that he would be playing for Saints the next season.

The demand for season tickets went into orbit, but there was little that could be done, other than announce that next season's matches would all be ticket-only. The situation was getting ridiculous. The Dell was taking on an aura of exclusivity.

Keegan's stay at The Dell was memorable. He hit up a great rapport with his former England colleagues, Alan Ball and Mike Channon, both of whom had returned. Channon had come back in the summer of 1979, while Ball was recalled, after an abortive attempt at management with Blackpool, in 1981.

Saints qualified for the UEFA Cup in both 1980-81 and '81-82. Unfortunately, Keegan was not around for the latter competition, having departed in a huff to Newcastle United in the summer of 1982. Mike Channon was off as well, on a free transfer.

Before Keegan left, in fact as soon as the 1981-82 season was over, McMenemy made a signing as significant as Keegan's, bringing Peter Shilton in from Nottingham Forest. Shilton was arguably the best goalkeeper in the world. This was something of a shock. Saints had not been noted for outstanding custodians since Ian Black – the only player ever to be capped for Scotland, while on their books – had left for Fulham in 1950.

Neither expedition into Europe raised Saints' kudos. They exited in the Second Round in 1981-82, having been blitzed at The Dell 4-2 by a very handy Sporting Lisbon. And the next year they went out in the First Round to Swedish part-timers, Norrköping, on away goals. Worse: the morning after the second leg in Sweden, Steve Moran and Mark Wright were arrested following an accusation of rape. The allegation turned out to be false, but it was the low point of a season to forget.

Saints surpassed all previous achievements in 1983-84, running champions Liverpool a close second. On their day, and at full-strength, they were arguably the best team in the country. But quality in depth – with a maximum gate of a little over 24,000, when the other contenders were getting gates of 35,000 plus – was beyond their means. They still took four points off Liverpool, though, drawing 1-1 at Anfield and winning a gloriously competitive game at The Dell with two spectacular goals by Danny Wallace (described in Chapter 28).

It was a commendable attainment, though the faithful could not help but question some inexplicable, if typical, contrariness in form. How could a side as good as Saints lose 2-0 at home to a team as bad as Notts County in November? How come they were held to a draw at an already-relegated Birmingham in May? Worst of all: how could any team play badly enough to lose against Everton in the semi-finals of the FA Cup?

Saints, as ever, one of football's great enigmas.

The 1984-85 season was the best of times, and the worst of times. Saints managed to win their first League game at their sixth attempt, a 2-1 defeat of Norwich City. Then McMenemy found himself at war with a significant proportion of his squad. Reuben Agboola was injured and then suspended by the Club after a night club fracas in town; then Steve Williams and Mark Wright began agitating for transfers. They, too, were suspended. Wright ended up staying, for the time being, but Steve Williams departed for Arsenal in December, at a price well under his true worth – and never played for England again – while Agboola left for Sunderland, and obscurity his skills did not deserve, in January.

It was symptomatic of Saints that, during all the controversy, they sustained the longest unbeaten run, 13 League games, that they had strung together since the 1920-21 season. In March, McMenemy chucked £20,000 at Brighton & Hove Albion for their superannuated ex-Liverpool midfielder, Jimmy Case. Much to everybody's amazement, he turned out to be what is known in coaching circles by the technical term, "a bloody marvel." Saints, against all probability, finished the season fifth and qualified once more for the UEFA Cup. Because of the blanket ban on English clubs, though, they were not able to compete.

At this juncture, Lawrie McMenemy resigned.

As noted above, Southampton had, and continue to have, a stalwart contingent of curmudgeons and a significant percentage of them would not admit Lawrie McMenemy was a good manager if they had their fingers crossed and a primed thermo-nuclear device strapped to their heads, but it cannot be doubted that he had raised both Saints' reputation, and the supporters' expectations, to a level that had not been enjoyed since the heady first decade of the 20th century – a reputation that had been lost in the pea-soupers of time, anyway. Yes, McMenemy was responsible for leading Saints into the Second Division wilderness for four seasons, but he had also led them into the promised land of Europe five times; in particular, he had seen them qualify for the UEFA Cup four seasons out of five. He would be a hard act to follow at the best of times. And the following five years would prove not to be the best of times – not for football and certainly not for Saints.

Chris Nicholl, who had departed from The Dell in 1983 and spent two seasons as player-assistant manager at Grimsby Town, was recruited to replace McMenemy.

His was an unenviable situation. Saints were trapped in a small stadium with no viable potential for significant enlargement; they had been denied lucrative UEFA Cup fixtures; football's attractiveness was not only diminishing but was under a constant barrage of hostile criticism from "right thinking" and "voguish" pundits; and there was absolutely no indication that the situation was going to improve. It was said interminably, around this time, that "football was a slum sport for slum people."

Meanwhile, between the 1981-82 season, in which Saints had finished seventh, and 1983-84, when they were runners-up, the average gate at The Dell had fallen from 21,841 to 18,050.

Nicholl's task was, first and foremost, to cut Saints' wage bill. His problem was articulated in Graham Hiley's "With the Saints" page in the Sports Echo of 8 October 1988. Nicholl was reported as telling the Club's AGM that, when he went into the transfer market, he had to consider the player's salary, as well as the fee:

> In his three years as manager Nicholl has not only changed almost all the players, but also made massive alterations to the club's wage structure to bring it in line with attendances.
>
> There is no way he could justify wages in excess of £150,000 a year to Peter Shilton and £60,000 a year to Mark Wright on gates of around 15,000.
>
> Saints have always prided themselves on their good housekeeping. They insist on cutting their cloth according to their means so when crowds fall they have to cut back on wages and transfer fees.

FULL-TIME *at* THE DELL

In other words, Saints were back to the days in the 1930s and '50s when they went round in ever decreasing circles selling players to pay the wages because of the diminishing gates, and saw them diminish further – but with one important difference. The dilemma now was that the same pattern was being repeated around the country and The Dell was not capable of catering for substantially-raised gates that might, possibly, come if a superstar or two was brought in or, by some implausible trick of fate, football become fashionable again.

It has to be said that Nicholl obtained some remarkable players and produced some great results, but the curse of inconsistency became even more marked under his stewardship than in the 30 years overseen by his two predecessors.

Nicholl's first term, 1985-86, was marked by Saints' centenary, two extended Cup runs and a short but worrying flirtation with relegation. The Milk Cup terminated in a Fourth Round replay defeat by Arsenal at The Dell. The FA Cup saw Saints take on Liverpool at White Hart Lane in the semi-finals. A game which they might have won but for the double misfortune of Mark Wright's sustaining a broken leg and the referee's benign indulgence of Liverpool's persistent employment of the "professional foul". Saints went down 2-0 and it must be said that Liverpool were the better team, however dubious their marking of Steve Moran and Danny Wallace.

League form was fitful. Perhaps exemplified by a 3-2 home defeat by Everton, the match that marked Saints' first 100 years. Everton were, at this time, an unremarkable team, not playing particularly well, but came determined to dampen the celebratory atmosphere. The referee, Mr Cotton of Camberley, was a remarkable referee, not performing very well, and was not in any mood to add to the celebrations either. Which is not to say that he deliberately set out to turn the game into an unpleasant farce, but the effect of his erratic and inconsistent decisions had precisely that effect. Still, as David Bull remarked in his "Eastanders" piece in the *Saints Matchday Magazine* of 20 December, "perhaps we shouldn't expect much of a grown man who can't tie his laces." Indeed, the most memorable part of the game was the referee's repeated attentions to his boots.

Saints got through the 1985-86 season fairly respectably, finishing in lower mid-table. Something of a disappointment given that they had finished among the leaders the previous year. This was, though, Chris Nicholl's first attempt at management, he was a popular former-player and not too many of the faithful were about to cast stones.

Nicholl was given six years to prove himself and never quite convinced either the supporters or, it would seem, the players that he was the man for the job.

His best season was 1989-90, when Saints finished seventh in Division One and pulled off some terrific performances – not least when champions Liverpool were annihilated 4-1, on 23 October, in one of the most

audacious and spectacular games The Dell ever witnessed (exceeding, in Oz's estimation, mere *Roy of the Rovers* stuff). What made the result all the more incredible was that, of the 12 players fielded by Saints that day, five were graduates from the youth team and only three had played First Division football before coming to The Dell. As Roy Facey pointed out in a letter to the *Sports Echo* on 12 December, Saints' team had been assembled for £925,000, a sum that wouldn't have purchased one of the Liverpool first-team squad. The most gratifying performances came from Dell debutant Jason Dodd, at right-back, who had arrived from Bath City the previous March; Rod Wallace; Alan Shearer; and Matthew Le Tissier, a precocious quartet that did not have a season's first-team experience between them. Qualified predictions were already being made in Southampton that Rod Wallace, Le Tissier and Shearer might be England's forward line by the time the 1994 World Cup was played. By the end of the season, it was considered inevitable.

When Chelsea came to The Dell in the early 1990s, a substantial police presence marshalled them into The Dell,
where more police officers were waiting in their new control box, to watch them in preference to the game

Given the previous campaign, the quality of the players emerging through the youth set-up, recruited by Bob Higgins and coached by David Merrington, 1990-91 promised much, but delivered very little – other than First Division survival. Frustration was manifest among the Saintly congregation and the *Sports Echo* letters page was dominated by complaints regarding Nicholl's management skills, ranging from his limitations as a coach to his public relations style.

Limited facilities

As for The Dell, the Milton and Archers ends remained as open terracing; and the "spliced" seating-with-standing arrangements under the East and West Stands remained as they were. The only fenced area continued to be the Archers end: hooliganism, despite a downturn following Heysel, continued to be a preoccupation.

Two contributory factors to the decline in unruly behaviour were almost certainly a realisation, on the part of those prepared to involve themselves in violence at football games (as opposed to those who went intent on inciting it), that beating people up was not just "a bit of a 'laff'"; and, in Southampton at least, improved policing. It was not perfect, because football games at The Dell, as everywhere else in the country, continued to be treated as a public order problem; but the police were, on the whole, polite and friendly, whereas further north, most notably in Luton, attending a game of football seems not infrequently to have been interpreted by the constabulary as an admission of base criminality.

Keeping "peculiar people" behind reinforced fences was regarded as one solution, but it did not prevent hooliganism, merely contained it. Identifying miscreants in a crowd is difficult – which is why football grounds are such a popular resort for poltroons. Thus it was that a close circuit television system was installed in time for the visit of Millwall on 15 February 1986, for a Fifth Round FA Cup tie.

It consisted of three cameras mounted to cover both the ground and the exits.

"They leave no hiding place for the hooligans," Chief Constable (Operations) Richard Stobart told the *Echo* of the day when Deptford's "finest" were expected in town.

Dockers' Corner survived the introduction of a CCTV box overhead,
but would succumb to the Archers "improvements" of the next Chapter

FULL-TIME *at* THE DELL

As for improvements to The Dell itself, these consisted of the usual maintenance to keep it neat and tidy, which it always was, and of up-rating the facilities.

An item in the *Echo* of 19 March 1988, headlined "Streamlining comes to end", more or less summed up the situation. The Club had gone as far as it could "in bringing about major changes." Guy Askham, who had taken over the chairmanship after the death of Alan Woodford the previous month, claimed that

> most of the major things we can do within the ground have been done. We have a very small area of land to operate in and there is little more we can do within the curtilage of the ground

The only way forward, he said, was for the local authority to build a "spectator arena" which Southampton could rent for matches. But having to share with other sports would be a problem and Saints themselves could not afford to pay "more than £6,000 per game using a municipal stadium – not unless people were prepared to pay more money to watch."

Two months later, at a meeting of the City's planning committee, a stadium on the Western Esplanade was back on the agenda. Although the original site near Central Station had since been occupied by a "superstore" owned by the giant retail group, *Toys 'R' Us* , the 40-acre swathe of land, on which the Pirelli cable works stood, was about to become available for development.

The *Echo* of 18 June reported that Conservative councillor, Brian Parnell, had suggested a new stadium could be sited there: "They would only need 10,000 seats." Which went down like a lead balloon with the Labour majority, who considered such a project "pie in the sky". Don Wark told the council meeting, Brian Parnell in particular, that, "People should concentrate on generating wealth before it is actually spent. We must find something that is going to provide money for us to use."

As another article in the same edition of the *Echo* pointed out, it was only because Saints had won the Cup in 1976 that making use of the land between West Bay Road and Western Esplanade was seriously discussed. The original plan was for the retail and leisure complex to facilitate the building of a stadium. Now, "with dreams of football glory fading," a stadium was being considered as a deterrent to potential investors.

Saints' secretary Brian Truscott was surprised by the latest political manoeuvring. He told the *Echo* that the Club, if approached, would look at the idea "with interest." But finance would be a problem: "We've invested a lot of money on The Dell, spending about £2 million over the past ten years." The article ended with the opinion that a new ground "must wait 12 more years at least." Which turned out to be uncannily accurate.

Money was still being invested in The Dell. The pitch was proving a nuisance, subsidence in the south-west corner being the main concern. New drains were installed and the pitch re-surfaced at a cost of £40,000 over the summers of 1987 and 1988. And Saints hit the national headlines in July 1987 when they sent out an appeal for worms. Brian Truscott told the *Echo:*

> There has been no worm activity in the pitch for years … some years ago we had too many of them at The Dell. We treated the soil to keep their numbers down but in doing so we killed the lot. Now we desperately need them back. We are not looking for any old worm. It's the blue nosed earth variety we are after.

A further facility was the conversion of the glassworks in the south-west corner of The Dell's car park into a "community office": an assembly place and social centre for members of the Junior Saints (whose development features in Chapter 26). It would also house the Pools and Youth Development offices. This was officially opened by England Manager, Bobby Robson, in December 1988.

And so to the 1988-89 season. It was not memorable. Some time in the future, children – wearing their first Saints' replica shirt and sitting saucer-eyed on a grandparent's knee – may be regaled by the story of Rodney Wallace racing in pursuit of a ball going wide of the Milton end goal like a torpedo and being brought down by Kelly, the luckless Newcastle goalkeeper; and how the new boy Ruddock, by converting the resulting penalty in the last minute of the game, gave Saints a 1-0 victory and their first win in 21 matches (an event recalled in Chapter 28 by Irene Mitchell).

Yet what will stick in the minds of most Saints' supporters about that season was something that happened well away from Southampton: the Hillsborough Disaster.

It was commemorated at The Dell four days later, when Norwich City visited:

> At 7.24pm Bristol referee Bob Hamer blew his whistle and silence hung in the air. Players, officials and fans remembered those who had paid the ultimate price.
> For a minute the raw, stark scenes of the dead and dying inevitably filled everyone's mind. Turnstiles stopped operating and the late arrivals waited patiently outside.

It was a sombre occasion, as John Hoskins's *Echo* account attests. He further observed that the three exit gates in the fencing at the Archers end were left unlocked: "Nobody expected any trouble – and none came."

The final Taylor Report was published in January 1990. Chapter Two is titled "A Better Future For Football" and begins:

> It is not enough to aim only at the minimum of measures necessary for safety. That has been, at best, the approach in the past and too often not even that standard has been achieved. What is required is the vision and imagination to achieve a new ethos for football. Grounds should be upgraded. Attitudes should be more welcoming. The aim should be to provide more modern and more comfortable accommodation, better and more varied facilities, more consultation with the supporters and more positive leadership. If such a policy is implemented it will not only improve safety. There will also be an improvement in behaviour, making crowd control easier.

19 April 1989:
"silence hung in the air"
for the victims of Hillsborough

The Taylor Report was an intelligent, decent and humane document. It was not received well in many quarters. This was fair enough, as there were plenty of holes that could be picked in his reasoning, but the fact is that there had been a number of intelligent, decent and humane documents produced on accidents at football grounds down the years, which had been received politely and had, to all intense and purposes, been ignored. The reason why Taylor's recommendations had to be enforced was that many football grounds were administered by buffoons. As Simon Inglis argued, in his introduction to *Football Grounds of Britain,*

> it was not Lord Justice Taylor who closed down the terraces… It was the footballing industry, by its own ineptitude. Instead of grasping the nettle and making the safety and comfort of supporters a priority, the majority of clubs abdicated responsibility for crowd management to the police (who treated grounds largely as a law and order issue and every fan as a potential hooligan), while regarding safety as something imposed upon them by the local authority and other outside agencies.

FULL-TIME *at* THE DELL

Football was in desperate need of a revolution. Taylor provided it and, while there were legitimate misgivings regarding such drastic measures, the days of paying good money to be treated like rubbish, and of club directors who believed taking money off people and treating them like rubbish was a divine right, were numbered. And – while I am no less nostalgic about the "good old days" on a heaving Milton end than the most strident traditionalist – it has to be said: good riddance to them.

To be fair to the directors of Southampton Football & Athletic Co. Ltd., it should be said that they had been making the best of a bad job at The Dell for a couple of decades. On a temperate day, for the standing spectator on the new Milton end, there probably wasn't a better place to watch football in the country. As for those caged at the Archers end on a cold rainy afternoon or evening… compliments from visitors are a rarity.

Taylor was correct in his conclusions. This did not make his recommendations any less devastating for Southampton FC. Booted out of Europe in 1985 and now compelled to carry out alterations to their ground that made it even more unviable as a first class venue than it already was. Early estimates of the capacity of an all-seater Dell varied between 12,000 and 14,000.

It appeared that Saints had been bracing themselves for such an outcome. Guy Askham told the shareholders at the AGM on 1 September 1989, that the Club were preparing plans to move away from The Dell, "or transform The Dell." Graham Hiley's *Echo* report of 2 September quoted the Chairman as saying:

> If we are to remain a First Division club of any status then we want a new ground… Land in Southampton is limited and we will need to find the right site and get planning permission.
> The problem with The Dell is…

But we already know what the problem with The Dell was.

Saints were not the only football club that the Taylor report would hit hard. Bringing every stadium in the country up to scratch was going to cost millions clubs had no idea how to raise. Furthermore, even if Saints could find a site and get planning permission instantly, it was unlikely they would be able to raise the money and build a new stadium before the 1995 deadline set for top flight clubs to remove standing areas.

Searching again

The Southampton board set out, once again, to find a potential site. Land in Lordshill, around the Europa Tennis Centre, appeared to have potential; and the Council arranged a meeting at the Oaklands Community School to discuss the matter with local residents. Twice as many as could be accommodated in the hall turned up, all of them angry. The meeting was abandoned and assurances that another would be convened, at a future date, at the Guildhall were given. The date was never fixed and Lordshill was off the agenda. The reason being, according to the 7 April 1990 edition of the *Sports Echo,* not the hostility of the locals, but the cost of the land.

The University playing fields at Wide Lane were also mooted. Advantages: a nearby airport; a railway station, Southampton Airport Parkway; and the proximity of Junction 5 of the M27. There were also two undisclosed acreages under review: "One on the outskirts of the city, one is more central," Graham Hiley revealed. Facilities being considered, along with the 25,000-capacity football stadium, included a 2,000-seater indoor venue for basketball, indoor soccer etc, an athletics arena, all-weather pitches, restaurants, a ten-pin bowling alley and parking for 5,000 cars and 80 coaches.

Meanwhile, football was about to have a revival.

Soon after the Taylor Report was published, analysts noted an upturn in attendances nation-wide. Saints were a case in point: having dropped to an average gate of 14,670 in 1987-88 from 15,810 in '86-87, they rose to 16,038 in 1990-91. Not a spectacular increase by any means – only a little over 1,300 a game – but it did mean that, if The Dell's capacity were cut, there would be a demonstrable loss of income. Not as in the bad old days when the gates closed on the faces of frustrated punters at two or three big games a season, but week in, week out. They were no longer in the position of politicians turning on them and saying there was little demand for the facilities they required.

There was another boost: after a dodgy start, the England football team had a very good run in the 1990 World Cup in Italy and, by the time the ink had dried on all the hyperbole in the tabloids about English yobs running wild in Sardinia and elsewhere in Italy, even the most faithful and gullible tabloid readers began to realise that the vast majority of English supporters had behaved decently.

UEFA was so impressed that it invited English clubs back into European competitions.

There was too another factor in football's rehabilitation: the television viewing figures for Italia '90 were phenomenal. As if by magic, simplistic, supercilious and sanctimonious pronouncements about the national game dried up. By the mid-nineties, many of the game's former detractors were including the team they had supported since childhood in their *Who's Who* entries.

This is not to suggest there was any hypocrisy regarding the decision of Southampton City Council's Labour administration to take up the problem of Saints' desperate need for a stadium. It was pragmatism pure and simple. The World Cup had brought home the simple fact that football was a big deal and that even a moderately successful English club could enhance the image of a city, or town.

On 8 March 1991, Southampton City Council announced that its Environmental Planning Department had assessed 14 sites and had decided that the playing fields at Monksbrook, Stoneham, would be an ideal, or at least a practicable, location for a Community Stadium.

A press release, from the SCC Public Relations and Marketing Unit, reported that the City Council had been working in partnership with Southampton Football Club, Eastleigh and Test Borough Councils, Hampshire County Council, Hampshire Constabulary and the Sports Council for nine months to find a site and that Stoneham would be suitable because:

- It is large enough to accommodate a stadium complex including a football pitch, an athletics track, indoor sports facilities, grass and all-weather pitches and plenty of car parking;
- It is on the fringes of the city next to good existing road and rail links;
- It is a self-contained area which could easily be landscaped to fit in with the existing environment and protect near-by housing.

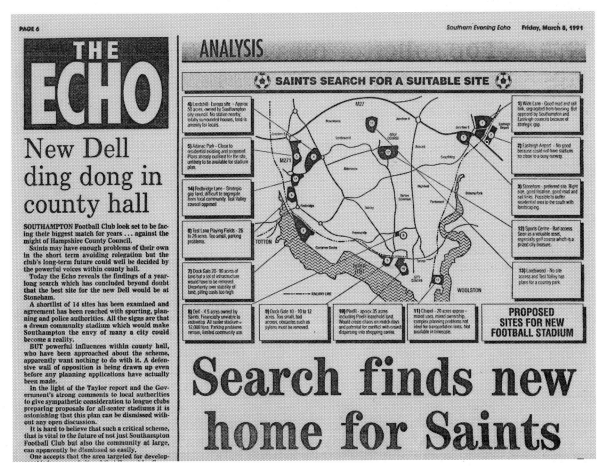

FULL-TIME *at* THE DELL

The stadium complex would be run by a management team representing Southampton City Council, Southampton Football Club, other interested parties and any financial backers. As it would not be a purely commercial site, the City Council could guarantee that the whole community would benefit from the facilities.

The County council has been asked to endorse the proposal in principle, and extensive public involvement in envisaged, together with studies aimed at assessing impact on the environment.

What happened then?
Dear reader, the world went mad.

"The site was unsuitable because…"

Chapter 25
Open Road to Northam

Politician, n. An eel in the fundamental mud upon which the superstructure of organized society is reared. When he wriggles he mistakes the agitation of his tail for the trembling of the edifice. As compared to the statesman, he suffers the disadvantage of being alive (Ambrose Bierce, *The Devil's Dictionary*).

On the official announcement that Monksbrook had been ear-marked for the development of a community stadium, every politician in Hampshire, including many so remote from Stoneham they might as well have been representing some hamlet on one of the outer moons of Saturn, decided to have an opinion on the matter. Given that Southampton was Labour-controlled and Hampshire Conservative-controlled (at the beginning of the debate at least), there was only one stance they were going to take: they would oppose it.

There is not the room – nor is there the inclination – here to follow the political shifts of power within Southampton City Council, Eastleigh Borough Council, Fareham Borough Council, Test Borough Council and Hampshire County Council, or the twists, U-turns, accusations, bad faith, counter-accusations, delaying tactics and plain inanity that Stoneham incited.

In brief…

The site was unsuitable because it was in a "strategic gap" – although it was not: it was in a *proposed* strategic gap". It was unsuitable because it was too close to a motorway junction. It was unsuitable because it was too close to housing in Southampton. It was unsuitable because it was too close to Eastleigh, the centre of which would become a no-go area on Saturdays, because of marauding Chelsea supporters. It would be unsuitable because the floodlights would confuse planes landing at Southampton Airport (a possibility that the Aviation Authority had failed to notice). It was unsuitable because the floodlighting would cause lorry drivers to career off the M27… well, it was just unsuitable; so there.

But mostly it was unsuitable because a council controlled by another party had set out the project.

The level of intellect which Hampshire County Council applied to the project was neatly, and unwittingly, encapsulated by Dudley Keep, who told the *Echo* that "there will never be a stadium on that site as long as I am chairman of the planning committee." So,

"Southampton will have to find somewhere else or stay at the Dell."

The saga reached one of its many nadirs in September 1995, when, as the official deliberations wore on, the *Echo* listed the councillors who had already declared they would vote against Stoneham – before anything was said; before any arguments had been heard.

Among those 29 councillors were the representatives of Kingclear & Tadley, eight miles north-west of Basingstoke; Alton, 16 miles north-east of Basingstoke; Cowplain, well over 20 miles from Stoneham; Andover, a good 20 miles from Stoneham; New Milton, practically in Dorset; Farnborough, Aldershot and Church Crookham, all of which are a good deal nearer the centre of London than Stoneham. One Southampton representative, Norman Best of Bassett, was among this crew. Norman Best, it will be remembered, was a leading advocate of the financially-untenable Western Esplanade scheme back in 1976.

One has to ask: how would a stadium between Southampton and Eastleigh make an adverse impact on the life on the citizens of Cowplain? Or for that matter, Farnborough, Aldershot and Church Crookham?

A further complication came in the shape of local residents. Not unreasonably, they felt that having a football stadium dumped on their doorsteps was not going to enhance their quality of life. Less reasonably, a substantial number of them were not at all interested in listening to arguments that might run counter to their pre-conceived assumptions. In fairness, it should be stated that most of those who were prepared to give Southampton FC and the City Council a fair hearing remained sceptical; it was not as if any of the Saints' directors had started looking for homes in the neighbourhood, after all.

Had Saints been setting the world alight, the spirit of '76 might have been rekindled and they might have got a better hearing, but this was not the case.

FULL-TIME *at* THE DELL

Chris Nicholl was still in charge when the prospect of Stoneham rose on the horizon beyond Portswood as a new Jerusalem, but the side that had promised so much in 1989-90 slumped in '90-91; and when it became evident that Rod and Ray Wallace – especially Rodney – were not to renew their contracts at the end of the season, supporter discontent grew from widespread to rampant. As letters to the *Sports Echo* demonstrate, the criticism of Nicholl was more in sorrow than anger but it was manifest that, as far as the faithful were concerned, he was not the man to lead Saints into the promised land.

The Board had come to the conclusion he was no footballing Moses either. A little over a week after the last game of the season, a 1-1 home draw with Wimbledon on 11 May, he was released from his contract.

Graham Hiley, in the *Sports Echo* of 25 May, observed that there was more to his departure than the disillusionment of the letter writers or the boo boys at The Dell:

> Many of the national press assumed the sale of the Wallace twins was the final nail in Chris Nicholl's coffin this week. Not so.
> His fate was almost certainly sealed with the humiliating 6-2 thrashing at already relegated Derby. If ever a team stuck two fingers up at their manager it was then!

If Nicholl left with any grudges, they have never manifested themselves in public. His restraint was admirable in the circumstances. Within weeks of the beginning of the 1991-92 season, many of those who had lobbied for Nicholl's dismissal relented.

All football managers have their critics, even successful ones. Ted Bates and Lawrie McMenemy came in for some stick over the years; and occasionally it became unnecessarily hostile and even vindictive. None of it reached the extremes that Ian Branfoot had to endure.

Branfoot arrived at The Dell having been, among other things, a youth team coach for Saints, manager of Reading and a coach of Crystal Palace. He had been accused of being a disciple of Charles Hughes, the then director of coaching of the FA. A fair evaluation of the Hughesian footballing philosophy would take a good deal of space to put across; but put simply – and unfairly – it amounted to booting the ball as far up-field as possible

and chasing it. This is not a bad tactic if you have a bunch of super-fit athletes with no ball skills and little intelligence to express, but somewhat counter-productive when dealing with real footballers. Whatever the limitations of the squad, even the most tactically ignorant Saints' supporter could have told Branfoot that his devotion to the "long ball" was, in the circumstances, a mistake. And they did.

It must be said of Branfoot that he had two qualities: he was personable and supremely confident in his own abilities. He also had two over-riding faults: an inability to grasp what made football a great spectator sport; and a stubborn streak that made him blind to the self-evident. He has protested – and his position is faithfully recorded by David Bull in *Dell Diamond* – that he was unduly burdened with the obligation to keep the wage bill down and sell his best players; but this hardly excuses the adoption of tactics that were the antithesis of the beautiful game.

The further the 1991-92 season progressed, the more obvious it became that Saints were a party of round pegs rattling around in square holes. More goals were conceded, fewer goals were scored, bookings soared and those goals that were scored seldom, if ever, emanated from a ball hoisted up-field, but rather from the determination of Alan Shearer or the genius of Matthew Le Tissier, who was establishing himself as one of the country's most outstanding players in the estimation of everyone but Branfoot and England manager, Graham Taylor. Given that Branfoot's preferred role for Le Tissier was wide left in midfield marking his opposing full-back, it is a wonder he made any impression at all.

Disharmony in the stands and on the terraces grew rapidly: before Branfoot could celebrate his first Christmas at The Dell, Saints were being greeted onto the pitch by choruses of booing.

Not unnaturally, those objecting to Stoneham were not averse to raising Saints' abysmal performances in their arguments against the scheme. A mantra was adopted in the suburbs around Monksbrook and in the council chambers of Hampshire: The Dell would be quite adequate for Second Division crowds.

The 1992-93 season saw a whole new, exciting epoch open up for English football (a dubious public was enthusiastically informed) – the FA Premier League. There was also a new television package: BSkyB had bought up the rights to broadcast Premier League games live with a deal worth £304 million, which gave the BBC the rights to highlights.

It was pointed out, quite forcefully in a number of quarters, that not everybody had satellite TV or wanted it. *When Saturday Comes* was especially scathing. Discussing the prospect of subscriptions and charges to watch certain matches, in its July 1992 edition, it posed the question of what would happen if subscriptions did not come up to BSkyB's expectations. Its answer was "hiked up" charges, although increased "admission prices for Premier League matches" would also make up the shortfall. "Either way," it concluded, "fans will be fleeced. Which is, after all, what the Premier League is all about."

Of more concern to regular supporters was what difference the Premiership would make compared with the old First Division. The answer was none at all. The same clubs, bar those relegated and promoted in time-honoured fashion, would be competing, just as they had the previous season, within much the same format as the 14 clubs that had started League football in 1888. The only difference was that, courtesy of BSkyB subscribers and stratospheric advertising rates, the 22 Premier League clubs would be receiving unprecedented incomes, provided they could maintain their place. In Saints' case, this looked progressively unlikely.

Negotiations over Stoneham were getting increasingly tiresome and it was difficult for the Club to know what to do for the best, as it explained in its occasional free tabloid, *Saints News,* in June 1992:

> THE UNCERTAINTY over the future of their ground makes it difficult for Saints to do any more than essential routine maintenance at The Dell. It is clearly not worth spending thousands of pounds on their present home if they are going to be moving in a couple of years. That money would be better invested in the new stadium.

Work would be carried out on the pitch during the summer and £40,000 was to be spent on improving the floodlighting, "increasing the lighting capacity by more than 50 per cent." An extra 40 lamps were to be installed, "but that money will not be wasted because if the club do move to a new ground, the lights can be transported to the new home." There was news on a new ground as well.

Saints had purchased the freehold on RS Southampton's ground near Marchwood, for use as a training facility.

RS Southampton had begun life in the parks' leagues as Road-Sea and had developed, meteorically, into a Southern League force: then, even more suddenly than they had emerged, they folded. The ground was later given the name Staplewood and, having been much expanded, remains Saints' training complex.

The first season of Premier League football was not propitious for Saints. The Dell's gates, against the national trend, declined and a significant number of those still putting in an appearance were openly hostile to the management. Saints finished the 1992-93 season one point clear of relegation. They had actually been mathematically safe from the drop with four games left to play, but it didn't look good on paper. Criticism of their play spread from the letters page of the *Echo* to the sports pages of the national press.

With the Stoneham debate ongoing, the Club had no option but to start converting The Dell in line with the Taylor recommendations. On 1 May 1993, the *Echo* announced that tickets for a place on the terraces – what was left of them – were going up by £1: "to £9 for gold games and £8 for silver." The article continued: "Within hours of today's final whistle against Manchester City the bulldozers move in to begin a £2m rebuilding programme at The Dell."

The spliced bench seating-and-standing arrangement on the terraces under the stands was to be dug up, new terracing laid and tip-up plastic seating installed. The Archers Road end was to be completely demolished and re-built. And the office accommodation around the main entrance was to be extended. Secretary Brian Truscott and his merry band of administration staff were to be condemned to a summer of conducting business from Portakabins in the car park.

Mr Truscott told the *Echo* of 11 May:

> Our priority remains relocation. We are still hoping to move to a new ground at Stoneham and, hopefully, that would mean we would not have to carry out next summer's work on the Milton end. But we cannot guarantee getting a stay of execution so we are having to press ahead with work now to ensure we meet all the obligations of the Taylor Report by the start of 1994-95 season.

FULL-TIME *at* THE DELL

The Archers end is demolished to make way for the
"Bike Shed" which can be seen (right) from the vantage point
of the Milton end, on the occasion of the final home game of 1994,
the last day you could stand on it

A word of sympathy here for director Brian Hunt who, in his capacity as a builder, had been overseeing construction and deconstruction work at The Dell since the early 1970s. "I am the man," he told me wearily in April 2001, "who reduced the Dell's capacity from 30,000 to 15,000. Of course, that wasn't done overnight."

The new Archers end was not an architectural masterpiece. In the circumstances, there appeared to be little point in pushing planning permission for anything radical. A cantilevered roof was erected and 1,800 seats were to nestle snugly beneath.

This proved to be a marvellous place, acoustically. A relatively few people could make one hell of a noise from it. Unfortunately, the Archers remained the designated "away end" and visiting choirs were at something of an advantage when it came to singing their team on.

The new Archers end had a further facility: a two-storey control box from which the police, with a battery of CCTV monitors, could scrutinize the crowd. It was another gratifying result of the Taylor report that the emphasis on the policing of football grounds was now on crowd safety, rather than crowd control. The difference is subtle, but important.

The new Milton

The following summer, with Stoneham still a matter of deliberation and procrastination, the Milton end was razed and – to employ a hackneyed phrase – like a phoenix from the flame, was born anew. Simon Inglis, in the 1997 revision of his *Football Grounds of Britain,* is

worth quoting on this last component of The Dell's metamorphosis from small, awkward and inadequate to smaller, less awkward and inadequate:

This has always been the unwieldiest part of the ground, measuring barely 5m from corner to pavement in the east corner, extending to around 30m in the west corner. Trying to convert such an area into seats, and cover it at the same time, therefore presented an unlikely challenge for the design team which consisted of the local architects, WH Saunders and Sons, and the structural engineers, Jan Bobrowski (who were responsible for Arsenal's North Bank Stand, plus many other stands, such as at Watford, Twickenham and West Ham).

The resulting stand is an unnerving collection of angles, all appearing different from various parts of the ground. The seating tier is a steeply raked, single deck which forms a just discernible parabola (to improve sightlines). This holds 2,897, arranged in bands of red and white seats. As the rows fall away towards the south-east corner, a sheer grey wall caps the rear.

But the cleverest bit is the roof's goalpost construction, but with the horizontal truss not parallel to the goal-line, as is normal, but angled away from the pitch, so that when viewed from inside the ground, even though the roof fascia is dead level, the truss appears to be twisted. Most unnerving, but fiendishly effective.

The Milton end has been demolished to make way for seating, which is being shown off (above) by Brian Hunt

Mr Inglis (who, being an Aston Villa supporter, can be nothing other than objective) signs off with a philosophical statement – one that should have been taken to heart all over the county:

> The best scenario for the residents of Stoneham would be for the Saints to plummet down the League, thereby negating the need for any more capacity than they already have at the Dell. But that would still leave the city, the region, and the whole South without a single decent venue between the coast and London. As the rest of the nation enjoys Euro '96, while the likes of Bolton, Sunderland and Stoke look forward to their own new stadiums opening in 1997, what can the south coast look forward to? …
>
> If that is what the people of Southampton and Eastleigh want, then fair enough. No one north of Gatwick is going to shed any tears. But if Stoneham should go ahead, they will not regret it. Just ask the people of Huddersfield and Middlesbrough.

Inglis made this very same point to Hampshire's politicians at a seminar on Stoneham at Winchester Guild Hall in March 1996. The *Hampshire Chronicle,* in its report of this event, considered Inglis's contribution to be "one of the most thorough presentations on the proposals so far." Both sides were heard – "the residents who are bitterly opposed and supporters who are keen to have a new home for the Saints" – but the *Chronicle* felt that "the overall impression was determinedly upbeat, in favour of a facility at Stoneham."

This seminar came about because the Liberal Democrats were holding the balance of power in Hampshire and were at least willing to give the scheme a fair hearing. The *Hampshire Chronicle* was correct: it really was an informative day.

An artist's impression of what all the fuss was about

Meanwhile, Saints' form continued to deteriorate. It seemed impossible that they could play worse in the 1993-94 season than they had in the two previous campaigns but, by the first week of December, they were three points and one place ahead of bottom of the table Swindon, with 14 points from 20 games.

FULL-TIME *at* THE DELL

Another impossible thing Branfoot had done in the interim was make himself even more unpopular with the supporters. These had basically broken into three main camps. The first were sitting on their hands, the second had come close to rioting in the car park after a defeat at home to Leeds United in September and the third just stopped coming.

On 15 December 1993, the *Echo*'s headline, after Queen's Park Rangers' 1-0 victory at The Dell, was

DELL CROWDS HEADING FOR 37-YEAR LOW

Reporting on how the jeers had been "comparatively muted… after a fourth consecutive defeat," Graham Hiley sardonically offered a dual explanation: "there were fewer home fans and… the rest could not be bothered to boo, such is the atmosphere of despair."

It was bad enough that the maximum capacity would soon be a tad over 15,000: the "official" gates were only 200 over 13,000 and falling.

Managerial merry-go-round

By this time, a fourth camp had emerged. The Board might have identified them with those who had laid siege to the car park, demanding *We want Branfoot out! We want Branfoot out!* And, beleaguered as they were, the directors might have regarded it as more of a fourth column than a camp; but, following the post-Leeds carpark protest, the editorial teams of the Saints' fanzine, the *Ugly Inside,* decided to get organised. A well-publicised meeting was held at the *Captains Corner* pub in Terminus Terrace. It was too well-publicised. Many people were unable to get into the hostelry; and of the 200 who were estimated to have squeezed in, many at the back could not hear what was going on at the front. It was agreed that something had to be done and that a boycott was not the answer.

Thus it was that the Southampton Independent Supporters Association was born. The main protagonists appeared to be Clive Foley, Perry McMillan and Nick Illingsworth of the *Ugly Inside,* but the editors of the other

The silent majority prepares, on 24 October 1993, for the game against Newcastle (described in Chapter 28),
in which the magic of Matthew Le Tissier postponed the inevitable

two Saints' fanzines, *Red Stripe* and *On The March,* were certainly enthusiastic about drumming up membership and supporting SISA's initiatives. There were other, less openly iconoclastic, committee members; but when a journalist was looking for a quote, it was the perspectives of Foley, McMillan and Illingsworth that usually ended up between inverted commas.

The Board took stock of the situation and then, in December, invited Lawrie McMenemy back to The Dell to take up the post of Director of Football. His first game at the helm, on New Year's Day 1994, attracted the largest gate of the season, over 17,000, but was, nonetheless, inauspicious: a 1-0 home defeat by Norwich City; and Francis Benali was sent off. Worse came the following week when Port Vale, of Division Two, came to The Dell and snatched a 1-1 draw in the FA Cup.

Clive Foley, in issue 29 of the *Ugly Inside,* recounted:

> Port Vale was truly the last straw as another mass red
> card protest had the desired effect. You can point to
> all sorts of reasons but one which I believe to have
> had a profound effect were the people protesting all
> around the Directors' box. It is very easy for
> Directors to ignore car park protests when they are
> entertaining guests in their sound proofed lounges. It
> is not so easy to ignore angry season ticket holders
> when they're waving red cards in your face.

On Tuesday 11 January 1994, Guy Askham invited Ian Branfoot to see him and handed over the metaphorical pearl-handled revolver. Whether Branfoot was sacked or resigned has never been firmly-established. What has been placed on record, by both Guy Askham and Lawrie McMenemy, is that "fan protests" did not influence the decision to replace Branfoot: it was down to results.

Whatever, Southampton took on a semi-carnival mood that evening, as cars drove up and down Shirley Road hooting their horns for joy.

By 22 January, Alan Ball, manager of Exeter City, had been re-canonised and was sitting in the dug-out for a potentially torrid Premier League fixture at Newcastle. Ball's record as a manager was hardly inspiring, although he had got Pompey into the old First Division for a season back in 1987-88; but the situation was so desperate that the faithful – and even the comparatively faithless – would have welcomed a stuffed yeti as a saviour.

Saints beat Newcastle 2-1. The winning goal: a 22 yard free-kick by Matthew Le Tissier, in the 83rd minute.

Saints' results did not improve dramatically, but they became a pure joy to watch. Le Tissier was given a free role and anything – even avoiding the drop – looked possible. Thanks to a 3-3 draw at West Ham on the last day of the season, it was: Saints finished one point clear of demoted Sheffield United.

They were tenth the following year. It all looked very promising, but then Alan Ball was lured away to Manchester City and reserve team coach Dave Merrington was elevated to manager. He was popular with the supporters, but he was somewhat conservative compared with Ball. Given the hard time many had given Chris Nicholl, criticism was muted. Saints left it until the last game of the season to save themselves yet again in 1995-96.

On 5 May, Southampton, Coventry and Manchester City, all on 37 points and all at home, were contesting the final relegation place – and Saints were playing Wimbledon, a team not noted for taking prisoners. As the last seconds ticked down, Saints, playing abysmally, were hanging on to a goalless draw, Coventry were drawing 0-0 with Leeds United and Manchester City had clawed back a two-goal deficit against Liverpool. An extremely pensive Dell crowd awaited news from Maine Road and Highfield Road, especially Maine Road.

Seconds ticked out like years... news rippled around the ground that City had drawn... the final whistle went ...there was a mass out-take of breath, followed by the most frantically celebrated dire, scoreless game in The Dell's long and exceptional history – probably? Saints, having got minus 18 goals as opposed to City's minus 25, were still in the Premier League.

On the afternoon of 14 June, Dave Merrington was sacked. Even those who believed that Merrington was not the man for the job were shocked by the manner in which the dismissal came – not least because his wife had been very seriously ill.

Graham Hiley observed, in an unusually confrontational *Echo* article of 15 June, that "twelve years of loyal service [had been] wiped out in a terse two-paragraph statement...The man who brought through Matthew Le Tissier, Alan Shearer, the Wallaces and many more appears to have been ruthlessly discarded like litter left on the terraces."

FULL-TIME *at* THE DELL

Next up for the management merry-go-round was Graeme Souness, the man who had revolutionised Glasgow Rangers and, according to Scouse devotees, come close to destroying Liverpool, before having an interesting time in Turkey with Galatasaray. He came, he saw, he conquered Manchester United 6-3 and left.

Reading Souness's autobiographical account of his brief encounters at The Dell one is left in little doubt that the reason for his departure was his perception that the Club was being transformed around him as he was trying to settle into the job; that and his suspicions regarding the new regime.

Late in 1996, Southampton Leisure PLC (formed by the Saints' directors) took over Southampton Football & Athletic Co. Ltd. and then did a reverse take-over deal with a company called Secure Retirement and announced they were to float the new company on the Stock Exchange. The *Echo,* of 15 January 1997, revealed that the Club's shareholders "have seen the value of their stake in the club increase an incredible 480-fold in just 24 hours." The deal gave Secure Retirements a 38 per cent stake in the Club and three of its directors, Rupert Lowe, Andrew Cowen and David Jones, appeared on the Board. Lowe became Southampton Leisure's chairman.

In April 1997, Guy Askham stood down as chairman of Southampton FC, and Lowe became chairman of both the Club and the holding company (by default, he says in Chapter 27 below), with Askham retaining his position as deputy chairman of the plc.

The more vocal of Saints' supporters, not least SISA, were not over enthusiastic regarding the development. For a start: "who was Rupert Lowe?"

Souness was uneasy with the situation too:

> We are talking about Southampton here. Their great strength over the years was their image as a family club and it had helped them through several crises. When the going got tough the fans rallied round and there was a bonding between them and the players which certainly helped to stave off the relegation threat on several occasions. Now that was all about to change and the supporters were quick to voice their disapproval. The news caused a storm through the town and hostility against the takeover began to mount. Public protest meetings were held, the media got involved and there were investigative TV

programmes on the subject as they attempted to unravel the details of the proposed takeover.

Having been introduced to Rupert Lowe, Souness was less than impressed. The new regime "were not aware of how a football club is run or were determined to implement their own ideas. At that stage I decided to grit my teeth and just get on with my job." In short, he did not like the cut of Lowe's jib. His "plummy" accent was certainly a minus point in the manager's estimation.

If there was outrage at the way Merrington had departed The Dell, it was restrained compared with the response to the resignations of McMenemy and Souness.

That Souness did not fancy working for Lowe can hardly be doubted. He was, however, big enough to reappraise him objectively at a later date. He decided, on a visit back to The Dell, that Lowe had changed: "He is not the first – nor will he be the last – businessman to discover that the world of football bears little relation to any other industry."

The occasion was the final game of the 1998-99 season, an emotionally-draining game for the chairman, which he describes in Chapter 28. Observing Lowe's palpable commitment that afternoon, Souness concluded that he had indeed become "a passionate football man", which was "good news for Southampton."

It would appear that the reason that Lowe was brought in was that the old Board, or at least Guy Askham, believed he had the gumption to make Stoneham a reality – both in getting the HCC to pull their finger out and in raising the capital to finance it. And to this end, things did appear, at long last, to be turning in Saints' favour. As Brian Hunt recalls, the Department of the Environment had actually overruled Hampshire's planning veto way back in 1994.

Hunt is fully convinced that, had the Liberal Democrats remained the majority party in Hampshire and their Pompey-supporting Leader Mike Hancock remained a leading influence in County affairs, Stoneham would have gone through. It is ironic, he observed, that the Conservatives were returned to power in Hampshire in 1997, on the very same day that they were ousted nationally.

By this time, Eastleigh was actually warming to Stoneham; but, with the *ancien régime* ensconced within the walls of Winchester Castle, it was back to square one.

What was now becoming a poisoned chalice was passed to former Everton defender and Stockport County manager, Dave Jones.

Progress under Jones was not spectacular; but under his guidance, Saints played neat, if traditionally erratic, football. And, given the budget he had to work with at The Dell, there was good reason to believe he would be just the man to build a side capable of challenging the top clubs, rather than fending off the other relegation nominees – when, and if, the extra gate money from playing in a bigger ground was available to him. There was one possible flaw: he did not appear to have quite the same, unquestioning, faith in Le Tissier that united the majority of supporters.

His second season, 1998-99, climaxed with Saints still needing to win the penultimate game of the season, against Wimbledon at Selhurst Park, to keep out of the bottom three. Wimbledon were no softer a touch on 8 May 1999 than they had been on 5 May 1996. The game was deadlocked in the 69th minute when Le Tissier was brought off the bench. Three minutes later, he planted a free-kick on Beattie's head and Saints were one-up. Eleven minutes after that, Le Tissier scored directly from a corner, or everyone thought he had; after intense study of the video playback, the goal was credited to Wimbledon's Robbie Earle. The following Saturday, at The Dell, Saints dispatched Everton by two goals to nothing. The perennial predictions of oblivion from the nation's sporting press had been confounded once again.

By the end of the previous, 1997-98, season, the Board might have been forgiven for approaching the City Council for planning permission to extend the Milton Road end over Milton Road, which had, by now, been converted into a *cul-de-sac* by the strategic placing of elevated brick constructions (in which the Council were attempting to cultivate plants) a few yards along the street from the rear of the East Stand. And maybe even propose a new Archers end, which would overhang the pavement.

The Dell remained pretty much as it stood in 1994, when the impressive, if somewhat *bijou*, all-seater Milton had been completed. As bright as a new pin, benign and fearsomely atmospheric.

After a crusade, mounted by SISA and other Saints' supporter organisations, the "Bike Shed", as the Archers had become dubbed, was allocated to the home crowd. It was quickly occupied, for the most part, by the more vocal, and musically-talented, of the Saintly host; and its reputation as an "end choir" earned renown from …well, it was well-regarded in Southampton.

New Dell?

The Board had not quite given up on Stoneham. Despite the fact that, as Brian Hunt admitted, as soon as Hampshire came back under Conservative control, "it wasn't dead, but it was most unlikely to go ahead – I think." But he was not blaming them. "Not totally, that is not my way … I think everybody did their best. I have no doubt about that at all." Mr Hunt is far too kind. I switched the tape-recorder off and asked if he cared to elaborate "off-the-record." He did, but not to the extent that he would in any way denigrate Freddie Emery-Wallace, Norman Best, Dudley Keep or anyone else who had laboured diligently to prevent Saints competing on an even playing field.

"Anyway," continued Brian Hunt, "Southampton [City Council] stepped in and said, 'you aren't going to get anywhere with this,' and offered us the St Mary's site."

The story broke on 8 July 1998. The *Echo*'s front page headline was COMING HOME?

On 30 July, the *Echo*'s leading story was

NEW DELL IS COMING HOME

One does get the impression from reading the stories – in between the lines – that the idea was mooted with the idea of forcing the HCC into making a positive decision on Stoneham, since Eastleigh, under the leadership of Keith House, were now getting enthusiastic about it. The City Council's decision to back the move to Northam was "unanimous", which is not to say that all present were happy about it.

Southampton's Council Leader regarded the turn of events as a "tragedy" for Southampton: "Whatever is done at Britannia Road will not be the first-class regional facilities we were working for at Stoneham." And he lashed out at Hampshire County Council and Eastleigh for blocking the Stoneham plans. "They will stand condemned," he warned.

An *Echo* article of 11 September 1998, devoted to the annual report of Southampton Leisure Holdings PLC, revealed that Saints had "spent nearly £700,000 chasing the doomed dream of providing a new Dell and

FULL-TIME *at* THE DELL

community facilities at Stoneham." Reporter Steve Flux quoted Rupert Lowe's observations on the negative return on the investment, which he put down to "a lack of political will" on the part of Eastleigh:

> Unless the borough and the county take a more realistic view of the magnitude of the Stoneham project, the outlook for the scheme is bleak and political obfuscation and intransigence will rob the region of a sporting focus.

At the time the above was published, Saints looked more than capable of dropping out of the Premier League. Dave Jones summed up the situation in his "Manager's Message" in the programme of 22 January 2000:

> There is no point in trying to hide behind excuses for our performances in the last two matches. They are simply not acceptable.
> But while I'm obviously disturbed at the situation there is certainly no need for panic. With 17 matches left, a lot of football remains to be played, plenty of time to put things right.
> That is not to say there is any complacency in the camp. Rest assured, everyone at this club is working extremely hard to improve results.

This was not a convincing message in the circumstances. The side may not have been world-beaters, but they were playing below their potential and the natives were getting restless again. Arguments relating to problems on the pitch were complicated by factors relating to Jones's previous occupation as a social worker on Merseyside. During the summer of 1999, he had got embroiled in an investigation regarding allegations of child abuse and before the close season was out he had been charged. As the winter dragged on, a trial date was awaited. Whether this was the reason that his team selection and tactics appeared to have gone to pot is impossible to say. Jones was not the most openly cheerful of personalities or the easiest of minds to read. He kept more or less the same dour expression whether Saints were winning or losing by two goals.

Richard Chorley, a spokesman for SISA, told the media he thought Jones should be given "leave of absence" until the trial had taken place. Jones was

indignant. The Club were indignant on his behalf … rumours, as they always do when the manager appears to be in a tight spot, began to circulate.

As it turned out, those "Manager's Notes" of 22 January were the last contribution Jones made to the programme. Despite the fact that Saints beat Everton 2-0 that day, Rupert Lowe gave him leave of absence until his trial was over. Jones was not inclined to be graceful about the turn of events.

Glenn Hoddle was installed *pro tem*, among much tabloid glee regarding faith-healing and Hoddle's own singular brand of Christianity. Whatever, it worked. Saints, despite a few hiccups, including a 7-2 slip at Hoddle's beloved White Hart Lane, marched into fifteenth place, and stayed there for most of the rest of the season. It was not European qualification form, but it was soothing for the nerves after some of the nail-biting conclusions of previous years.

In December 2000, Dave Jones, much to everyone's pleasure, left the court without a stain on his character. There was no question of his returning to Southampton, however. He had claimed, vehemently, from the point he had been given his "holiday", that it was a sacking by any other name; and it almost certainly was.

By this time, Hoddle had ably demonstrated his qualities beyond doubt. A team that was substantially the same as the one that had struggled under Jones (who could be said to have fared better at buying players than coaching them) was sitting pretty in ninth place. Nobody thought they were quite up to qualifying for the UEFA Cup, but that Saints would be playing Premier League football in their new stadium when the 2001-2002 season kicked-off was a near certainty.

At which point, Hoddle packed his bags and went off to manage Spurs. His decision to dump Saints was not well-received.

The stadium that Saints would be moving to was "St Mary's". The project had been made public in March 1998. The finance had been found, old Northam Gasworks had been demolished, the debris and polluted soil removed, an archaeological survey carried out and, despite some torrid weather, a new, state-of-the-art, football stadium was emerging, which everyone was confident would be ready by August 2001.

In nearly eight years of wrangling with the councils of Eastleigh and Hampshire, at the cost of nearly £¾ million

An exciting goal-mouth incident in the final game, as seen from the Upper West Stand

(the price of a useful Swedish midfielder), Saints had got nowhere. Dealing with Southampton City Council, Saints would get a 32,000-capacity ground in two years and 11 months. There is a moral here – one that is too obvious to spell out. The sad fact is that Hampshire had the opportunity of getting not just a first class football ground but a facility catering for everyone wishing to partake in sport and which would have been the envy of the nation. They ended up with what they started with: second-hand football and cricket pitches with decrepit changing rooms; and a stream full of household junk. It is even sadder when you consider that the County Council counted this as a triumph.

Coaches Stuart Gray and Dennis Rofe took over first-team management. They had a tricky run-in and Hoddle's perfidious decampment precipitated a distinct dip in Saints' form. The two final fixtures of 2000-2001 were both at home and, even though it appeared Saints would bow out with a whimper rather than a bang, there was no shortage of those wishing to savour the unique atmosphere for the last time and pay final homage to the greatest little football ground on the planet.

Which brings us back to where this story started. Unpredictable and contrary to the last, Saints beat the two top teams in England.

The icing on the cake: to complement Watty Keay's opener at the Archers Road end in September 1898, Matty's touch, turn and volley into the Milton end goal in May 2001.

You couldn't write it.

FULL-TIME *at* THE DELL

You've seen the goal in Chapter 1. James Beattie chases Matty to celebrate it.
And in the End… the scene after the Southampton and Arsenal players, and most of the crowd, had left The Dell behind

Part II (Chapters 26-30)   edited by David Bull

The Memories: introduction

This part of our book realises, in a round-about way, an ambition I first articulated 20 years ago.

In the close season of 1981, I watched two Southampton players, Trevor Hebberd and Malcolm Waldron, playing for the Diplomats in Washington DC. I came home, compiled a match report and sent it to Malcolm Price, Southampton's Commercial Manager, who'd been saying he wanted fans to be more involved in *their* club. Which is why my accompanying letter suggested that he assemble a rota of fans who would contribute a regular fans' page to the programme; and, if he agreed, then would he please consider my dispatch from Washington for inclusion?

The unanticipated outcome was that I got taken on in a rota of one. I'm now enjoying my third stint in that role. It's a privilege. But it's a privilege of a different kind – the kind I had in mind 20 years ago – to be able to *share* the pleasure of reflecting on Saints' fortunes and related matters. Which is why I have been so pleased with the feedback on *Match of the Millennium,* the book in which a dozen fellow-supporters joined Bob Brunskell and me in compiling reports on games of yesteryear and clearly demonstrated, for all to see, a widespread ability to write about their team.

The emphasis, here, is on "write". There were suggestions that this part of our farewell to The Dell should be an *oral* history. But that would have taken a lot longer to complete than inviting fans to write to us with their memories, under one or more of four headings – their First Game; Favourite Game; Worst Moment; and what they would Most Miss – and, following feedback, a fifth category of Weirdest Moments. Home games only in each case.

We received a pleasing number of responses – 78 fans (made up of 75 "customers", as they've started calling us, and three directors) join me, in Chapters 27-30, to recount their memories under at least one of those headings. I apologise if there is no evidence of memories you sent us. The most likely explanation for this is that your contribution was on Dave Juson's computer when it was stolen and that our various attempts – in the Saints programme and elsewhere – to advertise for re-submissions failed to come to your attention.

Of the responses securely to hand, there were plenty on "first games" – sufficient for a bumper chapter – and enough for a shorter chapter on "favourite games". But there were few takers either for "weird moments" – fans' memories recorded elsewhere suggest that away-day travel throws up the best anecdotes in that regard – or for "worst moments" (such suffering is best kept to yourself, maybe?), so it made sense to weave these two potential chapters into one.

Each of those three chapters of recollections is presented without editorial comment. The first two are clearly in match order. The third is as chronological as it can be, given that a particular match is not always identified. The remaining chapter, on what we'll most miss, is differently arranged: as I considered the recurrent themes in the contributions before me, I felt they could best be woven into a narrative. Chapter 30 is my attempt to weave it.

Chapter 26 follows a similar format. I'd become interested in mascots when I was loaned, for use in *Dell Diamond,* a photo that showed two little mascots welcoming Stanley Matthews to The Dell in 1963. My fascination with this rather special breed of fan might have stopped there, had it not been for a fortuitous introduction to June Sexton (*née* Nixon), a mascot of the 1930s. Kicking myself into pro-active mode, I then set about tracing June's predecessor and to locating a mascot or two from the species that we know today. The outcome is an incomplete history of 75 seasons of mascots at The Dell, but it felt, nevertheless, like a story that should be included at the start of Part II of this book, before we get into the memories of us fans who have recalled The Dell from our various vantage points on the non-playing side of the perimeter track (if you overlook those fantasists I've indulged as they sneaked into Chapters 27-30 their memories of *playing* there).

Having introduced you to Chapter 26, let me say a few words about the material received for the four chapters that follow it. You were queuing up to tell us about your Dell debuts. I have included all of your stories, some of them more severely edited than others. The principal challenge to any editor of this kind of chapter – and this goes for most of the chapters that follow – was how to avoid repetition. Well, nobody would get away with the cliché that he or she

FULL-TIME *at* THE DELL

was "hooked" upon first seeing the Saints at The Dell. But it would have disturbed the flow of many a memoir if I had ruled out repetition of how a newcomer to The Dell first climbed the steps of the West Stand or the Milton Road terraces – the two most-favoured points of entry, it seems – and had his or her first sight of the pitch and its surrounds. We didn't define "first" game so, while some treated reserve fixtures as a prelude to their first real game, others counted a reserves match, or even a schoolboys or youth game, as their Dell debut. And the odd contributor to Chapter 27 was permitted to write about the first game he or she could remember, as opposed to the first game actually attended.

Chapter 28 was much more straightforward: just tell us about your favourite game. Any submissions that included two or more games were, by and large, discarded – although Duncan Holley and I each slipped in a mention of our second-favourite game, the 4-1 drubbing of Liverpool in 1989. Perhaps surprisingly, that game never came to us as a first choice. And nor did the 6-3 win over Manchester United in 1996. The list of favourites is much less predictable than that. It reflects what different games meant to particular fans – maybe for a personal association, the extreme case being the incident that inspired Norman Gannaway to pick a 0-0 draw. And there's even a defeat – by Manchester United – from Ian Carnaby. Brave man.

The worst and weirdest moments are even more personal. Me, I especially like the near-juxtaposition of two tales about sweets: manager Dodgin made off to the dug-out with a bag of sweets belonging to two young fans; and, years later, trainer Gallagher was handing out sweets from the said dug-out. It must have been a big bag.

Acknowledgments

Over and above the debts acknowledged in the Preface, I want here to thank those who have contributed specifically to this part of the book. For a start, that means all of you who sent us your memories. I was happy to negotiate, with the two or three who wanted to, as to how their contributions should be edited, but most of the contributors approved an edited version of what they had submitted and gave me further licence to modify – which was just as well, given the tinkering so often needed, at the design stage, to fit the agreed text to the space available on any particular page.

The material for Chapter 26 was obtained by face-to-face interviews with Bert Baker, June Sexton (*née* Nixon), Alan Smith and Dave Warn; by correspondence and/or telephone conversations with Helen Adlem (*née* Cross), Morris Baker, Jack and Noel Broomfield, and Brian and Crawford White; and by recourse to Kevin Phillips's autobiography. Most of these loaned me photos from their personal collections, as acknowledged at page (iv). I am grateful to them all and to Gary Chalk and Brian Truscott for relevant introductions. Although we were unable to trace David Thackray, he left his rattle behind when he moved from Eastleigh, which enabled Gary Chalk to photograph it.

The majority of the photos in Chapters 27 and 28 are from the *Echo,* while most of the rest were borrowed from contributors: see the schedule at page (iv). You may wonder at why some games are generously illustrated while others have no picture at all. This was partly determined by considerations of layout but moreso by availability. For instance, I could put my hands on copies of all four goals scored in my own favourite game (and hereby invite you to admire my self-restraint in using only two of them), while there was one free-scoring match for which we had six sheets of negatives but could find no action of any interest. One photo I was determined to use is of the Doncaster game on page 175. Just look at that tiny crowd in the rain and consider where the Saints have come from there.

We had said we would present free copies of this book to the best response to a particular invitation – "First Game"/"Favourite Game", etc – but the unbalanced nature of the responses, with so many fans focusing on their first game, made that difficult. So we selected two contributors – Marian Thomas and Mark Fickling – for the outstanding quality of their writing across several chapters, in which they remained closer to the word-limit than some other essayists and left me with that feeling – a recurrent pleasure of the editing role – of "if only I could write like that!" Finding two or three runners-up from among a dozen or so other nicely-crafted pieces would have been invidious.

The object of the exercise, though, was not to award prizes for the few, but to offer space to the many. This is to say "thanks again" to all of those who responded, providing proof not only for my original supposition that Southampton has plenty of able scribes among its fans, but also of how much you *care* about the past of our club that is so passionately preserved in the next five chapters.

Chapter 26
Mascot Tales

Open any football encyclopaedia or A-Z at the "M" section and you ought to find an entry – somewhere between MANCHESTER UNITED and MATTHEWS, Stanley – on MASCOTS.

Ought to, but not in any of the compendia on my football shelves, you won't. And, even among the Football Association's collection, librarian David Barber and I could find only one entry, in *The Virgin Book of Football Records* of 1996, on the subject. This runs to three paragraphs, two of which are about World Cup emblems – dating from the lion that was "World Cup Willie" in 1966 – which were little more than logos representing the competition, as opposed to the *team* mascots that I have in mind here. The third paragraph is about a team figure, Ken Bailey, the England mascot who used to dress up like John Bull and "parade around the ground [including The Dell, occasionally] before games."

Younger fans are unlikely to recognize, in that quoted final phrase, a description of a "mascot", whom they doubtless expect to lead out the team; join in the salute to the crowd and maybe the kick-in; and then witness the toss-up and be photographed in the centre-circle. Older fans will recall, however, the days when a young mascot not so much paraded, as ran, around the ground before the kick-off, sometimes pausing to pick up coins thrown in his or her direction.

The history of mascots at The Dell essentially concerns those two models, the run-around kid whose origins seem to date from the establishment of the Supporter' Club in 1926; and the multi-purpose mascot, a creation of the Junior Saints, formed in 1978. That said, there were, from the early days, occasions – mainly for Cup-ties, it seems – when the run-arounders also got to lead the side out (or at least to greet them as they emerged onto the pitch) and/or to join the toss-up.

This chapter is about these youngsters in their various manifestations of the last 75 seasons at The Dell – to the exclusion of the two anonymous young men who dress up as what the Club calls "Character Mascots", known as *Super Saint* and *Sammy Saint,* and flop about the field before the game. A very recent innovation for Southampton, these figures are redolent of the time when Millwall had a lion as their "mascot". Bert Baker, who was

probably the first child to run around The Dell, adorned as what became known as a "mascot", remembers that lion as the only other mascot he met in his days as Southampton's prototype.

The run-around mascot

Resident in Woolston, in the house where Bert still lives, Mr and Mrs Baker liked to get themselves and their sons decked out for the Southampton Carnival. Morris would be a clown, while his younger brother, Bert, was Felix the Cat, after the comic cartoon character.

It seems that the 1926 Carnival coincided with a Saints home game, with the consequence that the five year-old Bert arrived at The Dell, that afternoon, as Felix, accompanied by Morris the Clown. Their gear took the fancy of some of his mother's fellow-Committee members of the recently-formed Supporters' Club. Bert and Morris were in business. Morris didn't think much of cavorting about as a clown, but had a couple of years of walking round, in civvies, at half-time with the Board announcing the winning numbers of the *Penny on the Ball* competition that the Supporters' Club had instituted – "except when it snowed hard. Father took it round then, because they threw snowballs at it."

So Bert – or, rather, Felix – had the stage to himself as the sole mascot. His duties were simple. Beyond scuttling round that narrow track that bordered the Dell pitch, "two or three times round the ground; and at half-time," he recalls collecting the ticket stubs from the *Penny on the Ball* vendors and hurrying them to the Supporters' Club room in a house in Burton Road, behind the East Stand. And never mind snowballs – he was used to having money thrown at him. His mother handed it on to the South Hants Hospital – a gesture that resulted, he believes, in his receiving free (pre-NHS) treatment there, as a teenager with appendicitis.

He was sometimes allowed into the dressing-room, where he had no favourites that he can remember – "everybody seemed to be nice" – and would then run out

FULL-TIME *at* THE DELL

with the team. He cannot recollect any pattern to this, save that "if they were going to take a photograph, they'd take me out with them."

It seems that the mascot had a good chance of being photographed – home or away – when Saints were Up for the Cup. And, in the period we're talking about, that wasn't very often. After reaching the semi-final in Bert's first season, Southampton would progress beyond the Third Round only once more, until 1946. We have photographic evidence of his being at Bradford for the Third Round tie in 1930.

As Bert recalls, the travelling fans "arrived at Bradford very early – about six o'clock, I think." The early arrival was typical, Morris says, of the trains laid on by the Supporters' Club: it seems that the way to charter a cheap train at that time was to travel through the night. This left you with lots of time before the kick-off, but the home supporters would often lay on hospitality: "whichever team we were playing," Bert recalls,

Bert Baker lines up, as "Felix", at Bradford before the team's annual Third Round defeat.
He is seen here with skipper Stan Cribb, in front of Rowley (left) and Stoddart

some people used to come and pick up some of the supporters and take them to their house… at Bradford some people were there and met us and took us … – as far as I can remember – to a little railway cottage. It was quite close to the railway. They had a big fire in there and they cooked us a lovely breakfast… The same used to happen at most football clubs in those days.

He has particularly fond memories of being entertained in Plymouth and of the reciprocal hospitality provided by his parents for Argyle fans. The annual Third Round exit in 1931, this time at Sunderland, also stands out for both of the Baker boys. As Morris recalls, this was when the train went off-course somewhere in the Midlands: "the 'Ghost Train', they called it." That was also the year, if Bert remembers correctly, when he gave up being Felix. He thinks it was soon after this – at least one *Echo* piece

on this development seems to date it, indeed, from 1933 – that the Supporters' Club produced another innovation: Bill Bray, a founding committee member and a *Penny on the Ball* vendor, would dress up in red-and-white and be a cheer-leader. It was not, however, the 36 year-old Bray who was photographed greeting the team onto the Dell pitch for a Fourth Round cup-tie in 1935, but a new mascot: three year-old June Nixon.

Birmingham City came to The Dell in 1935
for Saints' only FA Cup Fourth Round appearance of the 1930s.
June Nixon hands Bill Adams a good luck charm – which didn't work.

In fact, of all the moments in her life as a mascot, it is that of greeting the captain on such an occasion that June most strongly retains:

> The captain always used to kiss me and I probably gave him a paper horseshoe or something like that. And I can always remember their smell – of liniment – and most of them were chewing gum. That stayed with me. I can smell it now, the liniment they used to put on.

June cannot remember, though, how she came to get the job. Her maternal grandmother – who lived in Cook Street, opposite St Mary's Church, where June was born – was a fan, that's all. Like her predecessor, June ran round the pitch before the game and again at half-time, having money thrown at her – to the extent that when she completed her circuit, she "used to be weighted down with pennies" – and appears to have had her main photo opportunities when travelling to the west Midlands: so many old photos of the Saints were taken at Villa Park or the Hawthorns.

June Nixon joined in the line-up at Villa Park on 15 January 1938.
Standing (left to right): King, Sillett, Warhurst, Affleck, Woodford.
Sitting: Kingdon, Bevis, Bates, Hill, Holt, Osman.

After that Dell photograph from 1935, the next evidence

we have of a mascot at a home Cup-tie is for the visit of Blackpool in 1959. We see (*left*) the mascot accompanying the cheer-leader on the rattle. Goodness knows who this mascot was – the *Echo* caption-writer wasn't saying and Dave Warn, who was recruited by Bill Bray around this time, does not recognise him – but it was seemingly now the practice for the cheer-leader to find himself a young side-kick. Dave recalls how

somebody down the road gave me a placard to wear, which said UP THE SAINTS. And I was stood under the clock at the Archers Road end – in the corner where the half-time scoreboard used to be – and, one day, Bill Bray … saw this placard that I was wearing and he asked me if I had red-and-white Saints gear. And a rattle? The following home match, I did four laps round The Dell. I also used to go up to the Milton end and the chant used to be *Two-Four-Six-Eight. WHO DO WE APPRECIATE?* Sad, really!

Sad? Speak for yourself, young man. Responding to Bill Bray's invocation to join in that chant was the very essence of learning to be a Saints fan. Yet, according to Commentator, reflecting on "war-cries" in the *Echo* of 13 December 1947, the *Two-Four-Six-Eight* rallying cry had been borrowed from Saints speedway fans at the Banister Stadium. He regretted that supporters at The Dell seemed "to have lost the art of war cries" and effectively called for the revival of the "Yi! Yi! Yi!" shout about which we learned from Dave Juson in Chapter 6 above.

David Thackray's rattle, in particular support of the half-back line of Wimshurst, Knapp and Huxford

While Bill Bray led the chanting, his young sidekick (when he had one) was expected to accompany him on a rattle – a rattle supplied, as Dave Warn points out, by the mascot himself. Along with his kit. Dave's gear was "made-up" from assortments: "I had black shorts from the school team. I had socks from the school team. They weren't red-and-white hoops." His Saints shirt needed to be purchased, though, from Toomers, the sports outfitters. "My mum always used to say 'He's the mascot. Do I get a discount?'" She always did. But, then, Mr Walter Toomer was a Director of the Club, so it would have been churlish indeed to have refused her. When interviewed by the *Echo* in December 1961, Dave revealed that her haggling was worth 2s 3d (11¼p) to Mrs Warn.

Her son's mix of duties was much the same as for Bert Baker and June Nixon – although at half-time he walked behind that huge canvass target used for collecting money for the *Albion Band* and was expected to pick up stray coins and toss them into this oversize collecting contraption. But he got to keep the penny that the referee would give the mascot after the toss. The Saints goalkeeper, Ron Reynolds, was a lot more generous than that: "he always seemed to look after me. He always used to give me a couple of bob."

Dave had occasion to run out with a succession of captains. He got along with Cliff Huxford, even though he found his Gloucestershire accent impenetrable – "I could never understand a word he said" – but thought Terry Paine unsupportive. And then Tony Knapp took him "under his wing." After a while, he agreed to share his role with David Thackray, whose mother had accosted him: "They used to stand down by the trainers' dug-out. I was running round one day and she stopped me and asked me if her son could run round." So he did. They would come out and run round together, but Dave retained his part in the toss – and the penny that went with it, though he recalls that "when they played Portsmouth, it was always a two-bob bit." *Why?*

Mascots David Thackray (left) and Dave Warn (with his rogue socks) join in the welcome to Stanley Matthews in May 1963.

This lasted until 1965, about the time that Bill Bray retired, too. So Saints appear to have gone into the First Division with neither mascot nor cheer-leader. It was after their second promotion to the top flight in 1978 that Commercial Manager, Malcolm Price, set up the Junior Saints (who became the "Young Saints" in 1985 and "Team Saints" in 2001), which would provide the basis for a new breed of mascot.

Mascot for a match

Alan Smith, of the Commercial and Promotions Team, soon came up with the idea of a "members' benefit" for Junior Saints: they would all be eligible to be drawn, at random, to be a one-match mascot (although more than once a member's name has come up for a second appearance). He could remember how he'd seen mascots running out – at Fratton Park, his home-town ground – and regretted that this practice had "disappeared from the game. I thought 'Why can't we do it again?'"

The "it" in his scheme involves a lot more than running out. On reporting to the ground, the lucky youngster receives a replica kit (for keeps) and four tickets for the game. Then it's off to the dressing room for photographs with, and autographs from, the players. After a tour backstage, it's back to the dressing room door, to meet the team coming out and to lead them onto the pitch. Then, as the players kick in, the mascot hopes to get a touch. Finally, there's the toss-up and a place in a photo line-up, when the captains and officials are joined occasionally by a visiting mascot (perhaps once in every five games) and always, in recent seasons, by the Saints "Character Mascots" (initially just *Super Saint,* but later by his offspring, *Sammy Saint,* as well).

Initially, the Club bore the costs of this exercise – "lots of clubs charge," according to Alan Smith, now Head of Community Relations – but then found a succession of local businesses willing to sponsor it. *Wadham Stringer* came first, *Marshall Rolfe* had an especially long spell and *Redstone Telecom* were the final benefactors at The Dell. Alan enjoys ringing the lucky "winner": "The joy at the other end of the 'phone is always so special. The euphoria!" To his surprise, his overtures are sometimes rejected, though.

One parent who had reservations was Brian White: his son's spasticity would prevent him completing the mascot's routine. But Alan reassured him that, even if eight year-old Crawford could not join the kick-in, he could participate in the early stages of the mascot's day when Leeds came to The Dell – and were beaten 2-1 – on 22 November 1980. Brian remembers the "terrific conducted tour" that the Community team gave his son, while Crawford still enthuses about his reception in the dressing room by so many of the players – he mentions Golac, Waldron, Moran, George and Wells and has "very strong memories" of how "Ivan Golac was particularly good."

A year later, Saints again beat Leeds, to the *chagrin* of one of their celebrity fans, Jimmy Saville (seen, *right,* with that day's mascot, Helen Cross from Gillingham in Dorset). Helen was being filmed for *Jim'll Fix It* – not because she had written to seek Jim's intervention but because the producers of this TV programme had asked Alan

Smith to fix it, by arranging for the duly-drawn mascot to write the triggering letter retrospectively. Helen recalls

Chapter 26

Five stages in the pre-match routine of a modern mascot, as demonstrated by the four youngsters in matches identified in the preceding column or overleaf.

Clockwise, from the top left, they are:

Dressing room: Crawford White with (left to right) Steve Moran, Ivan Golac and Malcolm Waldron.

Leading out: Helen Cross leads the way for Kevin Keegan and Steve Moran

Saluting the crowd: Kevin Phillips with David Armstrong (left) and Peter Shilton

Kicking-in: Jack Broomfield accepts Dave Beasant's invitation to shoot at him.

Tossing-up: Jack Broomfield joins (left to right) Steve Bruce (in his first-half shirt), the match officials, Barry Venison and *Super Saint*.

FULL-TIME *at* THE DELL

how Saville reacted, as Saints went on the rampage, on the eve of her 10th birthday, to win 4-0: "He was bantering with Lawrie McMenemy – 'Couldn't you have left beating Leeds to another time?'" Unlucky Jim hadn't fixed it too cleverly.

If beating Leeds in successive seasons provided the fun 20 years ago, it must have been a special privilege in 1996 to be drawn as mascot for one of those two memorable wins against Manchester United. Jack Broomfield was the lucky one on 13 April 1996, when United turned up in invisible grey shirts (an afternoon recalled by his father, Noel, in Chapter 28 below). Pulling into the Dell carpark two hours before the kick-off, Jack "felt like a player arriving for the game." And, before long, he had changed into his red-and-white stripes and was in the home dressing room: "I couldn't really believe that I was there, rubbing shoulders with Matt Le Tissier and the rest of my heroes and listening to the dressing room banter." Then,

after a break, pitch-side, while the manager gave his team-talk, Jack was back with the team and "running down those steps and out onto the Dell pitch, alongside Barry Venison." The extent to which the mascot gets to join in the kick-in will vary and Jack was most fortunate: Dave Beasant invited him to take shots from penalty-spot range and he scored twice.

That wasn't enough to get him a trial, but several Junior/Young Saints have indeed gone on to become players. Only one of them has been a mascot, though: in October 1985, 12 year-old Kevin Phillips led the Saints out against Queens Park Rangers. We may all of us think it a pity that he never trotted out wearing Southampton's first-team shirt. But, hey, bringing on young players is not among the objectives of a scheme that has come a long way from those carnival days, 75 seasons ago, when a wannabe footballer called Bert Baker ran round The Dell dressed as a comical cat.

Chapter 27

My First Game

23 January 1915 v Millwall, Southern League, 4-2

The first game I can remember going to was the day Saints got promotion to the Second Division [6 May 1922] by beating Newport 5-0. I was 11. I distinctly remember that match, because we were going up from the Third Division (South).

George Muir, who was in the original Saints team [though see the debate, on the line-up, in Chapter 3 above] and who eventually became a referee and a Director of the Club, was my Headmaster at Mount Pleasant School. He went to London with another director and phoned the result through [of the game at Loftus Road that Plymouth Argyle had to lose, if Saints were to stand any chance of promotion]. We all waited at the end and when they came through, we knew we were there.

Four year-old Maurice Hockley (ringed) at his first game with his father

I used to tell people that was my first game at The Dell. But then my daughter started getting interested in the length of time I'd been supporting Saints and she found this postcard, that had been in the family for years, of me with my Dad when I was four. We lived in Rockstone Lane, about five minutes' walk from The Dell. We were at the Milton Road end – they called them the "Bob Bankers". You paid a shilling to stand on the bank: there wasn't much in the way of terraces.

Maurice Hockley, Maybush.

12 September 1936 v Bradford City, Division Two, 2-0

I was 12 years-old and very excited when my elder brother asked if I would like to go with him to The Dell. I can't remember the match in detail, but I was very impressed with the Bradford goalkeeper and told my brother so. Not long after, he signed for Southampton. His name was Sam Warhurst.

I later worked for British Gas for 39 years, more than half of which were spent on what is now the site of the St Mary's Stadium. So, as I sit with my grandson, watching the team my brother took me to see 65 seasons ago, we look out onto the pitch that was for long my place of work.

Sid Barfoot, Hedge End

28 January 1939 v Newcastle United, Division Two, 0-0

I was six when my father, on leave from the Royal Navy, took me to The Dell for the first time.

There are just a couple of things I recall about the game: the result, 0-0 and the fact that the Saints did get the ball into the net, but it rebounded out and, in my child's wisdom, I assumed this was the reason it was disallowed although I still do not know why.

My next visit was for a war-time game against Watford in September 1942. But not with my father, who had lost his life on *HMS Hood* in 1941. That pre-war game against Newcastle was, alas, the only time we went to The Dell together.

Brian Smith, Eastleigh

FULL-TIME *at* THE DELL

25 December 1941 v Bristol City, League South, 5-2

I remember very little about this Christmas morning game apart from the fact that three spectators were asked to play for Bristol City, who had arrived several men short. One of these, Jack Waterman, was a Brockenhurst player. The rest of the Bristol City team turned up by half-time. The reason they were late was that one of their cars had broken down *en route*.

Peter Ansty, Brockenhurst

11 March 1944 v Chelsea, League Cup (South), 1-5

To a 13 year-old boy already obsessed with anything related to football, this was an occasion never to be forgotten.

The accompanying adult on the train from Lymington was an uncle, Ron Veal – an Aston Villa supporter to such a degree that, in his later years, the Villa club extended to him a matchday invitation with full "guest of honour" trimmings.

There was for the boy something of incomparable magic to be guided by his uncle through pushing crowds up flights of stairs until able to look down onto the pitch itself. A consumer, from the age of eight or nine, of any scrap of football knowledge that chanced his way, he was already as familiar with some of the names on parade as he was aware of those who sat near to him at school.

Of the Chelsea players on view, there was none more widely known than Joe Payne. On 13 April 1936, when converted from half-back to centre-forward by Luton Town, he obliged with 10 goals against Bristol Rovers. The nickname "Ten Goal Payne" would last his career and beyond.

And the boy would soon have the much-treasured opportunity of meeting two of the Southampton players of that afternoon. Scoring for Lymington CC against Southampton Touring Club, he would have the thrill of being at tea with a visiting XI that included not only Don Roper and Albie Roles from the side that had lost to Chelsea but also the former Saints footballer, Arthur Holt.

If the match of March 1944 itself was generally memorable for Payne's adding three more goals to his tally, it is for a number of features – including the promise of young Scot Jimmy Bowie in the Chelsea forward line and of Eddie Shimwell, later of Blackpool and England, guesting at right-back for Southampton – remembered by the boy.

This was not only the first professional football match he had attended but also as far as he had ever ventured from home. It proved the start of an unswerving affection that would persist for the last 57 of Southampton Football Club's 103 seasons at The Dell. It would be optimistic indeed to anticipate as long a stay at the new ground of 2001.

Norman Gannaway, Lymington

29 December 1945 v Chelsea, League South, 7-0

Debut 1: Living in Lymington, my father Walter was one of the earliest employees at the Wellworthy piston ring company and was drafted, during the war, to Salisbury to help start a new factory there. I was a 15 year-old pupil at Brockenhurst Grammar School when, on the last Saturday of 1945, my younger brother Peter and I joined Wellworthy workmen on the works coach going to The Dell.

The visitors, Chelsea, were a team to be respected, especially with the redoubtable England centre-forward Tommy Lawton in their line-up. I remember his tall, lean figure, supremely fit, with his dark hair parted in the middle and slicked down with Brylcreem.

Southampton could seemingly do no wrong for, against all expectations, they were three-up at the interval. The restart could not have been more dramatic. In an obviously rehearsed move, the ball was kicked from the centre-spot to Ted Bates and next out to Bill Stroud, from whose cross Doug McGibbon scored without a single Chelsea player having touched the ball.

Doug McGibbon made the headlines (as below), assisted by team-mates pictured
with him on the opposite page (Stroud, top; and Bates, bottom left)

6-goal McGibbon scores in 4⅗ sec. —the fastest-ever

DOUGLAS McGIBBON, the Southampton centre, will only
remember the match with Chelsea—and not only
because he scored six goals.
One of the six was scored 4 3-5
secs. after the start of the second
half—more than halving the record
held by Iverson, who, playing for
Villa, scored 9 3-5 secs. after the
kick-off in the match with Charlton
on December 3, 1938.

The referee's stop-watch timed the goal at four and three-fifths seconds, a record. Lawton, who hadn't moved from the centre-circle, was convulsed in laughter. When my brother and I returned home, father inquired of the score. "Seven-nil," we replied. "Did they lose by that many?" he asked, then stood in disbelief when informed it was the other way round, with McGibbon bagging six of them. A memorable match and a memorable launch into a lifetime in local sport, including 40 years as sports editor on the local *Advertiser & Times*.

Brian Down, Lymington

Debut 2: Although Winchester-born, I was an Army child. So I spent my young life, including the War, abroad, ultimately as an evacuee to Australia. My most impressionable years having been given over to cricket and Australian Rules Football, I returned to Winchester in the summer of 1945, only to join the Regular Army as a Boy entrant of 14. Home for Christmas from Catterick Camp, I was taken by an uncle to The Dell.

As we left the ground, I asked him "Are Southampton the best team in the country?"

"No," he said, "but they are my team." And they have been my team, too, ever since – as a regular visitor to The Dell in the '50s and '60s, though latterly from afar.

Bill Harvey, Helston, Cornwall

1 November 1947 v Birmingham City, Division Two, 2-0

It was Charlie Wayman's debut and I was just 12. After the game, I went to the carpark to get his autograph. In my six weeks' summer holiday, I would spend most days at The Dell, watching them train. Ramsey, Bates, Ellerington, Rochford... I soon had all their autographs. But in the final season at The Dell, when I became 65, I was still collecting autographs in the carpark, as I had done for 54 seasons.

Ray Mursell, Bishops Waltham

23 October 1948 v Leicester City, Division Two, 6-0

At the age of 10 and against my parents' wishes, I joined my chums, Rhody Denham, Mickey Nuts and Tommy Whittaker, on the 47 bus from Winchester to watch the Saints for the first time.

We stood in the children's enclosure at the Archers Road end, West, on a sunny afternoon, and saw Charlie Wayman score five goals. Afterwards, we enjoyed beans on toast at Charlie's café before returning home.

Our parents found out when Mickey Nuts, who later became a C of E minister, told his dad. I was not allowed to leave home for the next few Saturdays.

But that did not stop me supporting the Saints, any more than living in Kent has prevented me being a season ticket-holder for the past 15 years.

Roger Gledhill, Maidstone

Charlie Wayman scores the first of his five, which was hailed,
by the *Echo*, as his 100th goal.
But that ton included 30-odd war-time goals, including five for
Portsmouth, that are excluded from "official" counts.

FULL-TIME *at* THE DELL

27 December 1948 v Nottingham Forest, Division Two, 2-1

I'd become a fan six months earlier when Mum's brother – never a follower of football and who today denies all knowledge of this aberration – took me to watch Salisbury City play Arsenal Reserves. There was no way Dad was going to induct me on a Saturday: as a bricklayer, he worked for his firm in the morning and moonlighted many an afternoon, sometimes taking me along to pour the water into his sandcastles from which mortar would materialise.

But now it was Christmas and Southampton were at home on the day after Boxing Day. Don't ask me how long I'd been following the world of football beyond Salisbury that existed for me in the *Daily Express* and *News of the World,* but I can remember an incident from January 1948 and the Fourth Round of the FA Cup. I was by then eight years-old and clearly fancied myself as a football forecaster. Taking the following Saturday's fixtures, as listed in the *News of the World,* I would underline my predicted winners. I'd tipped Blackburn to win at Soton – obviously a non-league outfit I'd never heard of – but when Uncle George explained the abbreviation, I went home and revised my forecast.

Correctly, as it transpired. Not that I knew anything about the Southampton side – either before or after the Forest game. I had a good view from down near the wall, but the only player I remember seeing that afternoon is Eric Day, the outside-right with whom the crowd joked when he came to take a throw-in. I enjoyed the way the adults around me joked among themselves, too, even when they tore up one of their programmes (vandalism horrified me even then) in order to draw the names of the ten forwards (those were the days!) and pay up on anyone who scored. You'll gather it all left quite an impression. Much more than anything that may have happened on the pitch.

Even so, my Christmas treat was like getting a puppy from Santa. It was for life.

David Bull, Bristol

23 April 1949 v West Bromwich Albion, Division Two, 1-1

My father, home on leave from the Merchant Navy, decided it was time to introduce me to the glorious game of football. In other words, to his beloved Saints. Just a small girl, I skipped along, clutching his hand, his white knotted handkerchief on my head to protect me from the heat of the blistering sun.

As we made our way along Archers Road, surrounded by hundreds of other fans, I felt very excited and very grown-up. After being in the ground for a while, though, and with the crowd growing quickly around me, I began to feel very hemmed in. I looked around at the sea of faces that seemed to go on forever and suddenly a feeling of sheer terror swept through me. I started crying, almost hysterically, and begged my father to take me home. The next thing I remember is being lifted and passed from person to person until I stood on the track surrounding the pitch. I ran as though my life depended upon it and could hear people calling out and whistling as I passed. I must have looked an odd sight – a small girl with an improvised sun hat, running like the wind, making for the nearest exit.

Fortunately, we lived only a few hundred yards from the ground, so I was soon home safe and sound. My father, on the other hand, did not fare quite so well. He received a telling-off from my mother for taking me in the first place.

That, I regret to say, put me off going to football for life. It was not only my first, but also my last, visit to The Dell.

Joan Bushrod, Waterlooville

17 March 1951 v Grimsby Town, Division Two, 5-1

I was only a toddler – well, three-and-a-half – and not really interested, but my uncle was a keen supporter and persuaded me and my cousin (of about my age) that we wanted to go with him. We stood on what seemed the vast expanses of the Milton Road terraces. It was a strange place for a small kid with all those concrete steps rising high up in the corner by the West Stand. My cousin and I ran up and down the terraces countless times all through the afternoon – or maybe it was only before the game started? All I remember about the football was that there seemed to be a goal every few minutes and each time the crowd made what seemed a helluva noise. Afterwards, we walked home to our house in Chapel and I recall sitting in front of the television that evening – we had a set even then – and seeing the football results. I suddenly thought to myself, "Wow! I was actually THERE!"

Dave Marden, Midanbury

29 December 1951 v. Sheffield Wednesday, Division Two, 1-4.

Although I had always supported the Saints, charmed at a distance by the exploits of Charlie Wayman, I was 16½ when I first saw them play. Although we lived only 30 or so miles away in Liss, this was (and still is) a rotten journey; and, as I went to a rugby-playing school, where Saturday morning lessons were part of the regime, getting to games at The Dell was impossible until I left school.

My enduring memory of my first game is of Derek Dooley, ably supported by a right wing of Jack Marriott and Albert Quixall and by Redfern Froggatt and Alan Finney to his left. The pitch was very heavy. The world-renowned B.M. Griffiths was the referee. Saints had most of the play and, I thought, played pretty well

All of this was eclipsed, though, by Derek Dooley, who scored two of Wednesday's four goals. On each occasion, he ploughed through the mud, through the home defence and past Mr Griffiths, with Henry Horton and other Saints defenders trying to hang on to him like despairing rugby players – all to no avail.

Dooley was wonderful that day. Sheffield Wednesday went on to win the Division II Championship, scoring 100 goals, of which Dooley claimed 46 in only 30 games.

John Wood, Petersfield

20 April 1957 v Barnsley Boys, English Schools Trophy Final, first leg, 1-0

If a team had a goalkeeper so good that he was impossible to score against, then world football domination would surely be theirs. Such a thought exercises the mind of seven year-olds about to begin a life a football addiction and here was I at my very first Dell game, witnessing just such a phenomenon.

Bob Charles had the advantage of considerable bulk, allied to great agility; so why, I demanded of my father, was he not in the Saints first team? – and, if England picked him, then the World Cup was surely a foregone conclusion.

I was amazed to hear that Bob had been beaten in the return leg. The trophy was to be shared. Bob never did become the world's greatest 'keeper, but he had a long run in the Saints' promotion team of 1960 and won a Championship medal; so he must have been a bit special, this goalkeeper whom I'd recognised as a future first-teamer.

I wonder if youngsters in Brazil were being similarly impressed by a teenage sensation who was to make a major contribution to winning the 1958 World Cup? What was his name, now?

John Parsons, Bassett

The Southampton Schools team of 1957 show off the Pickford Shield, the English Schools Trophy
and one of Bob Charles's England caps.

FULL-TIME *at* THE DELL

28 August 1957 v Walsall, Division Three (South), 4-1

Love came to me late in life. I was already 18 when first I took that magical trip through the Milton Road turnstiles. It was a blind date for, although my uncle had taken me to see Leicester City when I was 10 and living in Leamington Spa, I had gradually lost interest in football. But now, five years after we'd moved to the Southampton area, a friend suggested we go to see the Saints. I was not too keen to watch Third Division stuff but we were at a loose end that evening, so I agreed.

Immediately we entered the ground, the atmosphere overpowered me. There was a big crowd, 17,242, and we were tightly packed on the terraces. The noise and excitement was new to me, as was the passion when the ball hit the back of the net. We tumbled down the terrace in a way that would have horrified Taylor and his Committee. It was like being part of a tribe, all intent on the same aim – the destruction of the enemy.

The referee was Alf Bond, quite famous in those days and distinguished by having only one arm. From the start, Saints put on a tremendous attacking display. Don Roper, then in the twilight of his career, scored a cracking goal which was shortly followed by another from John Hoskins. However, the highlight was a marvellous individual goal from Derek Reeves who, just before half time, ran at terrific speed from the half-way line to slot the ball past the Walsall 'keeper. The second half was just as good, but with only one more goal from Hoskins and a reply from Hodgkisson of Walsall.

The most impressive player was Terry Paine, my exact contemporary, just starting his first full season with the Saints. His brilliance was evident even in those early days and, in my opinion, he and Mick Channon were the most exciting players out of all those who have graced the Saints these last 44 years.

I was truly smitten and for the next 35 seasons I hardly missed a home match. The Saints and I may since have drifted apart but it was just a temporary separation, not leading to divorce. I hope I still belong to the tribe which, I'm pleased to say, my sons have joined. One of them now sits with me at St Mary's – but being in a seat far from the action is not the same as in those far-off days, for which I still yearn, of excitement on the terraces.

Alan Cookson, Bursledon

2 November 1957 v Northampton Town, Division Three, 2-1

I arrived at The Dell at the rather late age of 13 years. Born and brought up in Winchester, I had spent my formative years following Winchester City. The 1950s were halcyon days for the Hampshire League and City were among its best teams, with regular gates of up to 1,000 and – for some of their wonderful runs in the Amateur Cup – of as many as 3,000.

They say the north-east is the hot-bed of football; but, in the 1950s, Hampshire in its own smaller way could rival the north for football fever. That was certainly true for me in that decade. From my first memory of the Infant School playground, life revolved around the round-ball game … next playing for my Junior School and then the Secondary School house team … evening games in the local park or on the roads under streetlights when it got dark … the thrill of getting that wonderful magazine, *Football Monthly*, every four weeks, then later *Soccer Star…* winter nights at a friend's house, watching big European matches on *Sportsview* with Peter Dimmock… and then the highlight of the fortnight, the trip to Airlie Road to cheer on Winchester City against the likes of Alton Town, Cowes, Fareham Town, Newport and Salisbury. No wonder Saints couldn't get a look-in. Who needed Division Three (South) mediocrity?

But then, suddenly in 1955, a young lad named Terry Paine made his debut for City. Such was his impact that, within a couple of years, he had signed for Saints and was in their first team. My mates and I were now very keen to see this City star playing for Saints. Which is why, early in his first full season, my friend, John Stepney, and I travelled in great anticipation on the No 47 bus to Stag Gates and then walked on to The Dell.

I don't remember much about the game except the feeling of awe at being there to watch this higher grade of football. But it obviously struck a cord with me and my affections switched – and remained when I moved to Bristol in the 1960s. I often wonder what happened to my friend John. We all know what happened to Terry.

Dave Adlem, Bristol

Chapter 27

25 April 1959 v Doncaster Rovers, Division Three, 1-1

It was wet and windy as the 12 year-old boarded the 13A bus at Bassett Green and paid his tuppeny fare to the conductor. He'd been struggling to keep his right-wing place in the school team but today he is going to see the professionals. He'd seen them before but only in the *Pathé* newsreels at the cinema, when glimpses of Cup Finals were shown. Twenty minutes later, he is walking down Archers Road and through turnstile No. 31, where boys can get in for a shilling and a programme can be got for 4d.

It's the last Saturday of the season and fewer than 6,000 have turned out in the continuous rain to watch mid-table Saints play already-relegated Doncaster on a quagmire of a pitch. So there is plenty of room for the new recruit to try the touch-line wall, decide against it and join those sheltering under the East Stand.

The *Albion* brass band gives way to the players and the

A brave few of the "crowd" of 5,782 had gathered at the Archers end to see a John Page free-kick tipped over, while Stephen Cheffy joined those "sheltering under the East Stand"

Saints defenders are soon left floundering in the mud as Fletcher, the visiting centre-forward, ploughs through it and squeezes the ball between Tony Godfrey and the far post. Injured in this action, Saints' left-back, Tommy Traynor, limps out to the left wing. Both goalkeepers are kept busy as the red-and-white striped shirts and the blue ones become a uniform shade of brown. Terry Paine uses the shallower areas on the right wing to display his trickery and in the second half it's Traynor who hobbles into the area to head the equalizer.

And that was it! Except the youngster being left to count the cost-benefits of the afternoon: one shilling and sixpence, a bit of a cold the next day and a life-time supporting the Saints…

Stephen Cheffy, Crawley

30 January 1960 v Watford, FA Cup Fourth Round Replay, 1-1

I couldn't see much. Mainly legs in front of me, and behind me, and above them burly bodies.

Between the bodies I caught an occasional glimpse of a patch of green, with red and white-striped men chasing a ball, too often foiled by other men (in yellow?). It was my first visit to The Dell, or to any professional game for that matter. I was with my father, not the most enthusiastic football watcher (he preferred his balls egg-shaped) but he obviously recognised his duty to his eldest son.

My memories of the game are, as I say, sketchy. One or another player was pointed out to me as "famous" but it didn't mean much. I know the visitors went ahead and I remember thinking, in the second half, that it showed very good sportsmanship that Watford, having scored their goal, were letting Saints (as I learned to call them from the voices around) have their turn at attacking. Unfortunately, all that attacking was at the Milton Road end – which perhaps explains why that was the only time I ever stood in the Archers.

My father, a tall man, took mercy on me and lifted me up (although I must have been too big to be on his shoulders). So I could just about make out that, at last, all the red-and-whites came back to the near end while everyone shouted and cheered. I knew enough about the game to realise that "we" had scored.

Despite further attacking, we did not score again. And I rather think we lost the replay. Although exciting, the experience was too frustrating to make it instantly addictive and it was not until secondary school, and the vagaries of the alphabet placing me next to a devoted supporter called Smith, that I was tempted by, and eventually hooked on, the drug which, despite long periods of abstinence, still has the power to drag me across land and sea to watch a "collection of muddied oafs" (as Kipling put it) kicking leather.

David Sweet, Belgium

FULL-TIME *at* THE DELL

29 October 1960 v Norwich City, Division Two, 2-2

I was fortunate. My baptism, as an eight year-old taken by my father, was a stirring match. It creates quite an impression on one so young. The roar of a large and largely partisan crowd... the Saints in their stripes as red as blood contrasting with Norwich City in their yellow and green, the badge of a Canary at their breasts... and the commanding green-jerseyed figures of Ron Reynolds in goal for us and Sandy Kennon for Norwich.

The football matched my anticipation. The crowd obviously approved, some of them thundering their feet against the wooden boards of the West Stand towering high above us as I watched open-mouthed from a vantage point some of us younger in years were able to find underneath.

I grew instantly familiar with names such as Terry Paine and John Sydenham and the rest of Saints' goal-hungry forward line. Time and again, Paine and Sydenham streaked away down the flanks, while the stocky figure of George O'Brien and the blond curly head of Derek Reeves together gave a defence, extremely well marshalled by City skipper Ron Ashman, no rest.

I thought my first Dell appearance had been enough to work the oracle. The industrious Reeves struck just before the half-hour, giving me my first taste of a home-crowd celebration. Bunny Larkin equalised but George O'Brien restored Saints' lead soon after the break. Saints looked as if they would retain this advantage until the end. But Norwich winger Billy Punton dubiously tumbled in the penalty area right at the death. Matt Crowe dispatched the resulting and highly controversial spot-kick and honours finished even.

Referee D.W.Smith of Stonehouse had to be safely escorted away by a police constable as a handful of the crowd ran on at the final whistle. My Dell debut had not been without incident and I greatly looked forward to my next visit.

George O'Brien shepherds in the first goal, scored by Derek Reeves (out of picture)

Chris Newman, Midanbury

12 November 1960 v Sheffield United, Division Two, 0-1

I was eight and had already been to a few Reserves matches where my Dad had lifted me over the turnstiles, as a mate of his was manning the gate. This practice was repeated for my first team "debut" (and the rest of that season) so I know the official attendance of 27,405 was out by at least one for that day and likewise for the remaining dozen games through to April.

Dad sent me down from the back, where he was standing, to the wall at the front of the Milton Road end where, as if by magic, a space was made for me to watch the game. It all seemed totally natural and there were plenty of us kids in the same boat with father (not many mothers in those days) somewhere to the back. The adults around us would look after us and wait until our fathers "claimed" us at the end of the game.

My other recollection of the game is of a splendid spread of colour photos in the next day's *Sunday Pictorial,* which I think still survive in my memorabilia box that covers the last 40 years of Saints supporting. The most recent of those years have been spent in South Wales, keeping in touch via the Saints internet List and Cardiff Saints. Through such media, I have been able to encourage my son to The Dell and, now 18, he has opted to be at Portsmouth University, specifically so that he might get a season ticket at St Mary's and/or a match day job that will supplement his meagre allowance from his tight-fisted parents.

Alan Horton, Colwinston, South Wales

11 March 1961 v Plymouth Argyle, Division Two, 1-1

I was just eight years-old, and knew nothing either of Saints' promotion the year before or of recent cup exploits, when Dad introduced me to The Dell. It was a debut in every sense of the word.

I was pushed down to the wall underneath the West Stand, at the Archers Road end. The sea of people on all sides, the seemingly massive stands, the atmosphere and sense of occasion made an enormous impression on me.

There was the *Albion Band* parading and the "target" tarpaulin to aim your pennies at, the mascots running round the pitch and the boys with rattles – I wanted one of those! At the end, there was that crush in the tunnel as everyone tried to leave at the same time, hemmed in tightly on all sides by (fortunately gentle) giants. I didn't feel at all frightened but, knowing what we do now, it was probably quite dangerous.

Using Harry Penk (No.11) as a climbing-frame, Tommy Mulgrew gets up to head home a Paine centre.

The football itself was almost incidental and in truth I can recall little about it, except that Tommy Mulgrew scored for Saints. What I do remember is the Plymouth trainer coming on and off the pitch half-a-dozen times and one player being helped hobbling round the perimeter, trying to walk off an ankle injury. The record books tell us that 18,949 were there. It was at least one more than that as my brother David and I doubled up to squeeze through the turnstile together for a two-for-the-price-of-one deal.

Dad wasn't really a football fan so I got to go to only the odd game for a couple of years. But, once I was allowed on my own, I was there for every home match. And, 40 years on, my love affair with the Saints continues – albeit at a distance.

Richard Atkinson, Macclesfield

7 October 1961 v Brighton and Hove Albion, 6-1

It was the summer when my holidays were interrupted by a burst appendix. When I was better, I was offered a special treat of my choice. It didn't take much thinking about. I wanted to go and watch Southampton.

In those days before regular televised football, I'd never seen what a proper football match looked like. I suppose I must have seen boys kicking a ball around in the playground, but my conception of the game was derived entirely from newspaper reports. We'd moved to Southampton a couple of years previously and, every week, I'd devour the reports, become more acquainted with the names of the players and look to see where Southampton were in the table. The fateful identification of myself with those players' names, that line in the league table, was forged before I even really knew what football was.

And so, perched beside my father up at the back of the East Stand, towards the Archers end, I watched the red-and-white incarnations of those names in the 'papers take on Brighton and Hove Albion. Of the match details, I remember little, except standing up and shouting *Come on Saints,* in imitation – and to the amusement – of the adults around me and my father pointing out a foul by Paine that the ref hadn't noticed. And I thought we'd added a seventh goal, only for it to be disallowed for what was to me a completely unfathomable reason, but my dad said it was something called "offside".

It seemed to me then perfectly natural and proper that a football match should be such an apparently effortless and triumphant progress for my team, with the fans cheering and the goals going in almost at will. I didn't know then the stories that lay ahead for me and for them over the years – where they'd take me – knew nothing of the desperate and ultimately glorious "Great Escapes" at Upton, Roker, Burnden and Selhurst Parks.

And I didn't dream that one day I'd watch a man from Latvia, with a first name like my own, scoring goals for my team. But I did know what football was.

Marian Thomas, Surbiton, Surrey

FULL-TIME *at* THE DELL

3 April 1963 v Nottingham Forest, FA Cup 6th Round replay, 3-3 (a.e.t)

The sixties were just beginning to swing and this 11 year-old schoolboy was at last beginning to untie mother's apron

George O'Brien (No.8) admires the late equaliser by David Burnside (out of picture)

strings. At a time when boys wore shorts to school until we were 13 and we didn't play outside the front gate on Sundays, the casual request to watch Saints on Wednesday night was a shock. Neither Dad nor my two older brothers played or watched football and nor did I. For me it was a chance to stay out late with my older, and streetwise, cousin and his mates. Until that day football didn't exist.

The walk from The Avenue down Northlands Road. The pace was brisk. One that my son in later years called the "going to the Saints walk." Skipping into the gutter to overtake the loiterers and herding together to squeeze along the narrow alley by the church that links Archers Road and Milton Road. We were bound for the "Boys' box" at the Milton end because it cost only 1/-. More squeezing and herding as we jostled for position in the huge queue. Through the turnstile, up the

narrow stairs and there it was. Why does the natural theatre of a football ground make everything look so big? And floodlights make it even bigger. And the noise! Everyone was singing the same song over and over again:

Aye, Aye, Aye, Aye, Reynolds is better than Yashin
Burnside is better than Eu-se-bi-o
And Forest are in for a thrashin'.

I didn't know who they were but it didn't matter. My cousin let me use his wooden rattle. I couldn't swing it. Street cred zero. And still an hour to kick-off. The facts of the game are well-known. Ron Reynolds, the goalie, wore contact lenses so couldn't see the ball in the floodlights. John Sydenham was faster than the Olympic gold medal winner. Tommy Traynor trained on whisky. David Burnside could have joined a circus as a ball juggler. I believed it all. And the captain's name was

The Milton End in Final mood

Knapp – nearly the same as mine and not the most common of names. We must have been almost related. By the end of the game I was telling everyone that we were.

I cannot remember being down-hearted even when we were 3-0 down. At 3-3 it was like all the best Christmases and birthdays together, all rolled into one. George Kirby is 6'6" tall and Cliff Huxford can hammer nails in with his bare hands. You don't choose to support the Saints. The Saints choose you.

Geoff Knappett, Whitchurch

22 May 1963 v Stoke City, Division Two, 2-0

I first became aware that The Dell existed in October 1959 when my parents bought a house in Archers Road and all of a sudden Saturday afternoons became a lot more interesting.

I watched fascinated from an upstairs window, as the motley crowd, heads lowered in conversation, hands thrust deep in overcoat pockets, made their way to this strange, noisy citadel down my road. Within a year or two I was old enough to be allowed out and would spend the afternoons outside the ground squeezing the horns on the parked motor bikes while listening to the "oohs" and "aahs" of their owners inside. Inevitably, one day when the gates opened – as they did then 20 minutes before the end – I wriggled into the crowd and caught my first glimpse of the green stage that would, for the next 40 years, fill, fuel and furnish not only the majority of my waking thoughts but most of my dreams as well.

My sneaking in like that makes it awkward to pinpoint my actual first visit but my first "official" game occurred when my father – a passionate Saints' fan and then a stile man at The Dell – took me to the last match of the 1962-63 season. I can still recall the overwhelming smell of tobacco smoke as I took my seat for the entry of the Division Two Champions, Stoke City, and most especially of Stanley Matthews, Footballer of the Year. Unfortunately, Matthews appeared only in a suit as he waved to the crowd prior to kick-off – forever denying me the opportunity of telling my grandchildren that I'd seen the wizard of dribble in competitive action.

Never mind! Saints won and their very own wizard of dribble, Terry Paine, scored both goals.

Duncan Holley, Winchester

Stanley Matthews is greeted by (left to right) Tony Knapp, Ken Wimshurst, David Burnside, Ted Bates and George Kirby

7 September 1963 v Preston North End, Division Two, 4-5

I was football crazy, football mad – in the words of the song – when I left The Dell, having watched an incredible game.

The memory plays tricks. I had thought until very recently that Saints won 5-4. But, hey, I was 10 years-old, it was my first visit and only the second professional game I had seen (the first being Exeter City v Lincoln City on my holiday a few weeks earlier). It turns out that we lost 4-5. There were seven goals in the second half and five in the last 10 minutes. It would have been no wonder to have lost track of the score.

I don't remember the Saints' line-up but it was mainly the side that had got to the FA Cup semi-final the previous season. I know Burnside, O'Brien and Kirby scored at least one each and remember that Knapp and Paine were playing. It was a magical match and the atmosphere in the Chocolate Box at the Milton Road end was stupendous.

No wonder I have been a fan ever since, latterly commuting from the distant east.

Andrew Collyer, West Malling, Kent

George Kirby (right) scores Saints' first goal against Preston

David Burnside (second right) scores Saints' second goal

FULL-TIME *at* THE DELL

4 January 1964 v Manchester United, FA Cup, Third Round, 2-3

I don't know any genuine fan who cannot remember his first game.

So said Charlie Whelan, erstwhile spin-meister to Chancellor Brown, when exposing phoney Tony Blair's dubious Newcastle United credentials. Wrong there, Charlie. I was simply too young to remember my Dell debut and I don't even know what season it was.

My apprenticeship for a life-time of devotion to the cause began, in the mists of time, on the Hythe ferry, with my father and his friends and then Shanks's pony to The Dell. We watched the matches from the Milton terrace – me with a grandstand view from my dad's shoulders. I later graduated to sitting on the wall by the players' entrance, which in those days had a sharply angled top – an early warning that the occasional pleasures of watching Saints would be juxtaposed with real pain.

In a quiet moment at The Dell, an artistic fan seized the moment to sketch Mark Fickling's father on a barrier

All of which explains how my first clear memory of The Dell is born of that pain and why I have required editorial indulgence to recount it in this chapter of debut memories. Scripted for revenge after United had literally kicked us out of the semi-final the previous season at Villa Park, Saints, clad again in old gold and black, roared into a 2-0 half-time lead, through Chivers and Paine. As the second goal went in, I threw my woolly hat into the air. Everybody went mad, nobody more so than Dad, when my hat landed several yards away and disappeared into the crowd. So, a severe rebuke from my father for the wanton abandonment of my hat, rammed home by the inevitable three second-half goals from United.

Mark Fickling, Rownhams

9 January 1965 v Leyton Orient, FA Cup, Third Round, 3-1

Arriving from Bitterne – probably on the No. 5 bus – for this cup-tie, Dad and I managed to stand just to the left of the Milton Road goal, right at the front. John Sydenham created the biggest impression and contributed to George O'Brien's second goal near the end. The Dell impressed me, too, as being so big – which, in reality, it never was, of course. I would get back there quite a few times, pocket money permitting, over the next few years – for some happy memories and some not so pleasant, such as when Peter Shilton scored for Leicester City on a very wet October afternoon in 1967.

Michael Hull, Northampton

18 September 1965 v Wolverhampton Wanderers, Division Two, 9-3

Debut 1: I was ten years-old when my pestering paid off. "I'll take you to see them play The Wolves," Dad said. Wolves had just been relegated from the First Division, but still had England's Ron Flowers playing for them.

A bus ride to Eastleigh Station, a train to Southampton and a long walk up Hill Lane until we reached the rosette- and programme-sellers outside the Catholic School. Dad bought me a rosette and the programme cost sixpence. I went into the boys' gate, which cost one-and-sixpence. Dad had to push the turnstile, which was too heavy for me. He went in the four shillings and met me on the inside. There we were in the Milton Road end, halfway up behind the goal, exactly the position I was in for the last match at The Dell. Dad lifted me up to sit on the crash barrier, legs dangling; other boys with their freshly painted red-and-white rattles, bobble hats and newly-knitted scarves; *Woodbine* smoke thick in the air; and not a replica shirt in sight. I remember cringing at seeing an almost bald player in our team called Jimmy Melia... We'd signed him from Wolves... A goal in the first minute! – our centre-half scores an own goal! Can't remember much about the match but the goals just flowed: Chivers four, Paine and Sydenham two each, O'Brien one. Their goalkeeper, Dave MacLaren? We signed him a year later.

Leon Burton, Horton Heath

Debut 2: I had been pestering my father for a long time to take me to The Dell. At last, he announced we were going, along with my Uncle Bob, to watch Saints play Wolves. We stood on the Milton Road end for the amazing 9-3 victory.

I was nine. So I recall the occasion, the incredible noise and excitement, more than any detail of the match. I can still see my uncle leaping in the air and twisting his ankle as he landed crookedly on the edge of a terrace step. The crowd took great delight in chanting *WE WANT TEN* but I did not realise until reading about it, years later, that all the goals were scored with 30 minutes to go. I had not only a sensational first match but an unforgettable first season, my first away game being at Leyton Orient where we effectively won promotion. And, as if that was not enough, my first international soon followed – against Uruguay at the start of England's World Cup-winning tournament.

Not surprisingly, after such a season of firsts, football – and Saints in particular – remains a lasting part of my life.

John Wilson, Warsash

Terry Paine twice rounded MacLaren to score as defenders covered in vain. This was the third goal, which he carefully copied for the ninth.

Debut 3: I had moved down from Liverpool, where I had watched Liverpool and Everton alternate weeks. And now I was standing at the Milton Road end, watching Southampton, with an ex-Liverpool player, Jimmy Melia, in their side.

Not an auspicious start! – 1-0 down within a minute to a Knapp own goal. But things were soon going Saints' way – all the way to that massive 9-3 win. From that moment, I was a Southampton supporter and Terry Paine was my all-time favourite player. Martin Chivers and John Sydenham were other stars of that match.

Saints got promotion in my first season. Perhaps I was a lucky omen: Liverpool were promoted the first season I watched them – with Jimmy Melia in the team.

David Thomas, Chandlers Ford

17 September 1966 v Liverpool, Division One, 1-2

It was a good time to be young in the 1960's and an even better time to be a student. No loans or tuition fees and you could even claim additional support for undertaking some extra study. Which is how I found myself back at Southampton University in September 1966, a few weeks before the start of term.

At an earnest teach-in on American involvement in Vietnam, the previous May, the attention of some of my friends had not been wholly on the subject. From the whispered messages and rising excitement as people slipped in and out to get the latest news, I gathered that it had something to do with Saints setting themselves up for promotion to the First Division. Not having much interest in football, I was a little surprised at the enthusiasm of people I had not suspected of such strange passions.

FULL-TIME *at* THE DELL

But all that was about to change. There was the little matter of the World Cup that summer and, like so many others, I was swept along with the excitement and success of the England team. So, back in Southampton that September, I needed no encouragement to join a group of friends to see the promoted Saints at The Dell. Coming from a remote rural area, I had never seen a proper stadium before and, although we later came to see The Dell as cramped and limiting, on that day, with its 30,000 (mainly standing) capacity, it seemed vast.

There was something slightly racy about standing on the terraces, a *frisson* of excitement that something might erupt. This was especially because my more experienced supporter friends had insisted we stand on the Milton Road terraces, where the hardened fans went. Needless to say, apart from the ebb and flow of bodies that is inevitable in a big crowd at exciting moments, there were no signs of any violence and, in all my subsequent years at The Dell, I was never near any threatening situations.

Being part of such a huge crowd was something new to me and revealed new forms of social etiquette. The opposition and the referee (and sometimes they were combined) could be abused as the personification of evil while I was united with thousands of others in a visceral, primitive surge of support for my own side. The players were professionals and had to play within the rules, but on the terraces we took no prisoners.

And yet, like supporters down the years, we privately shared our doubts about some of our heroes. Opinions were divided, for example, about Jimmy Melia. Was he the cunning schemer who would have been the architect of so many more goals if only his team-mates were as quick-thinking as he was? Or was he too slow to catch a cold and failing to play the obvious ball, while looking for something more ambitious? How we loved "Docker" Dave Walker – what a character and such determination! – but he was part of a defence that conceded goals as fast as that wonderful forward line of Paine, Davies, Chivers and Sydenham were scoring them.

The opponents that day would have tested any defence. Their own promotion from Division Two not many years behind them, Liverpool were not quite yet the force that they were to become. But most of the great Bill Shankly side was in place. Playing in an all-white strip, they looked enormous. Besides them, the Southampton players seemed almost puny, their legs white against the tanned limbs of their opponents. Saints were always going to be the underdogs and the game was not many minutes old when the odds tipped even further in Liverpool's favour. Right in front of us, Denis Hollywood collided horribly with Campbell Forsyth, Saints' imposing keeper, who was stretchered off with a broken leg.

In these days of specialist substitutes, it is strange to recollect that David Webb, the rock-like right-back, had to pull on the goalkeeper's jersey. He did a determined job, too, but the writing was on the wall and Saints went down to one of many home defeats that season.

So why did I keep returning to The Dell? Ah, but the style was there – and what else were the '60s about?

Malcolm Sykes, Limpley Stoke

14 January 1967 v Leicester City, Division One, 4-4

It had begun the previous summer when I watched the final stages of the World Cup on television. I was seven and members of the England team became my first heroes. Once the new season began, with Saints now playing in the top division, I had avidly followed the results and acquired some local heroes.

Then, one January evening, my father came home from work with two West Stand tickets. I was going to watch my new heroes play against England's Gordon Banks (not to mention a right-back called Peter Rodrigues).

That first game taught me that, if you follow the Saints, whatever sort of game you might see, it will never be predictable and very rarely dull. And whether we were ahead or behind, you could never rely upon the outcome. Against Leicester, we led 3-1, then 4-2, after Leicester had missed a penalty at 3-2. Although I had to settle for a draw, I had seen Ron Davies score a hat-trick and England's greatest goalkeeper beaten four times. I had been caught forever by the *Spirit of Southampton*.

Graham Hepburn, Chandlers Ford

28 October 1967 v Burnley, Division One, 2-2

Vague as the memories are of that damp Autumn day, I do remember standing with my father at the Archers end, just to the right of the goal, behind the railings long since gone. Aged nine, draped in a red-and-white scarf and hat, with a programme in my hand.

All I remember of the game is a penalty for Saints at the Milton end. Chivers took it but almost hit the corner flag. I lost my programme on the way home.

Gary Chalk, Eastleigh

26 December 1967 v Sheffield United, Division One, 3-3.

My recollections of this Boxing Day afternoon include… a white silk scarf, with SOUTHAMPTON FC in red letters and the old club crest at either end, purchased for me before the kick-off at the Club Shop on the corner of Milton Road and Wilton Avenue… entering through the turnstile under the West Stand and seeing these men dressed in white coats and thinking "What are these doctors doing at a football match?" (hey, I had just turned eight and hadn't been told about stewards) … the brass band playing… the *Watney* sign above the East Stand … a chant of *Zigger-zagger, zigger-zagger, SOUTHAMPTON!*… David Munks, a Sheffield United player with a name like mine.

If you like what you see on your first impression, you go back for more – most Saturday afternoons for the next 30-odd years, in my case. My first visit to The Dell will be in my memory until the day I become a Saint in spirit only.

Dave Monk, Bassett

(Above) With only the Burnley goalkeeper to beat from the spot, Martin Chivers fires wide of the camera-man.

(Below) With four Sheffield United defenders to contend with, he heads home

6 April 1968 v Peterborough United Reserves, Football Combination Division One, 1-0

Supporting the Saints was a family matter. My grandfather followed them home and away – he was the black sheep of the family, was Granddad; sometimes, he didn't return from away games until the middle of the following week and they still refuse to mention his name.

Uncle Ted travelled up from Poole for home games, while Uncle Malc, who kept promising to take me when I was old enough, came in from Kanes Hill. He would stop by, at our Thornhill home, always raising my expectations: was I to go this time? "No, maybe next time."

I think finally he'd had enough. OK, I go to the next game. "No he can't, he's not old enough," said Mum. You wear down one and another pops out of the woodwork. I could go only on one condition: it was to be a reserve game. I didn't care. I would have gone and watched the grass grow.

So came the big day. It's funny how it always seems like yesterday, yet I couldn't have told you the date. I couldn't sleep; what if it was called off; what if my uncle forgot; who would be playing? I remember driving past the Milton Road end, looking for a parking space. How much smaller it looked than I'd imagined.

We managed to find a space within a short walk back to the ground. I joined the children's queue and shuffled along with the crowd until I reached the turnstile. I was on my own now, until I rejoined my uncle inside. And then, there in front of me was the greenest green I'd ever seen. I walked down the steps of the Milton Road to the front. How much bigger it looked now!

The game itself went in a flash. Jimmy Melia scored with a header, a rarity I'm told.

Dave Webster, Fair Oak

FULL-TIME *at* THE DELL

21 March 1970 v Arsenal, Division One, 0-2

Chris Rawnson, my best mate at secondary school, started it when I was 12. Should we support a football team, he wondered; and, if so, should we go local or successful?

I had no idea who was successful, as I had no knowledge of the national game at all. My dad never mentioned football and I had never played it: my sporting life in Over Wallop consisted of climbing trees and generally being an outdoor kid, roaming the village and walking miles. Football never entered my mind – so much so that I remember the Aberfan disaster in '66 and the *Torrey Canyon* in '67, but not the World Cup win of '66.

So local we would go. Our opportunity came when Chris's older brother offered to take us to The Dell. He had a big car. Well, all cars were big to me as we didn't have one. And it was a big trip for me, a village yokel who'd never been to Southampton before. We stood in the Milton Road chocolate boxes. What a sight for one so naïve! A crowd of almost 24,000 was something I had never witnessed before. I had my programme (price 1/- with its free copy of the *Football League Review* as a centre-fold) and my pen poised to note the changes and the goals (something I do to this day – sacrilege, I know, but my programme is my record of my game).

I vividly remember Eric Martin and his hair; Joe Kirkup without; Big Ron Davies; and Mike Channon, who was to become my all-time favourite. Otherwise, my memory of the match has all but gone, although my annotated programme tells me that Jon Sammels and Charlie George scored for Arsenal and Frank Saul replaced Tom Jenkins for Saints. Pompey were one-up at Preston at half-time – I'd recorded the scores they used to display on the scoreboard at the far end, on hooks as with cricket scoreboards, or propped up against the wall around the pitch, under the letters A, B, C etc, relating to the list in the programme. I have also completed the crossword, but surely I must have looked the answers up, as I can't have known them at the time.

The journey home was all a blur (as other matches since have been, for different reasons). But I must have been bitten by the bug, because I remember collecting stickers for the 1970 World Cup in Mexico. My mate has been only a couple of times since, but I was there at the end, 31 seasons later. I wonder what my great grandchildren will have to say for themselves in their contributions to *Memories of St Mary's* when that compendium makes it to the Megastore in a hundred years or so from now?

Hayden Hopkins, Andover

15 August 1970 v Manchester City, Division One, 1-1

I had just returned from Australia with my parents and, after four years of watching Aussie Rules, it was a relief to come home to some proper football.

Francis Lee scored for City (not from the penalty spot) and big Ron Davies, the Welsh Warrior, for Saints, probably from a Terry Paine cross. Otherwise, the thing I remember about the match was that the Saints fans were giving Mike Summerbee some stick about his big nose (sounds familiar) so, in the second-half, he took the field wearing a big plastic nose, to the amusement of all the crowd. All in all, though, it was a typical first game of the season. Yet I was sufficiently impressed to come back. I would stand with my mate Richard, under the West Stand, just behind the old dug-outs, where we used to bang on the top of the home dug-out to encourage Ted Bates to put the sub' on.

Richard now lives in Australia, but I continued to come back – for another 31 years, over 600 games at The Dell and almost as many away.

Paul Nicholson, Basingstoke

13 November 1971 v Leeds United, Division One, 2-1

It was when Leeds were admired and despised with equal vigour and I was a football-mad seven-year-old. We lived near the Gaumont, a stone's throw from The Dell and on the critical path for police escorts from the railway station.

Grabbing my hand, Dad stomped me into town about 1 o'clock to meet Chuck, a big, bald, unshaven man, rather like Eli Wallach in *The Good, The Bad and The Ugly*. I remember the plethora of thick woollen scarves and rosettes and the unbridled excitement as we made our way from The Windsor Bar to Milton Road.

Chapter 27

Inside the ground, we took a position at the base of the West Stand, right next to the players' entrance. I swear that, in the subsequent years, my peering over the wall helped me to develop my current 6 foot 1 frame. On this first visit, as I hung over that wall, it was the whiff of liniment that got me hooked. Subconsciously, I can still smell it today, wherever I am in the ground. A smell from the '70s, never more pronounced than when John McGrath's ample thighs emerged from the tunnel.

I vaguely remember the team of the day, Channon, Davies, Painie… Most vivid, however, is the *Tra-La-La – Brian O'Neil,* sung to the tune of The Banana Splits, as he hustled and harried in midfield. The result merely added to the occasion. It was the smell and sounds of The Dell that I most remember and nothing can ever replace the first time.

Robert Harding, Maidstone

13 August 1974 v Leeds United, Ted Bates Testimonial, 1-1

Our next door neighbour, Ray Garvey, took us – his son Patrick, my older brother Matthew and me. He worked for Whitbread, who were very heavily into football at the time. They produced a yearly book that had a few teams in it, including Leeds. I could name every player in the Leeds squad but only a few of the Saints.

Although I do not remember the football at all, I can just barely remember going to the match and standing in the Archers. We were to the left of the goal (looking at the pitch), but, like any child of eight, I was probably in awe of seeing so many thousands of people. I do remember that we had to go the other end of the Archers for decent toilets.

Julian Sutton, London

27 September 1975 v Portsmouth, Division Two, 4-0

I'd been nagging my dad to take me to a Saints game for a while. He finally relented and, for my ninth birthday, I received a couple of tickets for the local derby with Portsmouth. Mind you, I had no idea that it was a local derby: we lived on the southern edge of the New Forest and I had never heard of Portsmouth (ignorance can indeed be bliss).

We arrived in Shirley in time to eat and look round the shops. I was looking for my fellow-supporters, those whose scarves matched my red-and-white bobble hat and my two red-and-white scarves tied around my wrists (very fashionable among nine year-old supporters of the day). We were bound for the Upper West Stand – my parents said I was too small to stand on the terraces, in addition to which my teacher, a season ticket-holder, used to regale us with stories of fans stretchered from the terraces having been crushed/stabbed within an inch of their lives. I guess that it was a good decision since, when we started to stand on the terraces a few years later, no matter how early you got to the ground and found a spot where you could see the whole of the pitch, you could always guarantee that some giant of a man would come and stand directly in front of you two minutes before the kick-off.

Going through the turnstiles was the most exciting thing ever to have happened to me (not a lot happens in small New Forest villages). We climbed the wooden stairs and made for the bar – a pint for my dad and a lemonade for me (by the time I was old enough to have a pint myself, alcohol had been banned from football grounds). Eventually, we headed up the few remaining stairs and there it was – The Dell in all its glory, the biggest ground in the world. Well, to a small boy brought up on a diet of local non-league football – Totton (in the pram), New Milton and Brockenhurst (both in short trousers) – it was the biggest, most colourful and noisiest place I had ever been to. It took a while to take it all in. The "chocolate boxes" at the Milton Road end, the advertising hoardings, the blokes on top of the East Stand to retrieve the balls – it was a completely new world.

When we started going to all of the home games a few years later, we stood on the terraces; but, in the late 1980s, I sat in the Upper West Stand for a couple of reserve games and again got that shiver of excitement walking up those steps and looking out over The Dell, just like that day back in 1975. No other area of the ground ever did that to me.

I've still got the 16-page *Matchday Magazine.* The striking difference from today's programme seems to be the number of advertisements – commercialism hadn't hit Southampton Football Club at that stage. The main concession to big business were the advertising hoardings around the ground – which I faithfully read and committed to memory in case anyone wanted to test me on them later.

FULL-TIME *at* THE DELL

I can remember the excitement when the team – including 10 of the 12 who would be at Wembley come May – came out on to the pitch. My recollections of the game itself are sketchy at best. I can picture the goals going in and the ground standing and cheering and I can recall who scored them – Mike Channon with a hat-trick and David Peach with a penalty – but I couldn't describe any of them.

The result fully vindicated my decision, made around the age of six, to become a Saints fan like my dad. I assumed that watching them would always be like this. Yet, if the outcome had been different, if I'd seen Saints play poorly and lose, then maybe I wouldn't have caught the bug, maybe I would have saved myself a lot of stress and money, maybe I would have saved myself a lot of ridicule at school, college and work over the years, but I don't regret a minute of it.

Nick Brice, Lordswood

3 January 1976 v. Aston Villa, FA Cup, Third Round, 1-1
My brother and I begged to be allowed to go to The Dell with our friends; but Dad, not himself a fan, was worried by the media coverage of hooliganism.

We were permitted, though, to go and watch Bournemouth and spent half a season in the away end – with so few people that we could chat to Harry Redknapp when he took corners. Our having survived that, Dad agreed to take us to The Dell for our first game: if all went well, we could then go it alone.

It was a cold, cloudy Third Round day. It seemed like the walk from the station up Hill Lane would never end but, on turning into Milton Road, I knew this was going to be a special place in my life. Dad took us under the West Stand, Milton end.

From my short 13 year-old height it seemed so dark and packed full. We were stuck at the back, the terrace-wise regulars having got their kids down to the front. But, the floodlight-developed glow, over all the heads at the front, looked brilliantly bright and produced an atmosphere I can't begin to put into words.

I saw frustratingly little of the game. My best view of the ball was when it was in the air and it

Bobby Stokes (No.9) and Mick Channon (No.8) watch Hughie Fisher score the equalizer that would have such an "impact on the rest of our lives"

seemed that Chris Nicholl's head was often high enough for me to get a glance. That's still how I remember Chris, even after he became our manager. But we knew what was happening, the moans and groans, swearing, cheering, singing and clapping providing a perfect indication of what I mostly couldn't see. We shared in the jubilation of Hughie Fisher's late equaliser but we were not to know about the impact it would have on the rest of our lives.

Dad approved of The Dell and never came with us again. We soon learned how to get in a decent position to see the actual grass. A useful lesson for the packed terrace at Wembley come that May.

Ian McWilliam, California, USA

16 October 1976 v. Hereford United, Division Two, 1-0.
I said "Yes" when my dad asked me, one grey Autumn's day, if I would like to go to football at The Dell. He stood at the Archers Road end and I sat on his shoulders.

His Hereford team-mates pause to let "the great man" jog the appreciative gauntlet of (left to right)
Peter Rodrigues, Mick Channon, Steve Middleton, Hugh Fisher and Jim McCalliog

My only real memories from the game are of the green-ness of the pitch, the noise the crowd made, especially when Nick Holmes got the winner, and a player in a white shirt getting a standing ovation for just walking onto the pitch.

To a baffled small boy, "Who was this man?" It was a certain Terry Paine and, although I never saw him play for the Saints, at least I saw the great man grace The Dell for the last time.

Andy Nunn, East Molesey, Surrey

7 December 1976 v Chelsea, Division Two, 1-1

I had sat in front of the TV seven months before, Cup Final Day, with all the dispassion of the neutral. Southampton v Manchester United. I guess I wanted the underdog to win, but I really had no strong feelings. In those days, games came no bigger than the Cup Final. An event not to be missed and an all too rare opportunity to see football live on TV. It mattered not to me that, in a few months, I would be leaving my school in Essex for "The Cup City", to start a degree. The two points had no connection.

Of course, I was a Chelsea fan. Never seen them, but Dad sort of supported them, and they had been good in the sixties as I grew up. That Tuesday evening towards the end of my first term at university was my first chance to see the Blues in the flesh. And my first time at The Dell, under the East Stand, close to the Archers.

It was like going to so many away grounds: few street signs, follow the strangers in front, ant-like, down the road, talking to friends, prepared for the weather, feeling self-conscious, looking for a programme, not knowing which turnstile, being outnumbered… *Come on you Blues!*

I was one of the 19,909. Another one was stabbed that night. Chelsea fans had a reputation and had probably earned it. I think the Saints scored first – through Ted MacDougall, my records tell me. The Chelsea scorer has long since been forgotten.

So what happened? Well, in my second year at university, I got in with a group of friends who were going to matches. I joined them. Again it was mid-week, against Reading, in a League Cup replay. The following mid-week it was Villa in the League. By the time of the League Cup semi-final, I had forsaken the Blue and was on my way to Wembley, I shall not be moved!

Peter Emery, Kenley, Surrey

FULL-TIME *at* THE DELL

20 August 1977 v Brighton and Hove Albion, Division Two, 1-1

Saints begin the new season against Brighton and Hove Albion at The Dell tomorrow knowing that they should be on their way towards promotion.

It was Saturday and I was listening to *Paranoid* by Black Sabbath on the radio and reading the prediction in Friday's *Echo*. I was 14 and was impressed. I could see Winchester station from where we lived and, as the noon crowds gathered, I felt I had to join them.

I already had the gear for it. Scarves were the order of the day, tied around a wrist or two and the neck. No shirts then – not too many at any rate. I had the *Admiral* striped one but that was for the all-important kick-around at the Arbour Park. The walk up Hill Lane, with a friend I'd met on the train, was a great experience. I was instantly absorbed and joining in the singing of *When the Saints Go Marching In* and the chanting of *Southampton! Southampton!*

I paid just £1.20 entrance fee and the programme was 15p. We decided to try the chocolate boxes, as a steward indicated spaces above. And then my first sight of The Dell and the Saints players warming up – Wow, what a view! It was high up but not that far away as to hinder pointing out who was who on the pitch. The stands looked great with their floodlights sitting on top and the whole ground appeared larger than on television.

The Brighton fans let free a mass of blue and white balloons to the chant of *Seagulls! Seagulls!* The Milton responded with *Seaweed! Seaweed!* – my introduction to the quick terrace wit of The Dell. The back page of the programme had the "line-ups", with a blank column for you to mark in the subs. The Saints included Alan Ball (7) and Ted MacDougall (11) and there was a lot of talk about the potential of Steve Williams (4). And Alan Mullery's newly-promoted Brighton had a certain Mark Lawrenson (6). MacDougall was full of running and the Milton cheered "Super Mac" as he latched on to any passes or loose balls. But Brighton were attacking as often as Saints and this worried me, even though Chris Nicholl was intercepting everything in the air and displaying good, close ball-skill on the deck.

Then, just before half-time, Saints scored. Peach took a free-kick and Williams just stopped it dead, for Ball to race in and shoot past Steel. What a goal! There was a great surge forward and a crush of bodies ensued. At half-time, some of the fans around me were talking of going underneath, behind the goal. This sounded worth a try and we battled through to the front, to the left of the goal. From my new position, I had a real close-up view of the action and was taken by the fact you could hear Ian Turner shouting instructions to team-mates defending the Milton end. The perspective was different, though, as we no longer had the advantage of looking down on the pitch.

Then Brighton sent on John Ruggiero who, with his first touch, just cut through the solid Saints defence. There was a moment of groans in the Milton, but then we all rallied with *Southampton! Southampton!* Towards the end, many a youth filtered down from the back of the terrace to the front in order to get onto the pitch. The whistle went and I raced out with them to greet the players. The stewards allowed us our brief invasion. Then we jumped back onto the terrace. I had passed my initiation into the Saints fold, a truly great experience to be repeated (without pitch invasions) across 24 Dell seasons. Meanwhile, the programme said Saints had Mansfield Town next at home. No problem. That's a win and I'd be there for it – and for the rest of a stunning season that would justify the *Echo*'s prediction.

Manny Choudhury, Eastleigh

26 August 1978 v Middlesbrough, Division One, 2-1

Growing up in isolated Chilbolton, I didn't have much exposure to football outside the *Grandstand* results and thought it existed only in exotic cities like Leeds. However, on 1 May 1976, I found out, via a car radio, that Southampton had a team and the next day I saw them on the bus proudly showing off the FA Cup.

Then, at the start of the 1978-79 season, my dad decided to take my eight year-old brother to The Dell. Maybe it was Saints being back in Division One; maybe Dad just thought my brother had come of age; but his reasons were pretty inexplicable to me at the time. Anyhow, my mum, being my mum, announced that she and her 13 year-old daughter were going as well.

Chapter 27

I had never seen a match either live or on television and had no idea what the rules were, or even what football really involved. We parked in one of the roads off Hill Lane and walked down to the ground. My excitement and curiosity were building as we climbed high up in the Milton and stood at the back. We were among the first people there. So we waited. Out came the thermos and sandwiches. And we waited. The ground started filling up, the old people in the seats in the stands, the lads in the Archers end.

Just when the ground seemed full, the moment arrived, the players ran out and suddenly The Dell erupted in sound. That was when I stopped being somebody who said they supported Saints and started being totally in love with the Club. I couldn't believe that such collective emotions could exist with such a large group of people. I couldn't believe the sound. I couldn't believe adults could get so openly emotional. It was wonderful.

I soon found out the players in red-and-white stripes were ours. I didn't know who any of them were, or even what the rules were. It didn't take long to figure out what goalies did and that the other players could not use their arms. As I had to rely only on observation to work out the rules, the offside rule baffled me. I just couldn't get why, as the build-up was developing nicely, the referee would blow his whistle and the other side would get a free-kick. I was too embarrassed to ask. Everybody else seemed to know the rules and I got the impression my dad wasn't too happy to have me there.

I was fascinated by the players' art and was frustrated to be at the back, so far from the action. I tried to gain knowledge from the shouts of the men around me: who the players were, what they did, whether they were any good or not.

All too soon it was over and I went home bursting with emotion. My mum enjoyed it too. My brother, on the other hand, spent his first match being bored and asking for sandwiches. Needless to say, 23 years later, only the female half of my family is still attending.

Tanya Lim, Donnington, Oxford

24 April 1979 v Liverpool, Division One, 1-1

No matter that we lived in West Wales, Southampton were our team. Granddad had been a Saints supporter from the 1930s and we would holiday in Southampton with my mum's family – Nan in Radstock Road and Auntie Doreen in Atherley Road.

On our December 1978 visit, my father produced two tickets for Saints v Liverpool, making a 10 year-old boy very happy – until the snow and frost made The Dell unplayable. The re-arranged fixture was squeezed into April on a Tuesday night and, after much pleading, begging and the crossing of fingers, I was granted two days off school and a 400-mile round trip to see 90 minutes of heaven.

What stays with me above all else is the sight that greeted me as we walked up the steps to the Milton Road terrace – the radiant green of the pitch lying proudly under the early evening floodlights. I still get a little shiver as I cast my mind back and I still love evening kick-offs.

What of the game? Liverpool, with Dalglish and Souness (who was not surprisingly booked), looked fantastic in all yellow. Saints wore what remains my favourite red-and-white striped number. David Johnson scored an unspectacular opener and the game never really came alive until the second-half. Roared on by the home support, Saints pushed Liverpool deeper and deeper and finally Steve Williams's cross was met perfectly by Nick Holmes to leave Clemence with no chance.

The sheer volume of the celebrations scared me at first but I then perceived the joy and relief that went with it. Seeing your team score a goal (especially at your end) is quite hard to beat, isn't it?

My father kept me on his shoulders from just before kick-off until the final whistle. I had pins and needles in my legs. I can't even begin to imagine how his shoulders felt. But, that evening, he gave me something special. I still hold it dear, 22 years later, and my love of football continues to grow. I feared one day I'd grow out of it, but I sincerely hope I don't.

Nigel Bowen, Cardiff

FULL-TIME *at* THE DELL

7 October 1980 v Wolverhampton Wanderers, Division One, 4-2

My Dell debut required six years of hard work. I lived in Leicestershire in a family of Leicester City supporters and, for some reason, decided, at the age of 12, to follow Southampton. This was in 1974 and despite relegation I stuck with them. I made a conscious decision then to go to Southampton University, where I arrived in 1980, along with Kevin Keegan. My first stop upon arrival was not my hall of residence, but the Dell ticket office – to pick up the batch of four tickets that I had ordered.

The first of these games was a night match. I had seen the Saints play away to Wolves, but this was the moment I had been looking forward to for years – my first home game. I was standing on the lower Milton Road terrace behind the goal and under cover and this is where I stood up until the all-seater era.

The atmosphere was even better than I had imagined it to be. I remember very little about the game itself, though. I was convinced the team was aware that this was my first time and would not let me down. Defeat was therefore unthinkable but I think we might have gone 1-0 down. However, we stormed back to record a 4-2 victory and I was sure Keegan must have scored at least one of them – until the editors assured me otherwise.

My love for Southampton FC was now transformed from a long distance relationship to a closer intimate affair. Although this closeness fluctuated over the years, as work assignments intervened, I am now a regular. That first game was a fabulous performance from a team that was beginning to challenge the big boys and it underlined the way Southampton liked to play at the time – just score more than the opposition. A fine philosophy.

Glenn Johnson, Arundel, Sussex

21 November 1981 v Leeds United, Division One, 4-0

In 1980, I was only four and had not decided on a favourite football team. But I did have a favourite player – Kevin Keegan. As soon as Lawrie McMenemy bought him, I had no more doubts. I wanted to be a Southampton fan. I had to wait for over a season, however, before my dad thought I was old enough to visit my first football ground and to appreciate the football – although I did have the kit and a Junior Saints scarf, which I still have.

Living 65 miles away in Surrey, Dad found it difficult to get tickets, but managed to get two at the Milton end. We arrived very early and I had prime position for a little boy, right at the front and near the tunnel, where I could almost touch the players as they ran out. I stood on a small step-stool, which we had painted red the week before, with SAINTS written on it *(retained – and reproduced below)*. The script could not have been better-written. The match was brilliant, the score 4-0 and Keegan got one of them. He ended up the highest scorer in the top three divisions.

I had become, and remain, a committed fan, nowadays following Saints from Italy via the web and my dad's match reports. I have seen many great games and teams and Juventus are now on my doorstep. Yet I shall never forget when I first raised my Junior Saints scarf above my head to cheer on Keegan and the Saints at The Dell.

Ian Simons, Turin, Italy

27 March 1982 v Stoke City, Division One, 4-3

Though only 19 years ago, a mere blink for some supporters, I can remember my first ever football match about as well as I can any others. The early eighties. The mighty Saints under Lawrie McMenemy were riding high enough in the league to be in with a chance of a EUFA Cup place. Lee Chapman, husband of Lesley Ash, was playing for Stoke that day.

What a game! The goals went in and I didn't fall from the red leaning posts on the Milton Terrace. My Dad kept a hold of me and looked very happy: 3-0 up at half-time and the sun was shining, too.

I don't really remember the goals, or who scored them, but I was amazed by the celebrations. I loved David Armstrong's bald head and thought Steve Williams was the coolest man on the pitch. Keegan's perm was at its peak and he wasn't playing badly either. One other name always stuck in my mind. Ivan Katalinic. Our 'keeper let in three goals in the second half and I remember the disbelief around the terraces. I prayed we would win and we did. I have been in that position many times at The Dell since, and the prayer power just hasn't worked as well.

A winner arrived and we won 4-3. I remember it as being Kevin Keegan – my favourite player – but my old man says it was Mark Whitlock in the closing minutes. In fact, any of the details could be wrong, but that doesn't matter to me. That's what I remember: it was perfect. That's my story and I'm sticking to it.

Arran Frood, Isle of Wight

19 September 1984 v Hamburg, UEFA Cup, First Round, first leg, 0-0
Debut 1: My first-ever trip to The Dell was for what turned out to be the last-ever European tie played there [for reasons explained in the next piece below].

I went along in the enthusiasm of young love with my then new boyfriend, now older husband, a born and bred Saints fan. We stood in the Archers Road end and I looked in vain for any footballers I knew. Being Scottish, I recognised only Mark McGhee and he was playing for Hamburg.

It certainly wasn't an immediate conversion to being a Saint: it took another five years and the skills of a young Channel Islander before I suddenly became the one organising my social diary around the Dell fixtures.

Linda McDougall, Shirley

Debut 2: The ticket was a surprise, an early 10th birthday present that would consummate the life-long love affair that had begun earlier that year, when I went to the FA Cup semi-final against Everton at Highbury.

My dad had managed to get hold of two tickets for the Upper West stand. I remember looking at them (at home in the loft) and being amazed at how much our seats had cost. I do not think we really had the money to pay for them but Dad worked hard and made sacrifices for us to be happy.

During my first game – the semi-final – I had become transfixed by Mark Dennis, Mark Wright and Steve Williams, but when I stepped into The Dell, I was completely and utterly overcome by the occasion and by everything around me. Passing all the fans outside the West Stand, buying the programme (which my brother has claimed), through the turnstiles and up the old wooden steps until the ground came into view, the pitch glowing under the lights and the crowd already singing and shouting.

Match report? I'm afraid I spent as much time watching the crowd as I did watching the game. As the Hamburg fans and the Saints fans serenaded each other, I was oblivious to whatever was being shouted between them. Although I had been at the infamous semi-final, the whole spectre of trouble never really hit home until Heysel; so, if there was any that night, I did not notice.

And how was I to know that my first game at The Dell would also be the last-ever European match there, thanks to the events in Brussels the following year?

During the second-half, I began to take more notice of the game. Then Saints scored – or so it seemed. Steve Moran, with a diving header (at least, it looked like that to me) and the crowd was going crazy. I was absolutely elated, but what followed was awful. The linesman ruled it out and I was devastated. Why had they disallowed the goal when it had seemed fine to me? Dad couldn't explain.

I anxiously awaited a victorious second leg in Hamburg. That never came, of course, but that first leg night remains one of the most amazing in my life. In some ways, the game was symbolic of life at The Dell... great hopes, anticipation, excitement and drama, joy, disappointment, dodgy decisions (although they probably weren't), intense atmosphere, people coming together for the cause and, of course, the stadium glowing like a beacon in the city long after the crowd had dispersed from one home to another.

I hope St Mary's is as special for the child still in me and for the thousands of others for whom The Dell was one of the most special places on earth.

Matthew Sanger, San Francisco, USA

FULL-TIME *at* THE DELL

3 October 1987 v Everton, Division One, 0-4

All I can really remember is the excitement around me, as I stood on the Milton Road, and how, even though we were easily beaten with Graeme Sharp bagging all the goals, the fans still stuck behind the team.

The biggest cheer of the day was when a skinny right-winger was brought on for Graham Baker and, with his first touch of the game, set himself up with a corker of a shot which forced the Everton goalie to palm the shot on to the bar. My step-uncle, who'd taken me, commented, at the end of the game, that this Matthew Le Tissier might be a bit of a find.

Matthew Bartlett, Basingstoke

26 February 1993 v Wimbledon, Premier League, 1-0.

I was seven years-old and I stood in the upper tier of the Milton Road stand with my dad. My mum was a steward at that end. She'd started working as a steward the previous season and she convinced me that I should start going – earlier than I otherwise would have – with my dad. It meant we got in free, while Mum worked nearby. There weren't many women stewards and she often felt that she was treated unfairly and disrespectfully.

She eventually resigned after complaining unsuccessfully that she should have been given a warm coat for blistering cold days like that February afternoon when Matthew Le Tissier scored a free kick late on in the game at our end to give Saints a narrow victory. I remember thinking that football was brilliant and Matt Le Tissier instantly became my favourite player.

Natalie Kitcher, Romsey

1 January 1994 v Norwich City, Premier League, 0-1

I owe my first-ever visit to The Dell to my disbelieving husband.

I had supported the Saints since 1974 (when growing up in Kent and before moving to Northern Ireland in 1983) and he could not credit that I had never visited The Dell while still living in England. We were due to visit our families, both now residing on the South coast, and he enlisted the help of his dad, who went into Southampton and bought us tickets for the upcoming game.

Saturday came and, on the drive across to Southampton, the anticipation began to build. We parked the car just off The Avenue and walked up to The Dell.

Ten minutes later, standing in the car park savouring the atmosphere, I felt like I had just come home. I was so delighted to be there that I spent the entire afternoon with a silly grin on my face.

The game itself was a forgettable one but not even the score took the gloss off the experience for me.

Oonagh Griffith, Belfast

24 February 1996 v Chelsea, Premier League, 2-3

Although we used to come down from north Surrey to visit my aunt in Southampton – she was the Mother Superior at the convent in Bitterne – it was as a Chelsea supporter that I first came to The Dell in 1996. I'd seen the Saints several times at Stamford Bridge, including the game earlier that season when newboy Ruud Gullit was among the scorers in a 3-0 home win. And he it was who ran through to score Chelsea's winner at The Dell.

While I have remained a Chelsea fan at heart, I became a "Blue Saint" of sorts, joining my friends from Godalming and another from Guildford for the occasional visit to The Dell.

We found the hospitality there – from the programme seller, the tea hut, the turnstile operator, to the stewards – so friendly. It's something you don't experience at Chelsea – with all the travel and parking problems, the jostling and expensive items – and where you are just treated as a number and not a real fan.

So you'll understand why I'm looking forward to marching into the St Mary's stadium to the same hospitality I received at The Dell.

George Holland, Banstead, Surrey

Chapter 27

6 April 1996 v Blackburn Rovers, Premier League, 1-0

Before Dad took me to The Dell on Easter Saturday 1996, I had no interest in football. He was an avid Saints supporter (see match of 11 March 1961, above) but, as we live near Manchester, I had never been to a match. I had no chance of being allowed to support United (something which I now thank my father for).

Blackburn were the reigning champions and Saints were facing relegation, so it was a crucial match. But the idea of football didn't thrill me too much. When it came to the big day, I threw a tantrum (I was only eight at the time) and my Dad had literally to drag me from the house.

I remember arriving and having to trek from the car to The Dell in a huge crowd, thinking "what the hell am I doing here?" But when I arrived in the ground, I warmed to the whole idea and I'm so glad that I did! From the moment the teams ran onto the pitch, I loved it, the atmosphere was electric, the crowd were all cheering and chanting and I held my breath every time Saints took a shot at goal.

The wonderful thing about Saints fans is that, even through the bad times, they never stop singing. It looked like being a 0-0 draw but everyone was still belting out *Oh when the Saints...* I knew then that I wanted to return. Luckily, Saints were awarded a penalty about 10 minutes from time. Matt Le Tissier took it – of course! Dad whispered in my ear, "It's a sure thing." I felt the whole crowd hold their breath as Matt ran up to take it. When he scored, everybody went wild.

I now go to The Dell as often as I can and try to go to a lot of the away games up North. If I couldn't go and watch Saints play, I don't think anybody else could compare. I can't imagine going to watch United or City: it's just not the same. To me, the best thing about football is the atmosphere and the atmosphere at The Dell was one of a kind.

Anna Atkinson, Macclesfield

18 September 1996 v Peterborough United, League (Coca-Cola) Cup, First Round, first leg, 2-0

For many, supporting Saints and going to The Dell always went hand in hand. Unfortunately, for me this was not the case for several long years. I was born and brought up in the north of Hampshire. My mother had been taken to The Dell many times by my grandfather: hence my support for the red-and-white. But she married a rugby player. There are several places my father would prefer to be than at a football stadium. Six feet underground being one of them.

So I would have to make my own way to The Dell. Once I had finally earned the money, I telephoned for a ticket, to be told I required a membership. Then came the frustrating bit – to get a membership you needed to go to four matches, but to get a ticket for a match you needed a membership. I'm sure I was not the first to be caught out by this vicious circle and doubtless not the last. There are many more like me, for whom Southampton is the nearest team, and who look to the city from which our county takes its name. Not being born in Southampton does not make people any less passionate supporters. Indeed, supporting Saints is all the more difficult when all you can do is listen to Radio Solent, read the (biased) press and watch the (20 seconds of) highlights on *Match of the Day*.

My luck changed in 1996. By happy coincidence I was working at the Boat Show when the Coca-Cola Cup match against Peterborough United was made pay-on-the-night. Feeling a bit like a five year-old kid, I paid my £10 over and went in. The first thing that struck you was the noise that the crowd made, even before you entered the stand proper, let alone the roar as the players came onto the pitch. Having been used to TV and radio, I found not having a replay took some getting used to. Fortunately I was looking in-line as Matt Le Tissier scored a screamer. I can remember thinking how solid and skilful on the ball Lundekvam looked. He was from that moment my favourite player. Gordon Watson scored the other goal.

I cannot remember much more of what happened on the pitch. I was in truth too busy looking round the ground and soaking up the atmosphere. I do, however, remember going to the ticket office so that I could get my membership application form stamped. One match down. Eighteen months and three away matches later, I would make my league debut at The Dell, against Newcastle (see match of 28 March 1998, below). It was certainly that one glimpse of Paradise that got me through my qualifying stages, with such dark times as Coventry 1 (Soltvedt) Saints 0.

Miles Parker, Liphook

FULL-TIME *at* THE DELL

19 October 1996 v Sunderland, Premier League, 3-0

It had all started two years before when a seven year-old boy came home from school and asked "Dad, what team do you support?" "Southampton, of course!" "Really? I'm a United supporter."

From that moment, it was my father's life quest to change my opinion. You might think that would have been simple, but two whole years it took for him to win me over. Then, early one Autumn morning, we travelled down to Southampton from Camberley to get tickets to watch Manchester United. But that meant we had to buy tickets for the previous Saturday as well, so my first game was against Sunderland.

What a day it was – sunny and a wonderful atmosphere. Ascending those Milton end steps to the music playing, the crowd shouting and the players kicking in was simply breathtaking. Dodd scored first. Then a Le Tissier penalty (which I was going to see many more of) and a well-earned goal from Neil Shipperley.

I came home thoroughly pleased but my father warned me not to expect a repeat the following Saturday: "these are the Premier League Champions." But Southampton's 6-3 win against the team I had wanted to support convinced me that my dad had rightly objected to my infant illusion.

Daniel Baird, Camberley

23 October 1996 v Lincoln, League (Coca-Cola) Cup, Third Round, 2-2

With so many supporters locked out of this pay-at-the-gate cup-tie, I was lucky to be inside, watching my first match. My previous experience of football had been playing it at school – along with other sports, especially hockey, the game at which I excelled.

It was a very exciting evening game. The atmosphere was electric. I was there expecting to be the chairman of a holding company, but would become the chairman of a football club by default.

With the team looking racing certs to go down and with me not wanting to be associated with failure, I got involved at the behest of the Board, principally Guy Askham, and took over, come the close season, his chairmanship of Southampton FC.

In my first four years, the Club achieved my twin objective: to move to a new stadium, still as members of the Premiership. And in the process, I came to appreciate what a community magnet football is. My experience as a player of so many sports had in no way prepared me for sharing with, and having a responsibility to, the people of Southampton and its hinterland.

Rupert Lowe, Chairman

Jason Dodd (left) congratulates Matthew Le Tissier on his 30-yard equalizing volley

Standing room only as the pay-at-the-gate cup-tie produced an unexpected lock-out

28 March 1998 v Newcastle United, Premier League, 2-1

Welcome to Andrei Zhezlov who has come all the way from Moscow to see the Saints...

As the half-time announcement spreads over the packed Dell, I am shocked and stunned and nailed to seat 25 in row 4 of the Milton Road stand.

I had begun to follow the Saints some 10 years before. We were playing one of the first football manager games at a computer class in a Moscow school and I just liked the name. Having then kept up with their results in the Russian sports papers for five or six years, I got an Internet connection and my first "search" was for Southampton FC. Then, every weekend and some midweek days, I would sit up late at night, staring at the computer and following the score updates – until Radio Solent's live broadcast became available online. And sometimes I would catch glimpses of the Saints when Russian TV turned to something like *Match of the Day*.

Early in 1998, Saints fan Miles Parker (see match of 18 September 1996, above) found my e-mail address on the Saints' Internet "List" and began to correspond. When he invited me to England, I obtained a visa from the British Embassy – after waiting for two months and queuing for two days. British Airways flew me to Gatwick and Miles drove me from his home in Liphook to Southampton.

Arriving at The Dell early for the "stadium tour", we visited the trophy cabinet and the dressing room, where the match kits were ready. I even managed to touch Le Tissier's shirt. Then we stepped onto the pitch and took some photos. And Miles had set up pre-match meetings with Per Opsahl, the president of Norway Saints Supporters Club, and Rod Armitage, who enjoys "SOG" (sad old git) status on the "List". We were back at the ground in time to watch Saints warming up and to take another photo – of Le God.

The first half was very scrappy and not so interesting but for me it was a real football festival. Difficult to describe my senses then. Being at The Dell and joining in the singing of *By far the Greatest Team the World has ever seen*. The second half was more entertaining. Newcastle scored but then Saints started to dominate the game at last. The crowd urged the lads on. We scored. Five minutes to go and Stuart Pearce handled in the box. A spot kick! The Magpies were protesting, though useless. Le Tiss scored the winner.

Insane happiness for the Saints supporter from a Moscow computer class.

Andrei Zhezlov, Moscow

Andrei Zhezlov had his photo taken on the Dell pitch, then donned his shades to meet up with (left to right) Per Opsahl of Norway Saints; and Miles Parker and Rod Armitage of Internet Saints

FULL-TIME *at* THE DELL

10th April 2000 v Coventry City, FA Youth Cup, semi-final, second leg, 0-2

Although still only four, I'd already been to a few Reserves matches, when my daddy decided he would take me to what he describes as my first "competitive" game. I have to bow to his labelling on that – and everything else, for that matter – as, although I'm now six, I still need him as my ghost-writer, you see. Having drawn at Coventry in the first leg, Saints were favourites to go through to the final. The 2-0 defeat was only one of the ways, though, in which the evening didn't quiet pan out as Daddy had expected. We arrived early, so that he could get good seats, from which I was able to see. We sat in the front row of the Upper West, in line with the half-way line, which Daddy said was the best possible view. But not the best position from which to get the gear that the Club had decided that the kids – who made up most of the crowd – should have. Like the flags that the stewards were giving out to the crowd in the Lower West Stand, but not in the Upper West, where Daddy had decided to sit for my sake. I was not impressed. If he thought the game would take my mind off my being denied a flag, he had another thought coming. It was a very one-sided affair, with little for Saints fans to get excited about, so I can hardly be blamed for cheering when Coventry scored their first goal. Daddy thereupon explained the nature of partisanship, so I didn't cheer their second. By the time we left the ground, I fully understood which side had outscored the other. "Saints weren't very good, Daddy," I'm told I commented, "they scored two and we didn't get any." Daddy says welcome to the club, son; I'd better get used to it.

He hasn't said how old I'll need to be before I get that cynical about my team.

Joshua John Ganley, Totton

The five o'clock shadows on Archers Road are as long as the fans' faces, after another home defeat – by Middlesbrough on 30 September 2000 – the last-ever September engagement at The Dell

Chapter 28
My Favourite Game

13 October 1945 v Newport County, League South, 0-0

Even for a football-addicted 14 year-old boy, this goalless draw would not have offered any greatly lasting memories had it not been for his experience on the return rail journey to Brockenhurst.

Standing in the corridor next to the boy during the 15 minutes or so of the train ride was a tall, fair-haired, youngish man wearing the uniform of an RAF corporal. Encouraged by the sight of a likely-looking hold-all at the airman's feet, the boy asked, in the polite fashion of that time, if he had been playing football. Indeed he had. He was Eric Sibley, Southampton's right-back that afternoon.

In the few minutes available, the boy plied the footballer with a flow of questions. What, for instance, had been the pre-kick-off instructions? He learned how the manager had introduced Sibley, whose first Southampton appearance this had been, to Albert Roles, the regular left-back, with the standard direction that Sibley at right-back would mark the opposing outside-left, while Roles would look after the Newport right-winger.

The journey passed all too quickly and almost all of what was learned of Eric Sibley was gained from later sources. Bournemouth-born, he had played for Bournemouth and Boscombe before being transferred to Blackpool, whence he guested six times for Saints in that 1945-46 season and later moved to Grimsby Town and then Chester City. Interest in his career might have been of distant nature had it not been for a second meeting, some 15 years after the first conversation, at a cricket match in Boldre. A considerable club cricketer, Sibley was playing for the visitors, Adastral, and there was an opportunity, afterwards at the *Fleur de Lys*, for the now grown-man to ask him further questions. Several of these concerned Blackpool, notably the experience of playing right-back to Stanley Matthews. These and other queries were equally patiently received; but, as at the initial meeting, the time passed too soon, with a dozen more questions unput.

That summer evening's word is treasured every bit as much as the meeting on the train. There remains an abiding appreciation of one person's infinite courtesy towards another – prompted by, and forever in the mind linked with, a match at The Dell in which neither Southampton nor Newport County were able to score.

Norman Gannaway, Lymington

Back row (left to right): Ellerington, Arthur Dominy (Team Manager), Evans, Ramsey, Stroud, Sibley, Warhurst, Roles, J.R.Sarjantson (Secretary-Manager), Jimmy Gallagher (Trainer).

Front row (left to right):Roper, Bates, McGibbon, Bradley, Hassell.

The Saints line up for one of Eric Sibley's six guest appearances (17 November 1945 v West Bromwich Albion)
The only guest in this side, Sibley continued, when the *Echo* recycled this photo over the years, to fox the caption-writers, who would shamelessly describe him as "Player unknown – wartime guest?"

FULL-TIME *at* THE DELL

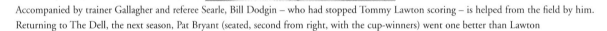

29 December 1945 v Chelsea, League South, 7-0

Having first gone to The Dell as a schoolboy in the early 1940s, when Ted Bates and Don Roper were my favourites, I am inevitably among the many [see the examples in the previous chapter] for whom this 7-0 win is an outstanding memory. And a triumph not just for Doug McGibbon, with his six goals and his record-breaking effort from the second-half kick-off, but for Bill Dodgin who never gave the great Tommy Lawton a look-in.

My fondest Dell memory, however, is a personal one, from playing there for Woolston Boys in the 1947 Youth Cup Final. Bill Dodgin Junior (whose father had by then, of course, become Saints' manager) was playing for Harefield Youth Club, but we beat them 3-1 and I scored our second goal at the Archers Road end – a tremendous strike from about two feet.

Pat Bryant, Bexhill-on-Sea, East Sussex

Accompanied by trainer Gallagher and referee Searle, Bill Dodgin – who had stopped Tommy Lawton scoring – is helped from the field by him. Returning to The Dell, the next season, Pat Bryant (seated, second from right, with the cup-winners) went one better than Lawton

11 December 1950 v Barnsley, Division Two, 1-0

Can it really be over 50 years since I stood on the ice-packed terrace in the Boys' enclosure at the Milton Road end? So much wanting to be part of the action versus Barnsley and identifying myself, in one of the following Monday's 'papers, among celebrity players captured on photo.

It wasn't my first match at The Dell. That had been the Cup replay against Northampton Town the previous season – the only time I saw the Dell legend, Charlie Wayman. He had scored both goals in a 3-2 defeat, but at 13, I was too young to appreciate his high profile among the Dell faithful. Now, though, he had departed for Preston and Eddy Brown had arrived in part-exchange. Eddy not only scored the only goal against Barnsley; he arrived in the goalmouth just too late to score another, but in time, as you can see, to join me and Danny Blanchflower on camera.

Tom Kelly (circled) leans into view as Danny Blanchflower (No.4) slips and Eddy Brown (No.9) strives to inherit the Wayman mantle

Tom Kelly, Christchurch

18 April 1960 v Reading, Division Three, 1-0

It was the win that ensured promotion to Division Two. It was a pivotal match in Saints' 20th century history, taking them for the second time up and out of Division Three. And this time, they would keep going upwards to the top division. On that Easter Monday afternoon, we were not, of course, to know of the success that lay ahead. This was simply the high point – to which clinching the Championship a few games later seemed almost incidental – of a sparkling season when some lovely flowing, attacking football took the division by storm (to say nothing of that famous 5-1 Cup win at First Division Manchester City). Heady days, indeed, for a teenager who had followed them all season, home and away.

This "wonderful panoramic *Echo* photo" of the long-range header from Brian Clifton (stripes, right) may have been revisited over and over, but who can possibly object to seeing it again?

The anticipation and excitement was quite special. The 25,042 crammed into The Dell saw Brian Clifton score the only goal after 15 minutes, when he met John Sydenham's cross with a powerful header from the edge of the box – a moment, coincidentally featuring my two all-time favourite players, forever enshrined in that wonderful panoramic Echo photo, so often revisited. If only they took photos like that nowadays!

Not the *best* Saints match I've ever seen, but for sheer occasion and importance my favourite.

Dave Adlem, Bristol

4 January 1964 v Manchester United, FA Cup Third Round, 2-3

If everyone else is recounting famous victories or fight-backs, there may be something novel in my recalling a defeat. But it happens to be the game I remember most vividly.

In the final years of The Dell, it had become hard to imagine 29,000 souls crammed into it. However, for the visit of the Cup-holders, many more than that would happily have queued all night. On their way to that Wembley win, United had beaten the Saints, somewhat fortuitously, in the semi-final. But Denis Law, scorer of the only goal, was missing on this occasion and Matt Busby relied on two fledgling wingers – Willie Anderson and a certain George Best, each playing only his second senior game. This was a magnificent cup-tie and there is no doubt the Saints should have won it. They led 2-0 at half-time, thanks to a sublime Martin Chivers goal, struck from distance as defenders appeared to have forced him away from the danger area, and a real collector's item – a point-blank Terry Paine header from John Sydenham's cross. The second came on the stroke of half-time and the match should have been over. Maybe the Saints tried to sit on their lead, maybe they were simply forced back. Nearly 40 years on, this observer is still unsure. But the fact is that Pat Crerand and Maurice Setters camped on the half-way line and set up the kind of relentless service which made 45 minutes seem a very long time indeed. And the goals came. Graham Moore, who did precious little else in his United career, and Bobby Charlton scored with headers, but the abiding memory is of Tommy Traynor flailing desperately on the goal-line as David Herd's effort crept in with just the hint of an apology. Setters, his face still streaming with sweat, told the world at large that Saints had let United off the hook. Well, perhaps. But it was a riveting, never-to-be-forgotten encounter. All five goals came at the Milton Road end, incidentally. No doubt there were United fans dotted around The Dell – there always were. But it is safe to assume that most of those who had watched the drama unfold went home sad.

Ian Carnaby, Nailsea, Somerset

FULL-TIME *at* THE DELL

30 April 1966 v Charlton Athletic, Division Two, 1-0

Memory 1: As a game of football, it was no classic. But, for sheer nail-biting drama and the significance of the result, our final home game in the promotion run-in of 1966 takes a lot of beating.

Saints had managed to put together a rather unconvincing eight-match unbeaten run during March and April, with a combination of scrappy draws and none too convincing wins. But our promotion rivals were falling away and now, with mid-table Charlton (a team we had walloped 4-0 and 6-1 the previous two seasons) coming to The Dell, surely Saints would regain their goal-scoring touch and save our nerves.

Pressed against the wall behind the goals was my natural habitat in those days; but, for the first time ever, I was sitting in the stands with my mother. It was a beautifully warm sunny day.

Things didn't go according to plan. My faded memory tells me that Saints attacked incessantly but in reality it probably wasn't quite that one-sided. Whatever, half-time came and it was still 0-0 and so it went on…and on…and on. Charlton held firm against intense and increasingly desperate pressure. Play was deep in Saints' half as the match went into injury time and a disappointing draw seemed inevitable.

Then came one of those rare football moments that are forever etched in the memory (like Bobby Stokes's winner at Wembley and that Le Tiss goal against Newcastle). Saints had two forward players of undoubted class at that time, Martin Chivers and Terry Paine, and they combined to devastating and brilliant effect.

Collecting the ball at the Milton Road end as a Charlton attack broke down, and urged on by the crowd, "Big Chiv" powered 70 yards down the right wing leaving several Charlton players trailing in his wake. As the ball was pulled back from the by-line, Paine nipped in between two defenders to score from close range. Few if any goals at The Dell can have been celebrated with more fervour or relief.

Moments later, the final whistle went and Terry Paine was chaired off. Ears were glued to radios. Other results went our way and I can still hear those magic words from *Sports Report*: "It looks as though we will be seeing Southampton in the First Division for the first time in their history."

It would take another tense affair at Plymouth Argyle and that famous night at Leyton Orient to clinch it (virtually) but, once the Chivers-Paine combination had created that golden goal against Charlton, promotion was there for the taking.

Richard Atkinson, Macclesfield

Memory 2: It had all started so brightly, with the programme sellers proclaiming "Last home game in the Second Division," as 22,000 of us poured into The Dell on that sunny April day.

But optimism had turned to anxiety as three times the woodwork and, on numerous occasions, Wright the Charlton goalkeeper had kept Saints at bay. The tension had grown tighter and tighter until, in the dying minutes, hope had all but evaporated. It wasn't going to be our day – they didn't want to go up, did they?

A far-from-fully-fit Martin Chivers got the ball near the halfway line. At his best, he might have dribbled through the entire opposition defence and have scored a sensational goal – but what hope now?

As he set off towards the goal, whether from choice or because he was so marshalled by the retreating Charlton defence, he hugged the touch-line. The crowd's murmur of expectation had turned to a groan of disappointment as he somehow made it to the goal-line and just about sent over an innocuous little centre that dribbled across the Charlton penalty area. Why the advancing 'keeper failed to claim it, or a defender get there to intercept and clear, will never be known; but "World Cup Terry" Paine appeared, as if from nowhere, to meet the cross and score.

The Dell erupted as only it could. No-one wanted to leave as grown men cried and delirium took over. There has since been many a last momentous game of the season at The Dell – but none with quite such a late winner until the drama of the last game of all [as recalled below] – and, although nothing was decided, the dream of the Promised Land was on again. The coach to Plymouth was soon booked, followed by a half-day bunked off school for the trip to Orient.

John Parsons, Bassett

Terry Paine finishes on the ground after rounding off the memorable run by Martin Chivers (still standing) against Charlton

16 September 1967 v Liverpool, Division One, 1-0

Those old enough to remember the scrapes Saints had with relegation during their first spell in the First Division will undoubtedly agree that goals were nevertheless plentiful "in them days", with the likes of Martin Chivers, Ron Davies and then a youthful Mick Channon. Yet the game I especially recall – from when Liverpool came to The Dell early in Saints' second season at that level – was not noted for its goals, but for the drama and tension felt by the crowd (of over 29,000) and the players alike.

Having broken his leg against Liverpool exactly a year previously [see the report, in the previous chapter, on the match of 17 September 1966], Campbell Forsyth was back in the Southampton goal. Saints' form had been inconsistent but Liverpool were leading the league. With only half a minute gone, Saints were awarded a free-kick some 30 yards out from the Archers end, where I was standing behind the goal. Paine chipped a "quickie" in and Chivers stooped to head home. I was reduced to nail-biting for 89 minutes of backs-to-the-wall resistance, in which a memorable display by Forsyth included a penalty save from Tommy Smith.

I'll never forget my evening paper-round. It took me till at least 8 o'clock to finish, because I kept reading the match report in the *Echo*.

Bob Weston, Spalding, Lincs

30 January 1971 v Stoke City, Division One, 2-1

It was not the "match" between Saints and the Potters that makes this my favourite but the match between two players who, at the time, were arguably the best exponents of their particular footballing arts in the world. The heading ability of Ron Davies was pitted against the goal-keeping skills of Gordon Banks, as Terry Paine supplied the ammunition, with a continuous supply of pinpoint crosses.

The game started in spectacular fashion when, after just five minutes, a typical Brian O'Neill thunderbolt was hit with such ferocity that even Banks could only stand and watch it hit the back of the net. Brian Greenhoff equalised with a neat header.

FULL-TIME *at* THE DELL

The hands of Banks await another header from the climbing Davies

It was in the second-half, with Saints kicking towards the Milton Road end where I was standing, that the contest became etched in my memory. Cross after cross came over from Terry Paine on the right and sometimes from Tommy Jenkins on the left. Almost all them were met by the head of Ron Davies and then, in turn, by the hands of Gordon Banks. Eventually, Davies scored but the battle between the two continued to the end.

Going home from The Dell, I knew that nobody in the world at a match that day would have witnessed a more compelling contest of football skills than that between the best header of a ball and the best 'keeper I have ever seen.

Rob Whatley, Freemantle

28 October 1972 v West Bromwich Albion, Division One, 2-1
I cannot recall very much about this game, except for one piece of action. I was at the Archers Road end with my mates, in the front where we always stood – if you were lucky, you might get your picture in the *Daily Echo* on the Monday.

Saints were attacking our end and Bobby Stokes was put through, one-on-one with the goalkeeper, Peter Latchford, younger brother of the more famous Dave and Bob. As Bobby got close to the goal, he lost control and Latchford rushed out to collect the ball. Now, Bobby wasn't a player to give up easily. The two of them collided near the penalty spot and were left in a heap as the ball went out for a corner. Bobby soon jumped up, but the 'keeper had picked up a nasty whack on his hands. The trainer came on with the magic sponge and bucket of water; and, before long, Latchford was OK. But, as he made his way back to

Dave Webster (ringed) and his mates are perfectly placed for the tap-in by Bobby Stokes (No.11)

his line in preparation for the corner, he dipped both of his (ungloved) hands into the bucket. He was very soon to regret that impulse. The corner was swung in too close to him and he gathered it with outstretched arms. Momentarily. The ball slipped from his grasp and dropped behind him. Where Stokes was waiting to prod it into the empty net.

Monday's *Echo* had a picture of the incident – Bobby Stokes scoring and my mates and I about to celebrate.

Dave Webster, Fair Oak

15 September 1976 v Olympique Marseille, European Cup Winners' Cup, First Round, first leg, 4-0
Having emigrated to Australia in 1972, I *had* to return in 1976 for the Cup Final – and stay, of course, for Mick Channon's testimonial, two days later at The Dell. Then I stayed on over the summer, so that I could get a few matches in, the following season, before returning to Australia.

The new season started disastrously with a 0-1 home defeat to Carlisle. We continued with two more defeats and a couple of draws and were only one off the bottom of the table as we came to my last game – home to Marseille. Everyone outside Southampton thought they would make mince-meat out of Saints. Yet Saints had a habit of losing to the bottom clubs, but beating the top clubs. So could they beat Marseille? I really can't remember too much about the match – apart from Saints being a transformed team, ripping Marseille apart. It was total demolition.

I left London that very same night for a coach-trip, through Asia to Australia, taking three-and-a-half months. What a fantastic way to say "Goodbye, England!" and "Goodbye, Saints!"

Peter Varnes, Cudlee Creek, near Adelaide, South Australia

Chapter 28

10 November 1979 v Nottingham Forest, Division One, 4-1

I can't say that I saw this game, at the time, as being an opportunity to avenge a defeat, a little over six months before, in the League Cup Final. Indeed, my memory of the game is one of *beauty*. Vengeance doesn't come into it.

The beauty that still lingers in the eyes of this beholder concerns two second-half goals, each of them by Phil Boyer at the Milton end. OK, so this image could have been re-inforced by my watching video snippets of the game and by rummaging among *Echo* photographs of it when I first came to write it up, as one of Saints' 100 most memorable games, for *Match of the Millennium*. That said, my recall of those goals is not from any of those camera angles, but from my perspective under the East Stand, way towards the Archers end. Twice the play swept away from me down the far touch-line. Twice the ball came in. Twice Boyer stroked it past Peter Shilton.

So what was so special about this – compared, say, with the 4-1 win over Liverpool in 1989? A hard call, but there's just something about that double helping of a surge forward and the sweep of the "early ball", to be met by a forward racing towards the near post, back-tracking defenders in his wake and a frozen 'keeper to beat. Geoff Hurst, in his autobiography, *1966 and All That*, claims that this kind of cross was West Ham's "trademark" in the 1960s, developed by Ron Greenwood from the Hungarian prototype of the 1950s. Maybe so, but I associate that era with Terry Paine, getting to the by-line and looking up to review options that would often include a pass pulled back *behind* the back-trackers. And, having been spoiled by the peerless Paine, we

Saints fans then watched Mick Channon, the disciple, perform at the by-line as the master himself dropped deeper.

But now, here I was, in the late 1970s, watching Channon, in his second coming at The Dell, playing an "early ball" in a majestic move. Alan Ball had demonstrated how it was done when, with the score at 2-1, he dispossessed Kenny Burns, skuttled 40 yards and slid the ball in low and early for Boyer to score. When Channon's cross ended in the same sweet way, the culmination of a move started in Saints' own half by Steve Williams and on to Ball to Boyer to Graham Baker to Channon and Boyer again, it had reporters reaching for their superlatives. Jack Welling thought it "a gem", while John Moynihan revelled in "a wonderful move" and John Parsons in "a masterpiece".

Yet the last word should belong to Brian Clough. His European Cup-holders had won in Rumania in mid-week, *en route* to retaining the trophy. Not for him, though, a Fergiesque whine about the demands of cross-continental travel. He acknowledged that "Southampton were incredible, better than us in every department."

"Incredible" says it nicely for me, Brian, know what you mean.

David Bull, Bristol

Phil Boyer twice evades the back-tracking defenders to beat Shilton for the third goal (top) and the ultimate "gem" (bottom)

FULL-TIME *at* THE DELL

16 March 1984 v Liverpool, Division One, 2-0

There are a lot of favourite games. Too many. This is my fifth – sixth? – attempt.

But it has to be this win over Liverpool.

Saints were great in 1983-84. Notwithstanding my conviction that the team of the 1962-63 FA Cup run could have beaten Brazil 1970 on their day – they never quite had enough days, though – Peter Shilton, Mick Mills, Mark Dennis,

Mark Lawrenson (No.4) waves to his growing band of Dell admirers as Danny Wallace becomes an inverted vertical flash to score his first goal

Steve Williams, Reuben Agboola, Mark Wright, Nick Holmes, Steve Moran, Frank Worthington, David Armstrong and Danny Wallace were, I say, the best Saints team ever. If only there had been a little more strength in depth, we might just have had the Championship.

It was a Friday night. The BBC were broadcasting the match live to the nation – not just to subscribers – and I stood on the Milton. Liverpool had been the best team in the country for over a decade and what made the game special was not that we won (beating Liverpool at The Dell was not unusual in an average year), but that we looked better than them player for player. There wasn't much between the teams, but if you had asked a passing Martian, who just happened to be a footy expert, to pick out the reigning champions, he or she would not have deliberated long in selecting Southampton.

The first goal, the bicycle kick into the Archer's, was not just a great finish, it was the sting to a classic counter-attack, catching the usually unflappable Liverpool going eleven directions at once. The second, Danny running in front of Hansen to head past Grobbelaar, was the result of a consistent edge in midfield.

Two sublime strikes that garnished a performance from heaven. But what made the goals all the more special is … they had a sense of humour. I do not recall any sense of triumphalism on the Milton that night. We laughed, or at least a lot of us did, not at Liverpool, but at the sheer impudence of Danny Wallace.

Dave Juson, Freemantle

7 March 1987 v Leicester City, Division One, 4-0

How to pick one match from a myriad of memories? I could have opted for the fabulous 4-1 "thrashing" of Liverpool, either of the 1996 victories over Manchester United or one of the many "Great Escapes".

So why that 1987 meeting with Leicester? It was a bitterly cold weekend. Heavy snow had put the game in jeopardy and the awful tragedy at Zeebrugge with the *Herald of Free Enterprise*, the previous day, had not left one feeling much like football. Nevertheless, I drove down from London to be among a paltry 11,611 crowd.

The many who had stayed away missed the arrival, on the League stage, of a man who arguably would become the Club's most important player and certainly its most gifted. Matthew Le Tissier had debuted earlier in the season against Spurs and already scored his first League goal at Hillsborough. The Leicester match was only his fifth league start; but, by the end of the game, we knew we had unearthed a rare and prodigious talent. His hat-trick on that freezing afternoon not only warmed the heart, but was also a glorious combination of skill, stamina, guile, control, poise and endeavour in conditions very unsuited to such virtues.

A star was certainly born that day, who would soon assume the mantle of The Dell's favourite son.

Duncan Holley, Winchester

Mark Wright (second from left), having headed down to Matthew Le Tissier (partly hidden by Gordon Hobson, No.10), celebrates as the rising star scores the first of his three goals against Leicester City

1 April 1989 v Newcastle United, Division One, 1-0

It really was a relegation match. Saints, without a win since early November, and Newcastle were both in the bottom three. The football was dogged – though not boring.

It was 0-0, almost the end, and I had come out of the Milton Road end to get through the car-park, en route to the *Winston*, to catch the bus home. I was nearing the exit, by the Shop, when there came this deafening roar. I went back in a little and asked the stewards and police if we had scored.

"No," they said. "It's a penalty."

I asked who was taking it. "Ruddock."

I asked if he had ever taken one before. "No," they said and made room for me to get in front of them to see it.

Yes-s-s! Bless him!

I am sorry to say we waved our scarves and taunted the Newcastle fans, as our bus battled to get through them. It was such an important win for us – it started a good run and we finished 13th but Newcastle sank to the bottom. Now 80, I have made my last early exit from The Dell, but I'll never forget that precious Dell moment.

Irene Mitchell, Bitterne

Neil Ruddock takes the vital penalty… and celebrates success

FULL-TIME *at* THE DELL

Felgate topples back, unable to stop Barry Horne's 35-yard equalizer

26 February 1992 v Bolton Wanderers,
Fifth Round replay, 3-2 (aet)

Having won their Fourth Round replay on penalties at Old Trafford – in the first season of FA Cup shoot-outs – Saints again went to a replay in the Fifth Round, this time at The Dell after throwing away a two-goal advantage at Bolton.

We took the lead in the first-half, thanks to a goal from Alan Shearer, but Bolton equalised from an error by Tim Flowers. After the interval, Bolton came out fired up and ready to have a real go. They looked, and played, like they wanted the victory more than us. The fans were, as usual, singing and chanting at top volume; but, with two minutes left on the clock, Darby put Bolton 2-1 up and we were stunned into absolute, total silence. The atmosphere just completely evaporated: this was such a shattering moment, such as I have never experienced before or since. People were shuffling out of the ground as soon as they had recovered, resigned to another Cup defeat.

But then Barry Horne struck a screamer from 35 yards to equalize. The crush from the fans pouring back in was a frightening, but amazing, experience. In the space of two minutes, the atmosphere had gone from disbelief to hysteria. To top this unforgettable Dell game, Horne went on to score the winner in extra-time.

To see Barry Horne score was a rare enough event. But twice – and on a night like this – just shows you never know what to expect as a Saints fan.

Simon Robinson, Basingstoke

Editor's note: *Apart from amendments to the first paragraph – necessary, as with most openings in this and the previous chapter, to fit a common format – this recollection is essentially unaltered from that written by Simon Robinson in 1995, as part of an "A" Level Media Studies project. Sadly, Simon, who was a Dell season ticket-holder, died in November 2000, aged 21. We are indebted to his mother, Lynn, for sending us this account and for approving the changes I have made.*

24 October 1993 v Newcastle United, Premier League, 2-1

One win, and five points, from the opening 11 games. No win in seven. Only Swindon Town below us in the table. The manager apparently at odds with our pre-eminent goal-scoring and creating talent. The Sky cameras have come, under the floodlights of a dank and dark Sunday twilight, to intrude upon our communal malaise.

Until well into the second-half, there was no real evidence that this was to be a match for the archives of the memory. Then, a ball played across in the left channel to Le Tissier, restored after a three-match lay-off. But the ball was behind him, missing his run. Somehow, with a sideways flick from the outside of his right boot, he retrieved the ball and brought it into the path of his stride. More upward flicks, the ball never touching the ground, and he'd fought clear of the encroaching defenders and was in free space, chasing the ball down into the area.

But the last flick had surely pushed the ball just too far ahead of him and into the path of the facing, last defender. Disappointed, I waited for the clearance. Then, as if defying the laws of ballistics – but, in reality, driven by backspin – instead of bouncing on forwards, the ball seemed to hold, for an instant, straight up in the air between attacker and defender. With astounding skill and spontaneity – or had he known all along that this would happen? – Matt chipped the ball over the defender, without breaking stride, rounded him and met it perfectly as it descended, to slide it precisely past the 'keeper and into the bottom corner. The sort of goal you fantasise about, but never believe you'll see, presented to us at The Dell.

Having brilliantly created the space, Matthew Le Tissier "perfectly" completes his come-back goal

Suddenly a great brilliance and passion in the murky evening. But Newcastle came back with a renewed barrage and, despite all Tim Flowers's heroics and defiance, eventually equalised. I felt deflated not just at the prospect of losing two, or even three, points, but also that a goal of such coruscating splendour was not to bring the victory it merited.

But then the ball's headed back to Le Tiss, some way outside the Newcastle area. As he flicks it up in the air with his thigh, I look at the line of dark blue shirts across the area in front of him. There's so little time left. I think I know what he's going to try. He let it drop, hit it on the volley and, from my vantage point high in the West Stand a little behind the goal-line, I could see almost as soon as it left his boot that it would beat the 'keeper's dive. But it would have to dip. It dipped, and I followed the flight, the ball a luminous white globe hanging under the lights, until I saw it safely under the bar and the criss-cross of the goal-net patterned on it.

And, in that instant, we were on our feet with a roar that acclaimed not just a goal, not just a win, but something like a great blaze of light, the knowledge that this was one of those matches people would recall for years afterwards and you'd think "I was there."

Marian Thomas, Surbiton, Surrey

13 April 1996 v Manchester United, Premier League, 3-1
The headline in the *Chippenham Gazette & Herald* had read YOUNG FAN MARCHES IN. The next day relegation-threatened Southampton would be meeting title-chasing Manchester United at The Dell and Jack Broomfield, a fourth-generation Saints supporter, was to lead out his side as mascot.

Most will remember the game for the "grey shirts" and for how much was made of this in the media afterwards. Saints fans, though, will remember the game for the nature of the 3-1 victory and for how Saints seemed to want the result far more than United did.

Eric Cantona fends off Barry Venison (left) and Jim Magilton

FULL-TIME *at* THE DELL

The scorer, Neil Shipperley (left), wheels away, pursued by Neil Heaney

One headline in particular, BUCCANEERS STILL, summed up the way Saints outplayed United and brought back memories of past Dell games. Yet my enduring memory of the day is of the delight that my son Jack experienced in the couple of hours before the kick-off and of how Alan Smith, Eileen Painter and the Young Saints team – together with Dave Merrington and his players – had given him a unique experience to remember (as, indeed, he does in Chapter 26 above). The slaughter of United was the icing on the cake. And Matty was on song, delivering a typical finish to score Saints' third.

And Jack? He wasn't just at the game, he was actually part of the Saints team that day – a real Dell memory.

Noel Broomfield, Corsham, Wilts

28 September 1996 v Middlesbrough, Premier League, 4-0.

This was a game that for me typified Saints' character and confirmed their right to be in the top flight. No matter that they would fall away and be relegated, Boro came to The Dell, boasting almost £16 million pounds-worth of foreign imports in Juninho, Emerson and Ravanelli and with the Italian striker already looking for his third hat-trick of the season. Saints, by contrast, had only two points to show for their seven games to date.

But, after Ravanelli had shot just wide, it was Saints who took the lead on 11 minutes through Oakley, following some determined work from Watson. Le Tissier now turned it on, first to be denied by Miller, the Boro 'keeper, a goal that would have competed for Goal of the Season; then unleashing a 30-yard drive that tested Miller again; and finally beating him, in the 29th minute, with a corner that flew into the far top corner of his goal.

He seemed to be offside, though, early in the second-half, when Watson chipped the ball over the static Boro defence, but he put the ball in the net and the goal stood. And Watson it was who started – and this time finished – the fourth goal with eight minutes remaining. There was still time, though, for Lundekvam to concede a penalty, which Ravanelli lashed against the bar, for the ball to rebound straight into the hands of Moss.

This stirring first win of the season was vital (as Oz appreciated). Not only did it spark a mini-run that included the 3-0 win

"One little win — and all I've had since Saturday night from Captain Kirk here is: We have lift-off!"

over Sunderland [reported in the previous chapter] and the famous 6-3 defeat of Manchester United; but it effectively meant that Saints survived, come May, at the expense of Middlesbrough who, after having three points deducted, went down on 39 points, compared with Saints on 41.

That's how important this game was. And what a glorious one.

Manny Choudhury, Eastleigh

Chapter 28

"Ale-House" Jake

21 February 1998 v Blackburn Rovers, Premier League, 3-0
A beautiful sunny Dell day and a sparkling performance from Saints to remind Tim Flowers and Jeff Kenna that the grass is not always greener away from The Dell. Uriah Rennie even gave a superb exhibition of refereeing. But with Saints already several points clear of the dreaded drop-zone, what made this game so special out of 40-odd seasons of Dell visits?

This was the match when my dad Albert, Bill Nicholas and I received an after-game invitation to the boardroom. Ordinary fans like us (even with around 150 years of Saints support between us) rarely got invited to sample the legendary Dell boardroom hospitality. The excellent win set us up nicely for an audience with "Mr Southampton" himself, Ted Bates. The legend lived up to his reputation and for the next hour we talked football, football and more football.

Just as we were thinking that Ted's family ought to have prior claim over him, big John McGrath (reporting on the match for a Lancashire radio station) arrived on the scene. Ted disappeared in a giant bear-hug and when he emerged it was introductions all round. A polite enquiry from my dad about "the ale-house brawlers" – you may recall that big "Jake" was the principal target of Bill Shankly's attack on the Saints side of the early 70s – launched John into his after-dinner routine. "Shankly was wrong about that," he regretted: "only seven of us were drunk; the other four were on drugs."

Mark Fickling, Rownhams

16 May 1999 v Everton, Premier League, 2-0
Memory 1: I was at The Dell a good half-hour before the kick-off. That was very early for an Archers boy, but the tension had become too much for me. At one point, I had had to leave the *Pensioners Arms,* as I could not sit there and drink my pint.

The Saints really had that look about them, after winning their previous two games. We were soon celebrating like crazy and hugging everyone in sight, after Pahars ran on to a Beattie knock-down, to drive the ball past the Everton 'keeper for 1-0. From then on, the support was getting louder and louder – although the second-half, as it sometimes would down The Dell, began slowly before hitting a frantic tempo around 25 minutes to go.

Everton were starting to come forward in numbers, with the dangerous Kevin Campbell threatening to add to his excellent recent run of nine goals in five games. But the best moment of my Dell life was about to happen. A block by Marsden sent Beattie scampering off to the by-line, where he nipped in a low cross for Pahars to score with a superb diving header. The relief and celebration afterwards was the loudest I ever witnessed at The Dell, as the whole ground united in a special song for Rodney Marsh.

Then came further celebrating in the pubs. Having proved all the doubters wrong, we managed to salute them in our manner, while watching the TV. The following day, it was still sinking in when the *Daily Mirror* gave Marians and our latest "Great Escape" a double page-spread.

Colin Graves, Totton

Memory 2: The uniqueness of our Club centres around "family" and the bond felt between all areas of our support. I think this has improved greatly over the past five years with Board and supporters now rowing largely in the same direction. This has been clearly visible for everybody to see since Glenn Hoddle's surprise resignation in April 2001. I am proud of this achievement as this cohesiveness and regional pride will be a very important contributor to our success in the new stadium.

It was probably at its peak during our last game of the 1998-99 season when we put the finishing touches to another of those "Great Escapes". I don't think I have ever enjoyed a day more or indeed caught up on so much needed sleep after the event.

Rupert Lowe, Chairman

FULL-TIME *at* THE DELL

19 May 2001 v Arsenal, Premier League, 3-2

The last League match at The Dell encapsulated the four things with which I had come to associate being a home fan:

- exciting matches in which we turned over the big clubs on an almost annual basis;
- a ground whose character somehow went hand-in-hand with the whole ethos of being a Southampton fan;
- last-day escapes; and, finally,
- a host of wonderful, wonderful goals by Matty.

I was by now 22 and had been going there since 1984, yet I didn't feel I had the same strong ties that so many Saints fans had been describing – on the internet, for instance – over the previous couple of weeks. So, unlike them, I was not going to get emotional on the "Big Day". But when Matty turned to volley home that late goal, I, too, felt my eyes well up. And me not being the smallest, either – there were some surprised faces among those I had sat with for the last 12 years in the Lower West. In that moment, and the subsequent minutes, I was moved to think of those four special associations.

The atmosphere and celebrations, although somehow more joyous, were akin to those days we had gone into the final game knowing one slip could send us tumbling. An atmosphere that I don't think could be created to that magnitude anywhere else in the country. I just hope we can go some way towards recreating it at St Mary's.

And Matty's goal will always remain special. Throughout my childhood he was my hero. And he still

So you saw him doing it in Chapter 1 – but we took it you wouldn't mind another look

is. Every time I see that strike, it will remind me more than any other event of the many, many afternoons I spent in that quirky little stadium with my dad. And yet I wish, in many ways, that Matty hadn't been given a new contract and that his Dell swansong could have been my last memory of the legend that is Matthew Le Tissier. I fear he will be unable, ever again, to bow out on such a high note and that he will just slip away on the conclusion of his one-year contract.

So, for me, that game against Arsenal will always be remembered as the passing of two great legends: of Matty and of our very old friend, The Dell. Moreover, I had not been born in 1976; so, unless and until 1 May 1976 is repeated, then 19 May 2001 will be stored in my memory bank under the heading, "MY CUP FINAL."

Andrew Carruthers, Cardiff

Chapter 29
Worst and Weirdest Moments

Various members of my family took me, as a kid, to a game against Arsenal. We had been queuing at the Archers Road end when two very tall gates opened and the crowd surged forward, packed liked sardines, towards those open gates. Suddenly, a voice cried out "There's a child down." Quick as a flash, a voice boomed back "We'll pick 'im up."

We were swept into the ground and, to this day, I owe the Club 10p (plus interest) for the only time I got in and watched the game free – until I joined the Board 50 years later.

Michael Withers, Director

It had started so well. My first visit to The Dell had been the ten-goal thriller with Plymouth Argyle in August 1945. But Dad was in the Merchant Navy, spending much of the year overseas, which meant that there was quite a gap before my second visit.

Yet my attendance at the 2-2 draw with Bradford in September 1948 came about through Dad's work. He was serving on the *Andes,* which had conveyed the team to Brazil for their close season tour of 1948, and Mr Stranger, the director who had organized that tour, had invited him to watch a match from the Directors' Box.

It was my first sight of Charlie Wayman who obliged with two goals. But it was a non-football moment that will always remind my sister Jean and myself of our VIP day out. Rationing was still in force but Dad had brought some sweets home from his latest South American trip and we dutifully passed the bag around. When the bag reached the manager, Bill Dodgin, he took a sweet, winked his thanks to my sister and continued to watch the action.

Then disaster struck! Bill was suddenly summoned to the dug-out, with our precious bag of sweets still in his pocket. He never returned to the box and we never saw our sweets again. At the time, losing them was worse than dropping a point – we were not to know that it would cost Saints promotion come April.

We obviously forgave Bill as I remain an avid Saints fan, while Jean maintains a close interest, principally through her son Leon, who follows them home and away. But you'll understand what I mean when I suggest that managing Southampton was once as easy as taking sweets from children.

John Warren, Chiswick

It was anticipated that I would follow my father into the "family business". My father was Ron Reynolds, Saints 'keeper during the early 1960s.

So it was that I reported, one May morning, a few seasons after he'd retired and when I was 15 or 16, for a trial match at The Dell. I had no idea what was about to hit me, as we changed, listened to a briefing, selected teams and walked out into a dust bowl that was The Dell at the season's end. Grass non-existent, goalmouth like concrete. After 10 minutes of non-stop action, mostly at my end, I began to wonder if I was really cut out to be a professional footballer. I played only the first-half, during which, despite my valiant efforts, one opposing forward hit three past me, while another live-wire scored a screamer that I never saw.

Both players were magic, a cut above everyone else, obviously destined for a bright future. The hat-trick scorer was Bobby Stokes, whom I'd previously encountered in Portsmouth youth circles. The other was Micky Channon – a teenager like the rest of us, but with a few first-team appearances behind him. Ted Bates must have put him on to make it a real "trial" for our defence – and the hapless goalkeeper in particular. My one and only game at The Dell. My worst moment. The beginning of the end of my professional career.

I have since followed Mick's career with special interest. Every now and then I put a few bob on one of his horses – he still does me no favours, though.

David Reynolds, Haslemere, Surrey

FULL-TIME *at* THE DELL

We would get there early to lean on the Saints' dug-out. We liked to exchange refreshments with the trainer, Jimmy Gallagher. When Saints scored, he used to give me a sweet. Conversely, there was a lady near us who used to make home-brewed wine. This particular one looked like whisky and when she gave Jimmy a glass, thinking it was the real thing, he downed it. When she gave him a second one, we never saw what he did with it before handing back an empty glass.

Ada Sims, Bournemouth

The January 1964 cup-tie against Manchester United was a memorable match [even appearing among "Favourite" games in the previous chapter].

I was 13 and by then a terrace regular, though on this occasion I sat with my mum in the East Stand. A 2-0 half time lead – Martin Chivers, with a rising drive from the edge of the area, and Terry Paine with a header – and the heights of ecstasy that perhaps only young teenagers at football matches can ever know. But then, in the second-half, United asserted themselves and Saints faded away to lose 3-2. It was all dreadfully disappointing and this disappointment was to be re-awakened, some 35 seasons later, when *Dell Diamond* was published and we discovered just why Saints had failed to contain United's second-half revival. It was, in the words of *Dell Diamond*, "a shame of two halves"; and the shame was on those players for whom the attractions of Butlins Redcoats and plenty of drink at the Club's match-preparation venue had proved too much and who were short of energy to withstand United's three-goal comeback.

I think I felt rather let down when I read all this. These things count for a lot when you are 13.

Dave Atkinson, Chester

It was grey. It was probably raining. And on the last day of 1966, we were playing Blackpool, the team anchored at the bottom of the table. As the excitement of Saints' first season in the top flight took on an edge of anxiety as to whether we would retain that status, this was a match we must, and surely would, win.

It didn't seem to matter that Blackpool scored first: I have a mental image of Ron Davies rising improbably high above a cluster of tangerine shirts to equalize with a majestic, trademark header, accompanied by a great sense of relief that the natural order of things had been restored and that now, surely, against Blackpool of all teams, everything would be all right.

But Blackpool scored again … and again… and again. As realisation grew that it was my team out there that had degenerated into miserable capitulation and disarray, I watched in wretched disbelief, wishing I was in another time, another place. I simply hadn't seen this sort of thing happen before to them. And then, when another cross came over and Ray Charnley, from almost the edge of the area, soared virtually unchallenged to head his hat-trick goal high above Dave MacLaren's reach, it seemed like a mocking reprise of Davies's first-half goal. One newspaper called it a "storybook" header. Not my kind of book, I thought.

It's not that easy to single out "worst" Dell moments – defeats mostly have a certain bleak sameness, while each victory has its own special vibrancy. Most typically, of course, the gut-wrenching injury-time goal, conceded to surrender some or all of the spoils, is the one guaranteed to pull you down into denial and irremediable bad humour. Yet, for all that the match was already lost, that header of Charnley's, to make it 5-1, still stands out in my memory, 35 years on, as a defining moment of utter humiliation – my first in the cause of Southampton Football Club.

Marian Thomas, Surbiton, Surrey

Worst moment? It has to be the last goal in the worst – non-Branfoot era – match I've had the misfortune to endure.

It was played out in continuous rain. Leicester City were winning 4-1 and had barely been out of their own half. There were only two players in the Saints' half when the gods decided to have a laugh at our expense. Some deity or other was responsible, because… well, what happened was that the teenage Shilton dropped-kicked the ball upfield, Stringfellow chased after it with no great enthusiasm and the gallant Campbell Forsyth rushed out of his goal. The ball was dropping out of the grey sky on a parabola that would see it land, with a splash, a yard or so outside the area.

Chapter 29

Only it didn't land. It bounced. Now take a football down to Crosshouse, when the tide is out. Get way out into the mud and fling it down with all your force. You may get a face full of noxiously odoriferous slime, but the ball will just sit there. Well, the surface of The Dell on 14 October 1967 was so near the same consistency of Itchen mud it made no difference, but the ball bounced. It bounced high and true over Forsyth and into the goal.

I know this because the score is on record. I actually have no memory of the ball doing anything other than pass, on an impossibly elevated trajectory, over Forsyth's head and… that's the point when I wake up.

Dave Juson, Freemantle

It was 1967-68, our second season in the First Division; and, while we had no chance of winning the League, you always had a chance in the FA Cup. We'd drawn 1-1 at The Hawthorns and had come out of the hat with Pompey for the Fifth round (if they won their replay at home to Fulham and we won ours). A golden path to the last eight beckoned with the thrill of a local derby along the way.

With an expectant home crowd behind them, Saints attacked from the outset and soon the dream seemed all but a reality. Frank Saul, the recent Chivers-deal makeweight, not only succeeded in scoring but semi-concussed the Albion goalkeeper, John Osborne, in the process. With full-back, Graham Williams, taking over in goal for the second-half, the match was there for the taking. Sadly, it all went wrong from then on. This was the Albion of Kaye and Astle, Clark, Hope and Tony Brown – a talented side and, it has to be said, they performed superbly. Against all the odds, they played an increasingly desperate Saints off the park. They led 2-1 at half-time, but a Hughie Fisher goal looked like taking the game into extra-time – surely Saints would then prevail – but, sickeningly, Jeff Astle applied the *coup de grace* with an injury-time goal. I was inconsolable – all the more so when I learned of Pompey's victory over Fulham.

Albion would go all the way and beat Everton 1-0 at Wembley.

Richard Atkinson, Macclesfield

Our first foray into Europe – in 1969-70 – and already in the Third Round. Saints were never going to win the league but cup glory was always a possibility. Hopes were high after a battling 0-0 draw at St James' Park and they rose even higher when Mick Channon scored an early goal and Saints dominated the first-half of the second leg. Surely it was only a matter of time before more goals came and the match was ours. There were to be no more goals from Saints but a deserved win still seemed on the cards as the final minutes ticked away.

Our little group of regular supporters had been joined in the Milton by a school friend called Nick who had previously lived in Newcastle and who claimed rather unconvincingly to support the Magpies. He was pretty quiet throughout and remained so until a last gasp "Pop" Robson equaliser had him in rapturous celebrations while all around him stood in dejected silence. We stopped liking Nick at that moment.

Newcastle were through on that iniquitous away goals rule. We felt cheated and so disappointed. To make matters worse, they went on to win the trophy. Nick's gloating just rubbed salt into open wounds. To this day, I have never again accompanied the supporter of an opposing team to The Dell for a match. And now I never will.

Bob Cushion, Dubai.

When Leeds United came to The Dell in October 1979, I gave my season ticket to my son, Sean. Hoping to be remembered as a generous father, I would let him sit in the West Stand while I watched the match from the Milton Road terrace. It was, of course, still pay-on-the-day for supporters and, with Leeds as always proving a major attraction, I found myself locked out of The Dell's biggest – 23,259 – crowd of the season.

What to do? Stay at the ground and endure the torment of wondering whether each roar from within greeted a goal; or take myself off to the city centre and maybe browse through some bookstores? I decided on the latter, arriving back just in time for the final whistle and briefly to catch a glimpse on the *Match of the Day* monitor of Alan Curtis, later to join Saints, scoring a marvellous solo goal in Leeds's 2-1 win.

Tom Kelly, Christchurch

FULL-TIME *at* THE DELL

It was the mid-eighties and we were playing all-conquering Liverpool, an arrogant bunch then and not too high up on my list of most-loved clubs. I was sitting half-way up the bench seats underneath the East Stand when, all of a sudden, the ball came to me in the crowd as Liverpool gained a throw-in. Mark Lawrenson or Ronnie Whelan (I can't remember which) gestured impatiently to me to return the ball and the red mist suddenly descended. I decided to hurl it at him at full force.

Unfortunately, as I brought my arm forward, the ball slipped slightly from my grasp and, instead of flying forcibly at the Liverpool player, it travelled no more than three rows of seats and hit some poor, unsuspecting Saints fan smack on the back of the head. Understandably, he was not too happy and, while the crowd roared with laughter, I felt more than a little foolish.

If you were that fan, I'm truly sorry – but Liverpool used to get to me like that.

Duncan Holley, Winchester

Of all the weird and wonderful moments we have experienced at The Dell, one of the greatest oddities must surely be Francis Benali's goal. An oddity, because it was the only one.

Francis's lack of a goal had long been a talking point, not least because he'd been a forward in the Youth team. In nine seasons and some 280 first-team games, he had never scored and was always the rank outsider in the betting odds for the first goal in any game. As a full-back, though, he rarely ventured into the opposition penalty area, a bit of a draw-back when it comes to goal-scoring. When he occasionally played centre-back, he would usually go up for Saints' corners, which always struck me as odd – as if the change of position somehow conferred extra height.

It finally happened in December 1997, against Leicester, a side known for its large centre-backs. Francis went forward for a free-kick, to be taken by Le Tissier, over on the far, right-hand touch-line, level with the edge of the area. While everybody jostled on Matt's side of the box, Benali took up station over to the left. What was he doing there? Nobody marked him – but, then, we joked, Leicester knew that nobody needed to.

It looked a good position, though. Le Tissier thought so, too, and hoisted the ball over the waiting bundle right on to Benali's head. He headed it back across the Leicester goalkeeper, into the top right-hand corner of the net, as if he did it regularly. I'm sure there was a split-second of stunned silence before an almighty roar erupted. Surely it wasn't Benali? Yes, it was! The winning goal as well. Francis looked as surprised as anyone.

After the match, you had that feeling of a special satisfaction. You'd been there. You hadn't missed Benali's goal. What's more, you knew there probably wouldn't be another one.

Philip Twelves, Stoke Gifford, Bristol

On Boxing Day 1998, the match – Saints v Chelsea – was irrelevant and the result – a 2-0 defeat – didn't matter. We had learned, over the public address system, of the death the previous day, of John McGrath, aged 60.

My post-match meeting with him earlier in the year had been so entertaining that I think of the occasion as "My Favourite Game" (see the match of 21 February 1998, in the previous chapter). How I loved his stories of life as a manager at Halifax Town Nil, as he called it – especially when he enlisted the coaching services of Frank Worthington, who'd been a silken-skilled Saint for that one season of 1983-84, when we finished second in the top flight and were FA Cup semi-finalists. "Other managers are running up and down the motorways in Mercedes", Big Jake had told us, "me and Frank are on a tandem and I swear that half the time he isn't pedalling."

In recalling my meeting with John McGrath, I repeated his send-up of the "Ale House" label famously bestowed by Bill Shankly, the wit who took issue with those who thought football was a matter of life and death: it was much more important than that. On Boxing Day 1998, though, football took a poor second place to life and death.

Mark Fickling, Rownhams

Chapter 30
What Will We Most Miss?

So what shall we most miss, now that we are no longer spending our rightful Saturdays, the occasional Wednesday and too many Skydays at The Dell?

In posing that question, I'd envisaged responses in terms of *matchday* experiences that fans feared might not be replicated at St Mary's. But **Marian Thomas,** living in Surbiton, expresses a wider sense of loss. The Dell had long been an "anchor" to her past:

> For more than 25 years, since family and friends moved away too, the reason for my visiting the city again and again has been to see Southampton play at The Dell… St Mary's is the future, but it slips some of the cables that keep me in touch with my past.

Those "cables" include not just the repeated experience of "parking around the same roads we parked in when I was a kid, walking the same route to the ground," but associations from all the other days when her walk took her *past* the ground, on her way from her school, just "a short walk down Milton Road," to the school's playing fields. She always hoped to see a player or two. She seldom did, but there was that lunch-time when she was walking down Bedford Place and she wondered

> who were these good looking, but strangely familiar, faces coming towards me? A few steps closer and I recognized Mick Channon, Tommy Jenkins and Hugh Fisher, it being surely mere coincidence that the nearest bookies to The Dell was a few yards further down the road. Even 30 years later, I could always get a *frisson* of illicit pleasure from walking up Bedford Place to an evening match, eating chips – school rules had dictated white gloves and no eating in the street; and it was chocolate bars they were thinking of, never mind chips.

But for those of us who think of The Dell only as the place where we went to watch our team, what aspects of the ground will we mourn? **Tom Kelly** is concerned to maintain the quality of its "playing surface, generally accepted for quite a while to be among the best in the

country. A complete contrast to my experience of playing there, in May 1960, for Christchurch in the Hampshire Intermediate Cup Final, when the pitch was almost bereft of grass." Let's hope, Tom, that, come May 2002, when Matthew Le Tissier steps out for his testimonial, he'll enjoy an immaculate carpet at St Mary's more worthy of his skills than The Dell proved for you and your repertoire in 1960: unless there's something about the geology of the Itchen's west bank that we've not been told, a superior playing surface is surely one feature we might expect to be transported across town.

By contrast, **Duncan Holley** has come up with a list of *non*-transferable attributes:

> Its name for a start. It seems so natural to say "are you going up/down The Dell?" and it's certainly going to take a long time to get used to asking "are you intending to visit the Friends Provident St Mary's Stadium?" Physically, I shall miss its higgledy-piggledy shape, its nooks and crannies, its Archibald Leitch stands – virtually unchanged since the day they were built – and the half-way line walk it forced the managers to make.

Over and above such geological and architectural concerns, the feature of The Dell that cropped up most often in Miss-Lists was its *intimacy*. This is mainly about the *atmosphere* inside the ground, generated by what Marian Thomas calls "the tight-onto-the-pitch stands," which enabled her to stand "almost within touching distance of Sydenham haring down the touch-line or Dave Webb sliding across to take the ball (plus man) onto the gravel track." More of that intimate atmosphere in a moment; but **Ray Mursell** feels he is forfeiting two kinds of opportunity "to get close to the players" – not only when they were on the Dell *pitch* but, before that, as they made their way across the *carpark*.

As a fan who latterly discovered (once I no longer needed to get in early to "reserve" my elbow-room on a

FULL-TIME *at* THE DELL

"Friends in a buzzing carpark before kick-off."
The scene on the afternoon of The Dell's final league game

barrier) the capacity for pre-match meetings in the carpark, I soon came to appreciate opportunities to loiter with Ray Mursell, who would point out so many ex-players I would never have recognized. But it was also a place to meet up with friends from whom you'd been separated by the removal of the standing option, which is why I empathise with **Chris Newman,** whose catalogue of "silly things" he expects to miss includes "meeting friends in a buzzing carpark before kick-off."

For **Herbie Taylor,** the carpark remained a universal, an unchanging feature of a ground whose innards were periodically chopped about – in ways charted in Part I and with impacts to which I return below. That's not to say that the matchday contents of the carpark have remained unchanged. Herbie's memories go back to the War, when "you might see just one or two cars, belonging to the Chairman and directors, parked out there; but generally players and fans arrived either on foot or on a bike… hundreds of bikes left unattended in the carpark along with all the accessories such as saddle bags, cycle pumps and so on. No locks or chains and no thought of them being stolen."

But what of the atmosphere *inside* the ground?

Dave Juson has a word for it – *ambience:*

> There was no place like The Dell, nor could there be, on a dark winter's evening, under floodlights, with the crowd roaring the team on. The atmosphere was often electric; and, being so close to the players, you felt part of the effort. I have on occasion walked up Milton Road afterwards every bit as drained – I swear – as the players.
>
> There was no place like The Dell on a sunny Saturday afternoon, either. The Milton end was a

glorious place when the sun had its hat on and the Saints were on song, hitting those one-touch passes to each other.

Offering a few examples of games played in this "electric" atmosphere, **Richard Barraclough** includes the Fairs Cup quarter-final in December 1969, when a 1-1 draw took Newcastle through on an away goal. It is significant that he should include an effective defeat – since many who fear a loss of "atmosphere" talk of surrendering a "tightly-packed fortress", as **Noel Broomfield** puts it.

So, Fortress Dell? Judge for yourself from the statistics, in Appendix I, of games won and lost. But if those are the *numbers,* most of the rest of this chapter is concerned with the *perceptions* – of contributors, from fans to directors; and from the early press conferences at St Mary's.

In **Mark Fickling**'s estimation, "the proximity of the crowd to the pitch and the noise swirling around to drive Saints on was always worth a goal – or sometimes three, as Liverpool would testify last season;" and Duncan Holley is equally convinced that the "much-vaunted proximity" of the fans "to the pitch caused so much trepidation among the opposition." **Rupert Lowe** is in no doubt, as Chairman, of the need to transport this "massive" factor in "the success of our Club" to St Mary's:

> Atmospheric, threatening, tight, unique and awkward are all adjectives to describe its effect on all the teams who have visited over the last century. The move to the Friends Provident St Mary's Stadium is crucial to the future success of the Club but we will be doing our best to transport as much of our history as possible across Southampton, a large part of which centred around The Dell.

These sentiments are amply endorsed by the colleague who joined the Board with him: **Andrew Cowen.** With the advantage of having been born just up the road – in Winchester – Andrew readily apologises for having been unable to bring with him, to the boardroom, "a long history of active Saints support …I did attend The Dell once as a small boy, taken by a family friend whilst my parents were on holiday, but my family were not football people and were otherwise occupied on Saturdays; so no stories about being passed over everyone's head to the front of the terraces for me."

Hence the memories he has taken with him from The Dell "are primarily those of the workplace. The offices were never designed to accommodate the staff necessary to run a Club in today's Premier League and, unlike the *Tardis,* The Dell was no larger on the inside than it was on the outside." But, always "a staunch supporter of all things Hampshire, particularly in an era where the influx of a growing commuter population has diluted its identity as a County," Andrew Cowen thinks of The Dell as having been

> a beacon of all things South Coast, competitive in its intensity and passion with anything north of the end of the stagecoach at Watford Gap, a passion that arrived, during my time at The Dell, in the Directors' Box… The banter and wit of the crowd, particularly the Archers end, never ceased to amaze – from early memories as a Director (speculation as to how Rupert occupies himself when alone) to the reception in our final month at The Dell ("give it to Wesley" – for the own goal that broke a scoring famine). I just pray that this sort of support – worth more than goal difference will ever be – is transferred lock, stock and two chanting barrels to St Mary's.
>
> I only hope that, in maybe 100 years when the Club moves to the Solent MegaCity Hyperdrome (or whatever football will then be played in), that that generation of fans will hold St Mary's in the same high regard and tenderness that today's fans have held The Dell.

Chairman Lowe puts this more soberly: "Change can often have unpredictable consequences, which should not be under-estimated, but the pleasing statistic is that many more people will be able to come and watch the Saints in action. I hope they, like me, will enjoy the opportunity of supporting their local club with great passion in great comfort."

Fine words, Mister Chairman, uttered with all the passion (as demonstrated in your contributions to Chapters 27 and 28, alike) of a convert to our cause. But, for reasons I'll come to, I'm concerned that these words may not be easily translated into action. That said, you are right to remind sceptics like me that many people who have had limited opportunities to contribute to the atmosphere at The Dell will have a chance to make their presence felt at St Mary's.

Which brings me to a related point that was put to us more than once: while we could never have been in any doubt that our new stadium was going to be very different from the only one any of us had ever known, we should not forget that The Dell we left in 2001 was different from The Dell we knew 30, 20 – even 10 – years ago. So when we sentimentalise about the Dell atmosphere, we should note that The Dell that some fans miss had ceased to exist – whatever Duncan Holley may say about the unchanged Archibald Leitch stands – long before the bulldozers and dynamiters moved in. Mark Fickling is especially poetic about it:

> What I will miss the most had long since gone – FA Cup ties in the rain and dark and a wall of smoke racing up through the floodlights over the West Stand. The FA Cup had been diminished; smoking had been banned; and the Milton Road terrace, from which I witnessed those magical sights, demolished.

And even before the Milton end was surrendered to seating in 1994, it had been "remodelled a couple of times and didn't quite feel," to Mark, "like home anymore." That 1993-94 season was for me a last, somewhat symbolic, chance to *stand* and watch. Having been evicted from under the East Stand where I had leaned on the same barrier for years ("reserved", as I say, by dint of a 1.40-ish arrival), I went back to my schoolboy perch, high on the Milton, for a couple of games. Being obliged to sit thereafter, I not only discovered a whole new pre-match world in the carpark, as mentioned above, but I was freer to wander, at half-time, meeting friends who might previously have come over to "our" barrier for a pre-match chat or even to join us for the duration.

So, unlike so many who have raised this point, I surprised myself – unadventurous creature of habit that I am – by adapting to change and have no sense of loss about any particular manifestation of The Dell or about any particular terrace from which I watched the action.

Director **Michael Withers** is of a similar disposition: it is the very fact that he has watched Saints, for 64 years, "from every vantage point at The Dell," befriending those who stood or sat next to him, that he will miss most. He concludes that, wherever you stood or sat, "you were always so close to play you almost felt part of the team. I hope that feeling will survive at the new stadium."

FULL-TIME *at* THE DELL

Hardly! – not if being "close" means that you could almost touch the players in the way that Marian Thomas illustrated above. That special kind of intimacy is no more. OK, so it was available, anyhow, only to those right down on the wall where so many of us were initiated (see Chapter 27); but what did this closeness mean to the players, especially those trying to do their stuff out on the aptly named *touch*-line?

I am reminded of Kevin Keegan describing his experience of coming to The Dell with Liverpool and venturing down the line: it was bad enough knowing that Denis Hollywood was bound to clatter him, but he always feared that one of the crowd might lean out to similar effect. A whimsical sound-bite harking back to his first visit in the season of Hollywood's final flourish; but, in so far as such apprehensions about being hemmed in were shared even a little bit by visiting players, this should have contributed to the "fortress" effect. The moreso, obviously, if the home team was lifted, conversely, by the feeling that their opponents were troubled by sensing such pressure from the crowd.

The chicken-and-egg relationship between the perceptions of the two sets of players was apparent after that August 2000 comeback against Liverpool. Matthew Le Tissier captured this for me when I asked him to relive, for the ultimate match of *Match of the Millennium*, the closing stages of that game: when the first goal of the revival went in, "you could see them just sort of jittering a bit," he reckoned. "And when the second one went in, they *did* panic."

So can that advantage be re-captured at St Mary's? Not according to the post-match reactions either of Chelsea's Frank Lampard (after the stadium's Premiership baptism: *Daily Mirror* and *Guardian,* 27 August 2001) or of Arsenal manager, Arsène Wenger (after his side had made it three home defeats out of three for Saints: *Guardian,* 15 October).

Lampard found St Mary's less daunting than The Dell overall: "the new stadium is the type of place you enjoy playing at and we certainly did;" and the away dressing room is less intimidating than the Dell hell-hole to which Nick Holmes alludes in his foreword – "it was so small," Lampard recalls, that "they kind of put one over on you before a ball was kicked."

But can Saints fans somehow compensate for those surrendered weapons? I had my doubts from when the plans for a stadium at Northam were unveiled and I read somewhere – I cannot recall where; and whenever I raised this with any of those managing the move to St Mary's, I was met with blank incredulity – that a single-tier stadium was bound to have less atmosphere than a two-tier structure like The Dell, where a second, upper level of fans had enjoyed proximity to the pitch. No matter that I failed "O" Level Physics, I felt I understood this argument. Indeed, it seemed distressingly obvious.

Yet, when Rupert Lowe was interviewed at the start of the new season at St Mary's, he seemed to treat it as self-evident that a single-tier would positively *contribute* to the atmosphere. With Saints pointless at home as they came to their third game at St Mary's – against Arsenal – he returned to this theme in the *Matchday Programme,* dismissing "media discussion about our stadium being less intimidating to our opponents than was the case at The Dell [as] unfounded 'tittle-tattle'."

That's not how Arsène Wenger saw it, though. His side had experienced "less pressure" from the home fans, whose favourites had not "looked in control" the way they invariably were at The Dell. As their team coasted to a 2-0 win, the Arsenal fans put their manager's sentiments to music (well, to a tune approximating to *Blue Moon*):

Two-nil, Two nil,
You should have stayed at The Dell

If any sentimentalists thought that an option, then Part I of this book should surely have disabused them. The argument is not about whether we should have stayed at The Dell, but about replicating at least some of its perceived structural advantages. Who better to discuss this with than Simon Inglis, the expert on ground design so often cited in Part I? He rejected my concern about a single-tier: the issue, he suggested, was less about architecture than about the capacity of the home fans to take their passion from one kind of stadium to another. Which is what Rupert Lowe was urging us, in that Arsenal programme, to do.

In support of that position, Inglis cited the ready transfer of the "Roker Roar" to the Stadium of Light. By that yardstick, the challenge to Saints fans is clear: notwithstanding the reduced hostility of the dressing room and the pitch, can we yet make St Mary's our Stadium of Fright?

Appendix I
Dell Statistics

A. Attendances

There are no really accurate gate enumerations until Saints went into the Football League. Before 1920, we have to rely on press guesstimates based on gate receipts disclosed by the Club (as for the 1899 cup-tie below). This said, there are numerous photographs of spectators sitting on the roofs of houses and stands, as well as hanging out of trees, that suggest that the Dell's capacity was stretched down the years. Even in the age of turnstiles that could count, we are not always better informed. For instance, the figure given for the Mike Channon Testimonial on 3 May 1976 is 29,508. There is no reason to doubt that this is an accurate calculation of those who paid to get in; but given the number of spectators who had to be accommodated on the running track and the impossibility of assessing how many managed to find alternative ways into the ground on the night – such as over, rather than through, the turnstiles – the official figure is almost certainly inaccurate. Which is a way of saying that the Channon Testimonial, in all probability, saw the biggest crowd ever crammed into The Dell, but there is no way of confirming that.

When considering the landmark figures below, it should be borne in mind (if you are peeking at this page before reading the book) that The Dell's capacity was continually reduced for public safety reasons over the last 30 years of its existence. By 1986, the maximum capacity was 24,000; and, in its incarnation as an "all-seater", the capacity was a little over 15,000. Thus, the record Premier League gate at The Dell was set on the first day of the first Premiership season – 1992-93 – a year of precious little entertainment and some appropriately abysmal gates.

These milestone figures show how the record FA Cup attendance took a few jumps from the disputed figure of 1899, to peak in 1937, while the Football League record went up in two flurries, in the 1928-29-30 and 1947-48-49 seasons, to peak in 1949, then remain unchanged for 20 years, when the ultimate ground record was established in 1969. The respective records for FA Cup, Football League and Premier League are shown in bold.

Whatever else these figures tell us, a glance at the months would suggest that Dell-goers were not fair-weather fans.

25	February	1899	v	Derby County	FA Cup Third Round	estimated	23,000
26	December	1902	v	Tottenham Hotspur	Southern League		14,000
11	March	1908	v	Everton	FA Cup Fourth Round		21,690
26	December	1913	v	Portsmouth	Southern League		19,291
28	March	1921	v	Crystal Palace	Football League Division 3		20,277
27	December	1921	v	Queen's Park Rangers	Football League Division 3(S)		20,940
7	February	1923	v	Chelsea	FA Cup Second Round replay		25,000
1	September	1928	v	Tottenham Hotspur	Football League Division 2		22,574
9	March	1929	v	Chelsea	Football League Division 2		23,829
26	December	1929	v	Tottenham Hotspur	Football League Division 2		25,203
26	January	1935	v	Birmingham City	FA Cup Fourth Round		28,291
16	January	1937	v	Sunderland	FA Cup Third Round		**30,380**
13	March	1948	v	Newcastle United	Football League Division 2		26,780
4	September	1948	v	Queen's Park Rangers	Football League Division 2		27,303
6	November	1948	v	Tottenham Hotspur	Football League Division 2		28,800
19	February	1949	v	Sheffield Wednesday	Football League Division 2		29,445
23	April	1949	v	West Bromwich Albion	Football League Division 2		30,586
8	October	1969	v	Manchester United	Football League Division 1		**31,044**
15	August	1992	v	Tottenham Hotspur	FA Premier League		**19,654**

B. First-team record at The Dell (friendlies excluded)

Cups

	P	W	D	L	F	A
FA Cup						
1898-1915	22	13	5	4	48	28
1919-1939	26	15	7	4	42	21
1945-2001	81	43	23	15	168	82
Total	**129**	**71**	**35**	**23**	**258**	**131**
Football League Cup						
1960-2001	77	48	17	12	159	131
European Competitions						
1969-1985	11	6	4	1	25	12
Southern Charity Cup						
1902-1914	10	7	1	2	26	12
Hampshire Benevolent/Rowland Cup (v Portsmouth)						
1905-1936	18	6	3	9	34	37
Hampshire Combination Cup/Professional Cup						
1931-1984	8	3	1	4	18	18
Southern Professional Floodlight Cup						
1957-1960	4	2	1	1	5	3
Super Cup						
1985-86	2	0	1	1	2	4
Texaco Cup						
1974-75	5	5	0	0	9	2
Anglo-Italian Cup						
1976-77	1	1	0	0	1	0
Full Members, Simod & Zenith Data Cups						
1986-1992	7	5	0	2	15	6
War Cups						
1939-40	1	0	1	0	1	1
1941-42	6	4	1	1	14	9
1942-43	3	3	0	0	7	2
1943-44	3	1	0	2	5	8
1944-45	3	3	0	0	18	5
Total	**16**	**11**	**2**	**3**	**45**	**25**
Cup Total	**288**	**165**	**65**	**58**	**597**	**381**

Leagues

	P	W	D	L	F	A
Southern League						
1898-99	12	9	2	1	34	9
1899-00	14	11	0	3	51	14
1900-01	14	13	1	0	44	12
1901-02	14	13	0	1	54	9
1902-03	14	12	1	1	53	7
1903-04	17	12	3	2	43	15
1904-05	17	9	4	4	29	21
1905-06	17	13	2	2	32	11
1906-07	19	9	6	4	31	18
1907-08	19	11	5	3	32	21
1908-09	20	13	4	3	44	26
1909-10	21	11	7	3	39	25
1910-11	19	8	3	8	25	28
1911-12	19	9	3	7	29	27
1912-13	19	7	7	5	28	25
1913-14	19	11	2	6	36	23
1914-15	19	14	3	2	56	28
1919-20	21	13	4	4	51	22
Total	**314**	**198**	**57**	**59**	**711**	**341**
Western League						
1898-1909	74	53	7	14	198	80
United League						
1898-99	10	10	0	0	40	5
Southern District Combination						
1899-00	8	5	1	2	17	10
Southern Alliance						
1912-14	16	8	3	5	37	28
War Leagues						
1915-19	39	23	7	9	111	57
1939-46	95	47	17	31	284	203

Appendix B shows the record for all competitive fixtures – even war-time games and "Mickey Mouse" cups – but excluding friendlies.
Appendices C and D exclude those war-time games and dubious cups, focusing on those fixtures that *count* in the "official" statistics.

Appendix I

Football League

Division Three

Season	P	W	D	L	F	A
1920-21	21	14	5	2	46	10

Division Three (South)

Season	P	W	D	L	F	A
1921-22	21	14	7	0	50	8

Division Two

Season	P	W	D	L	F	A
1922-23	21	10	5	6	28	21
1923-24	21	13	5	3	36	9
1924-25	21	12	8	1	29	10
1925-26	21	11	2	8	39	25
1926-27	21	9	8	4	35	22
1927-28	21	11	3	7	54	40
1928-29	21	12	6	3	48	22
1929-30	21	14	6	1	46	22
1930-31	21	13	4	4	46	22
1931-32	21	10	5	6	39	30
1932-33	21	15	3	3	48	22
1933-34	21	15	2	4	40	21
1934-35	21	9	8	4	28	19
1935-36	21	11	3	7	32	24
1936-37	21	10	8	3	38	25
1937-38	21	12	6	3	42	26
1938-39	21	9	6	6	35	34
1939-40	2	1	0	1	4	3
1946-47	21	11	5	5	45	24
1947-48	21	15	3	3	53	23
1948-49	21	16	4	1	48	10
1949-50	21	13	4	4	44	25
1950-51	21	10	9	2	38	27
1951-52	21	11	6	4	40	25
1952-53	21	5	7	9	45	44

Division Three (South)

Season	P	W	D	L	F	A
1953-54	23	17	5	1	51	22
1954-55	23	16	6	1	49	19
1955-56	23	13	6	4	60	30
1956-57	23	15	4	4	48	20
1957-58	23	16	3	4	78	31

Division Three

Season	P	W	D	L	F	A
1958-59	23	12	7	4	57	33
1959-60	23	19	3	1	68	30

Division Two

Season	P	W	D	L	F	A
1960-61	21	12	4	5	57	35
1961-62	21	13	3	5	53	28
1962-63	21	15	3	3	52	23
1963-64	21	13	3	5	69	32
1964-65	21	12	6	3	49	25
1965-66	21	13	4	4	51	25

Division One

Season	P	W	D	L	F	A
1966-67	21	10	3	8	49	41
1967-68	21	9	8	4	37	31
1968-69	21	13	5	3	41	21
1969-70	21	3	12	6	24	27
1970-71	21	12	5	4	35	15
1971-72	21	8	5	8	31	28
1972-73	21	8	11	2	26	17
1973-74	21	8	10	3	30	20

Division Two

Season	P	W	D	L	F	A
1974-75	21	10	6	5	29	20
1975-76	21	18	2	1	49	16
1976-77	21	12	6	3	40	24
1977-78	21	15	4	2	44	16

Division One

Season	P	W	D	L	F	A
1978-79	21	9	10	2	35	20
1979-80	21	14	2	5	53	24
1980-81	21	15	4	2	47	22
1981-82	21	15	2	4	49	30
1982-83	21	11	5	5	36	22
1983-84	21	15	4	2	44	17
1984-85	21	13	4	4	29	18
1985-86	21	10	6	5	32	18
1986-87	21	11	5	5	44	24
1987-88	20	6	8	6	27	26
1988-89	19	6	7	6	25	26
1989-90	19	10	5	4	40	27
1990-91	19	9	6	4	33	22
1991-92	21	7	5	9	17	28

FA Premier League

Season	P	W	D	L	F	A
1992-93	21	10	6	5	30	21
1993-94	21	9	2	10	30	31
1994-95	21	8	9	4	33	27
1995-96	19	7	7	5	21	18
1996-97	19	6	7	6	32	24
1997-98	19	10	1	8	28	23
1998-99	19	9	4	6	29	26
1999-00	19	8	4	7	26	22
2000-01	19	11	2	6	27	22

	P	W	D	L	F	A
Football League/Premier Total	1551	847	387	317	3020	1760
League Total	2107	1191	479	437	4418	2484
League & Cup Total	2395	1356	544	495	5015	2865

FULL-TIME *at* THE DELL

C. Appearances at The Dell – the main men

Name	League	SL	WL	SDC	SA	UL	FAC	FLC	EUR	Total
Paine, Terry	353 (3)						28	19	4	404 (3)
Channon, Mick	254 (2)						20 (1)	16	5	295 (3)
Holmes, Nick	224 (1)						17	19	6	266 (1)
Le Tissier, Matthew	201(32)						13	21 (4)		235(36)
Traynor, Tommy	204						16	6		226
Shelley, Bert	194	9					21			224
Sydenham, John	183 (1)						19	11	3	216 (1)
Day, Eric	187						11			198
Dodd, Jason	155(11)						18	18		191(11)
Woodhouse, Stan	181						8			189
Dominy, Arthur	109	57			3		19			188
Rawlings, Bill	149	16					21			186
Lee, Bert		128	37	1	4		9			179
Williams, Steve	143						9	12 (1)	6	170 (1)
Fisher, Hugh	141 (5)						12 (1)	11	4 (1)	168 (7)
Allen, Tom	146						20			166
Bradford, Arthur	153						5			158
Huxford, Cliff	137 (1)						13	7		157 (1)
Reeves, Derek	136						11	5		152
Meston, Sammy		86	41	7		9	7			150
Benali, Francis	128(16)						8	13 (6)		149(22)
Martin, Eric	126						11	8	4	149

D. Goals at The Dell – the main men

Name	League	SL	WL	SDC	SA	UL	FAC	FLC	EUR	Total
Channon, Mick	121						10	7	6	144
Rawlings, Bill	103	15					13			131
O'Brien, George	99						16	4		119
Paine, Terry	103						8	6	1	118
Le Tissier, Matthew	88						8	19		115
Day, Eric	98						6			104
Harrison, Fred		51	49				3			103
Reeves, Derek	90						5	8		103
Dominy, Arthur	45	42			1		11			99
Davies, Ron	85						6	4	3	98

Key.

League = Football League and FA Premier League   *SL* = Southern League

WL = Western League   *SDC* = Southern District Combination   *SA* = Southern Alliance

UL = United League   *FAC* = Football Association Cup   *FLC* = Football League Cup etc.

Eur = European Fairs Cup, European Cup Winners Cup & UEFA Cup

Appendix II
Programme's progress

Before they had programmes at The Dell, they had team-cards, which were the size of a folded postcard. The front cover showed a small black-and-white player portrait (*see below*), along with the match details, while the centre-fold had the line-ups and the back page an advert' for the printers.

This format continued until the 1919-20 season, when an eight-page programme – still printed by Waltons of St Mary Street – was introduced, the colour of the paper varying from match to match. There was now room for the inclusion of fixture lists, with up-dated results – for both the first team and reserves. The studio photograph of a player on the cover remained.

Notwithstanding – or maybe because of – their dire financial straits (described by Dave Juson in Chapter 14), the Club expanded its programme to 12 pages in 1930 and raised the price to 2d. It included the "Programme of Music" to be played by the *Albion Silver Band* and a key to the latest innovation at The Dell: the half-time scoreboard described in Chapter 15.

When its length was doubled later in the 1930s, the programme's price remained at tuppence – but, then, there was the revenue to be had from the advertisement for the Polygon Hotel that adorned the front cover. New features included "Club Chatter", "Today at The Dell" and a complete results chart for the Second Division.

During the Second World War, what with rationing and the paper shortage, the programme became a single sheet. Initially nothing more than an 8"x 4¾" line-up, printed at the Shirley Press, it had expanded, by the end of the War, to 8½" x 6½", with room on the back-side for the fixture list and brief club notes. The design was attractive, with a red-dotted border and an impressive white-on-red banner proclaiming

SOUTHAMPTON FOOTBALL CLUB.

This version survived beyond the War, to be replaced, in 1948, by a folded sheet that had much the same contents. This lasted only a season before it gave way to a larger sheet, folded so as to offer three double-sided, 10"x5" pages. Now printed by A.R. Simmons & Co, the programme retained this format for seven seasons, although the price went up in 1951 to 3d – a hike of 50 per cent, but the first price-rise since 1930. Its successor, in 1956 – with the Club now in the Third Division – was

a more conventional 24-page publication. It remained at 3d for a couple of seasons but cost 4d from 1958.

With minor changes and variations, this was the format for many years. The price remained unchanged upon promotion to the Second Division in 1960 but went up, the following season, to 6d.

The next promotion, in 1966, saw two changes: the price rose to 9d; but there was a free supplement – the *Football League Review* – which had itself a price-tag of 6d and which became a feature of that era in programmes across the country.

Southampton Football & Athletic Co.

Official Team Card, Saturday, Mar. 11th.

BRISTOL CITY
Southern League.

GLOBE PHOTO CO., SO'TON

Yours truly,

D. STEVENS

By 1970-71, the price was 1/-, changing with decimalisation in February, of course, to 5p. It had gone up to 7p, when Saints were again relegated in 1974. For the first season back in Division Two, the programme cost 10p. Printed by Ward & Woolverton, its manager's message was headed by the photo of The Dell that appears on our cover. More significantly, the cover of the programme was now in full-colour. It would feature a few action photographs – the same photos from match to match, so that the 1976-77 cover had five photos from a day out at Wembley, by which time the printers were J.B. Shears & Sons and the price 15p. There was only one colour photo on the 20 inside pages – a shot of Saints' fans above the editorial – and still not a sponsors' pic in sight.

After that, colour gradually spread to the inside pages and, by the time Cedar Press became the printers in 1993-94, the programme had doubled in size and cost £1.50, the pound-barrier having been broken in 1988. The programme for the last competitive fixture at The Dell (see page 2) was just four pages longer than that and cost £2. But then, to send us off bursting with nostalgia – and broke – we had the £5 souvenir programme for the visit of Brighton & Hove Albion.

The illustrations are the programme that survived
the Second World War;
the tall distinctive fold of the 1950s;
and Andrew Murray in his shop at The Dell

This brief history of the Saints programme has been compiled mainly from details supplied by Andrew Murray, who ran the Saints Programme Shop ("Collectors Corner") at the Milton end of The Dell and who is now to be found, on matchdays, on the Chapel Concourse at St Mary's.

The shop stocks a wide variety of programmes, including Saints issues going back to the pre-colour days recalled above. When Saints are not at home – or if you can't find your way onto the Chapel Concourse – you can reach Andrew at his home:
6 Goldcrest Gardens, Lordswood, Southampton, SO16 8FG or on his mobile: 07702 588 275.

Sources

The most important research tools for this work have been, as ever,

Gary Chalk and Duncan Holley, *Saints: a complete record of Southampton Football Club 1885-1987* (Breedon, 1987)
Duncan Holley and Gary Chalk, *An Alphabet of Saints: A Complete Who's Who of Southampton FC* (ACL Polar, 1992).

Other Reference Books and uncited sources

Two other reference books to which we have had repeated recourse are the relevant editions of those two dependable annuals: *Rothmans Football Yearbook* and the *News of the World Football Annual.* Other invaluable sources that have been much consulted but never actually cited in the text are

Mike Collett, *The Guinness Record of the FA Cup,* Guinness Publishing, 1993
Bill Dawson, "A Trainer's Story" *Football Echo* (a 1924 series)
Rev J.S. Davis, *A History of Southampton,* Gilbert & Son, 1886
Norman Gannaway, *Association Football in Hampshire until 1914,* Hampshire Papers No.9, Hampshire CC, 1996
Maurice Golesworthy, *The Encyclopaedia of Association Football,* Hale, 1956 edition
Paul Harrison, *Southern League Football: The First Fifty Years,* Paul Harrison, 1989
Barry J. Hugman (ed.), *The PFA Premier & Football League Players' Records 1946-1998,* Queen Anne Press, 1998
J. Lemon, *Reminiscences of Public Life in Southampton* (two volumes), Southampton, 1911.
A.G.K. Leonard, *Stories of Southampton Streets,* Paul Cave, 1984
A.G.K. Leonard, *More Stories of Southampton Streets,* Paul Cave, 1989
J.A. Mangan (ed.), *Pleasure, profit, proselytism: British culture and sport at home and abroad, 1700-1914,* Cass, 1988
Tony Mason, *Association Football and English Society 1863–1915,* Harvester, 1981
F.J. Montgomery, *History of Deanery Cricket Club,* privately published, 1921
A. Temple Patterson, *A History of Southampton 1700-1914* (vols II and III), Southampton Records Society, 1971-75
William Pickford, *The Hampshire Football Association: Golden Jubilee Book,* Bournemouth Guardian, 1937
Lawrence Popplewell, *Against the Grain: the Manchester and Southampton railway dream,* Melledgen Press, 1986
Dave Russell, *Football and the English: a social history of association football in England,* Carnegie, 1997
Peter J. Seddon, *A Football Compendium,* The British Library (second edition), 1999
Gordon Sewell, *Echoes of a Century: The Centenary History of Southern Newspapers Limited,* Southern Newspapers, 1964
Sir Montague Shearman, *Football,* The Badminton Library 1904
Wray Vamplew, *Pay up and play the game: Professional sport in Britain,* Cambridge University Press, 1988.

Archives & Libraries

The British Newspaper Library, Colindale
Football Association Library
The Hartley Library, University of Southampton
Hampshire Football Association, Southampton
King Edward VI School, Southampton
The Lansdown Library, Bournemouth

Southampton City Archivists' Office
Southampton City Library (Local History Collection)
Southampton Football Club
Winchester Libraries
University of Leicester Library

FULL-TIME *at* THE DELL

Newspapers & Journals

Over and above the sports pages of the many national newspapers to which we have referred in the text, we have relied upon the following local 'papers and specialist journals, reference to each of which is to be found in the text:

Southern Daily Echo; Southern Evening Echo; The Football Echo & Sports Gazette; The Sports Echo, The Pink

The Athletic News; The Bournemouth Guardian; Chums (October 1899, in the Terry Gregory Collection); *The Hampshire Advertiser* (including several articles by F.J. Montgomery in the 1920s and 1930s); *Hampshire: the County Magazine; Hampshire Football Association Handbook* (annual); *The Hampshire Independent; The Morning Leader; S. Mary's Parish Magazine; Southampton Amusements; The Southampton & District Pictorial* (including 1912-13 series on "The History of Southampton Football Club") ; Southampton Football Club programme (under its various titles); *The Southampton Observer & Winchester News; The Southern Referee: an Athletic Journal for Hants, Wilts & Dorset; The Southampton Times & Hampshire Express; When Saturday Comes*

Cited books and articles

The books and articles we have cited in the text, mainly in Part I, are:

Arnold Bennett, *The Matador of the Five Towns,* London, 1912

Philip Brannon, *Picture of Southampton: or stranger's handbook,* Philip Brannon, 1850 (Lawrence Oxley reprint, 1979)

Tony Brode, *The Southampton Blitz,* Barry Shurlock, 1977

David Bull, *Dell Diamond: Ted Bates's first 60 seasons with The Saints,* Hagiology Publishing, 1998

David Bull and Bob Brunskell (eds.), *Match of the Millennium,* Hagiology Publishing, 2000

Sir Arthur Conan Doyle, *Memories and Adventures,* London, 1924.

Alfred Gibson & William Pickford, *Association Football and the Men Who Made It* (Four Volumes) Caxton, 1905-06

Geoffrey Green, *The Official History of the FA Cup,* Naldrett, 1949

Geoff Hurst, *1966 and All That: my autobiography,* Headline, 2001

Simon Inglis, *Football Grounds of England and Wales,* Willow, 1983

Simon Inglis, *League Football and the men who made it,* Willow, 1988

Simon Inglis, *Football Grounds of Britain,* (second paperback edition), Willow, 1997

John Mann, *Southampton People,* Ensign Publications, 1989

Bert Moody, *Southampton Railways,* Waterfront Publications, 1992

Kevin Phillips, *Second Time Around: two seasons with Sunderland FC,* Collins Willow, 1999

J.B. Priestley, *English Journey,* Heinemann, 1934

Adrian Rance, *Southampton: an Illustrated History,* Milestone, 1986

Jack Rollin, *Soccer at War 1939-45,* Willow, 1985

Nevil Shute, *What Happened to the Corbetts,* Heinemann, 1939.

Graeme Souness with Mike Ellis, *Souness: The Management Years,* André Deutsch, 1999

G. Stavart, *A Study in Southsea: the unrevealed life of Doctor Arthur Conan Doyle,* Milestone, 1987

Rt. Hon. Lord Justice Taylor, *The 1999 Hillsborough Stadium Disaster 15 April 1989:* Interim Report, HMSO, 1989

Rt. Hon. Lord Justice Taylor, *The 1999 Hillsborough Stadium Disaster 15 April 1989:* Final Report, HMSO, 1990

The Virgin Book of Football Records, Virgin, 1996

Interviews

Bert Baker	– May 2001	Alan Smith	– September 2001
Brian Hunt	– April 2001	Ken Sweet	– August 2001
June Sexton	– October 1999	Dave Warn	– July 2001

Presentations & Subscriptions

We are pleased to present copies of this book to:

Gary Chalk, Norman Gannaway and Duncan Holley of Hagiology Publishing

Our associates, in the production of this and other books,

at SOUTHAMPTON FC and the *Southern Daily Echo.*

Marian Thomas and Mark Fickling for their outstanding contributions to Part II of this book.

1	Dawn Adams, Owslebury	31	Don McAllen, Pennington	61	Graham Feast, London
2	Dave Adlem, Bristol	32	Den McAllen, St Denys	62	Mick Grayson, Sheffield
3	Albert Fickling, Milford-on-Sea	33	Jack Baker, St Denys	63	Danny Powell, Charlton
4	Bill Nicholas, Hythe	34	Geoff Cotton, Lordshill	64	Malcolm D.E. West, Colchester
5	A.M. Quigley, Wimborne	35	Jamie Cotton, Southampton	65	Alister Betts, Maiden Bradley
6	David Brindley, Gosport	36	Mark Wood, Petersfield	66	John Betts, Somerton
7	Manny & Wendy, Block 5, Archers	37	Paul Wood, Williamsport, USA	67	Martin Murray, Sompting
8	Glen Williams, Sarisbury Green	38	Robert Dodd, East Dean	68	Andrew Tappern, Tilehurst
9	Andy Nunn, East Molesey	39	John Hammill, Jersey	69	Barry Gale, Woking
10	Ann Chalk, Eastleigh	40	Chris Stones, Reading	70	Martin Ellwood, Windsor
11	James Anderson, Holly Hill	41	Dave Pickard, Bournemouth	71	Richard Buckingham-Smith, Eastleigh
12	Colin Young, Reading	42	Cliff Pickard, Andover	72	M.J. Bennett, Andover
13	Pete Lacey, Southampton	43	Kim Hooper & Graham Lawrance, Ash	73	Anthony Coombes, Southampton
14	Ian Strickland, China	44	David Steele, Carlisle	74	Raymond Coombes, Southampton
15	Barry Roberts, Southampton	45	Daniel Thomas, New Barnet	75	Desmond Martin, Southampton
16	Lee Curtis, Bournemouth	46	Michael Baker, Hythe	76	Paul A. Clark, Broadstone
17	Peter F. Moody, Portchester	47	Maurice O'Connor, Southampton	77	Ian Whitworth, Wakefield
18	Stephen Cheffy, Crawley	48	John James O'Connor, Everton	78	John Warren, Chiswick
19	Paul Cheffy, Brighton	49	Roger Wash, Newmarket	79	Bob Warren, Chandlers Ford
20	Roger Airey, Wareham	50	David Stephens, Hamble	80	Leon Simon, Marchwood
21	Phil Snarr, Woolston	51	Anita Leach, Newbury	81	David Hole, Bishop's Sutton
22	Robin Lovelock, Southampton	52	John Lovelock, Southampton	82	Philip Joslands Rawlings, Fair Oak
23	Derek Edwards, Hedge End	53	Vivienne Broadway, Botley	83	Ian Barron, Southampton
24	Chris McShane, Glasgow	54	Richard Broadway, Fair Oak	84	K. Payne, Shirley
25	Nigel Burgess, Hoddesdon	55	Malcolm Wing, Eastleigh	85	Graham Watford, Locks Heath
26	Steve Molyneux, Bolton	56	Ron Kingston, Netley Abbey	86	Lewis Hodder, Whitely
27	Martin Walden, Chandlers Ford	57	Stephen John Northover, Southampton	87	Andy Fancourt, Hedge End
28	May Irwin, Salisbury	58	Malcolm Golding, Woolston	88	Scott Fancourt, Hedge End
29	Mark Wood, Thatcham	59	Dave Watkins, Hinckley	89	Scott Leicester, Bournemouth
30	Nigel McAllen, New Milton	60	Edward Paul Feast, Seaford	90	R. J. Gaiger, Winchester

91	Stephen Hoare, Salisbury	131	Derek Wicks, Bassett	172	Oonagh Griffith, Belfast
92	Mike Shelton, Kidderminster	132	B.T. Middleton, Banbury	173	Matthew Sanger, San Francisco, USA
93	Tim Newman, Shaw	133	Kevin John Quick, Shirley	174	Bert Weavers, Southampton
94	Nancy Toni, Swindon	134	John Culley, Lewes	175	M.J. Graham, Saint Johns, NB, Canada
95	Andrew Beach, Christchurch	135	Ray Mursell, Bishops Waltham	176	Julian Sutton, Nunhead, London
96	Martin Thear, Steyning	136	Donald Ingram, Hythe	177	Damian Sutton, Glasgow
97	Maurice Mascall, North Harbour	137	Tony Lovett, Stoke-on-Trent	178	Matthew Sutton, Woking
98	Brian A. Smith, Eastleigh	138	Jack Thomas, Ivybridge	179	Maxine Sutton, Brighton
99	Maurice Hockley, Maybush	140	Mike Young, Hoeford	180	Antony John Borowiec, Totton
100	Brian Barendt, Bartley	141	Alan Brackstone, Basingstoke	181	Dave Webster, Fair Oak
101	Marcus Betts, Hedge End	142	Ted Thomas, Hong Kong	182	Miles Parker, Liphook
102	Brian Hooper, Church Crookham	143	Christian May, Sydney, Australia	183	Lasse Gram-Hansen, Aalborg, Denmark
103	Gary Wilkins, Lordshill	144	Tim Evans, Poole	184	Andrei Zhezlov, Moscow, Russia
104	Albert Wilkins, Southampton	145	Gareth Evans, Dorchester	185	Ted Tarbart, Isle of Wight
105	Brian Dawkins, Romsey	146	Daniel Evans, Eltham	186	James Law, Chester
106	Christopher Dawkins, Romsey	147	Janet Evans, Hythe	187	Brian Fisher, Dibden
107	Joan Rozenberg-Summers, Romsey	148	Peter Horne, Hebden Bridge	188	Ted Porter, Andover
108	Noël Broomfield, Corsham	149	David L. Witt, Marchwood	189	Matthew Cox, Andover
109	Tim Bowden, Nailsea	150	Alan Hicks, Southampton	190	Andrew Ross, Andover
110	Martyn Parnham, Waltham Chase	151	Mark W. Adams, Bitterne Park	191	Phillip Cox, Andover
111	Jerome James, Isle of Wight	152	Steve Adams, Bitterne Park	192	Des Earl, Bitterne Park
112	Julian James, Isle of Wight	153	Robbie Hallwood, Eastleigh	193	Jeffery H. Pain, Midanbury
113	Barry Markham, Hythe	154	Bella McDonnell, Eastleigh	194	Lewis H. Pain, Fond-Du-Lac, USA
114	John Rawnsley, Pudsey, West Yorkshire	155	Jerry McDonnell, Eastleigh	195	Jonathan Short, Woolston
115	Keith Fray, Reading	156	Michael McDonnell, Eastleigh	196	The Aldworth Family, Southampton
116	Richard Manley, West Coker, Yeovil	157	Nick Brice, Lordswood	197	Alan Jones, St Denys
117	Peter Hole, Alresford	158	Trevor Brice, Barton-on-Sea	198	Martin Callinan, Bitterne Park
118	Karl Mitchell, Solihull	159	Jonathan Bushrod, Waterlooville	199	Jill White, Portswood Park
119	Karl Darley, Merryoak	160	Lee Martin Robinson	200	Ainsley Adams, St Denys
120	Paula Phillips, Whaddon	161	Andy Rogers, Stubbington	201	Ian McWilliam, Irvine, California, USA
121	Gary Ford, Hedge End	162	Phil Rogers, Titchfield Common	202	Bert Baker, Woolston
122	Connor Arnold, Southampton	163	Sid Barfoot, Hedge End	203	Norman and Norma Thomas, Poole
123	Andrew Kershaw, Chandlers Ford	164	Rob Moody, Southampton	204	Mark Thomas, Ashtead, Surrey
124	Steve Morris, Hove	165	Geoff Knappett, Whitchurch	205	Richard Atkinson, Macclesfield
125	Malcolm Lewis, West End	166	Terry Knappett, Whitchurch	206	David Atkinson, Chester
126	Malcolm Chamberlain, New Milton	167	Paul Noon, Walsall	207	Peter Atkinson, Fordingbridge
127	Paul Martin, Denmead	168	Peter Sharp, Bitterne	208	Bob Cushion, Dubai, UAE
128	Adam Martin, Bedhampton	169	Dave & Beth Currie, Southampton	209	Alan Horton, Colwinston, S. Wales
129	Simon Martin, Petersfield	170	Terry Bowen, Milford Haven	210	Peter Varnes, Cudlee Creek, S.Australia
130	J.H. Vahid, Ramsgate	171	Nigel Bowen, Cardiff	211	Peter Emery, Kenley, Surrey

HAGIOLOGY PUBLISHING

Formed in 1998, Hagiology Publishing is a collective of Saints fans committed to the collection and dissemination of accurate information on the history of Southampton FC.

Its first publication, in 1998, was *Dell Diamond,* the story of Ted Bates's first 60 seasons with the Saints.

Its second, *Match of the Millennium,* was most generously promoted by Matthew Le Tissier. In gratitude for those efforts as our Patron Saint, we were pleased to present him with a framed copy of his memorable "Great Escape" free-kick at Upton Park in 1994:

Matthew accepts the token of gratitude from (left to right) Duncan Holley, Dave Juson, David Bull and Gary Chalk
(inset: Norman Gannaway, the fifth member of the original Hagiology collective)

Its third venture, *FULL-TIME at THE DELL,* is its second publication within an agreement with Southampton FC and the *Southern Daily Echo* to produce a series, over the next few years, on aspects of Saints' history.
The next three books in the pipe-line are:

SAINTS v. POMPEY – a study of the rivalry (due 2002)
CONSTANT PAINE – a biography of Terry Paine (2003)
IN THAT NUMBER – a major update and expansion, in two volumes (2004 and 2005), of the two Chalk & Holley books, *Saints – a complete record* and *The Alphabet of the Saints*

Please address enquiries about *FULL-TIME at THE DELL* to the appropriate member of the Hagiology collective as indicated below:

Individual (incl mail-order) enquiries

Dave Juson (Chair)
The Flat, 44 Shirley Road
Southampton
SO15 3EU
Tel: 023 80 221410

All retail and review enquiries

David Bull (Editor)
170 Westbury Road
Bristol
BS9 3AH
Tel: 0117 962 2042

Photographic Orders

The *Echo* photographs listed on page (iv) of this book can be obtained from the *Daily Echo*. Simply complete a photocopy of this form and return it to the address below.

Newspaper House, Test Lane, Redbridge, Southampton
Telephone: 023 8042 4777

Photographic order from *FULL TIME at THE DELL*

Page number/s

Brief description of Picture/s contents

I would like   7" X 5" copies @ £4.50 each

I would like   10" X 8" copies @ £8.00 each

Plus 50p post & packing per order. Sizes are approximate. Larger sizes available on request.

IMPORTANT: This service applies to *Echo* photographs ONLY. Please check the *Echo* photos listed on page (iv). Payment and address details: please make cheques payable to NEWSQUEST SOUTHERN

I enclose   Name

Address

Postcode   Telephone